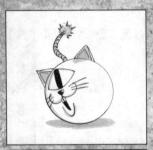

GEGE AKUTAMI

I feel like I haven't
grown as a person at all.

GEGE AKUTAMI published a few short
works before starting *Jujutsu Kaisen*, which began
serialization in *Weekly Shonen Jump* in 2018.

JUJUTSU KAISEN

VOLUME 10
SHONEN JUMP MANGA EDITION

BY GEGE AKUTAMI

TRANSLATION Stefan Koza
TOUCH-UP ART & LETTERING Snir Aharon
DESIGN Joy Zhang
EDITOR John Bae
CONSULTING EDITOR Erika Onabe

JUJUTSU KAISEN © 2018 by Gege Akutami
All rights reserved.
First published in Japan in 2018 by SHUEISHA Inc., Tokyo.
English translation rights arranged by SHUEISHA Inc.

Printed in Canada

Published by VIZ Media, LLC
P.O. Box 77010
San Francisco, CA 94107

10 9 8 7 6 5 4 3 2 1
First printing, June 2021

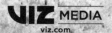
viz.com

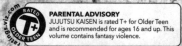

JUJUTSU KAISEN

10
EVENING FESTIVAL

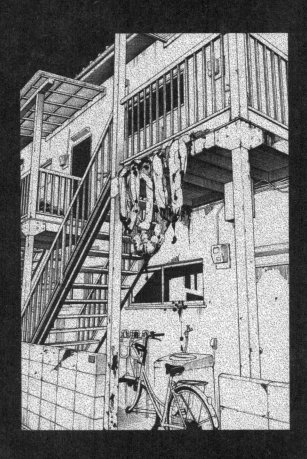

STORY AND ART BY GEGE AKUTAMI

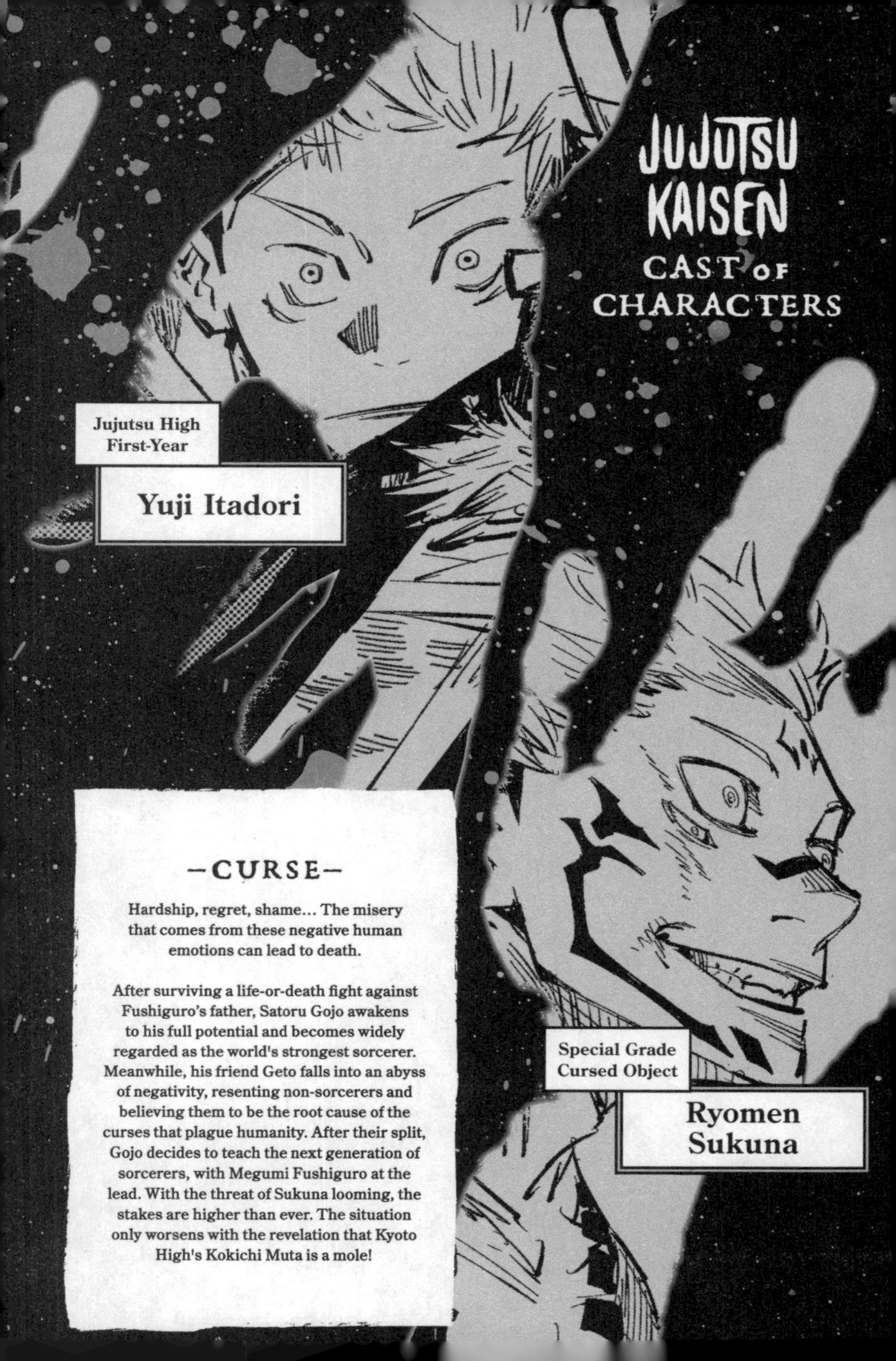
JUJUTSU KAISEN
CAST OF CHARACTERS
Jujutsu High First-Year
Yuji Itadori
Special Grade Cursed Object
Ryomen Sukuna

—CURSE—

Hardship, regret, shame… The misery that comes from these negative human emotions can lead to death.

After surviving a life-or-death fight against Fushiguro's father, Satoru Gojo awakens to his full potential and becomes widely regarded as the world's strongest sorcerer. Meanwhile, his friend Geto falls into an abyss of negativity, resenting non-sorcerers and believing them to be the root cause of the curses that plague humanity. After their split, Gojo decides to teach the next generation of sorcerers, with Megumi Fushiguro at the lead. With the threat of Sukuna looming, the stakes are higher than ever. The situation only worsens with the revelation that Kyoto High's Kokichi Muta is a mole!

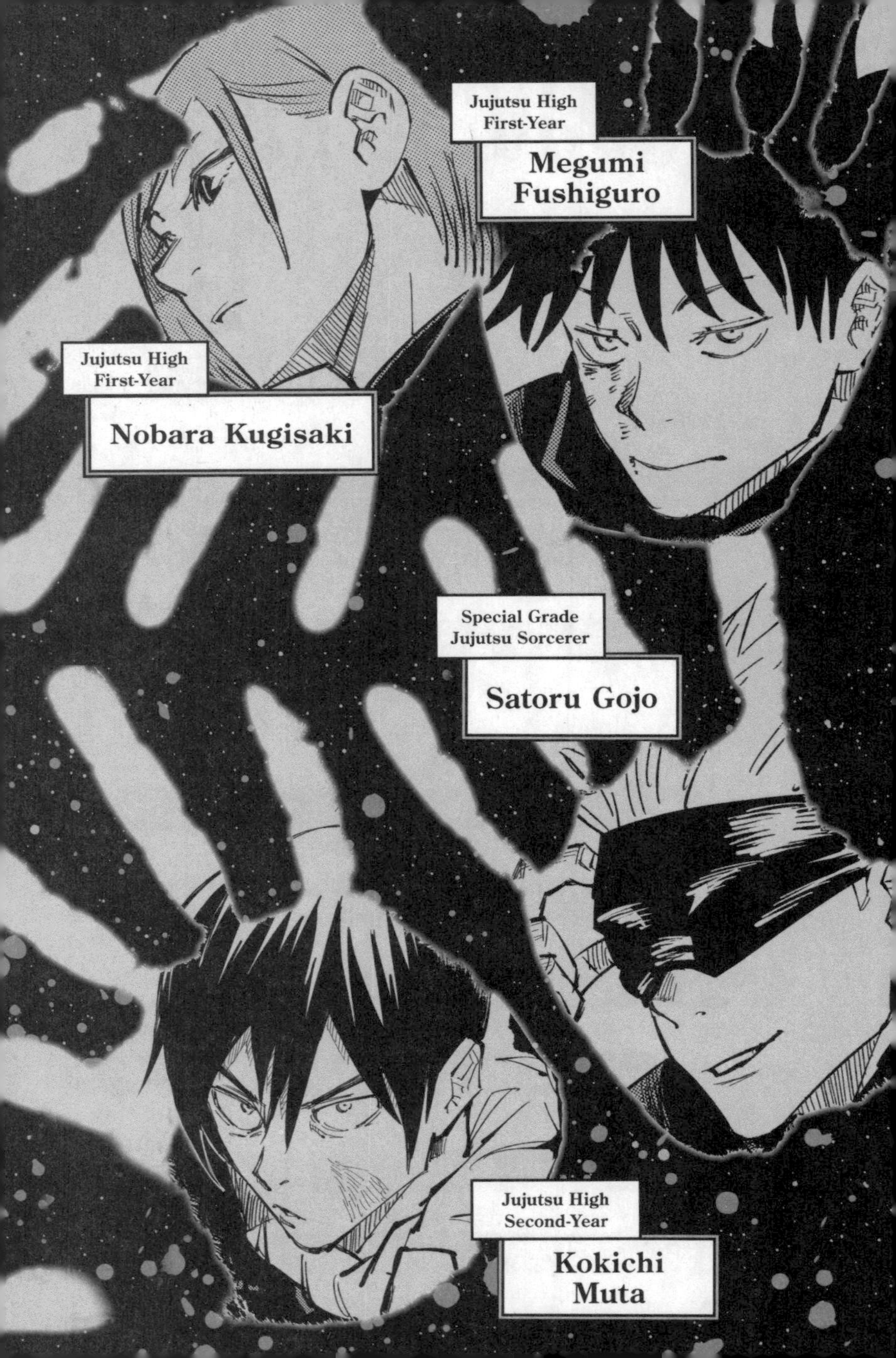
Jujutsu High First-Year
Megumi Fushiguro
Jujutsu High First-Year
Nobara Kugisaki
Special Grade Jujutsu Sorcerer
Satoru Gojo
Jujutsu High Second-Year
Kokichi Muta

JUJUTSU KAISEN

10

EVENING FESTIVAL

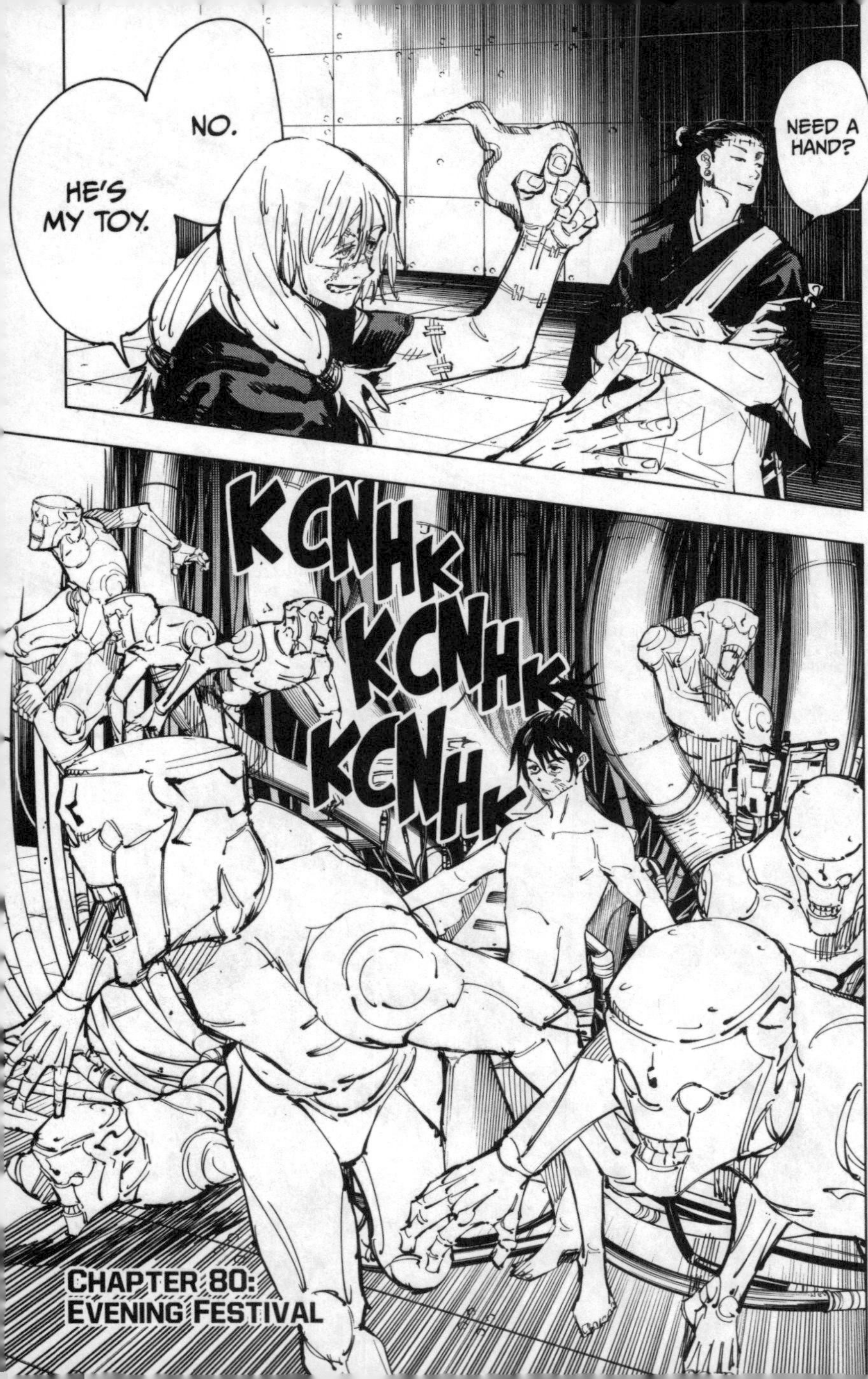
NEED A HAND?
NO.
HE'S MY TOY.
KCNHK
KCNHK
KCNHK
CHAPTER 80:
EVENING FESTIVAL

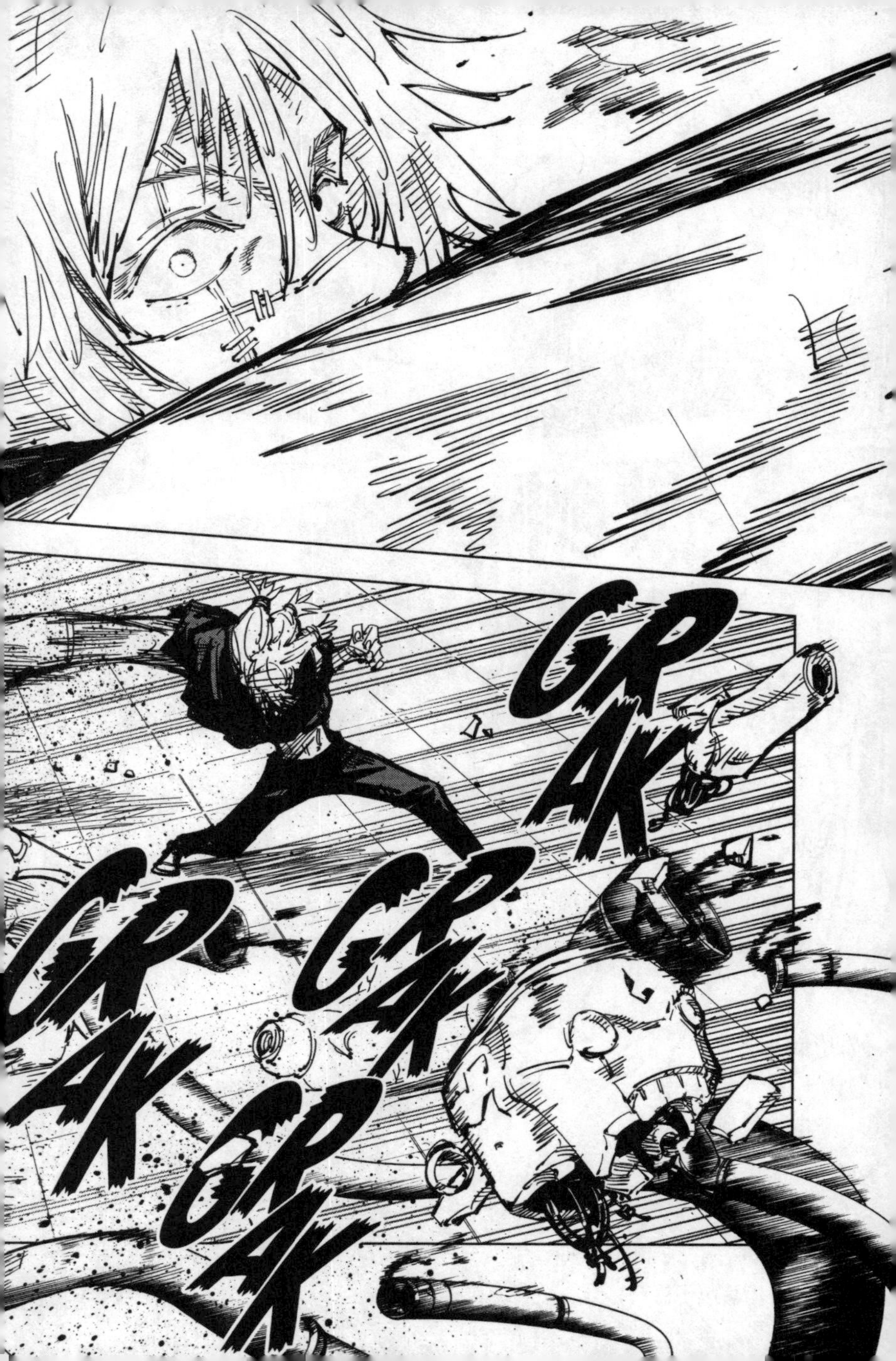
GRAK
GRGAK
GRAK
GRGAK

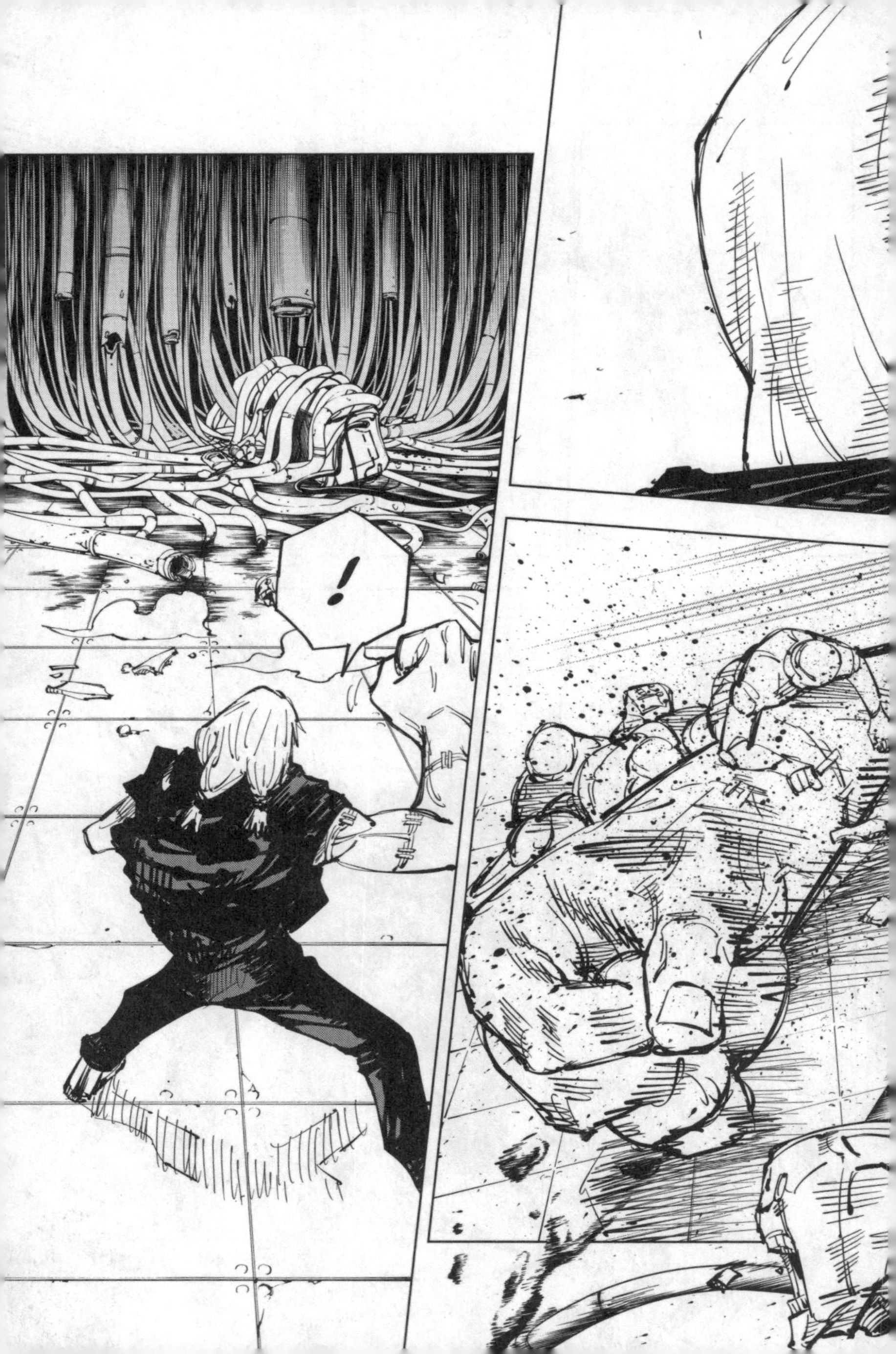
!

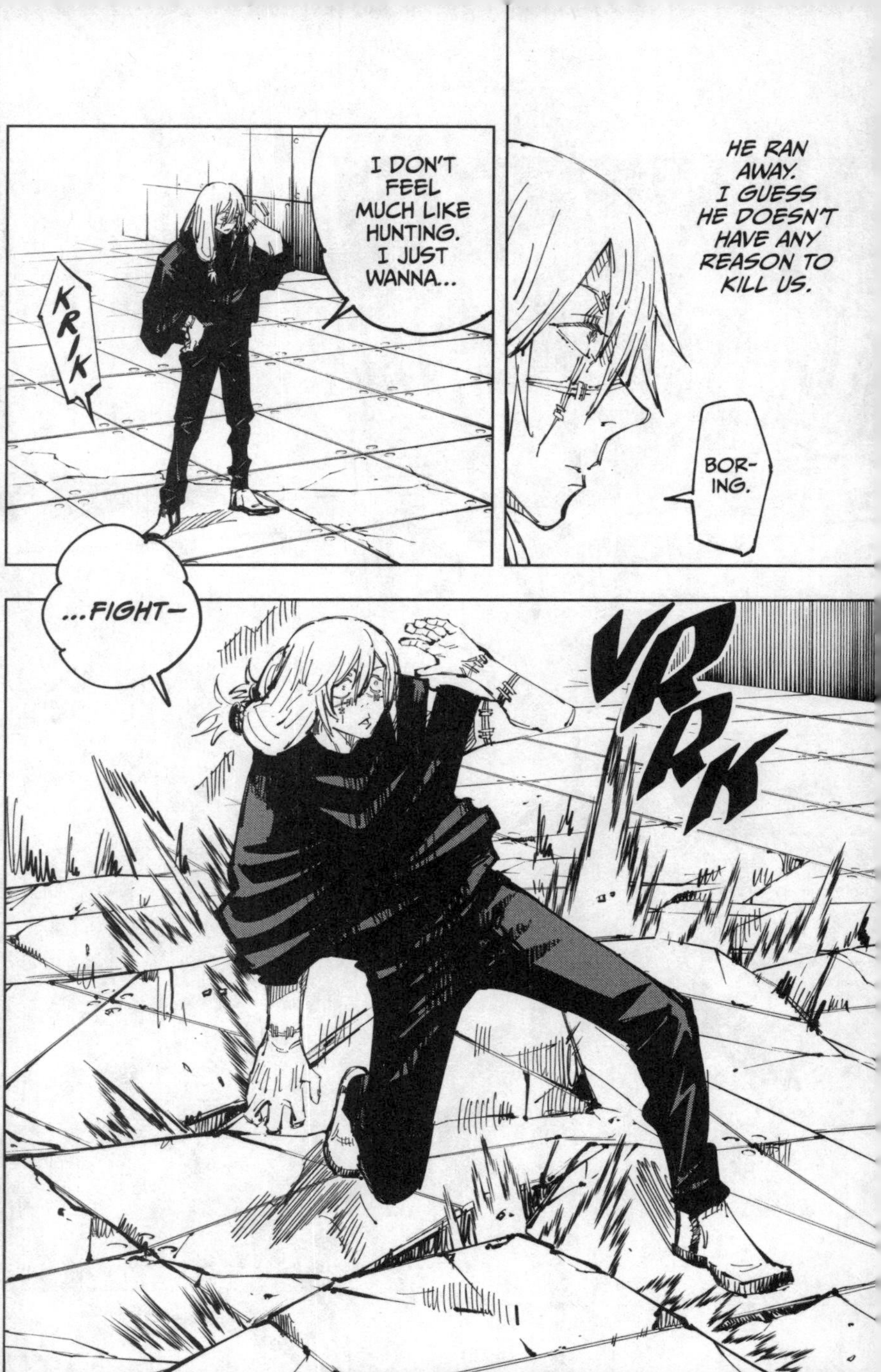
HE RAN AWAY. I GUESS HE DOESN'T HAVE ANY REASON TO KILL US.
BOR-ING.
I DON'T FEEL MUCH LIKE HUNTING. I JUST WANNA...
KRIK
...FIGHT—
VRRK

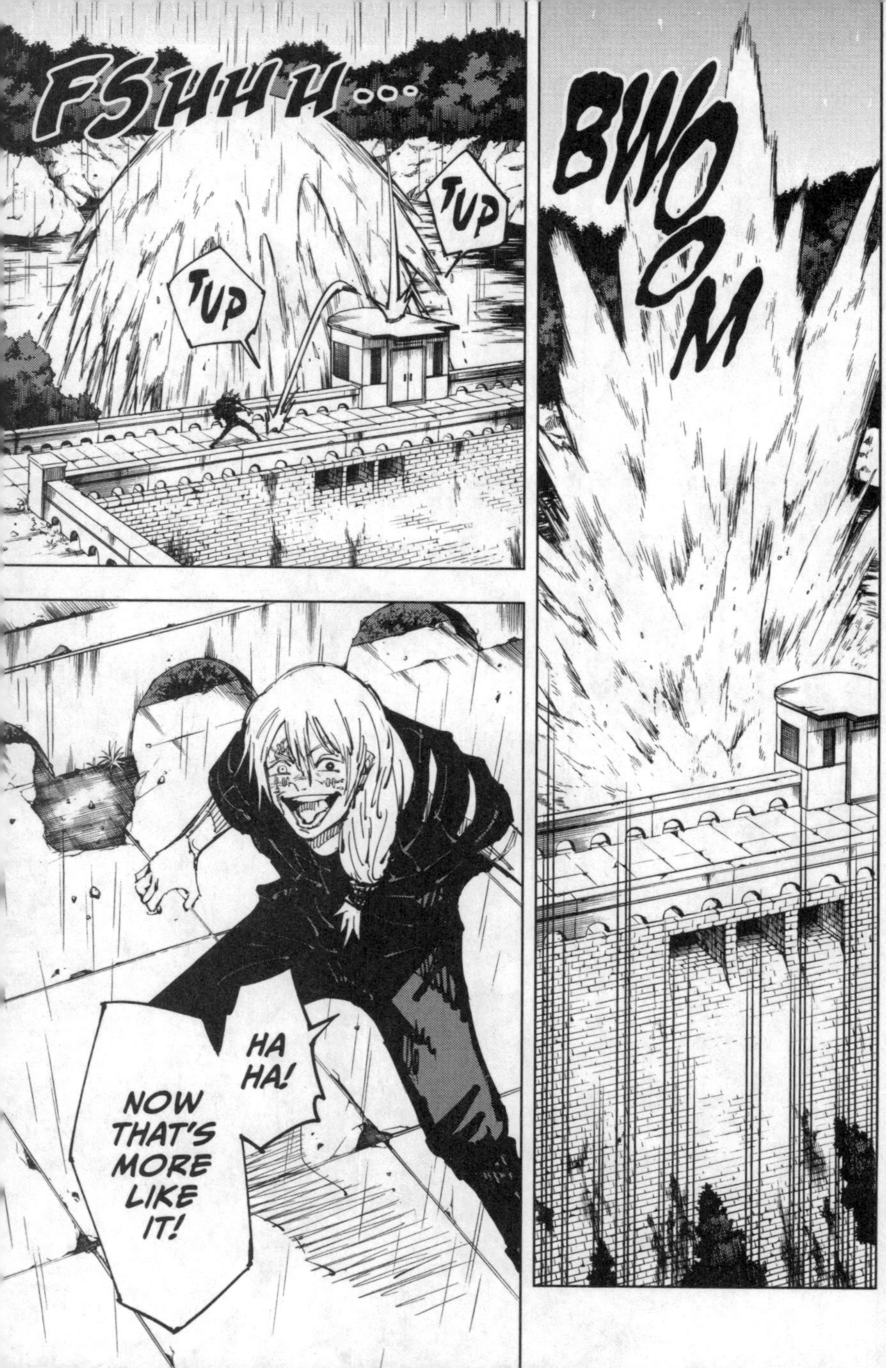
BWOOM
FSHHH...
TUP
TUP
HA HA!
NOW THAT'S MORE LIKE IT!

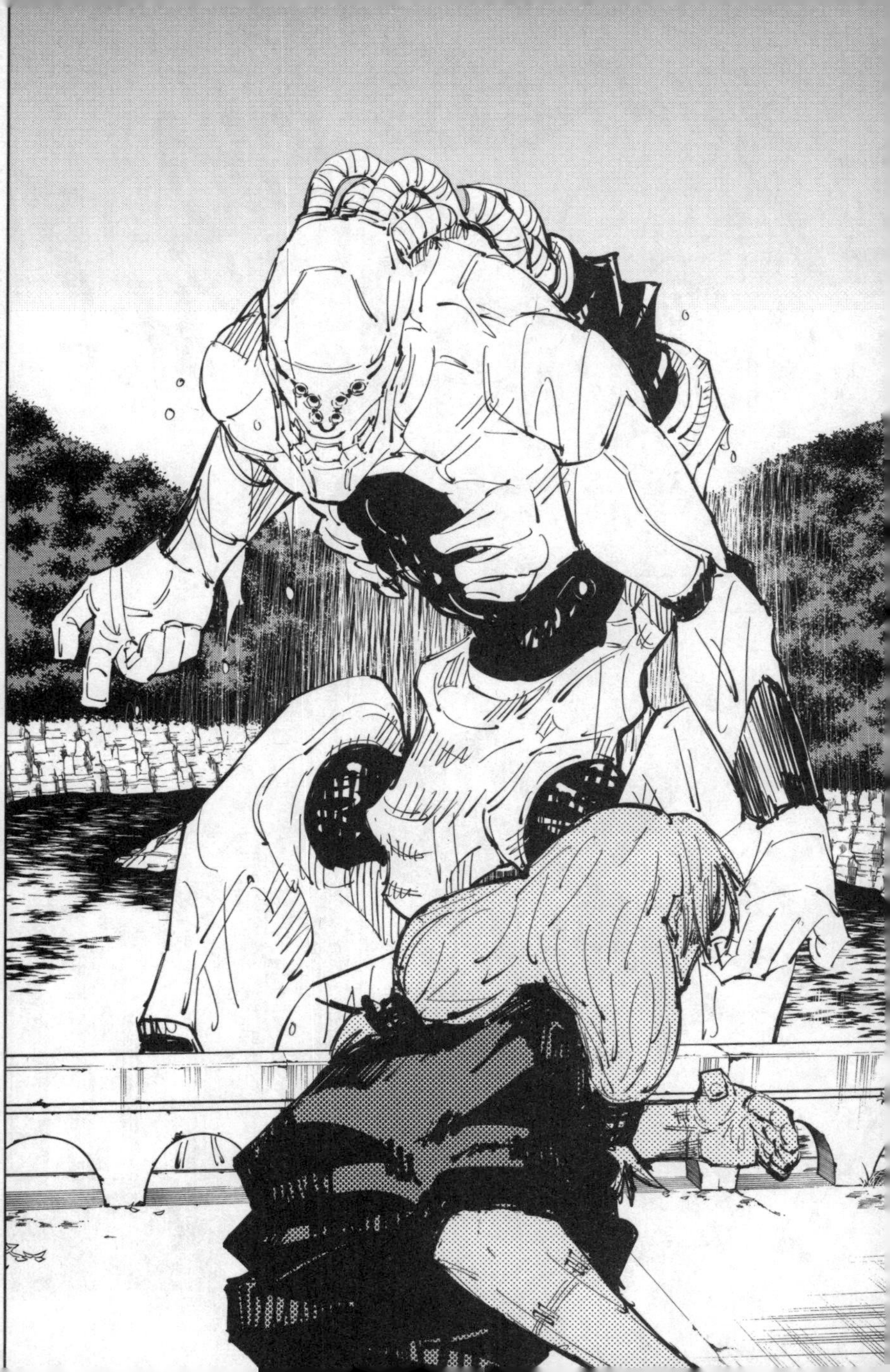

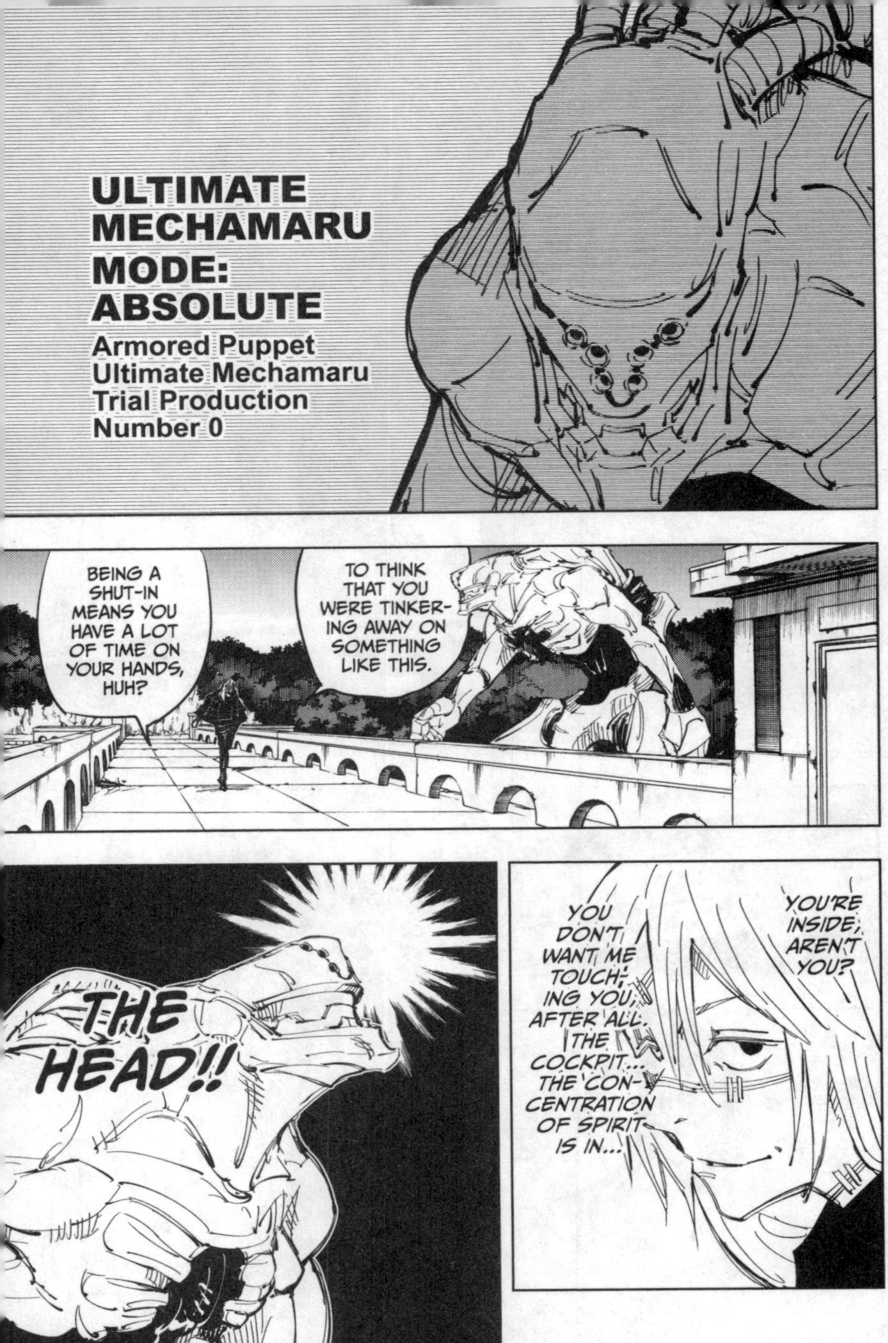
ULTIMATE MECHAMARU MODE: ABSOLUTE
Armored Puppet Ultimate Mechamaru Trial Production Number 0
TO THINK THAT YOU WERE TINKERING AWAY ON SOMETHING LIKE THIS.
BEING A SHUT-IN MEANS YOU HAVE A LOT OF TIME ON YOUR HANDS, HUH?
YOU'RE INSIDE, AREN'T YOU?
YOU DON'T WANT ME TOUCHING YOU, AFTER ALL. THE COCKPIT... THE CONCENTRATION OF SPIRIT IS IN...
THE HEAD!!

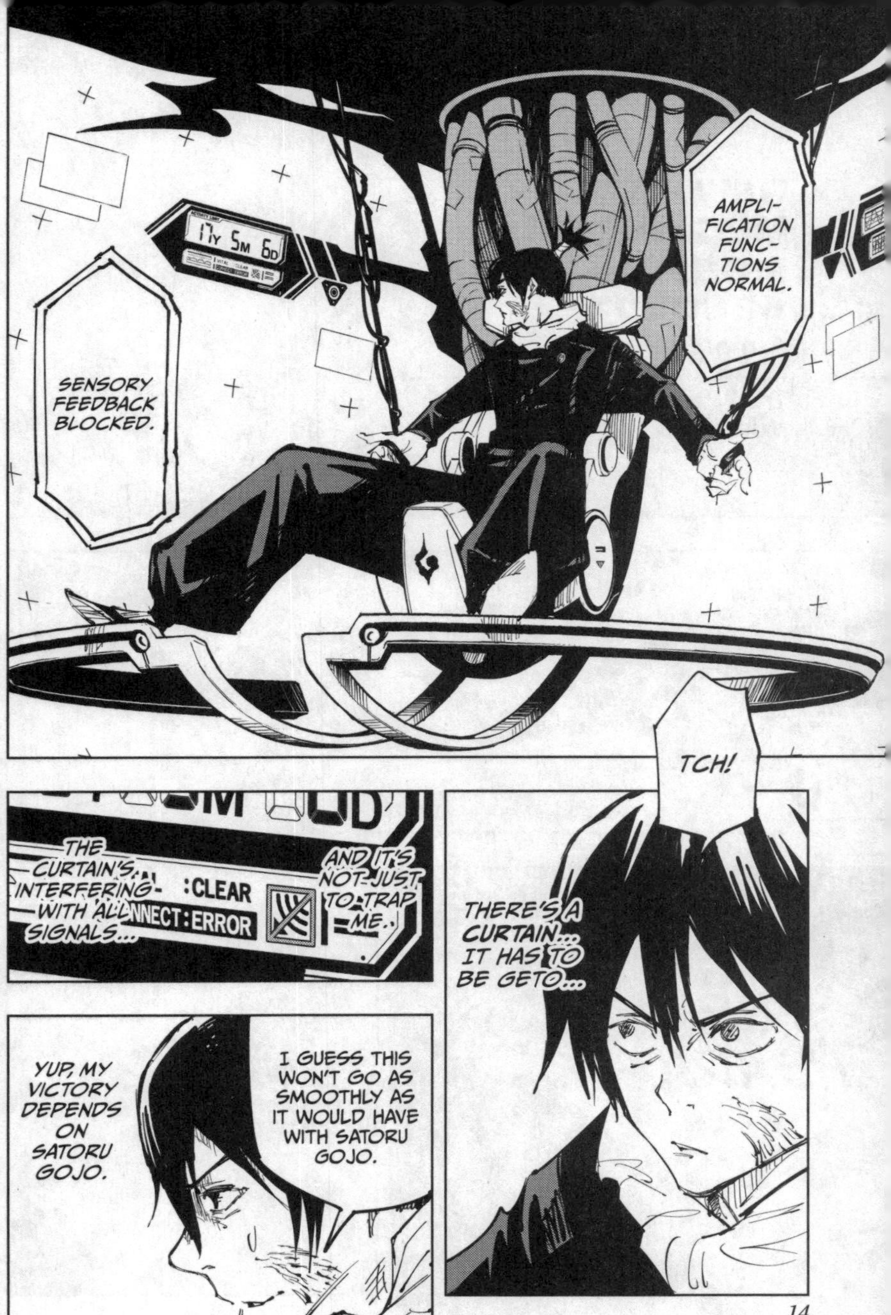
AMPLIFICATION FUNCTIONS NORMAL.
17Y 5M 6D
SENSORY FEEDBACK BLOCKED.
TCH!
THERE'S A CURTAIN... IT HAS TO BE GETO...
AND IT'S NOT JUST TO TRAP ME.
THE CURTAIN'S INTERFERING WITH ALL SIGNALS...
:CLEAR
NNECT:ERROR
I GUESS THIS WON'T GO AS SMOOTHLY AS IT WOULD HAVE WITH SATORU GOJO.
YUP, MY VICTORY DEPENDS ON SATORU GOJO.

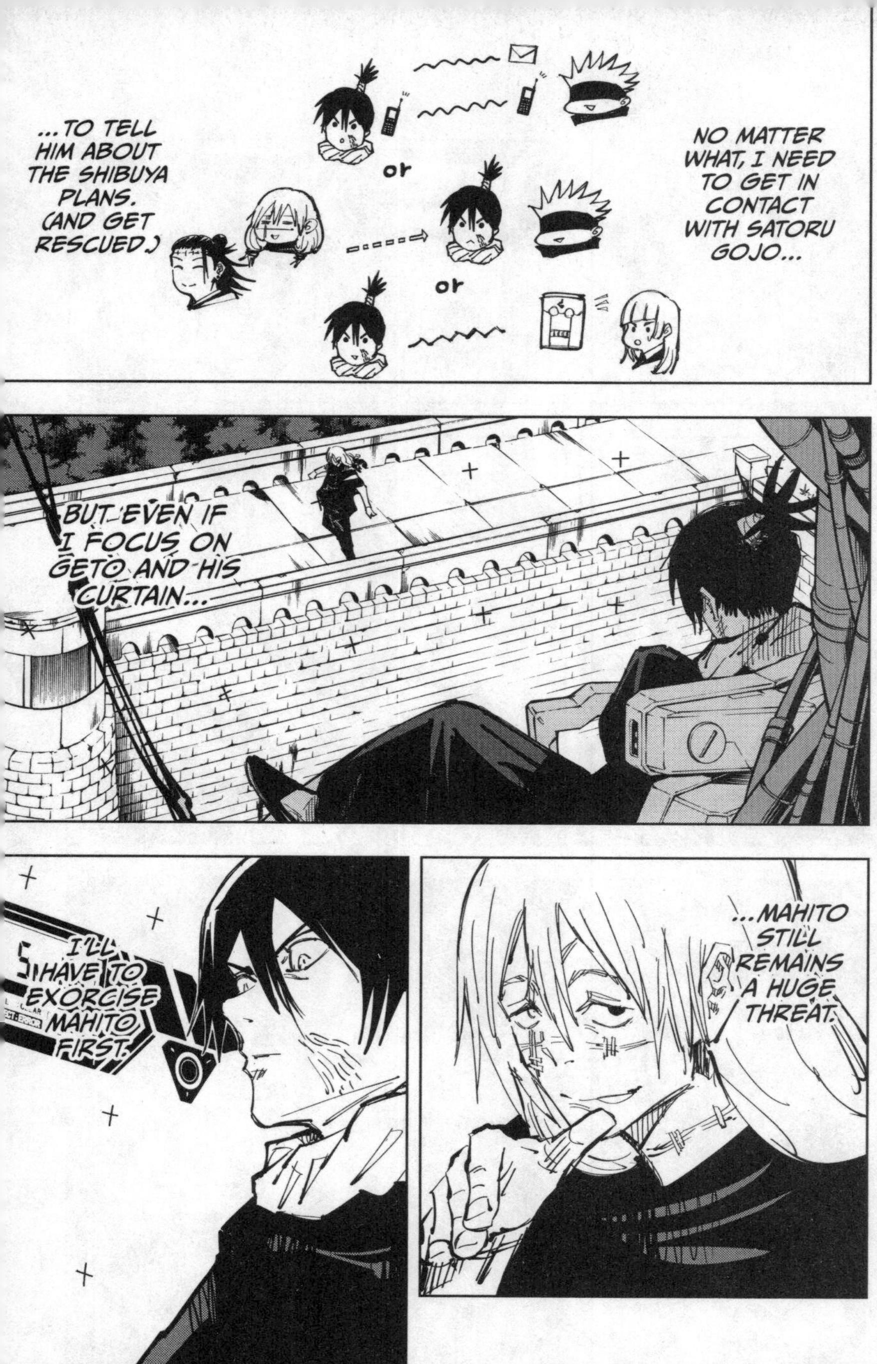
NO MATTER WHAT, I NEED TO GET IN CONTACT WITH SATORU GOJO...
...TO TELL HIM ABOUT THE SHIBUYA PLANS. (AND GET RESCUED.)
or
or
BUT EVEN IF I FOCUS ON GETO AND HIS CURTAIN...
...MAHITO STILL REMAINS A HUGE THREAT.
I'LL HAVE TO EXORCISE MAHITO FIRST.

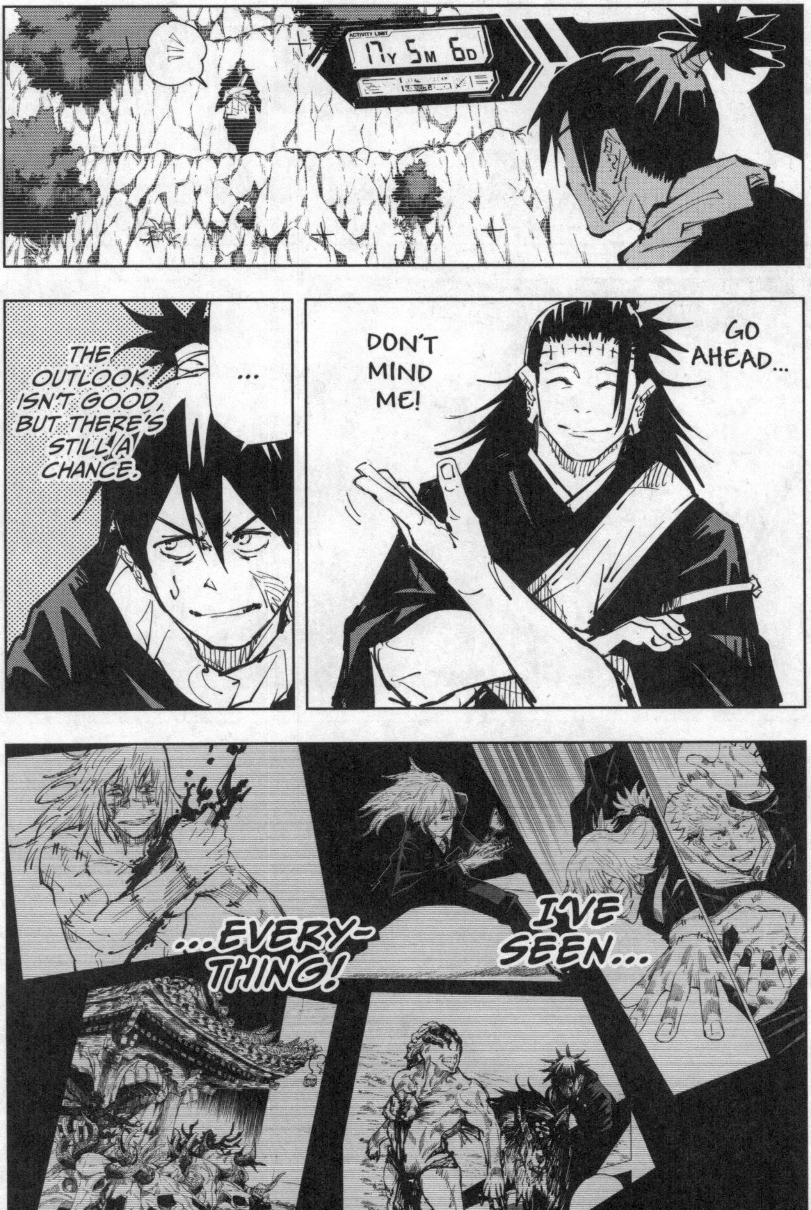
ACTIVITY LIMIT
17Y 5M 6D
GO AHEAD...
DON'T MIND ME!
...
THE OUTLOOK ISN'T GOOD, BUT THERE'S STILL A CHANCE.
I'VE SEEN...
...EVERY-THING!

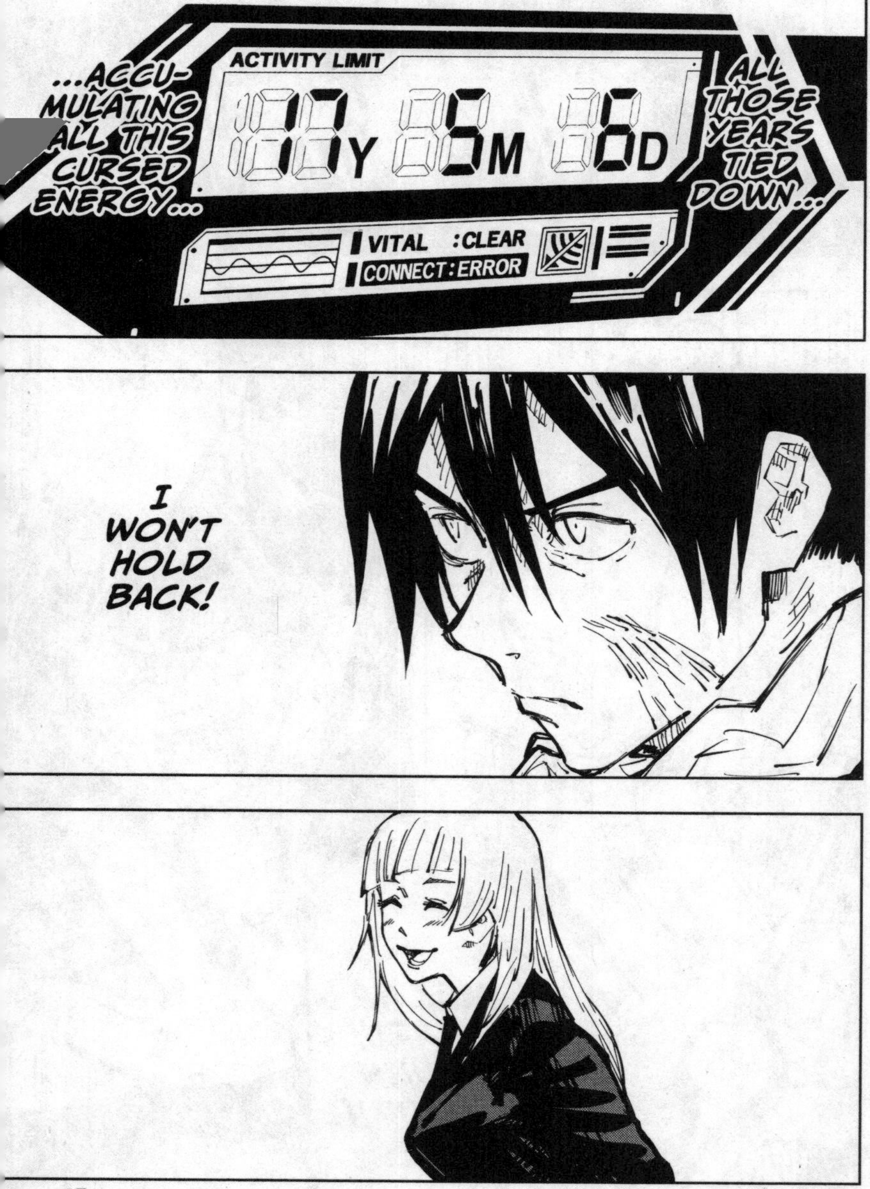
ALL THOSE YEARS TIED DOWN...
ACTIVITY LIMIT
17Y 5M 6D
VITAL :CLEAR
CONNECT:ERROR
...ACCUMULATING ALL THIS CURSED ENERGY...
I WON'T HOLD BACK!

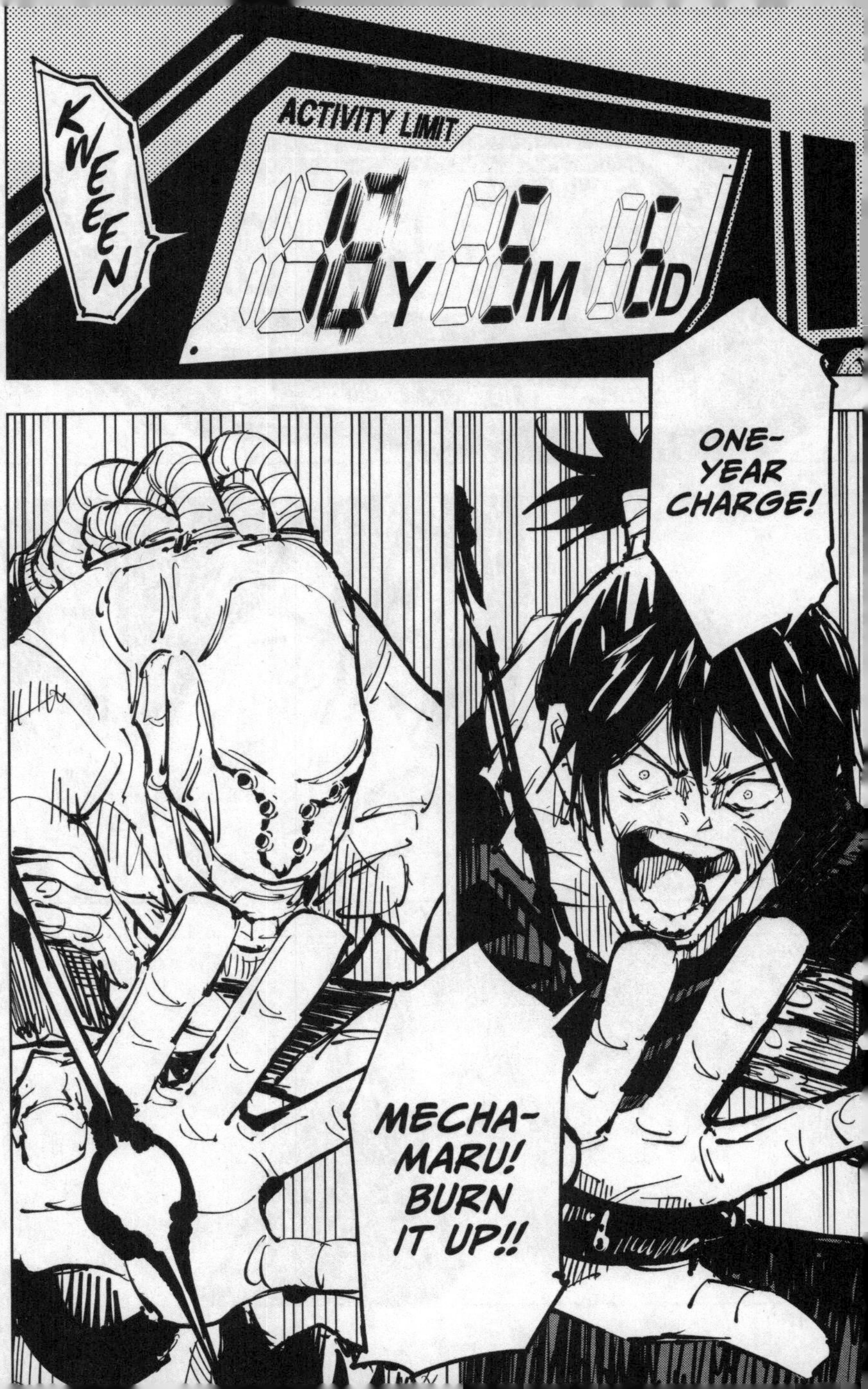
ACTIVITY LIMIT
KWEEEN
ONE-YEAR CHARGE!
MECHA-MARU! BURN IT UP!!

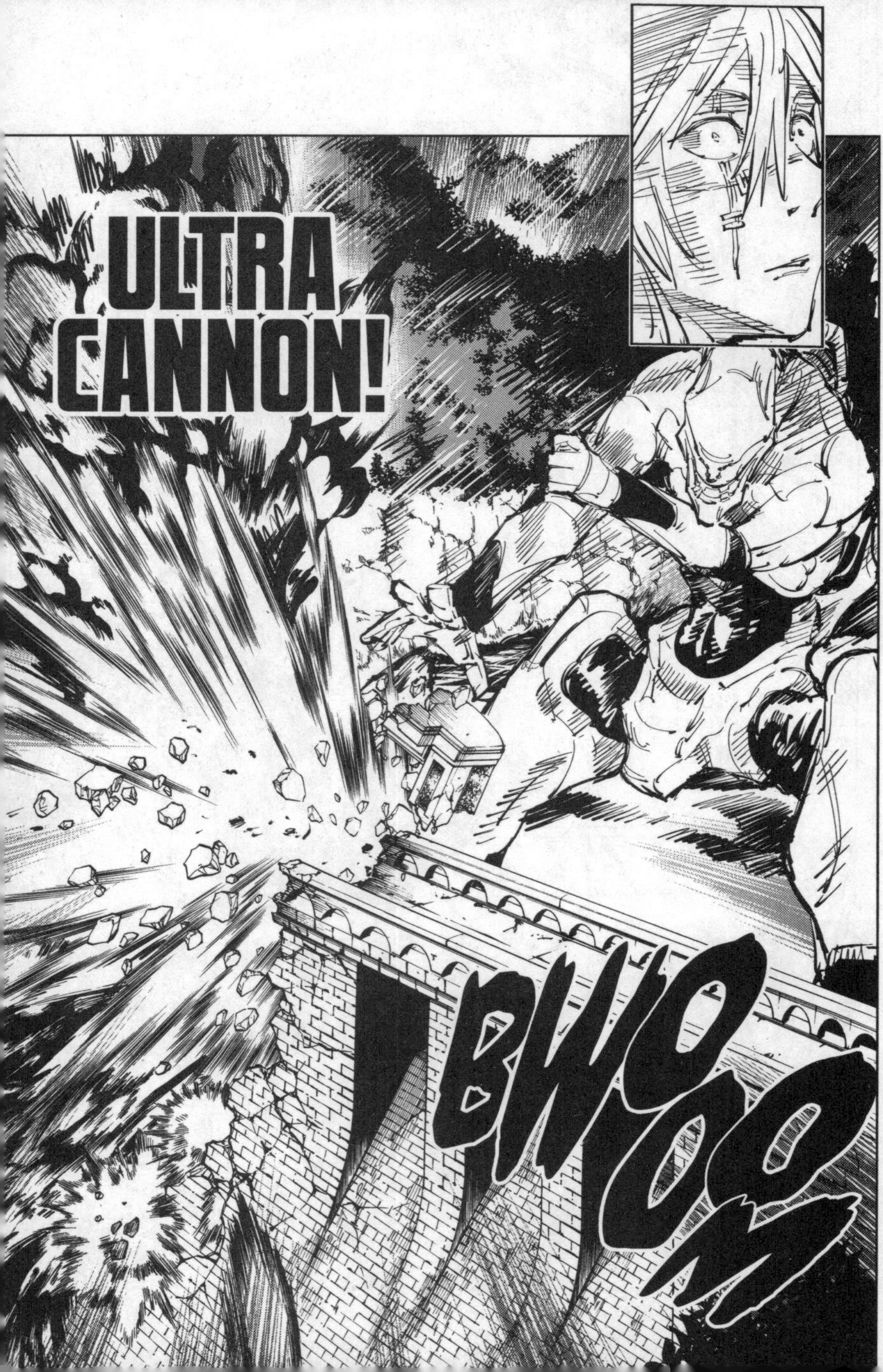
ULTRA CANNON!
BWOOM

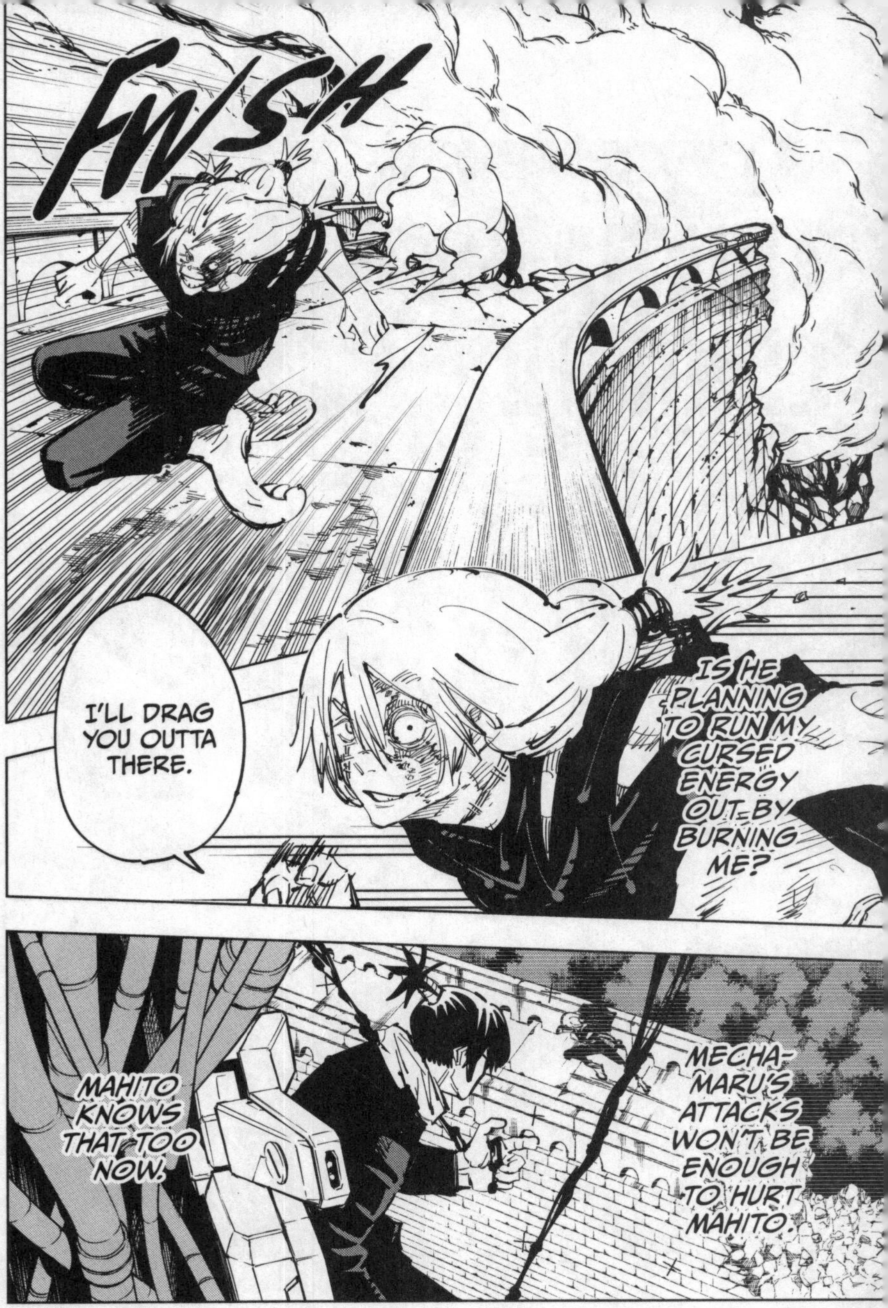
FWISH
IS HE PLANNING TO RUN MY CURSED ENERGY OUT BY BURNING ME?
I'LL DRAG YOU OUTTA THERE.
MECHA-MARU'S ATTACKS WON'T BE ENOUGH TO HURT MAHITO.
MAHITO KNOWS THAT TOO NOW.

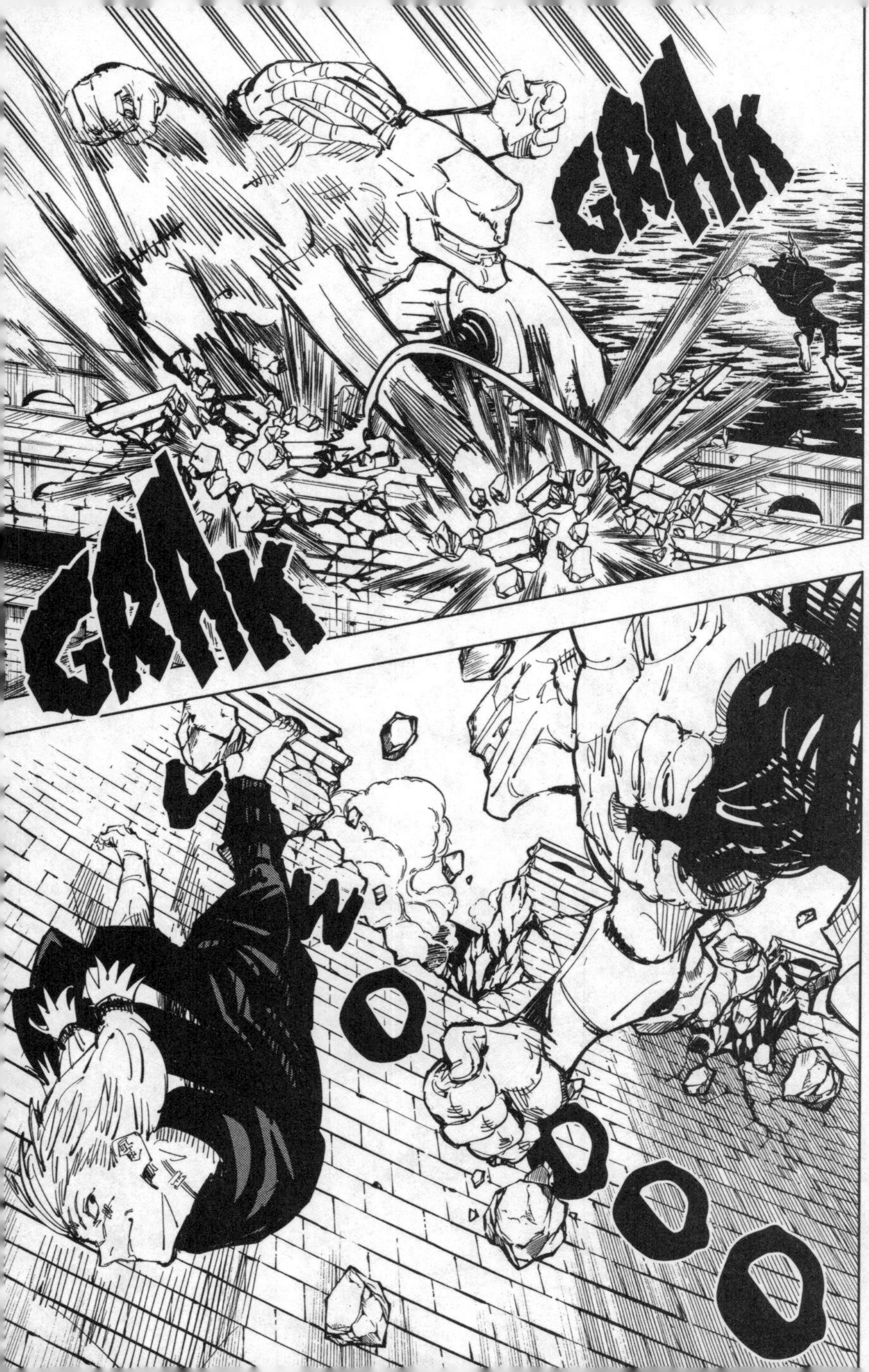
GRAK
GRAK
WOOOO

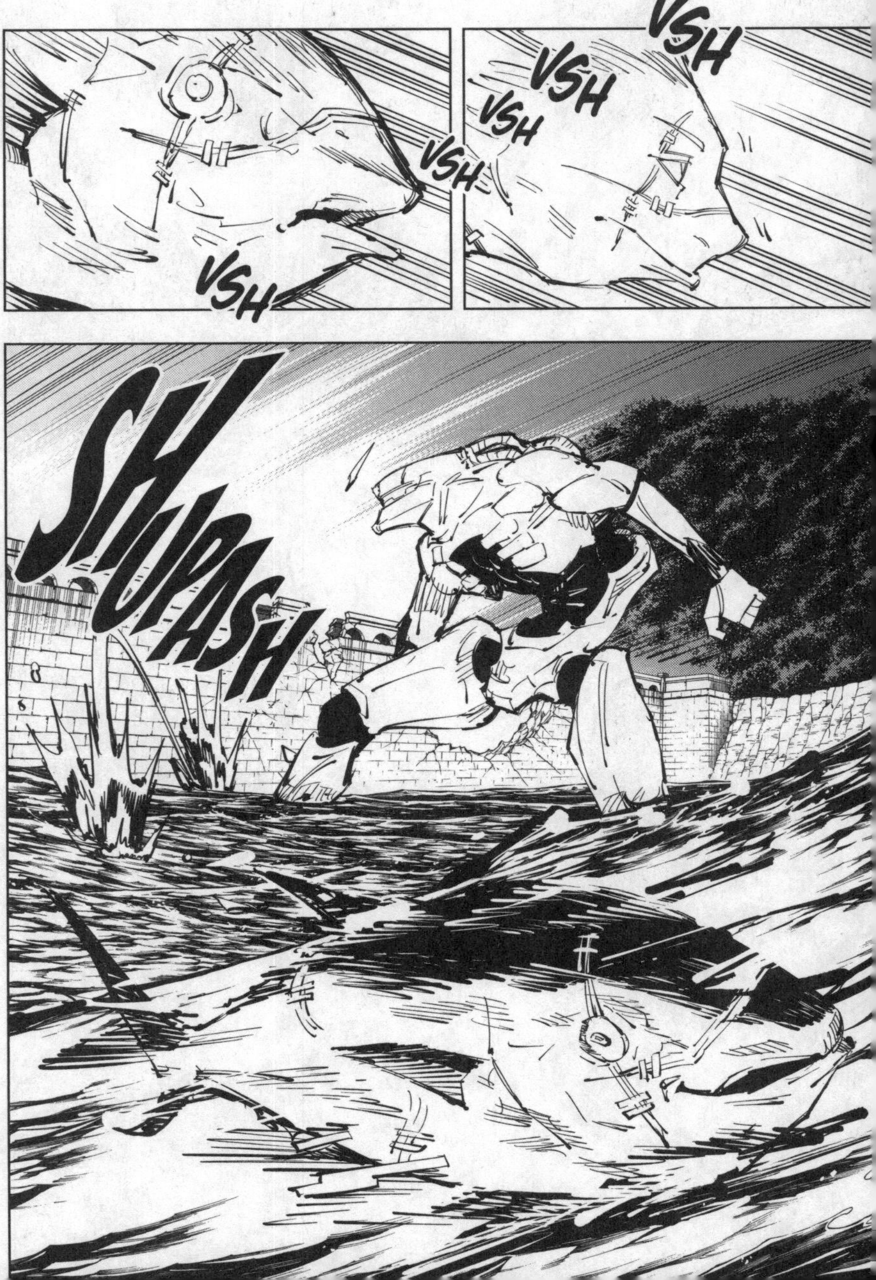
VSH
VSH
VSH
VSH
VSH
SHUPASH

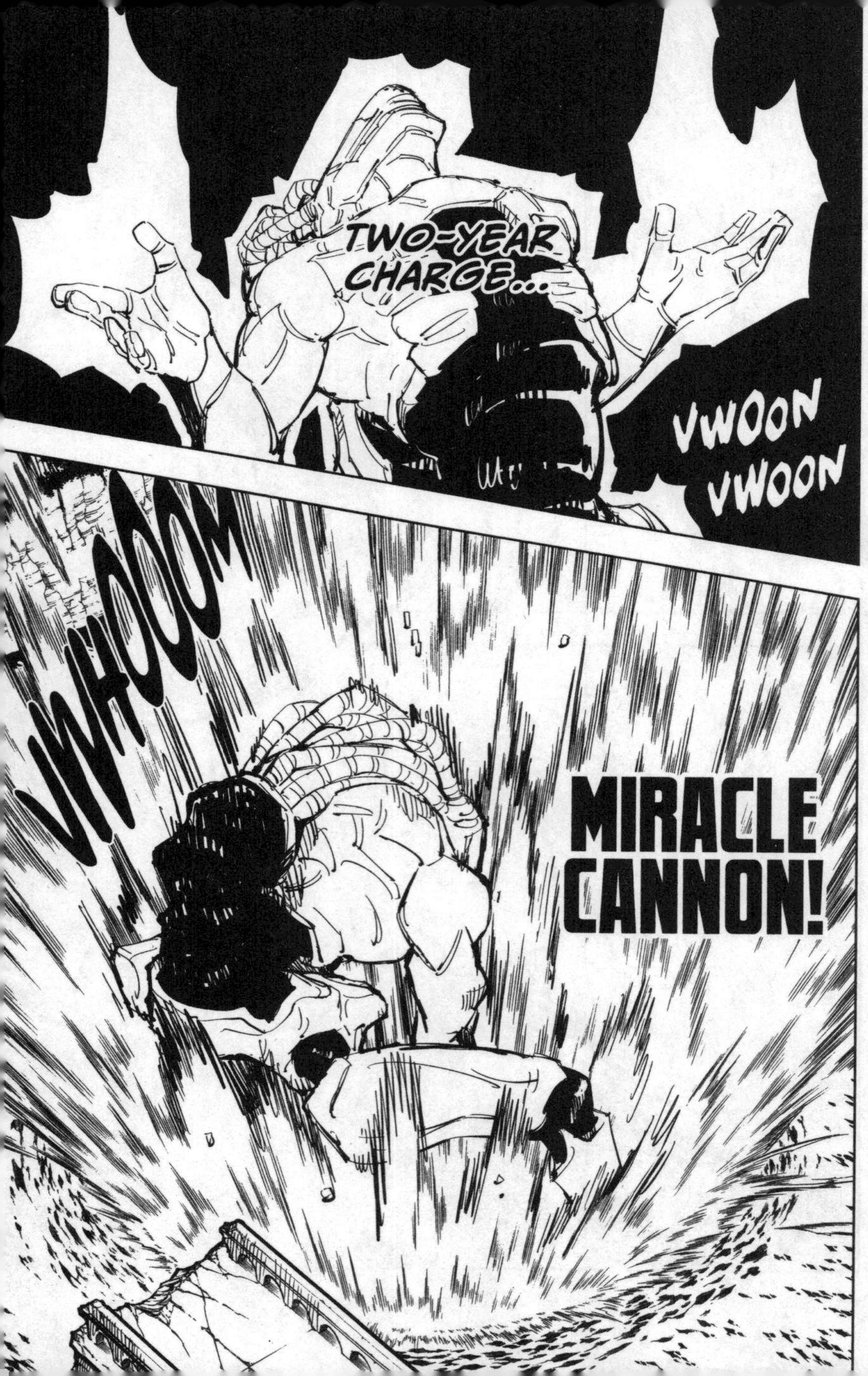
TWO-YEAR CHARGE...
VWOON VWOON
MIRACLE CANNON!
VWOOOM

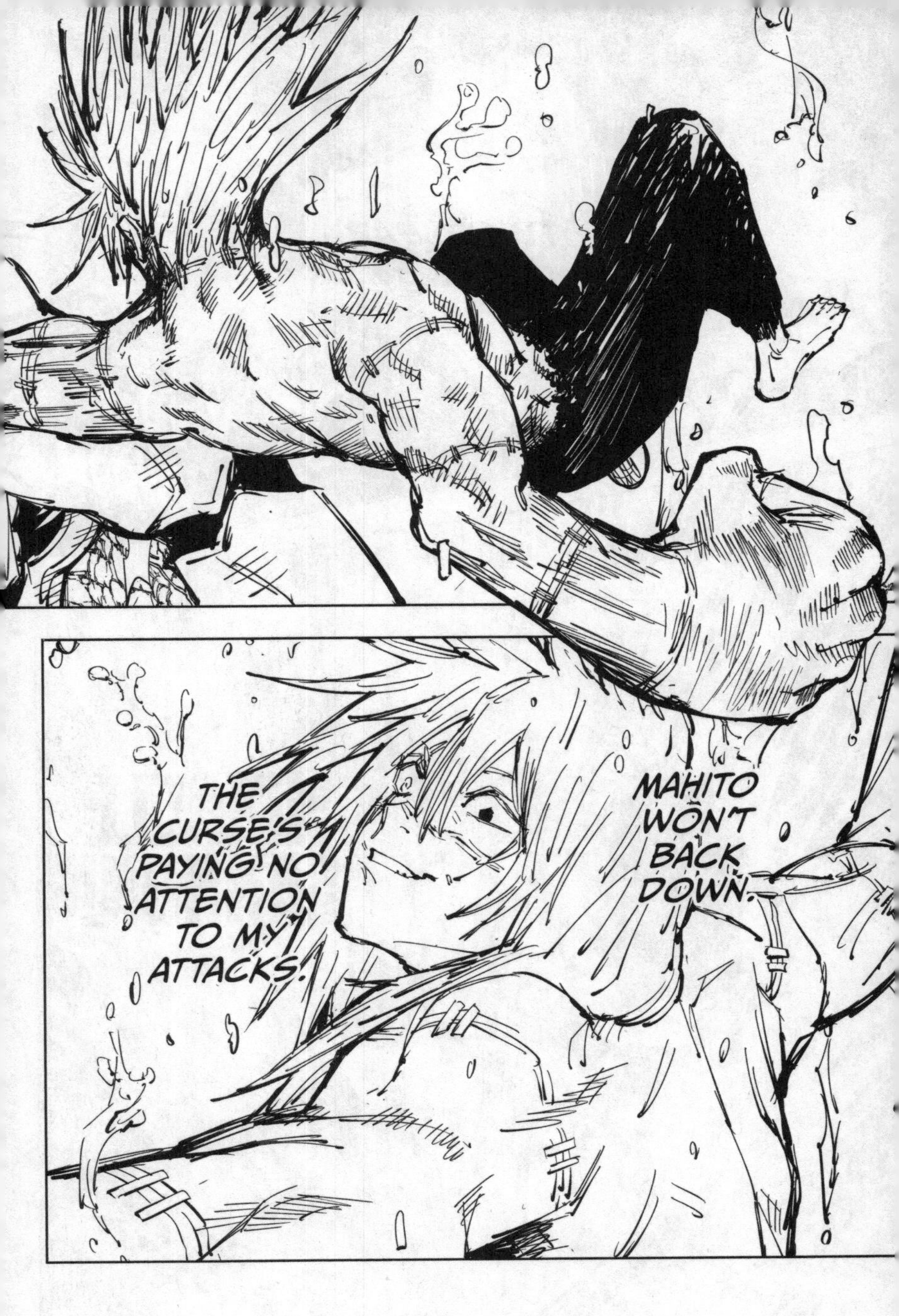
MAHITO WON'T BACK DOWN.
THE CURSE'S PAYING NO ATTENTION TO MY ATTACKS.

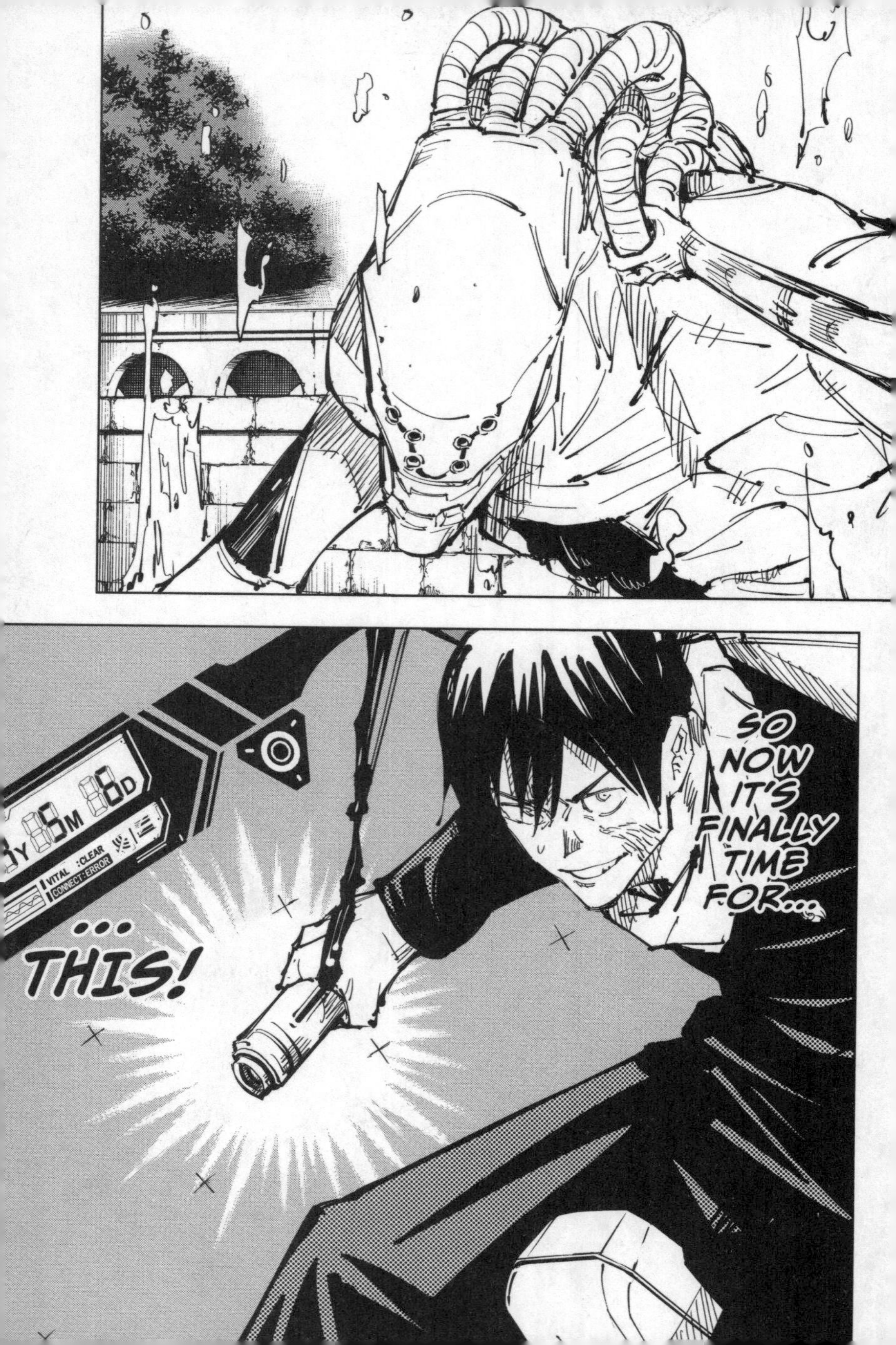
SO NOW IT'S FINALLY TIME FOR...
VITAL :CLEAR
CONNECT:ERROR
...THIS!

MAHITO

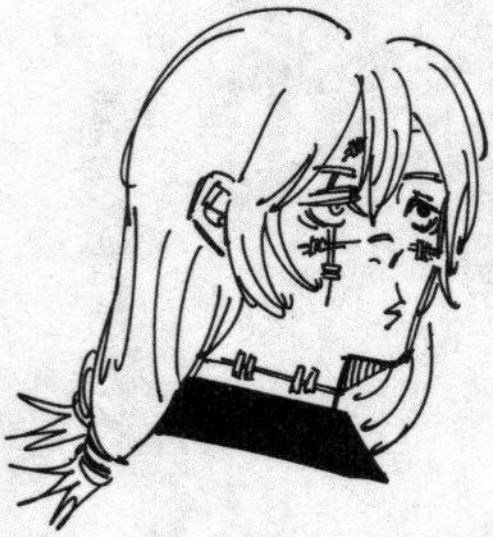

TUNA

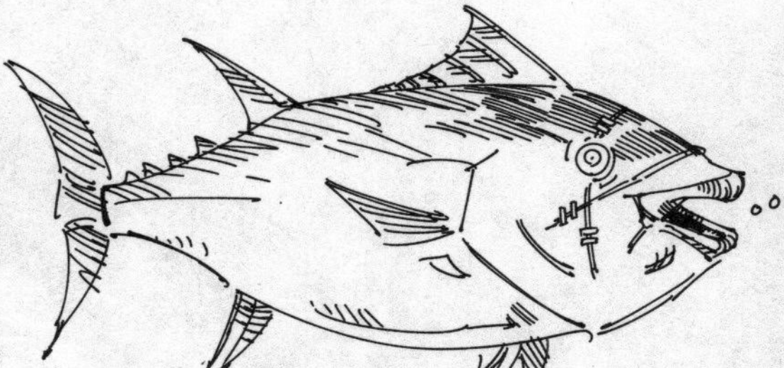

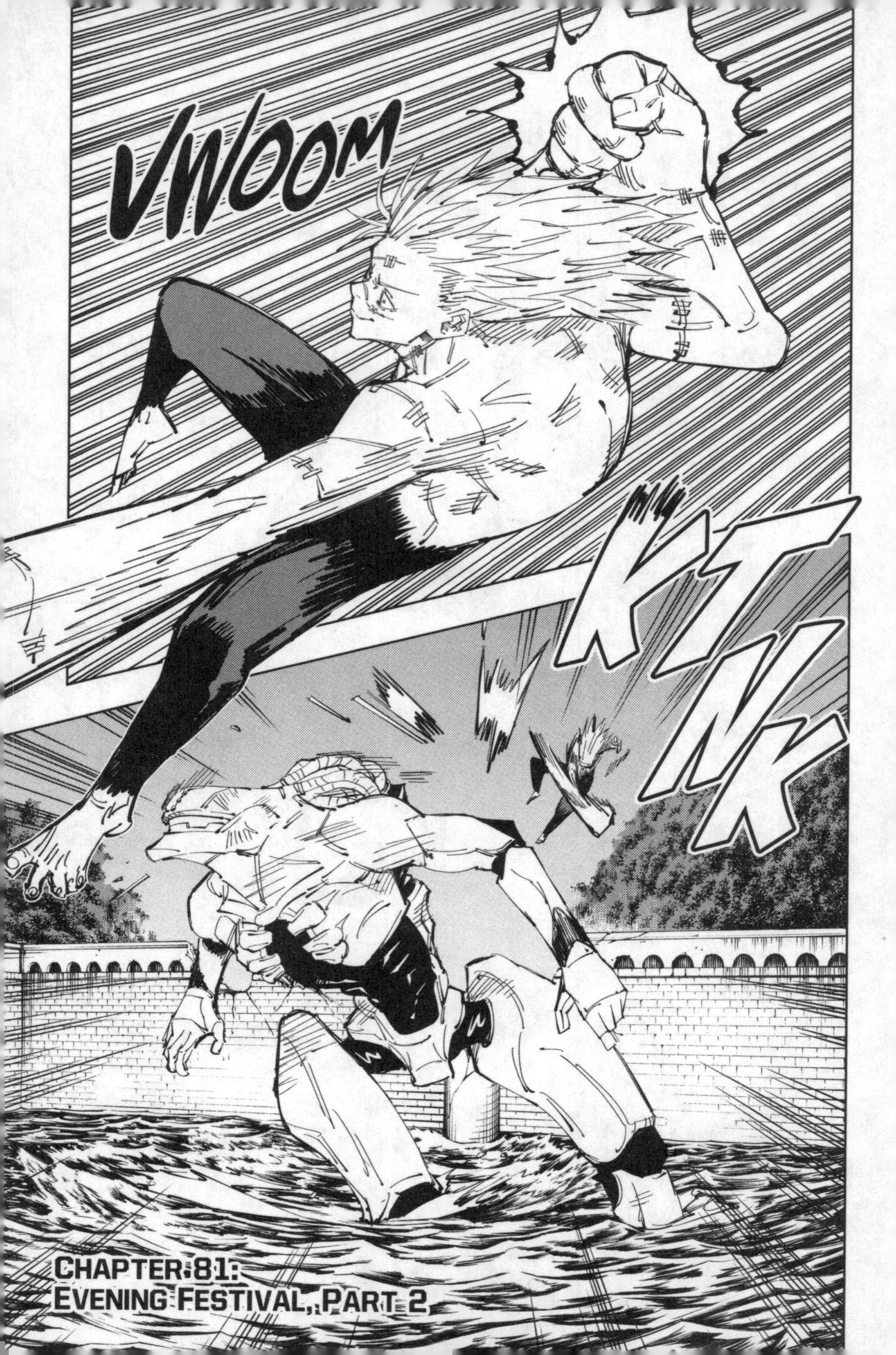
VWOOM
KRUNK
CHAPTER 81:
EVENING FESTIVAL, PART 2

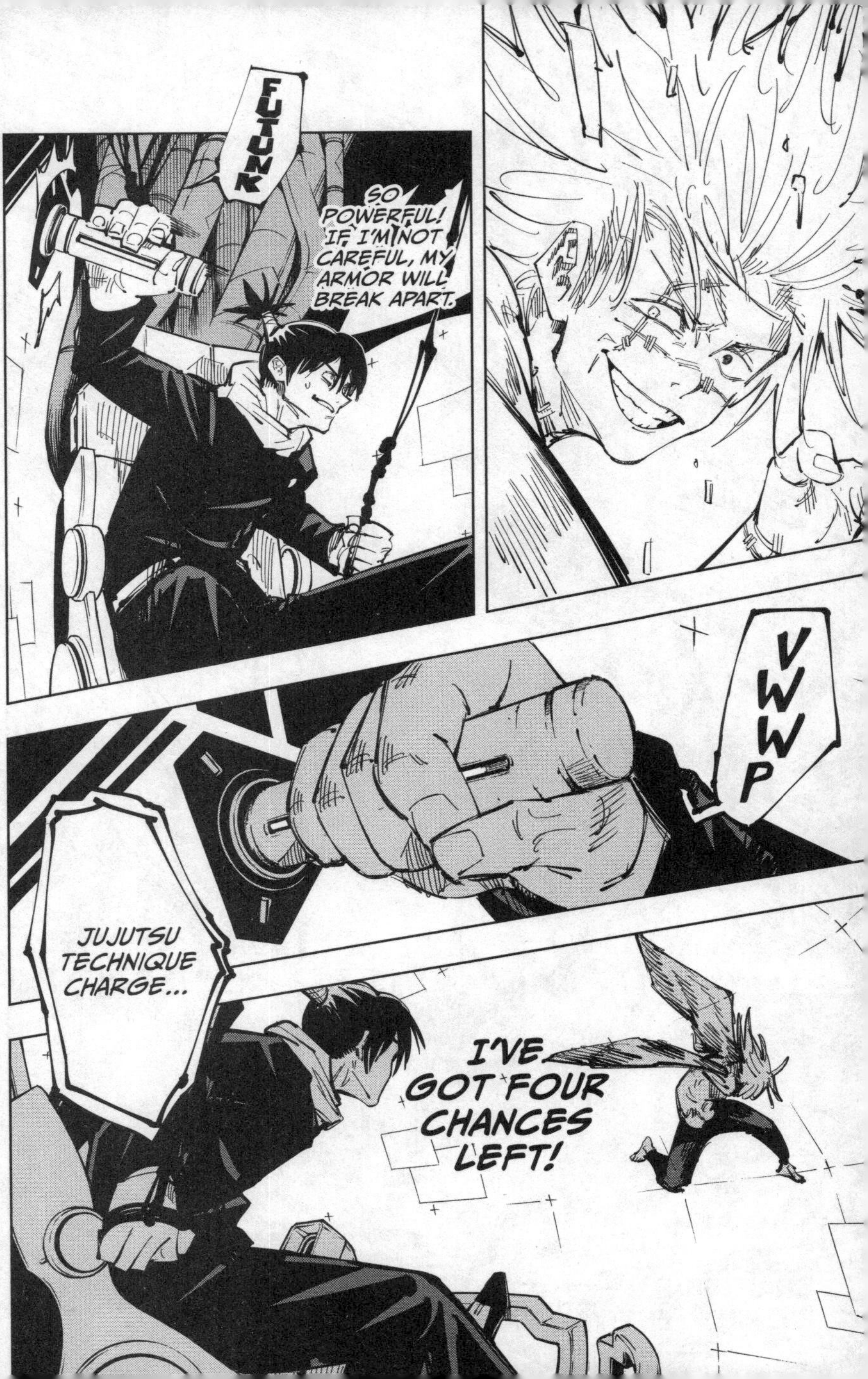
FUTUNK
SO POWERFUL! IF I'M NOT CAREFUL, MY ARMOR WILL BREAK APART.
VWWP
JUJUTSU TECHNIQUE CHARGE...
I'VE GOT FOUR CHANCES LEFT!

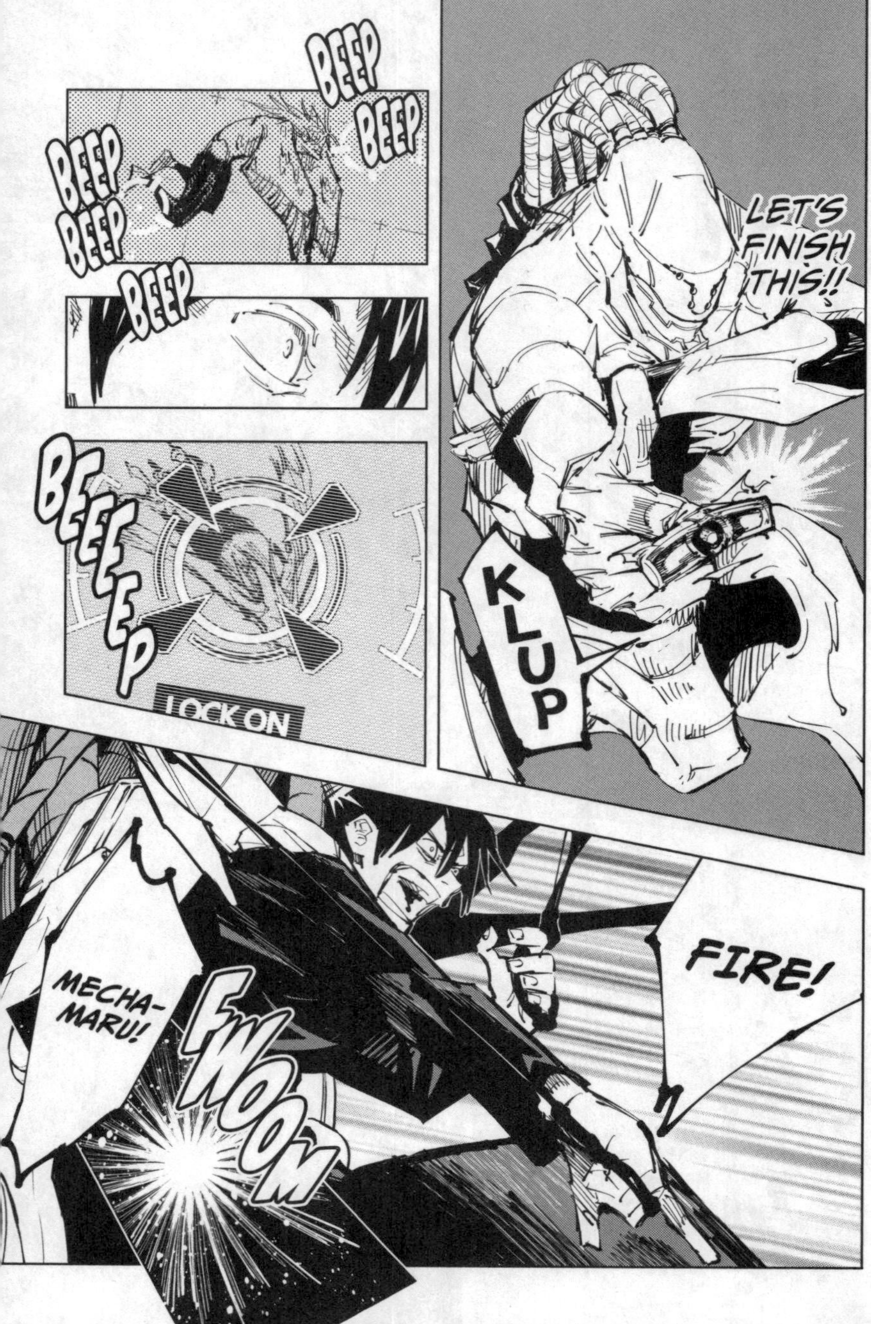
LET'S FINISH THIS!!
KLUP
BEEP BEEP
BEEP BEEP
BEEP
BEEEEEP
LOCK ON
FIRE!
FWOOM
MECHA-MARU!

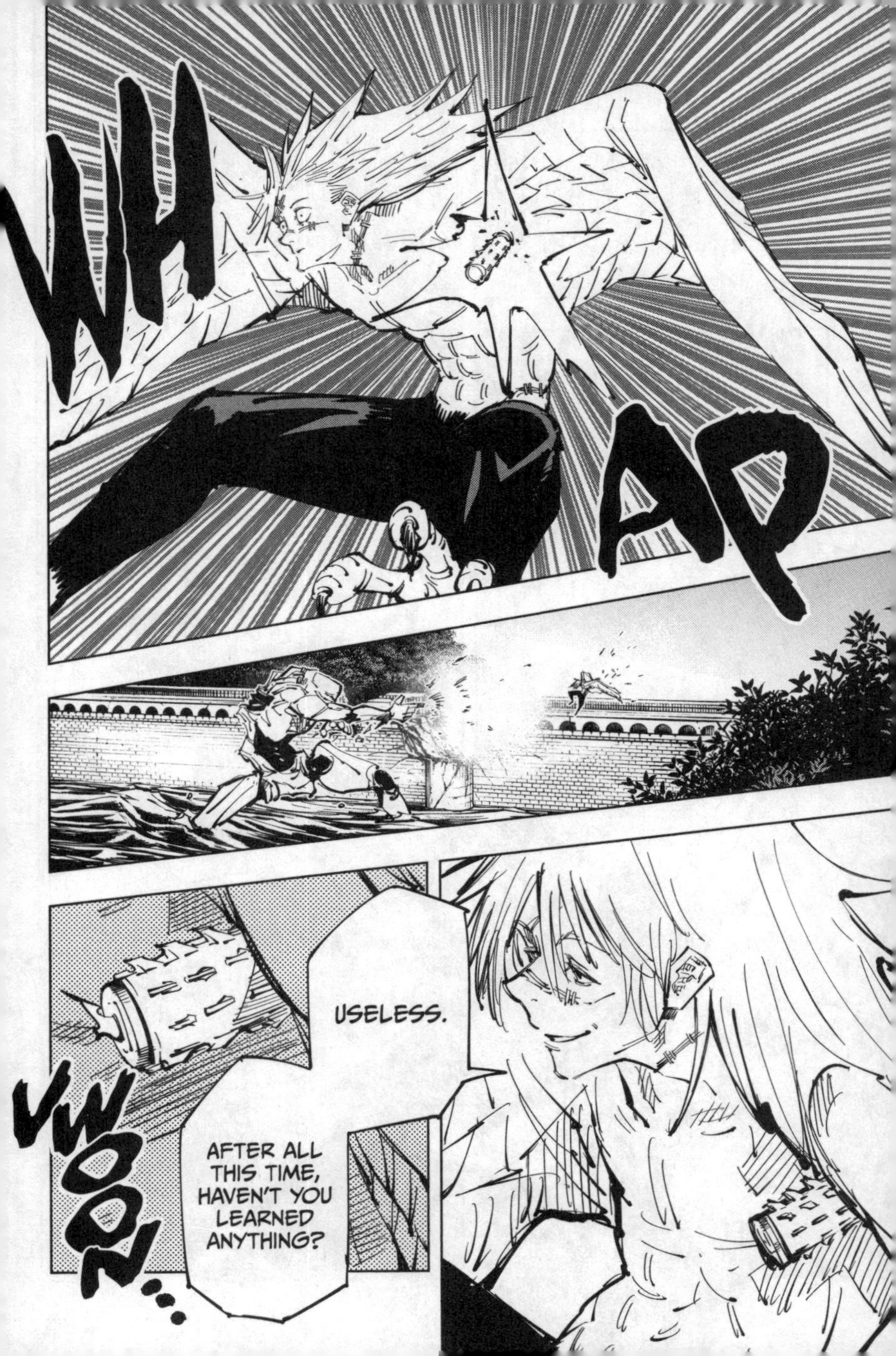
WHAP
USELESS.
AFTER ALL THIS TIME, HAVEN'T YOU LEARNED ANYTHING?
VWOOM...

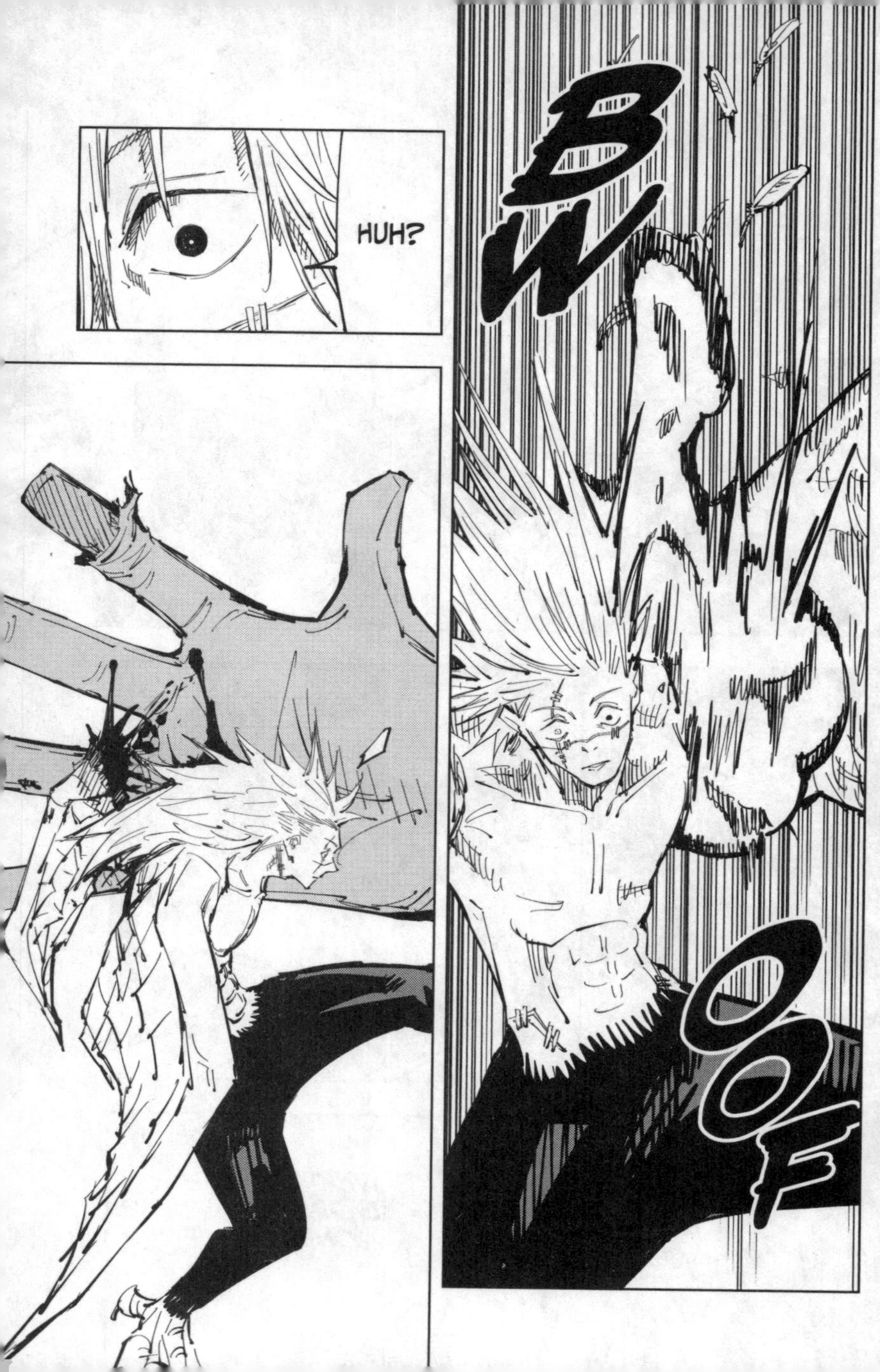
BW
OOF
HUH?

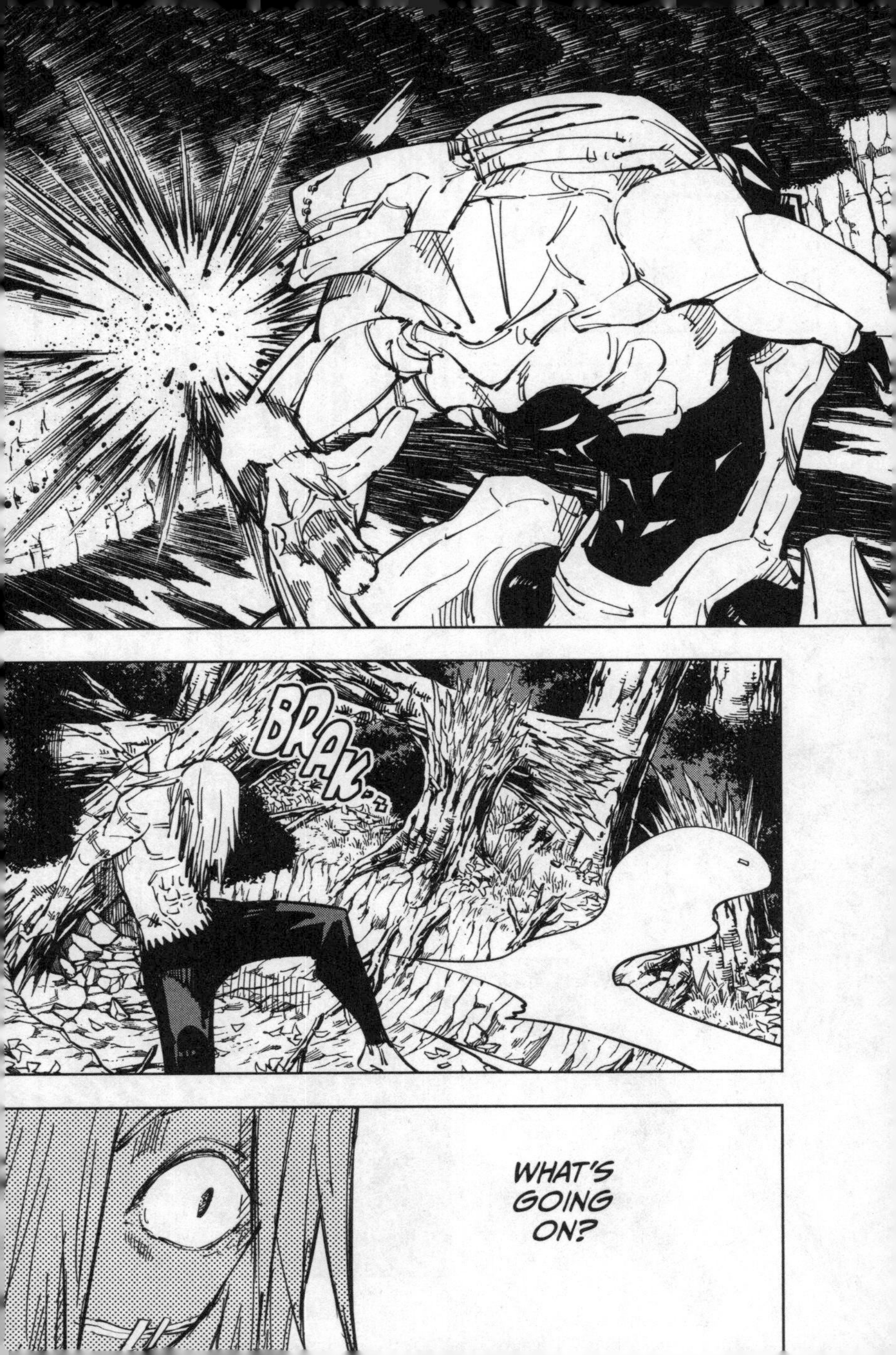
BRAK...
WHAT'S GOING ON?

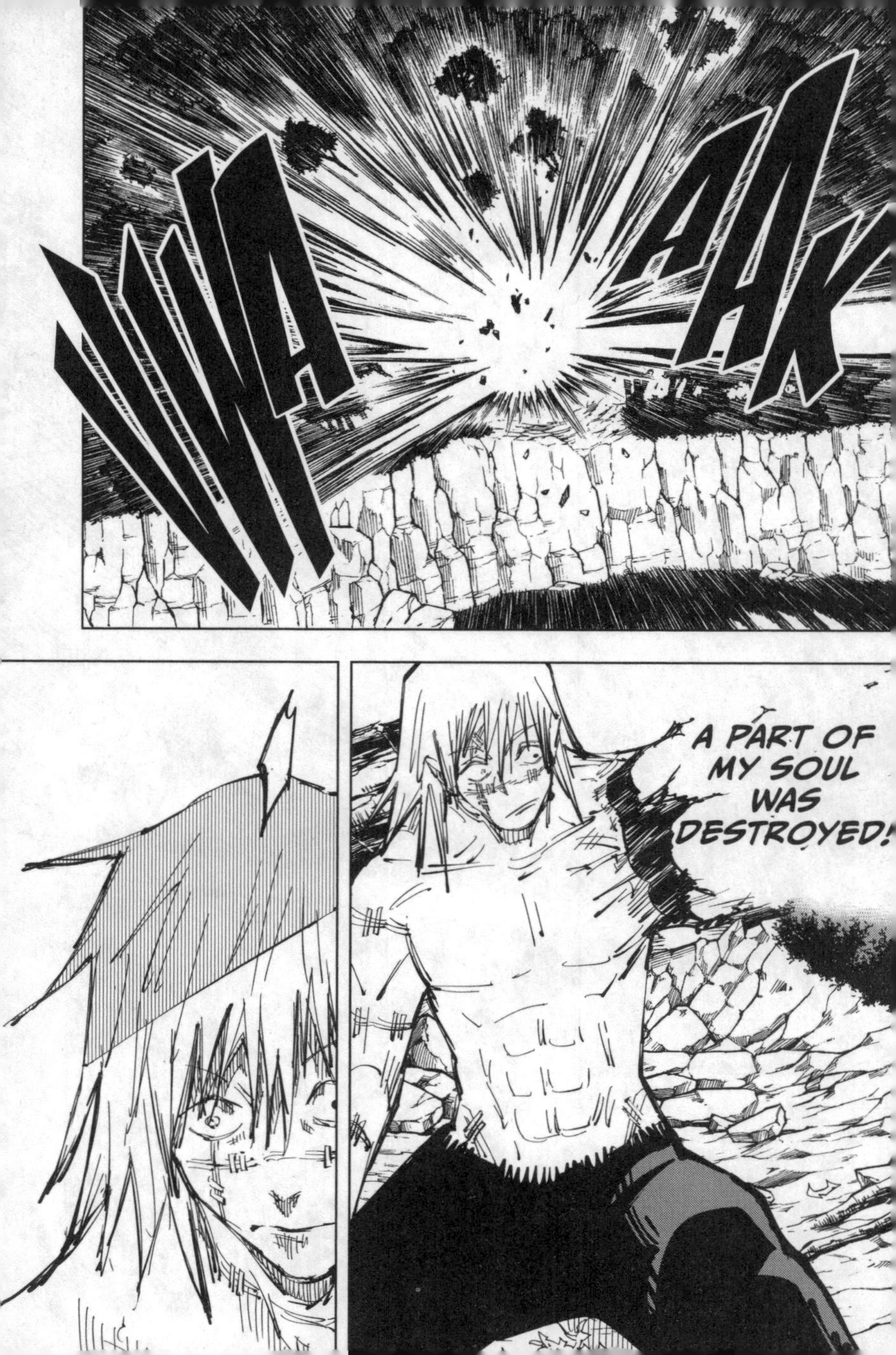
A PART OF MY SOUL WAS DESTROYED!

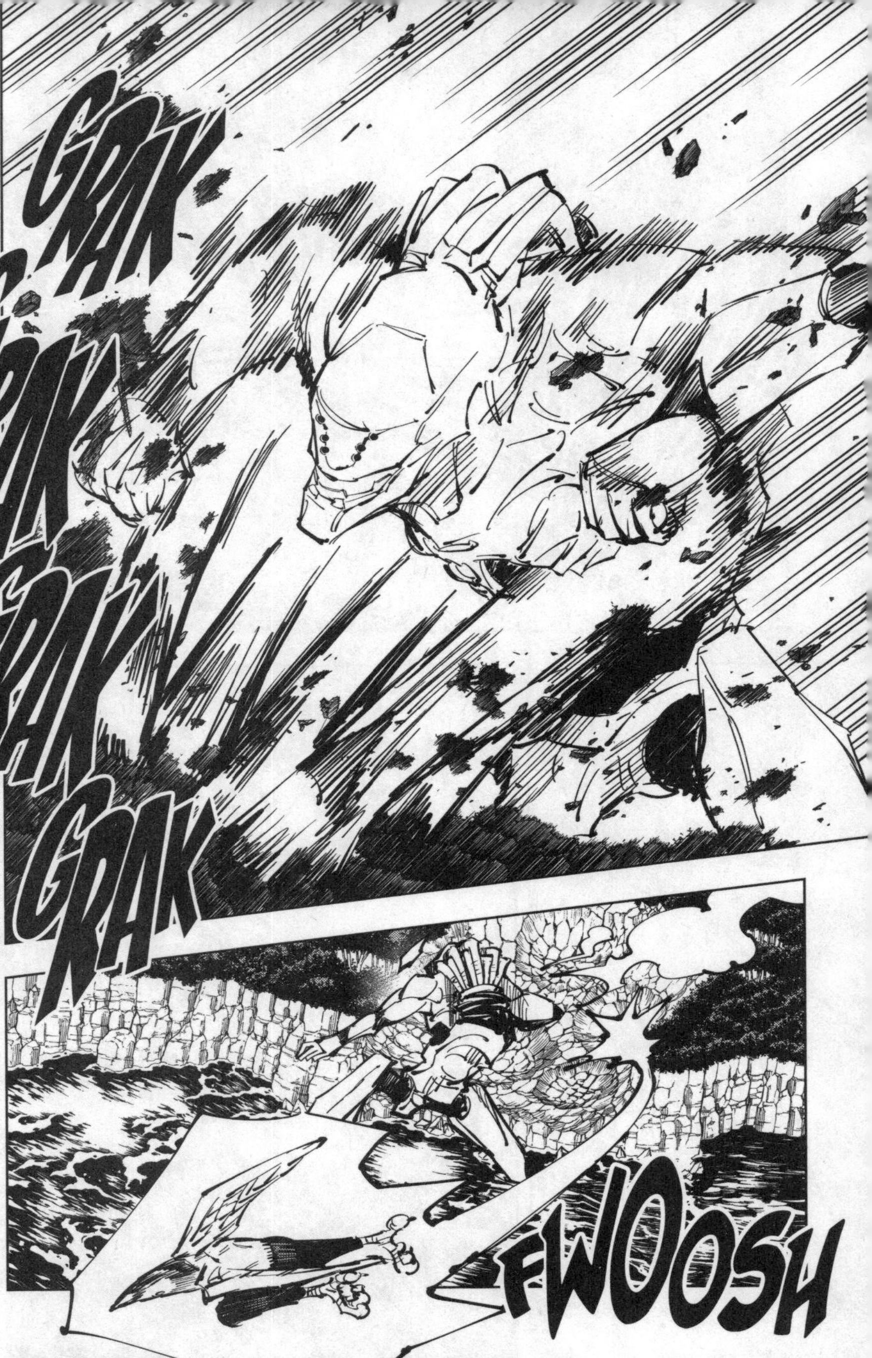
GRAK
GRAK
GRAK
GRAK
FWOOSH

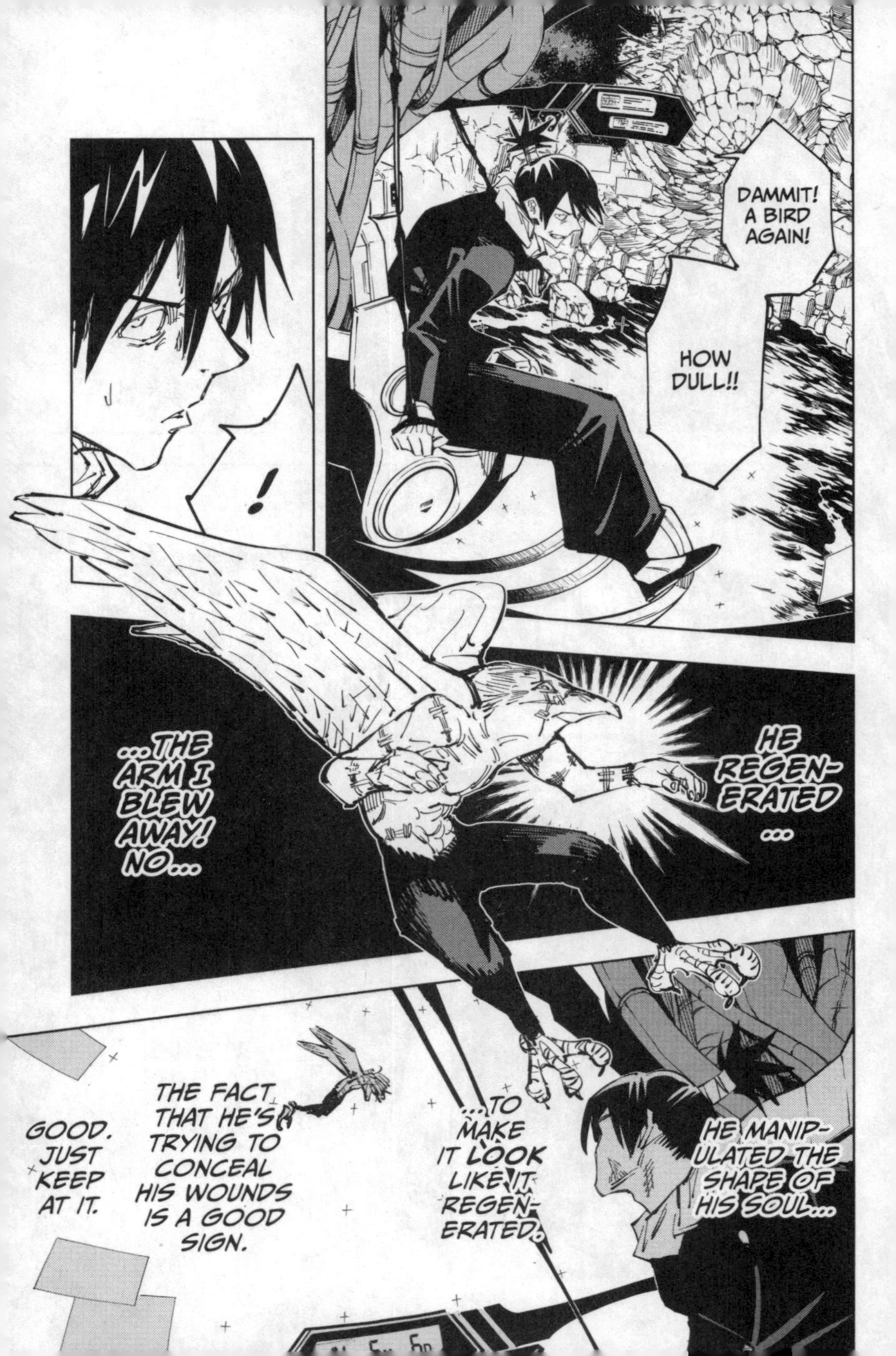
DAMMIT! A BIRD AGAIN!
HOW DULL!!
!
HE REGENERATED...
...THE ARM I BLEW AWAY! NO...
HE MANIPULATED THE SHAPE OF HIS SOUL...
...TO MAKE IT LOOK LIKE IT REGENERATED.
THE FACT THAT HE'S TRYING TO CONCEAL HIS WOUNDS IS A GOOD SIGN.
GOOD. JUST KEEP AT IT.

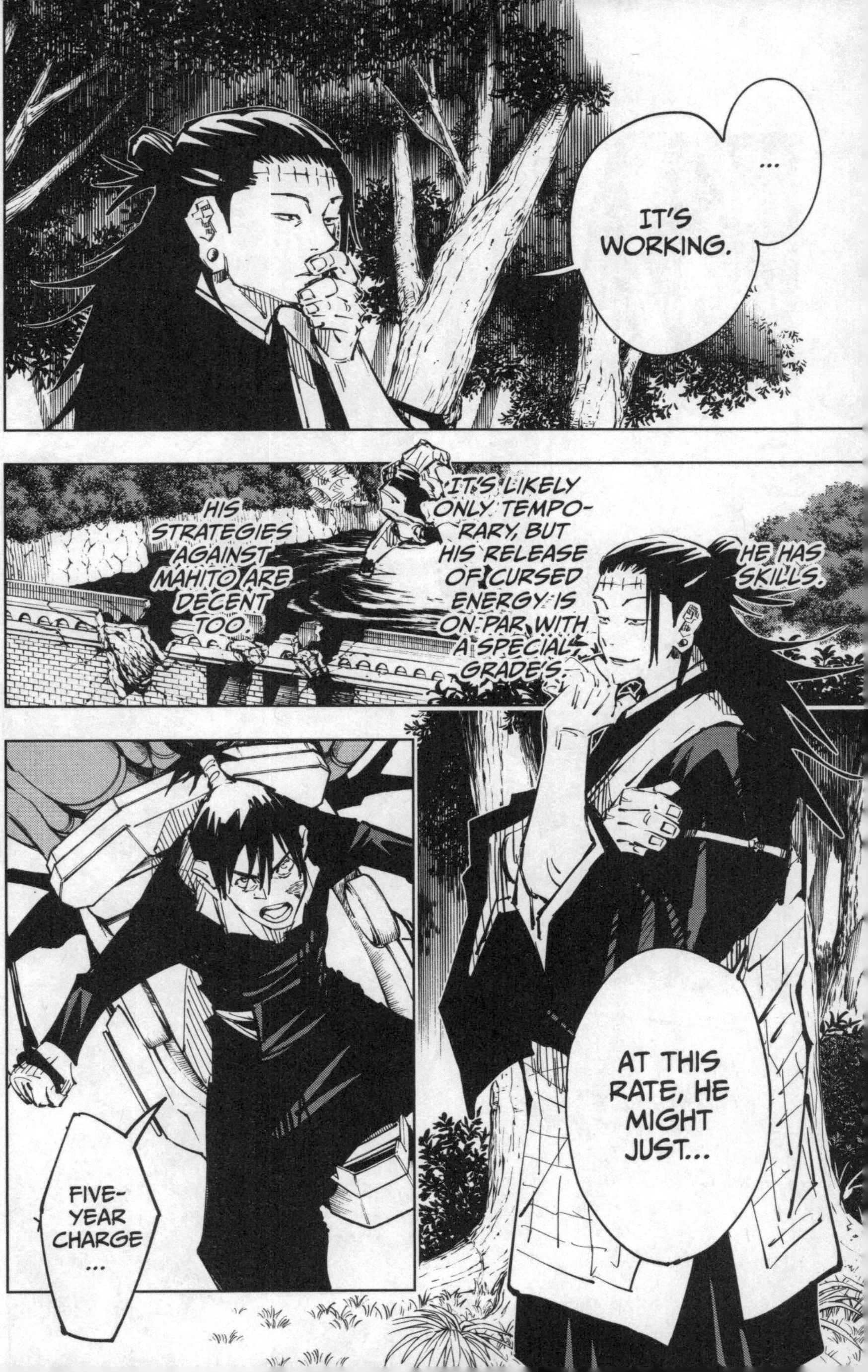
... IT'S WORKING.
HE HAS SKILLS.
IT'S LIKELY ONLY TEMPORARY, BUT HIS RELEASE OF CURSED ENERGY IS ON PAR WITH A SPECIAL GRADE'S.
HIS STRATEGIES AGAINST MAHITO ARE DECENT TOO.
AT THIS RATE, HE MIGHT JUST...
FIVE-YEAR CHARGE ...

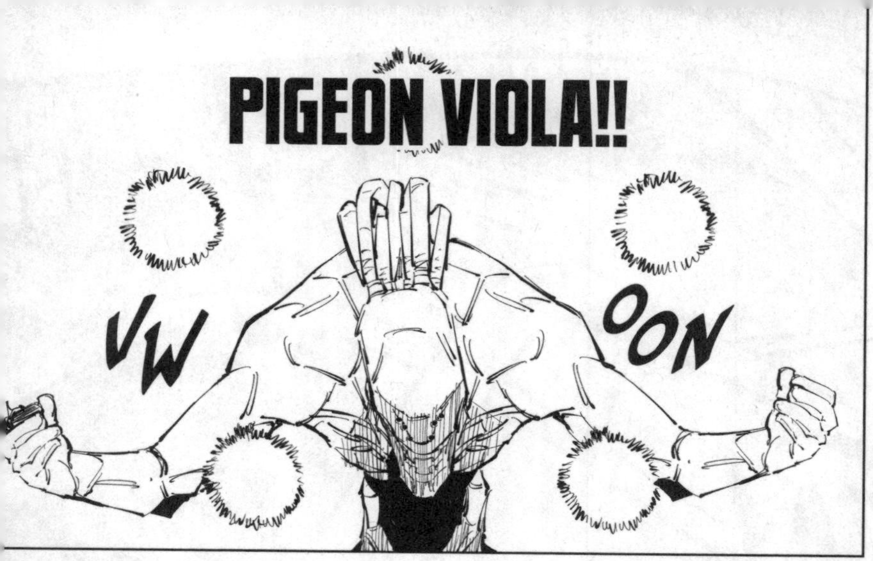
PIGEON VIOLA!!
VW
OON
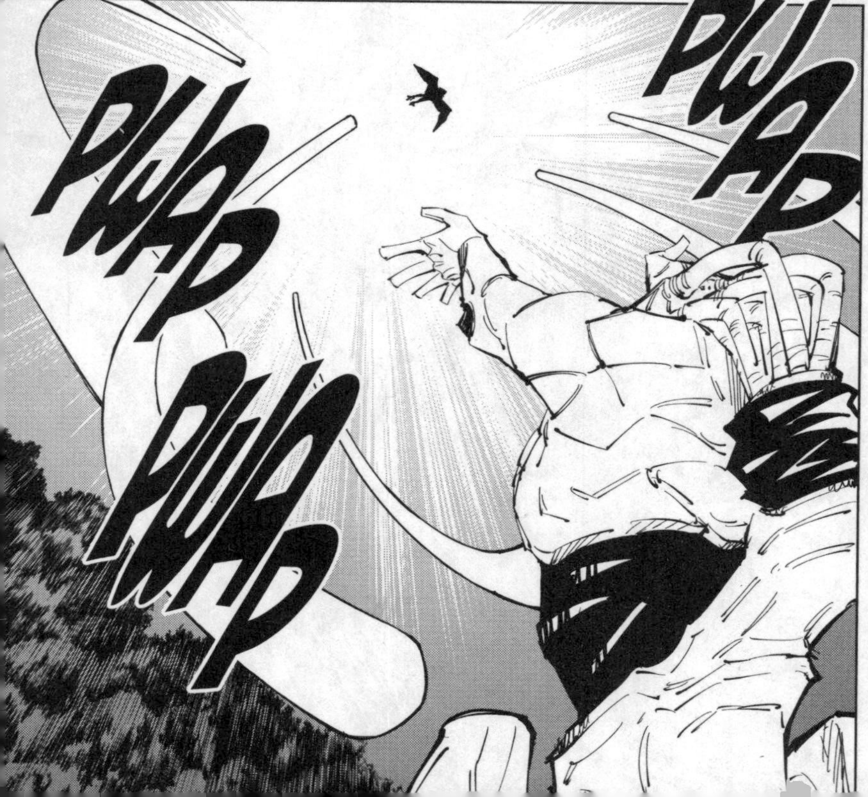
PWAP
PWAP
PWAP

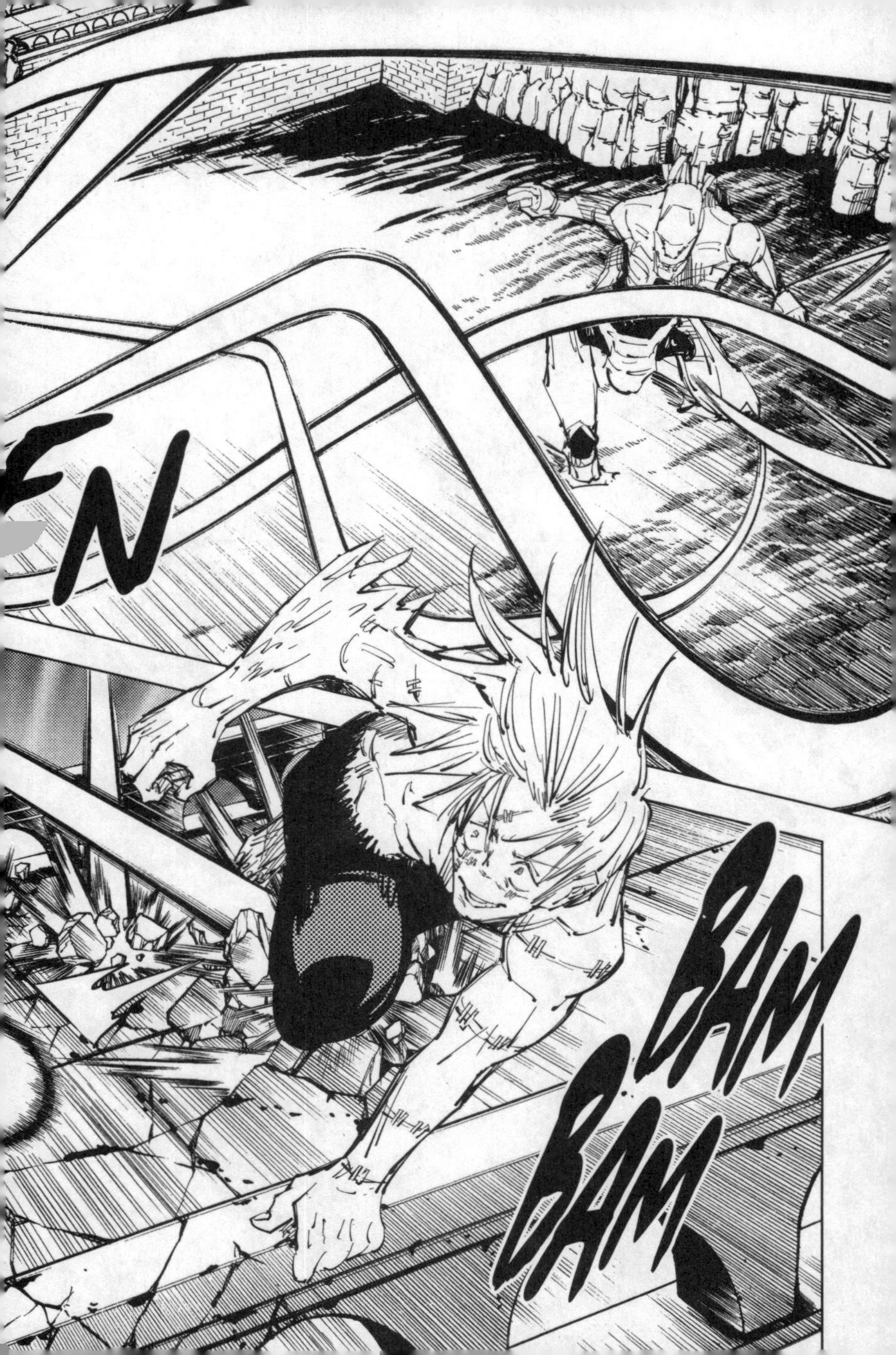
EN
BAM
BAM
BAM

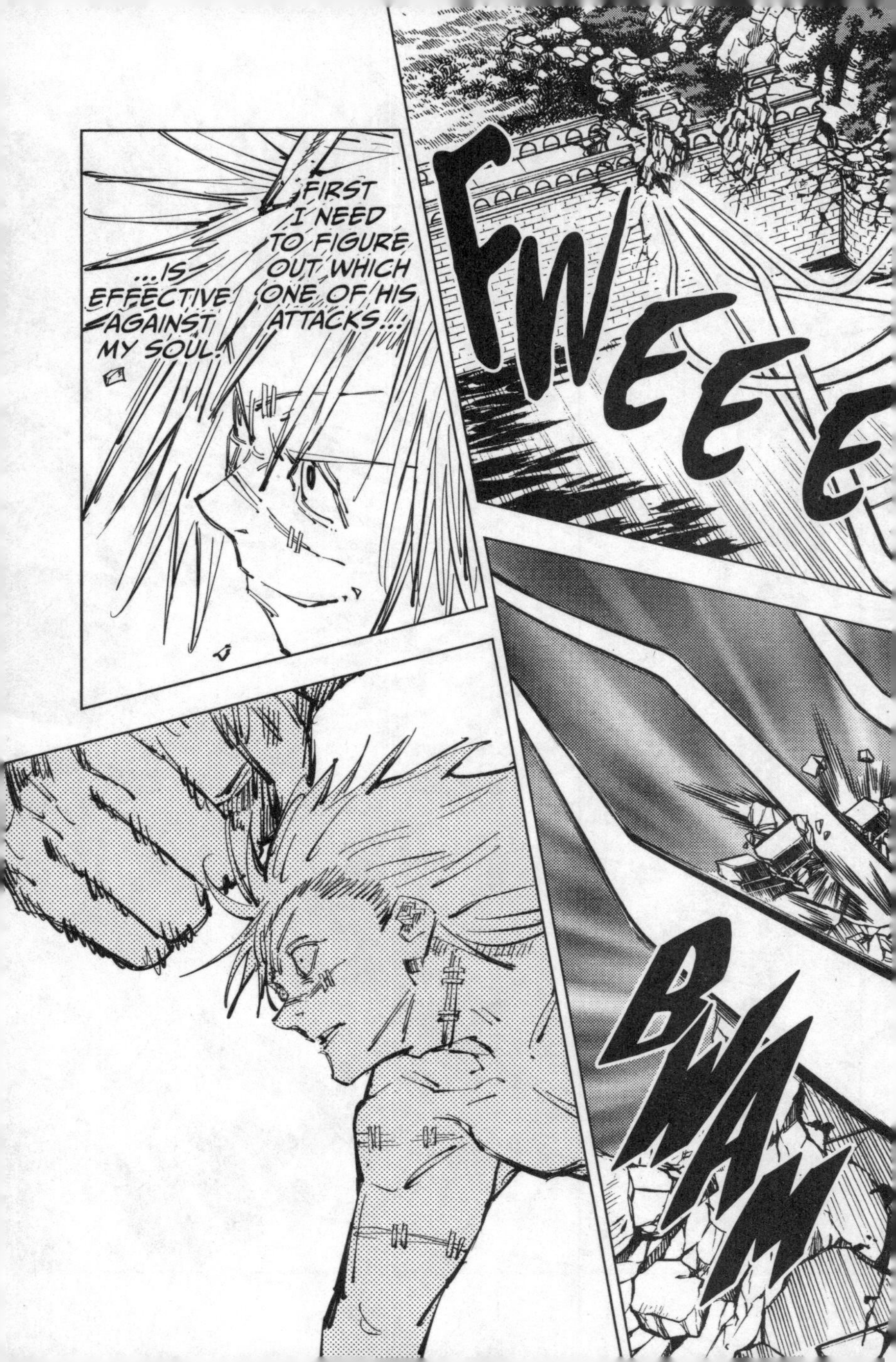
FWEEE
FIRST I NEED TO FIGURE OUT WHICH ONE OF HIS ATTACKS...
...IS EFFECTIVE AGAINST MY SOUL.
BWAM

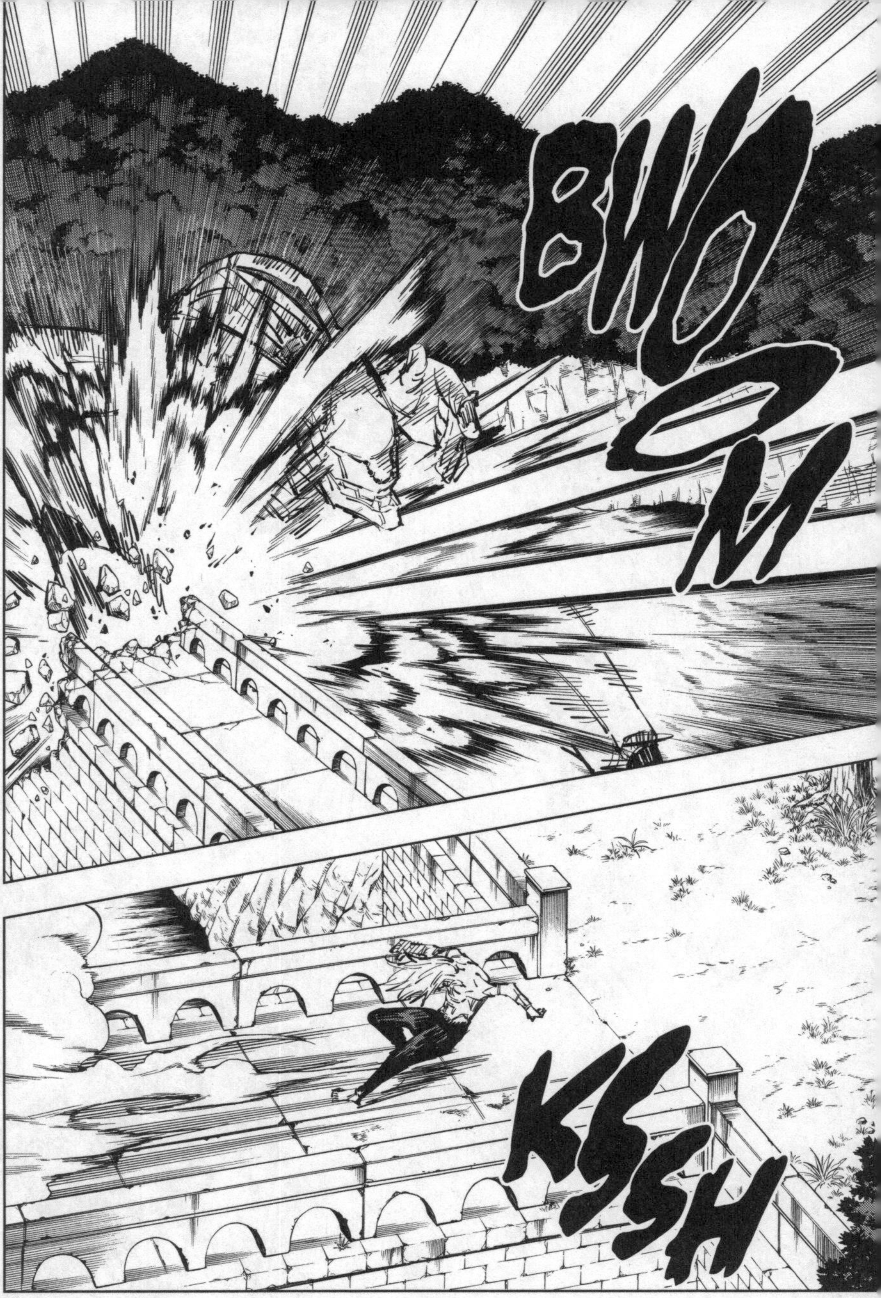
BWOOM
KSSH

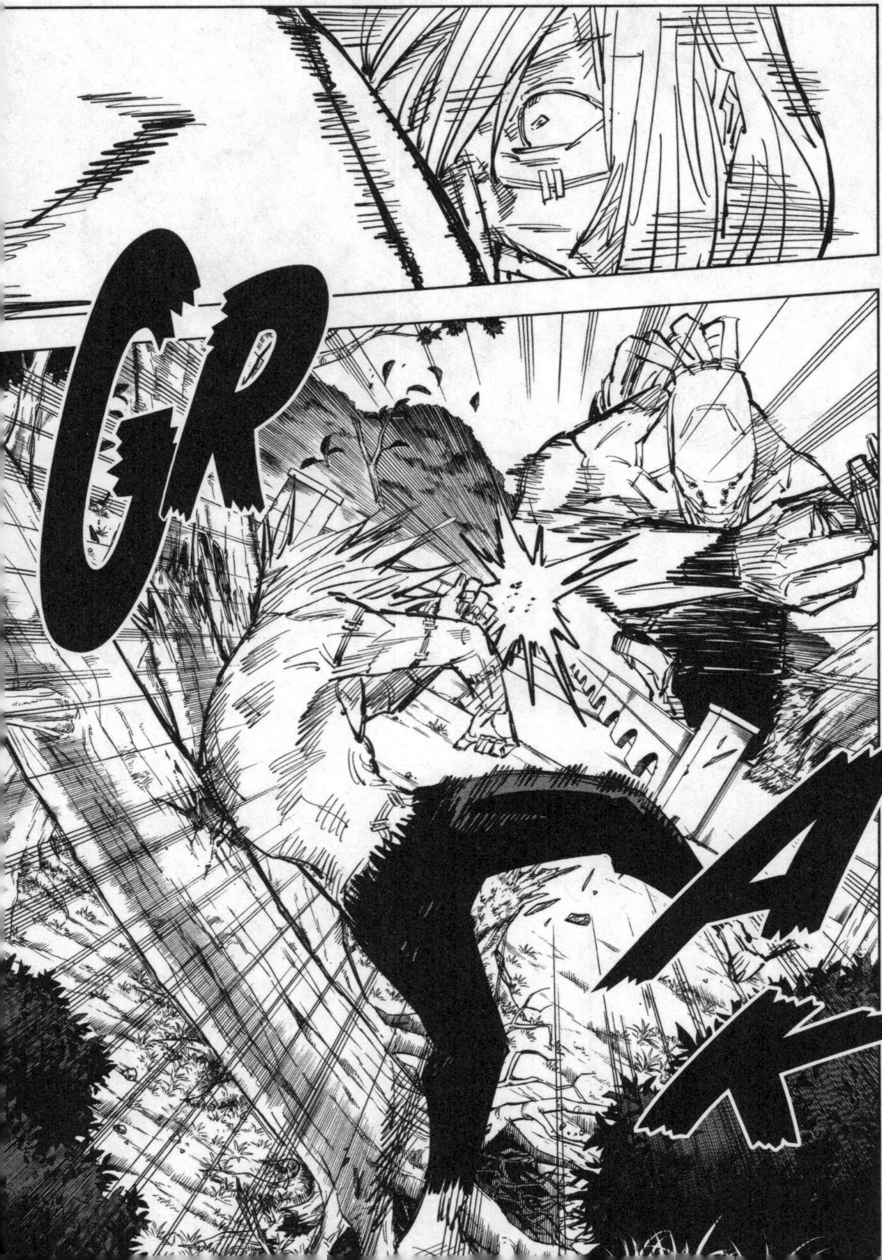
GRACK

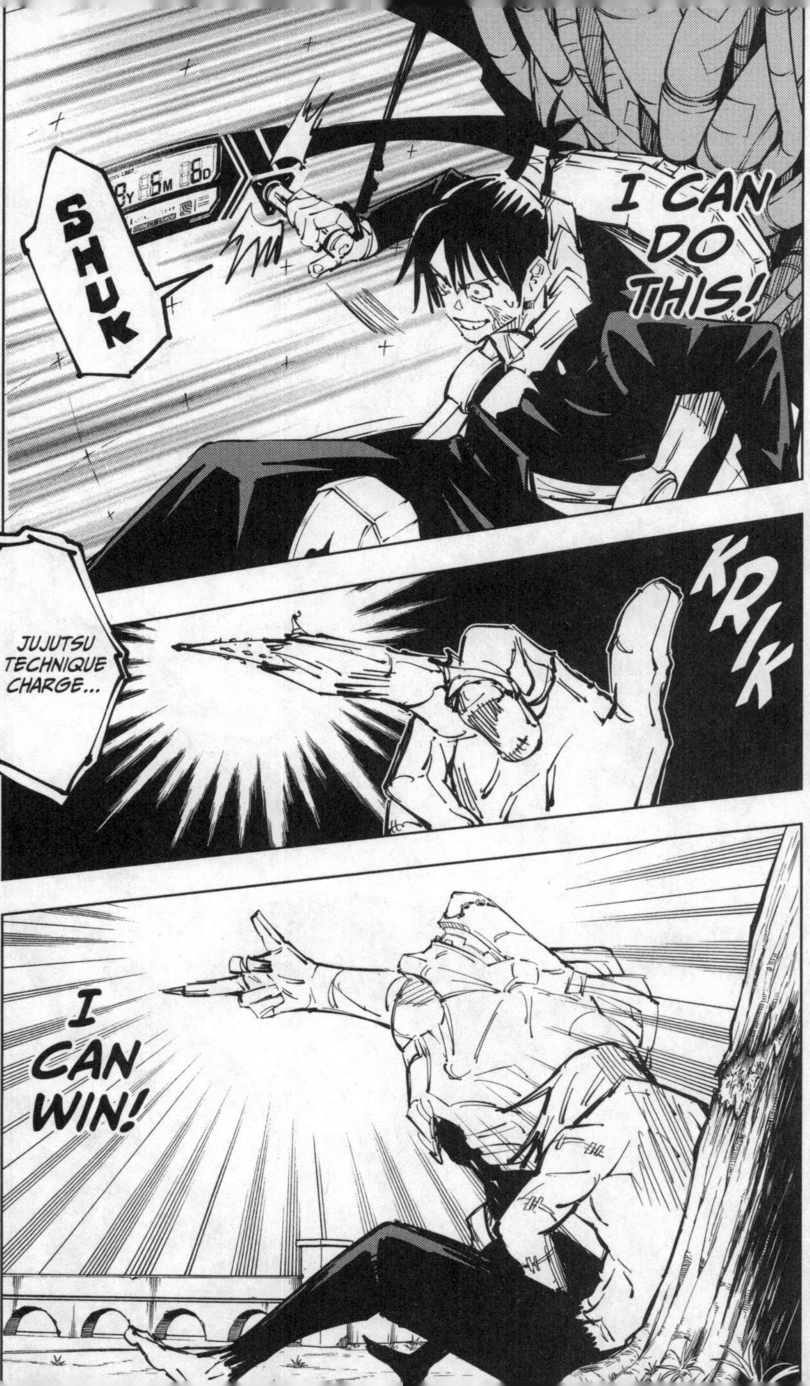
I CAN DO THIS!
SHUK
KRIK
JUJUTSU TECHNIQUE CHARGE...
I CAN WIN!

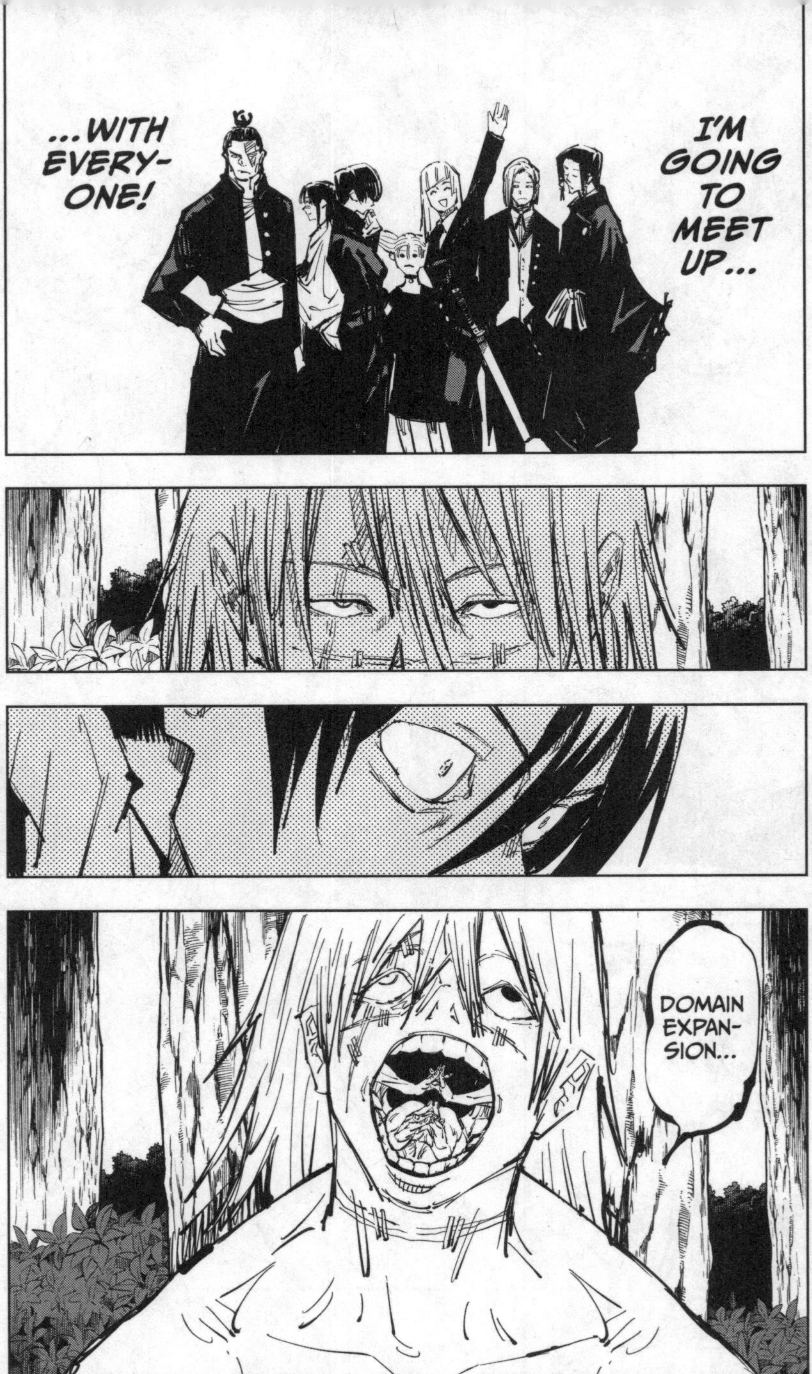
I'M GOING TO MEET UP...
...WITH EVERY-ONE!
DOMAIN EXPAN-SION...

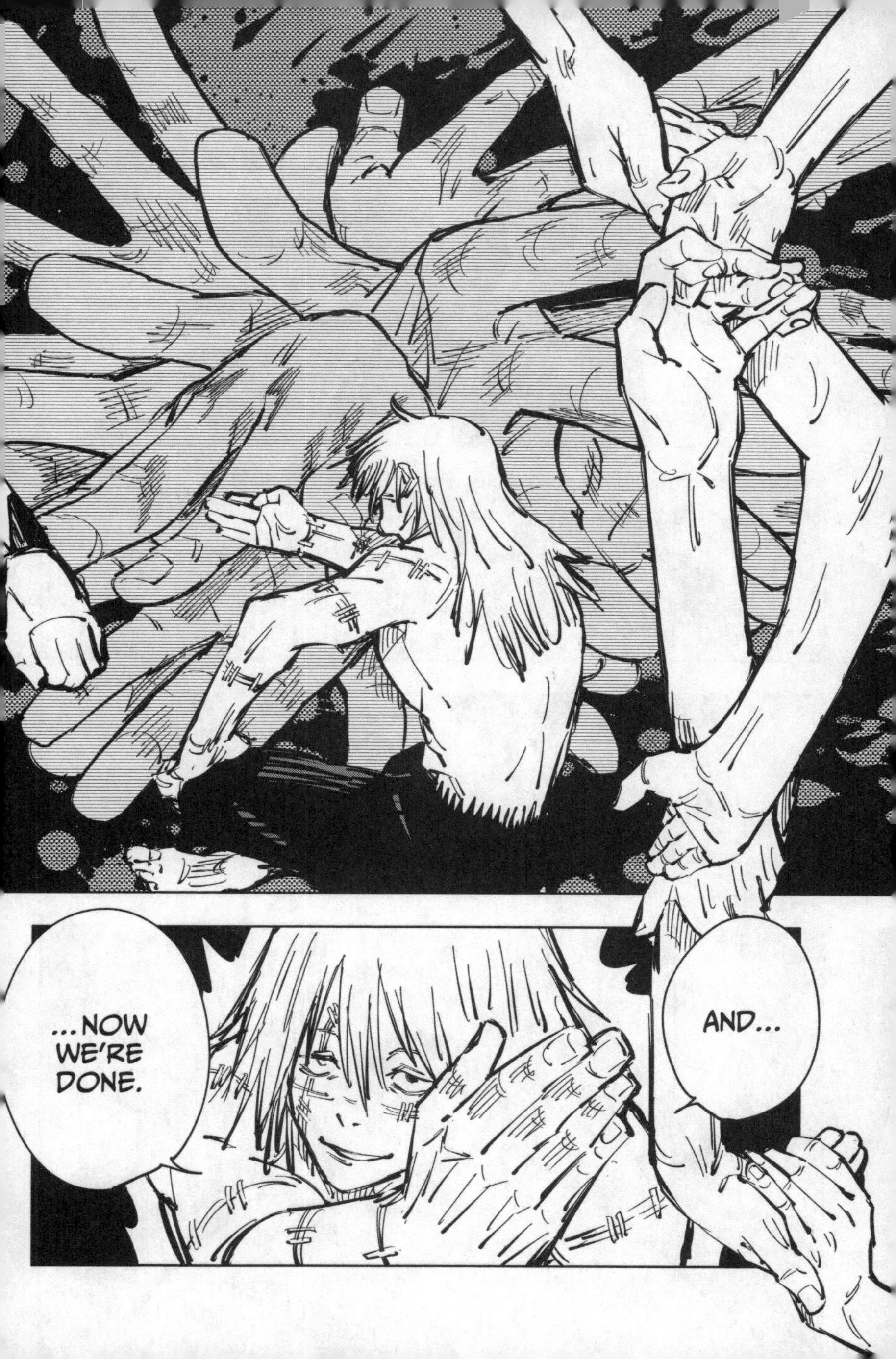
AND...
...NOW WE'RE DONE.

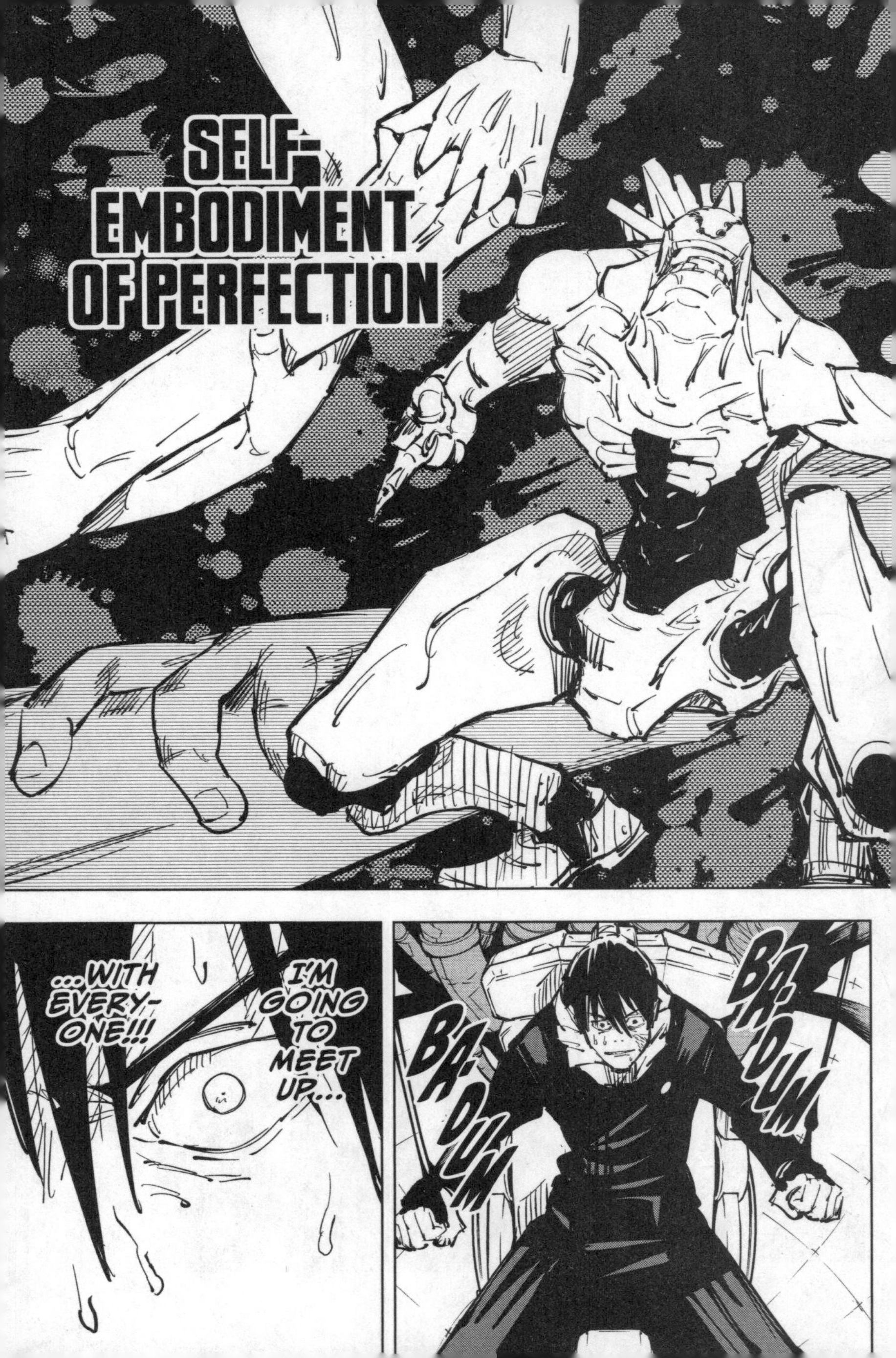
SELF-EMBODIMENT OF PERFECTION
BA-DUM
BA-DUM
I'M GOING TO MEET UP...
...WITH EVERY-ONE!!!

FIRST-
YEAR

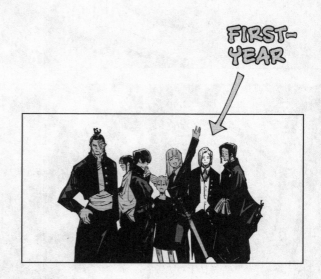

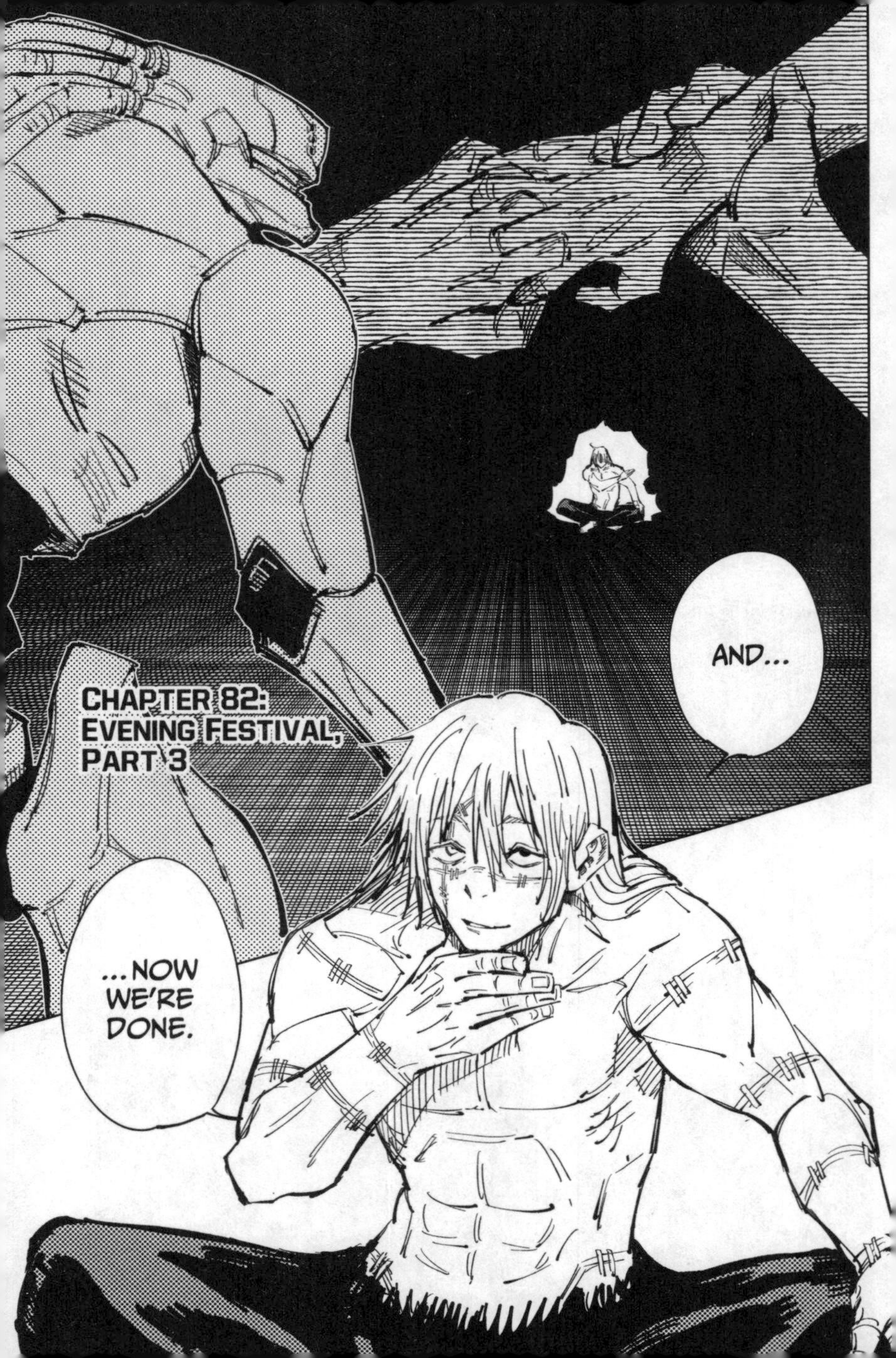
AND...
CHAPTER 82: EVENING FESTIVAL, PART 3
...NOW WE'RE DONE.

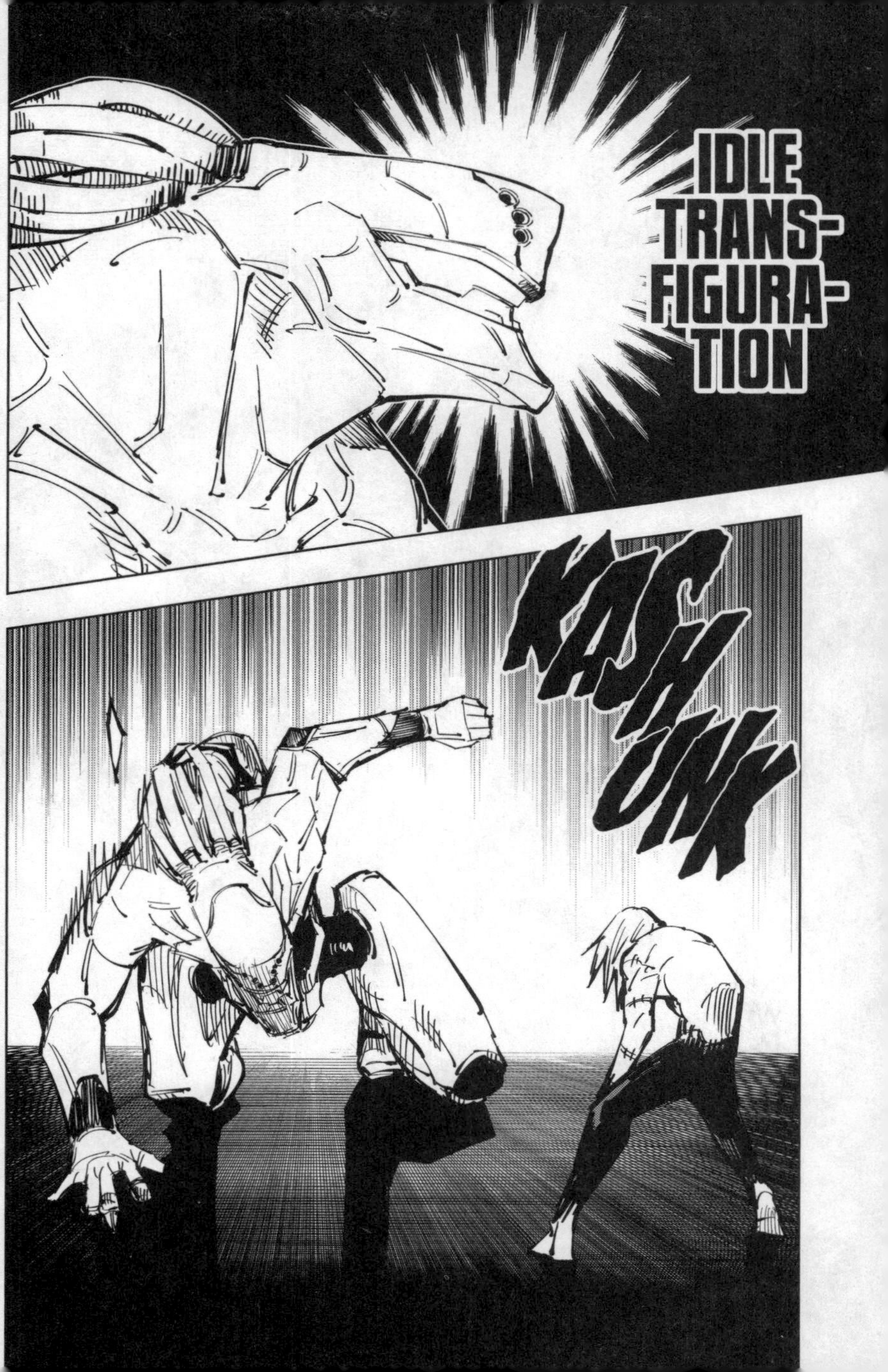
IDLE TRANS-FIGURA-TION
KASHUNK

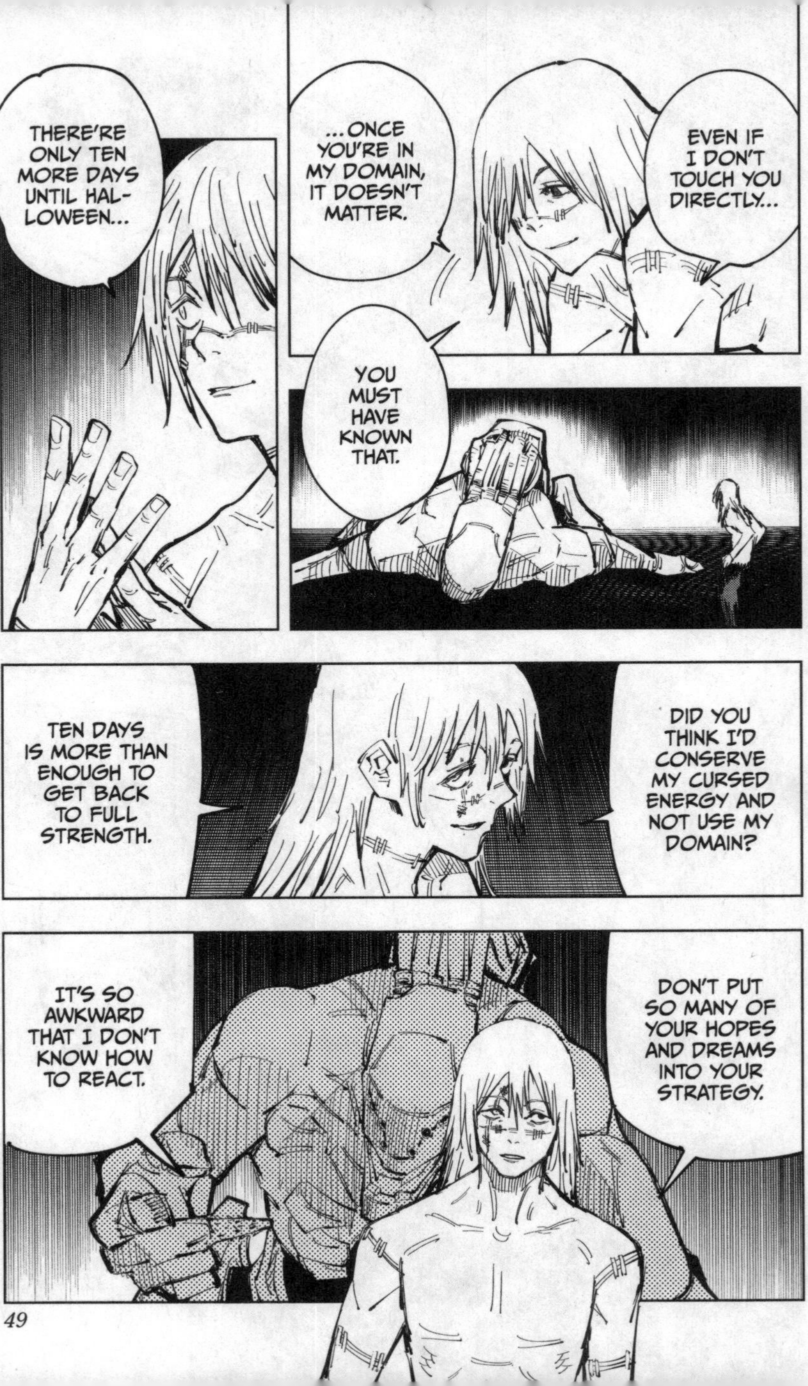
EVEN IF I DON'T TOUCH YOU DIRECTLY...
...ONCE YOU'RE IN MY DOMAIN, IT DOESN'T MATTER.
YOU MUST HAVE KNOWN THAT.
THERE'RE ONLY TEN MORE DAYS UNTIL HAL-LOWEEN...
DID YOU THINK I'D CONSERVE MY CURSED ENERGY AND NOT USE MY DOMAIN?
TEN DAYS IS MORE THAN ENOUGH TO GET BACK TO FULL STRENGTH.
DON'T PUT SO MANY OF YOUR HOPES AND DREAMS INTO YOUR STRATEGY.
IT'S SO AWKWARD THAT I DON'T KNOW HOW TO REACT.

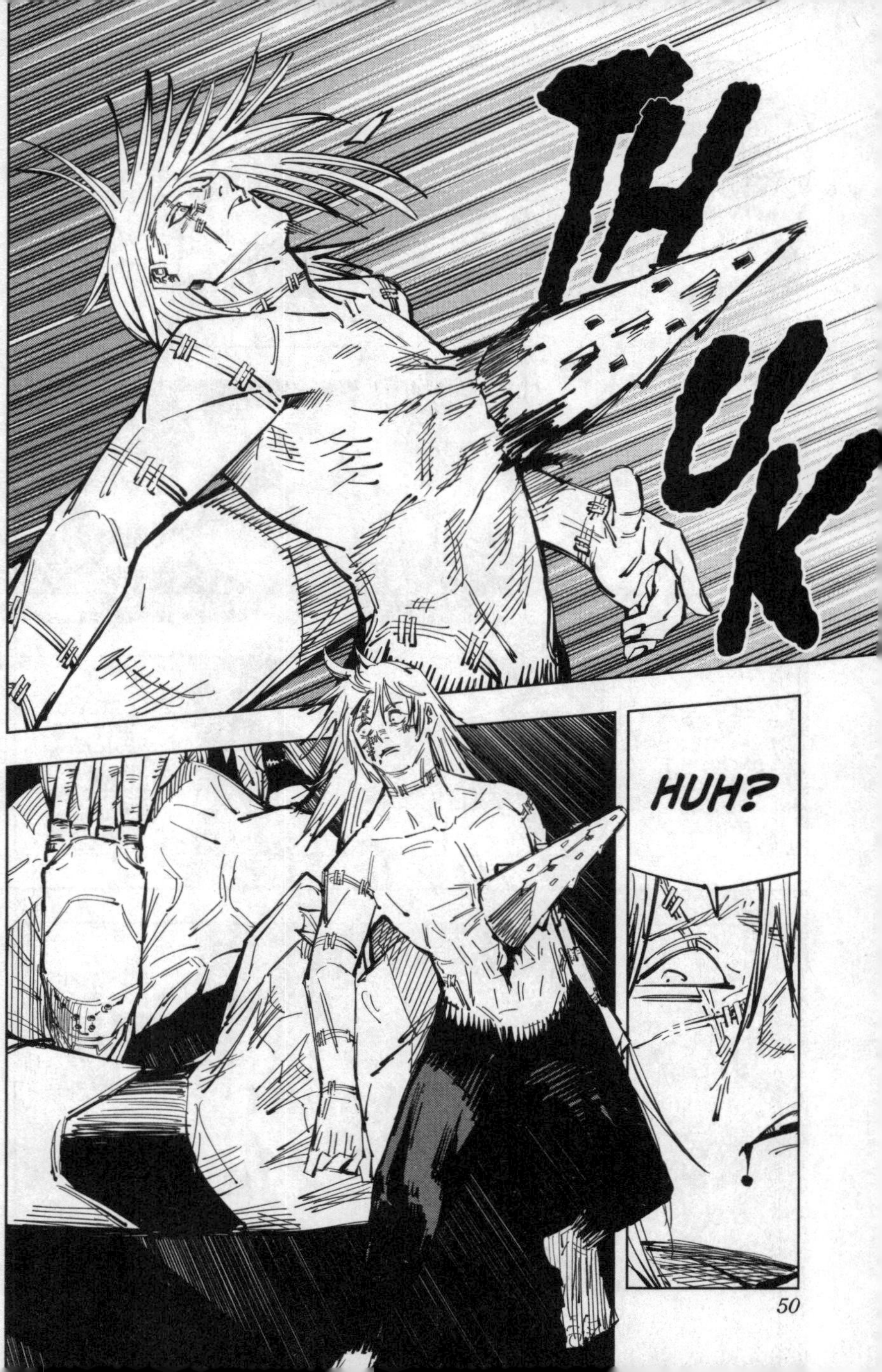
THUK
HUH?

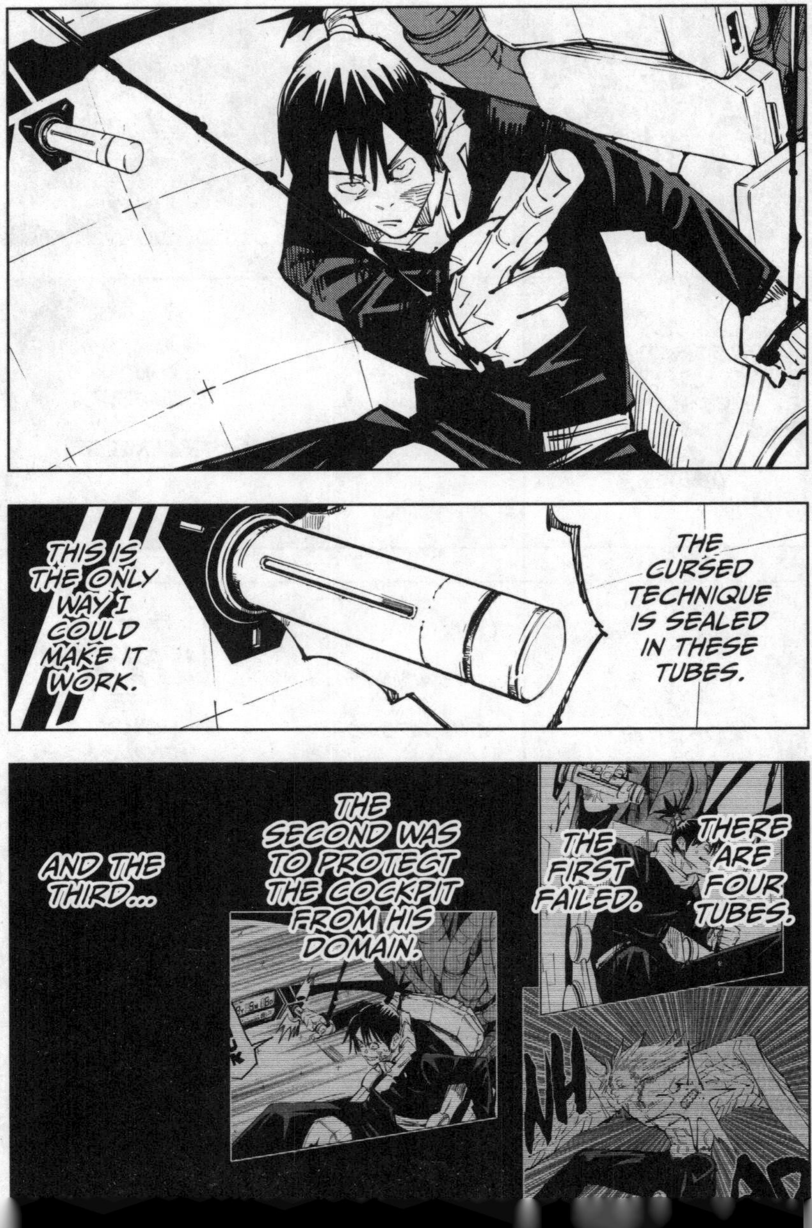
THE CURSED TECHNIQUE IS SEALED IN THESE TUBES.
THIS IS THE ONLY WAY I COULD MAKE IT WORK.
THERE ARE FOUR TUBES.
THE FIRST FAILED.
THE SECOND WAS TO PROTECT THE COCKPIT FROM HIS DOMAIN.
AND THE THIRD...

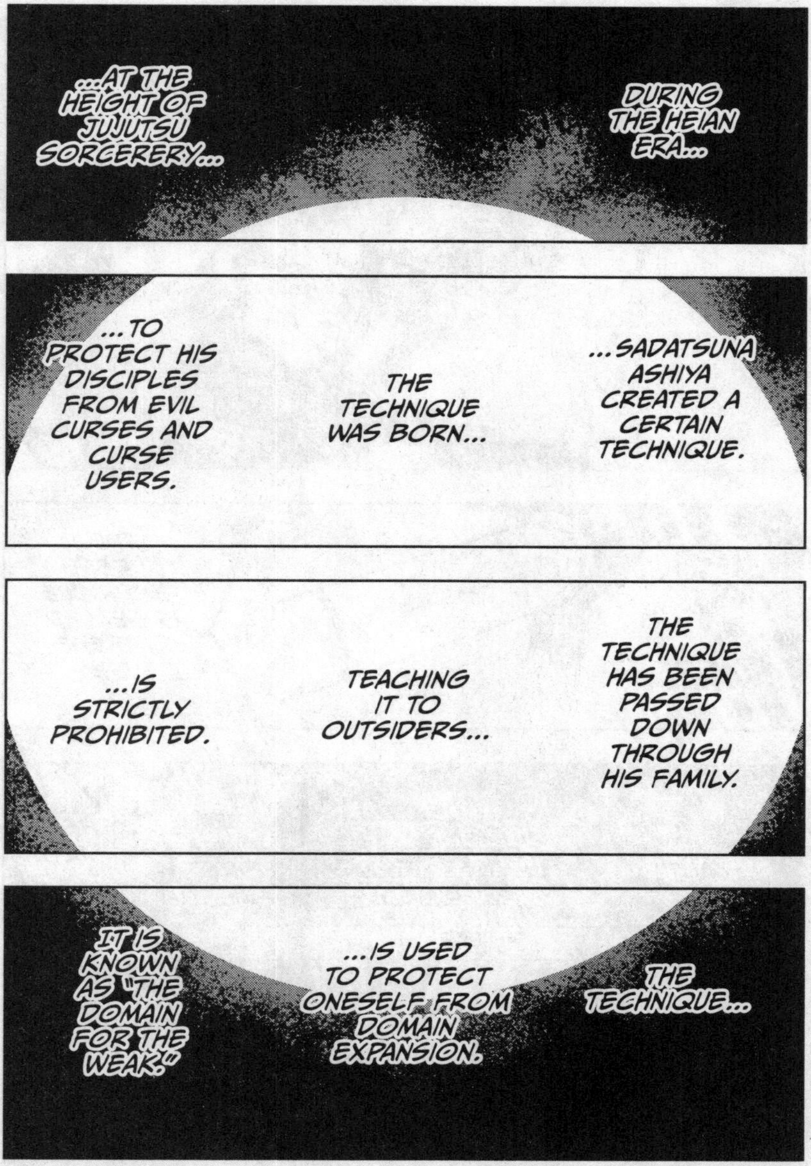
DURING THE HEIAN ERA...
...AT THE HEIGHT OF JUJUTSU SORCERERY...
...SADATSUNA ASHIYA CREATED A CERTAIN TECHNIQUE.
THE TECHNIQUE WAS BORN...
...TO PROTECT HIS DISCIPLES FROM EVIL CURSES AND CURSE USERS.
THE TECHNIQUE HAS BEEN PASSED DOWN THROUGH HIS FAMILY.
TEACHING IT TO OUTSIDERS...
...IS STRICTLY PROHIBITED.
THE TECHNIQUE...
...IS USED TO PROTECT ONESELF FROM DOMAIN EXPANSION.
IT IS KNOWN AS "THE DOMAIN FOR THE WEAK."

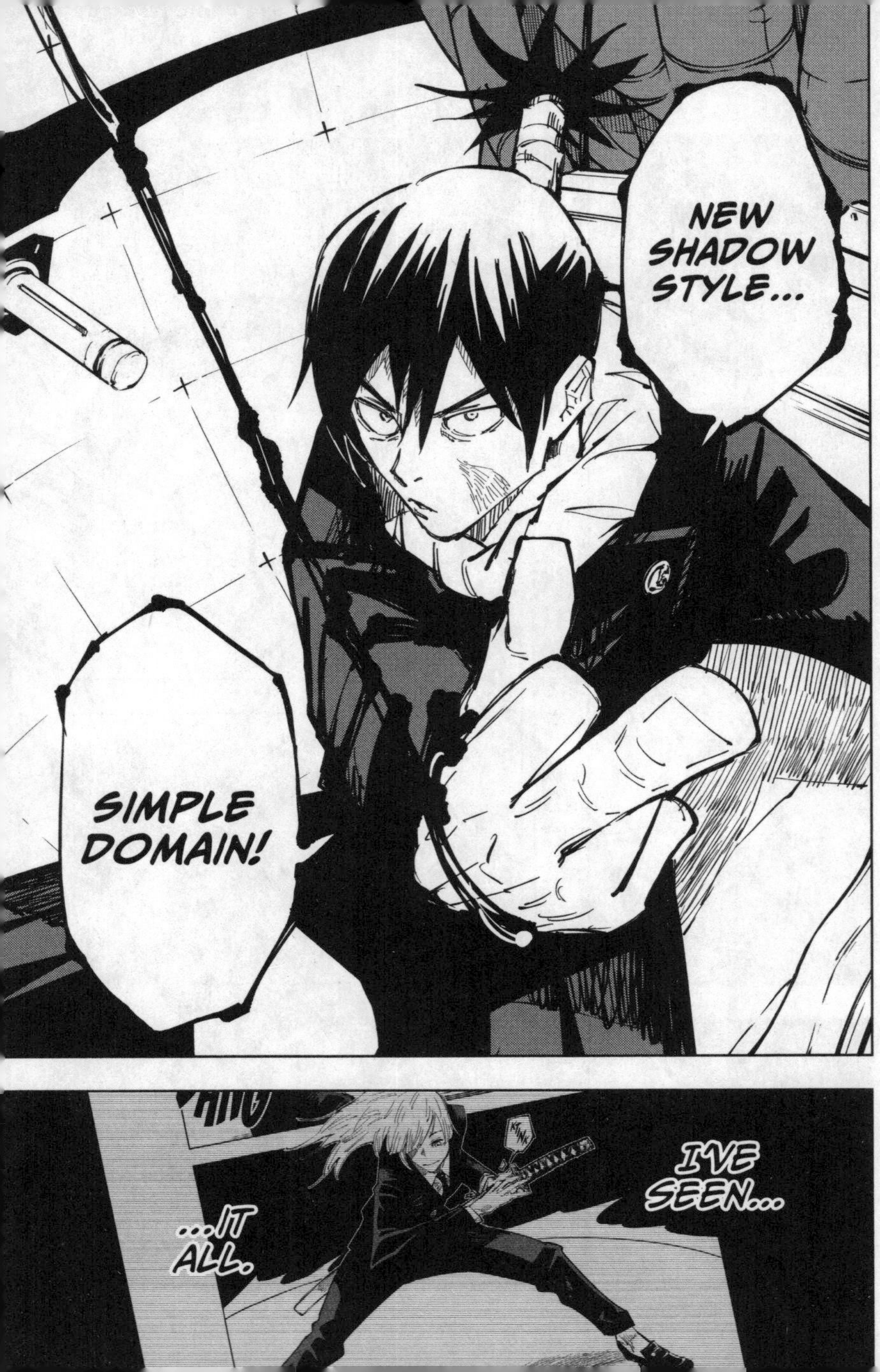
NEW SHADOW STYLE...
SIMPLE DOMAIN!
I'VE SEEN...
...IT ALL.

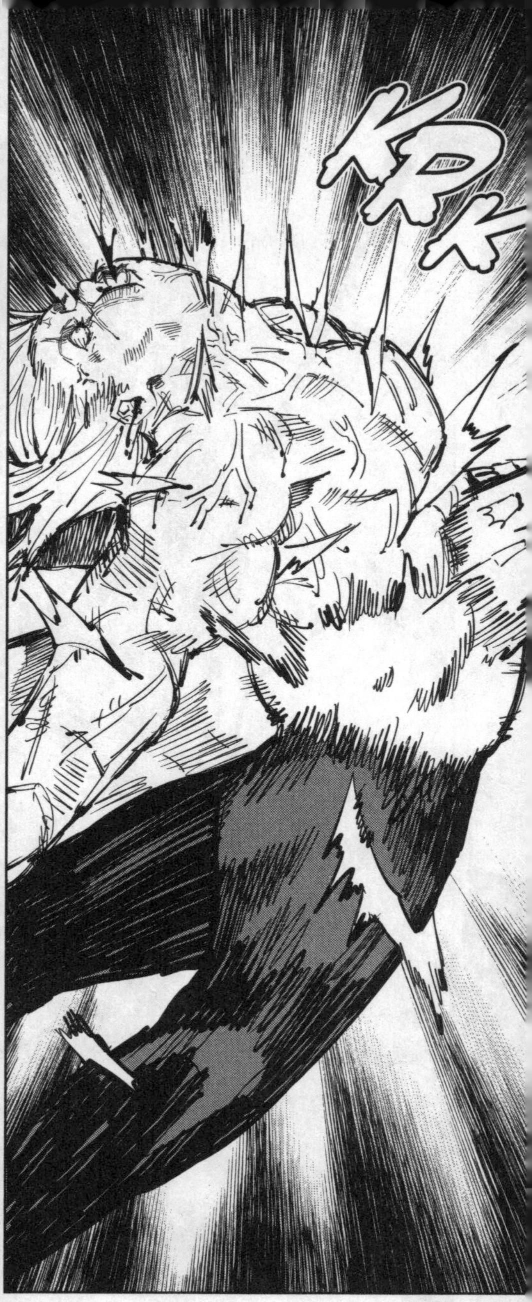
KRK
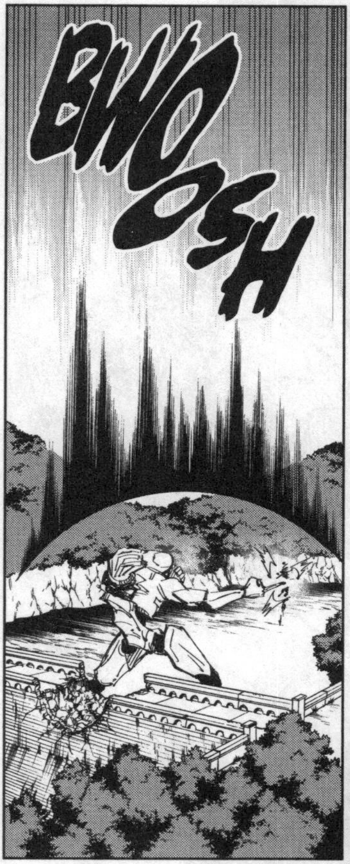
BWOOSH
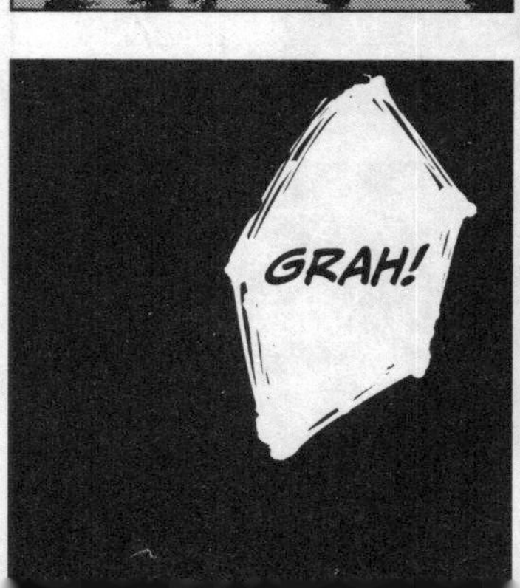
GRAH!

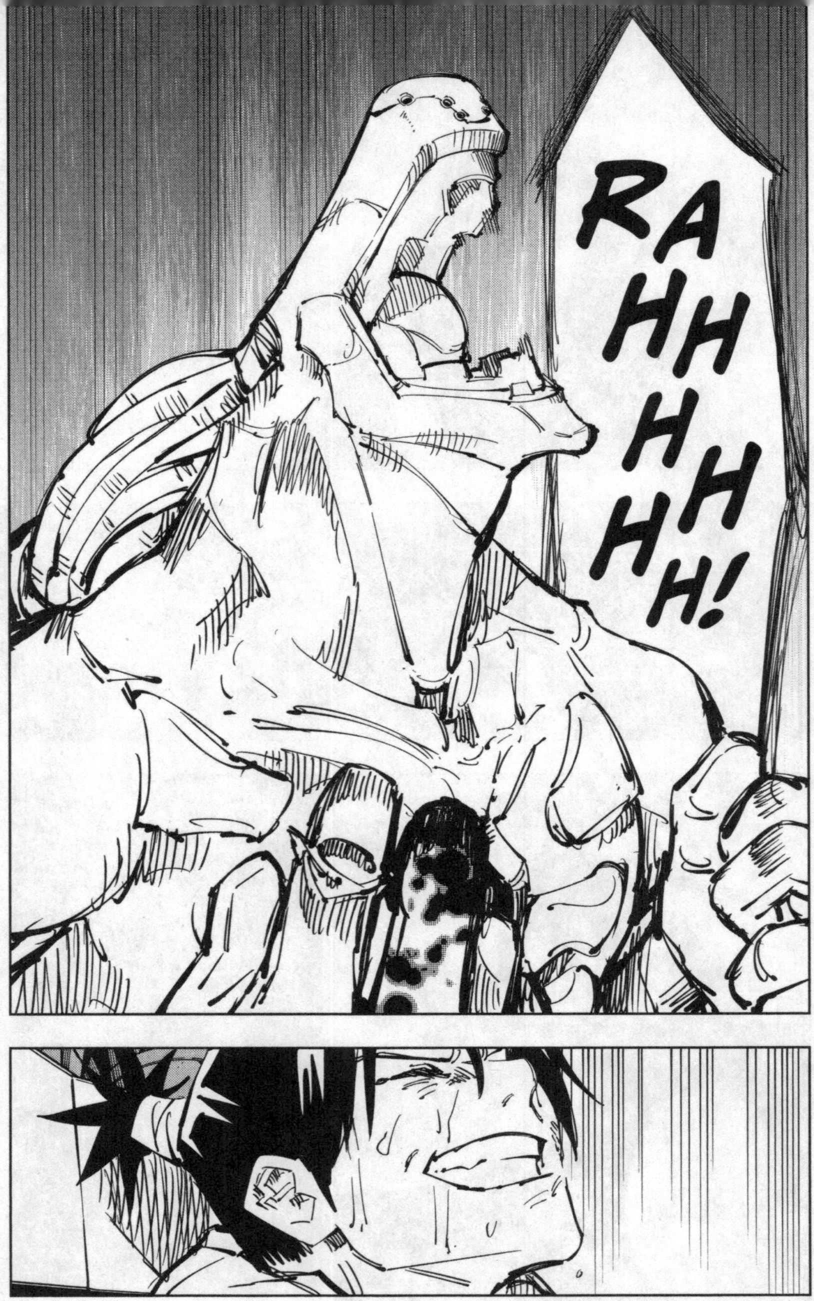
RAHHHHHH!

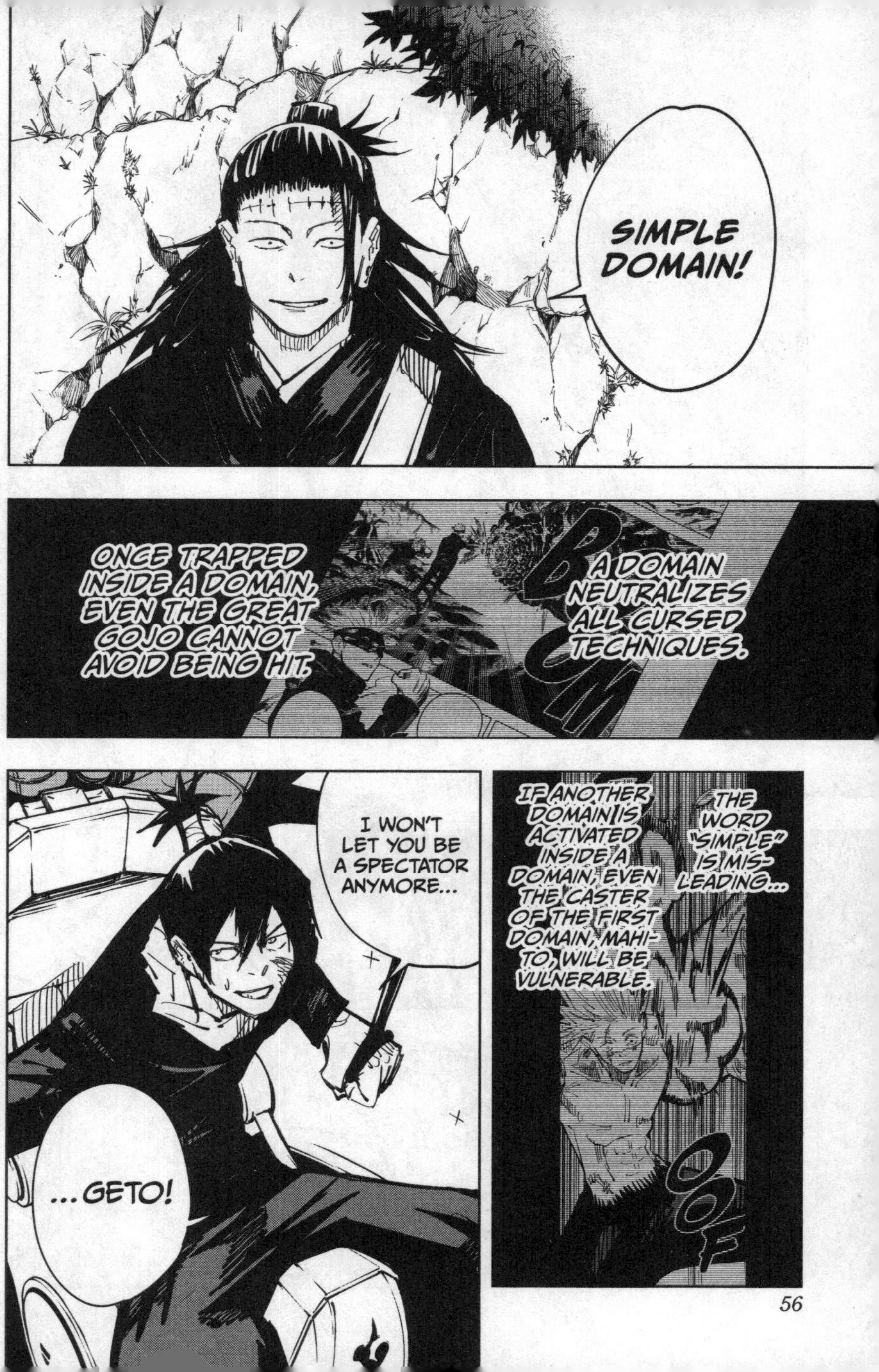
SIMPLE DOMAIN!
A DOMAIN NEUTRALIZES ALL CURSED TECHNIQUES.
ONCE TRAPPED INSIDE A DOMAIN, EVEN THE GREAT GOJO CANNOT AVOID BEING HIT.
THE WORD "SIMPLE" IS MIS-LEADING...
IF ANOTHER DOMAIN IS ACTIVATED INSIDE A DOMAIN, EVEN THE CASTER OF THE FIRST DOMAIN, MAHI-TO, WILL BE VULNERABLE.
OOOF
I WON'T LET YOU BE A SPECTATOR ANYMORE...
...GETO!

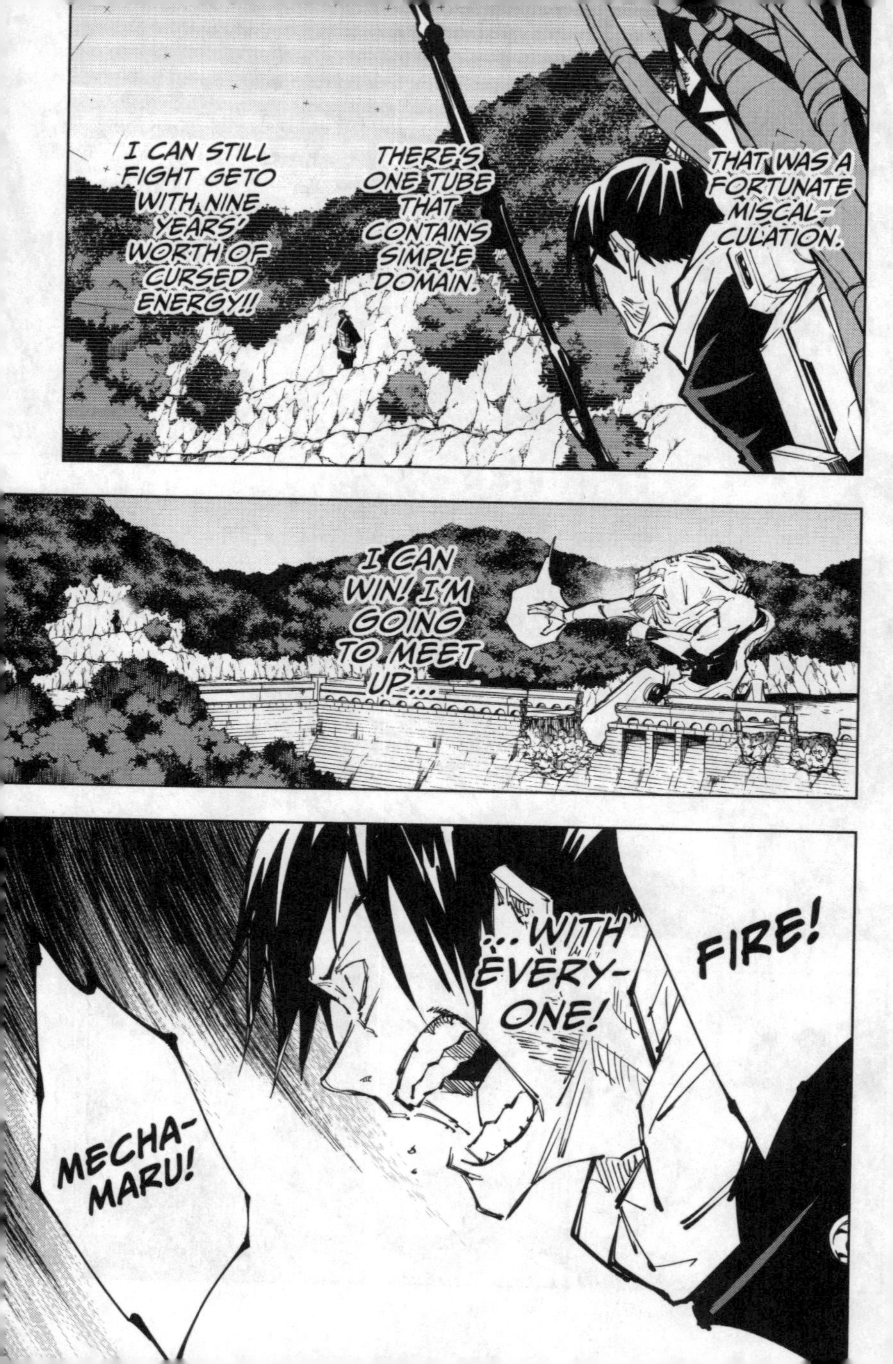
THAT WAS A FORTUNATE MISCAL-CULATION.
THERE'S ONE TUBE THAT CONTAINS SIMPLE DOMAIN.
I CAN STILL FIGHT GETO WITH NINE YEARS' WORTH OF CURSED ENERGY!!
I CAN WIN! I'M GOING TO MEET UP...
...WITH EVERY-ONE!
FIRE!
MECHA-MARU!

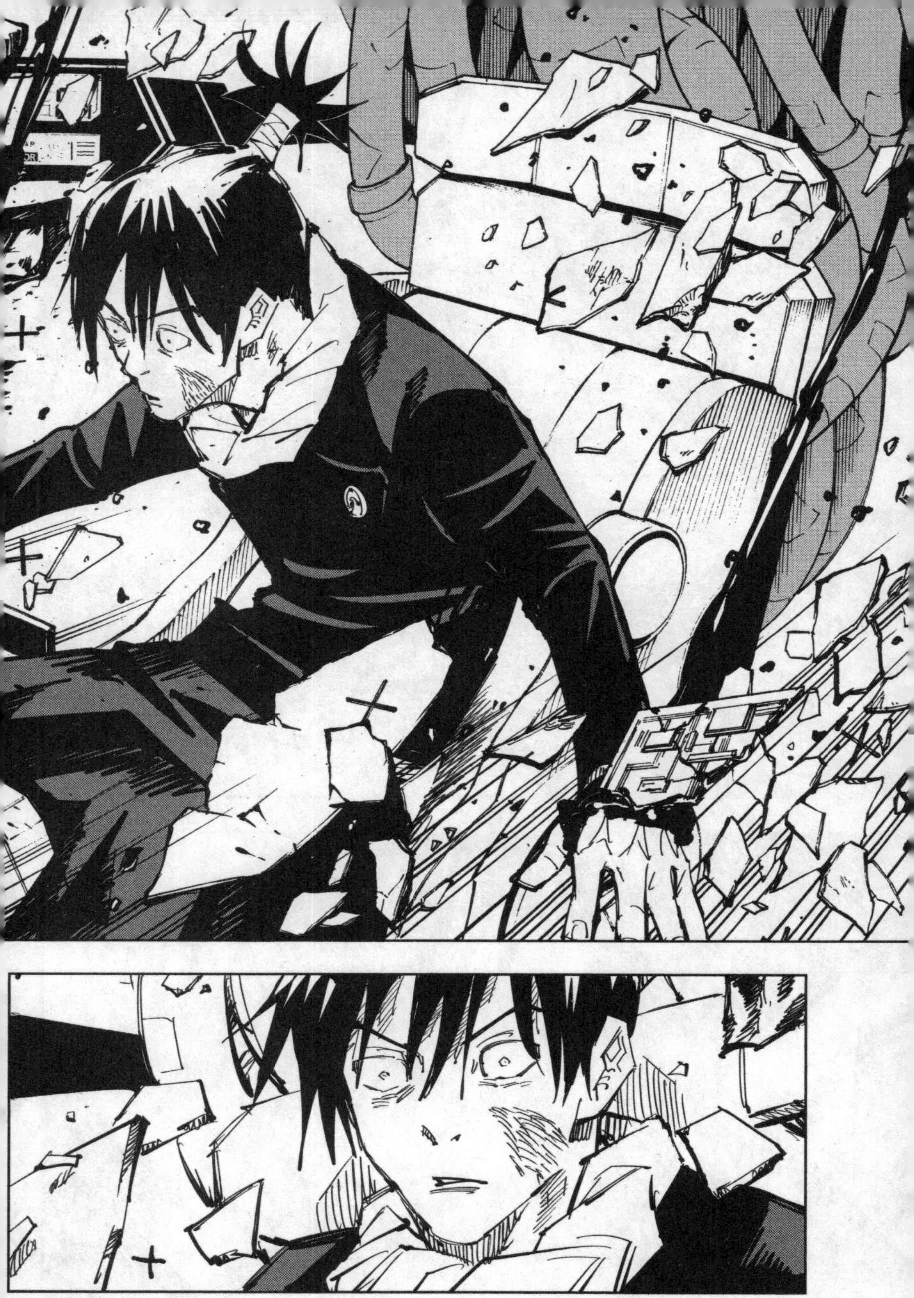

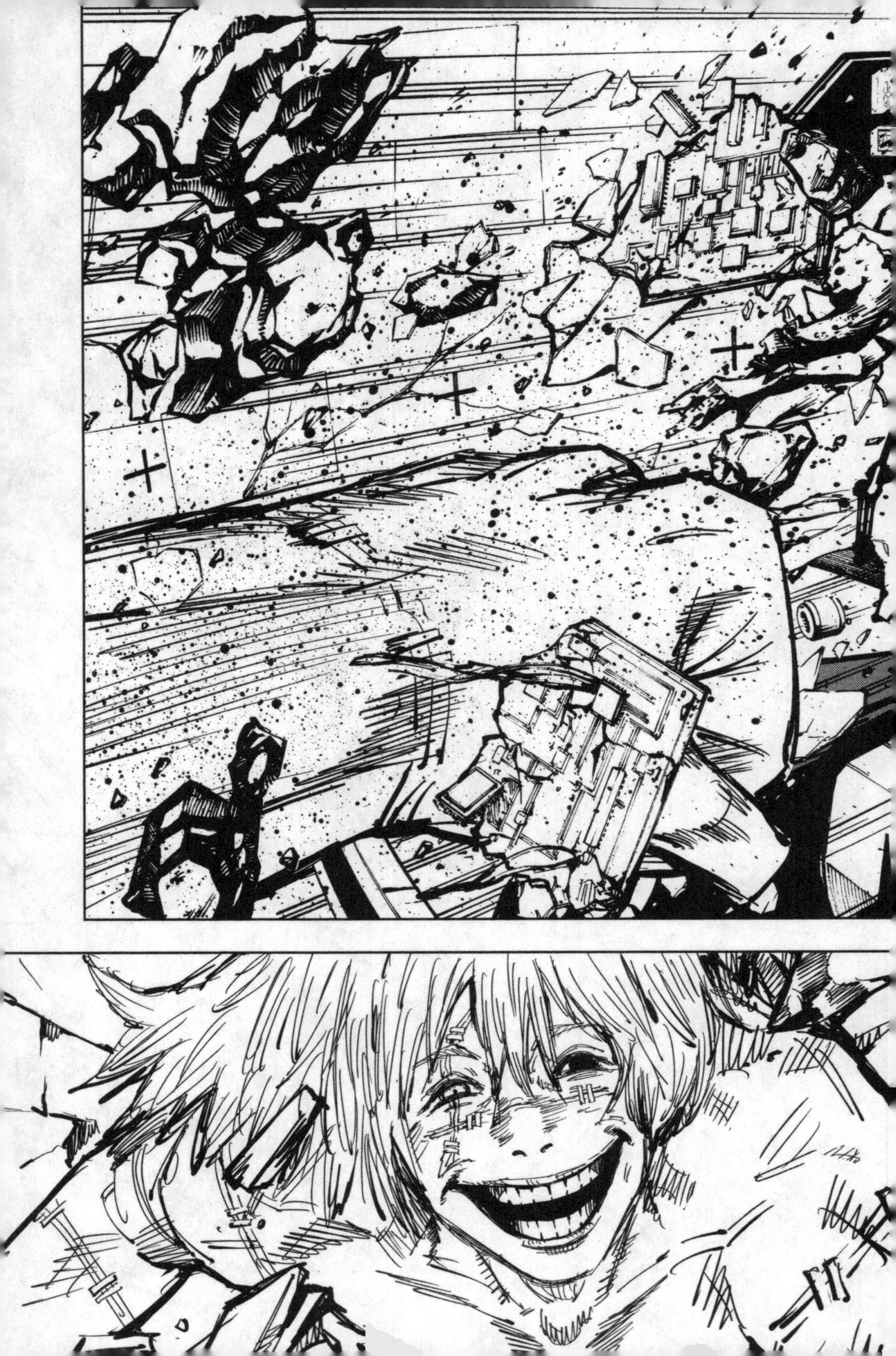

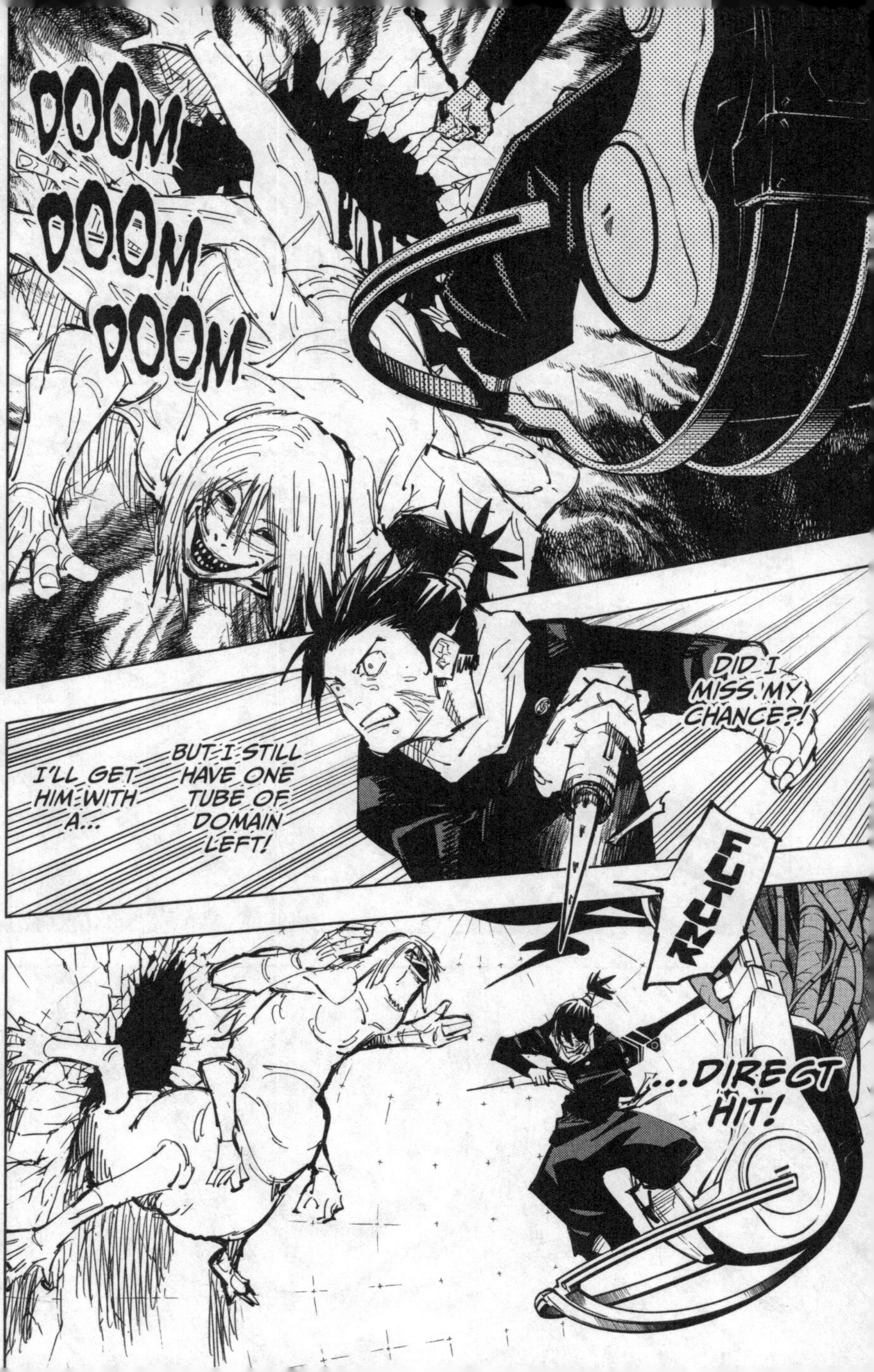
DOOM
DOOM
DOOM
DOOM
DID I MISS MY CHANCE?!
BUT I STILL HAVE ONE TUBE OF DOMAIN LEFT!
I'LL GET HIM WITH A...
FLITUNK
...DIRECT HIT!

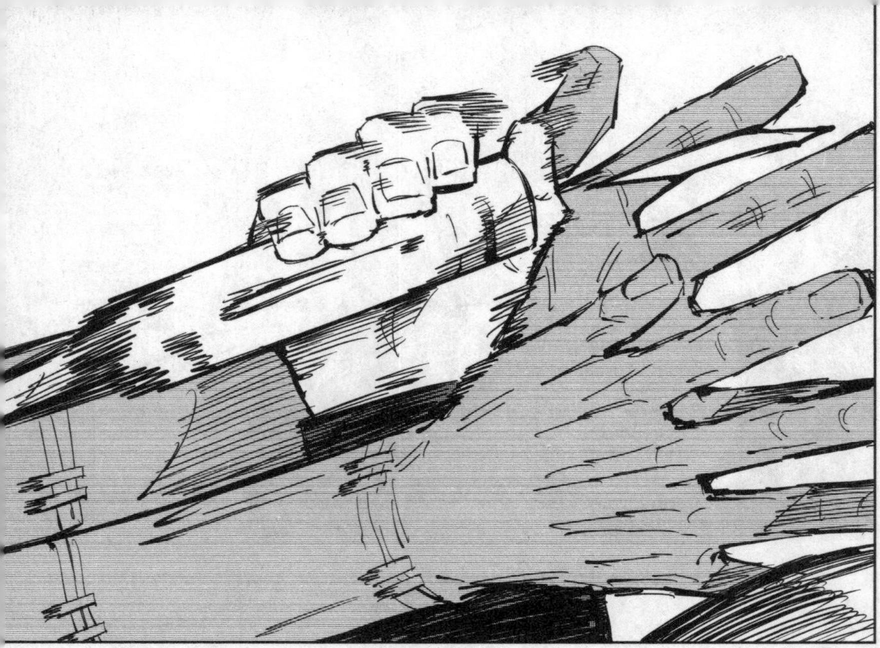

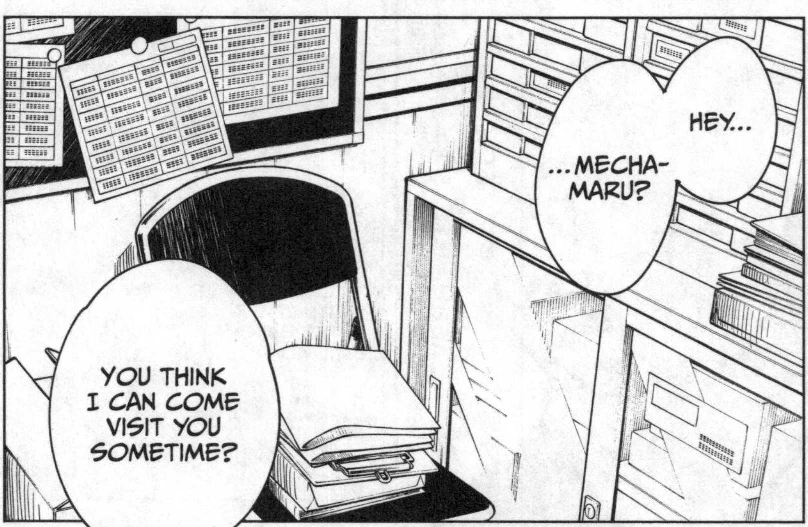
HEY... ...MECHA-MARU?
YOU THINK I CAN COME VISIT YOU SOMETIME?

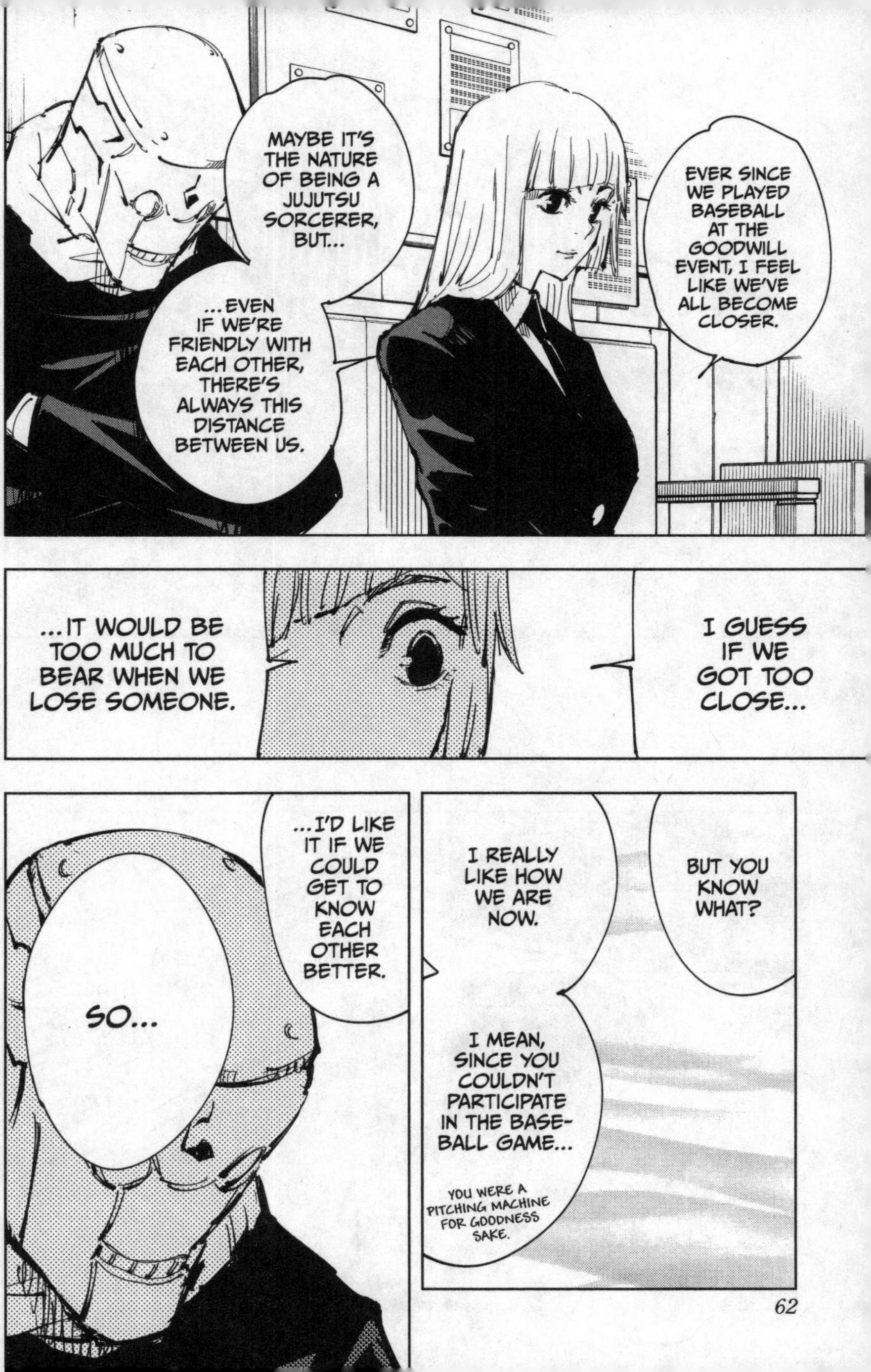
EVER SINCE WE PLAYED BASEBALL AT THE GOODWILL EVENT, I FEEL LIKE WE'VE ALL BECOME CLOSER.
MAYBE IT'S THE NATURE OF BEING A JUJUTSU SORCERER, BUT...
...EVEN IF WE'RE FRIENDLY WITH EACH OTHER, THERE'S ALWAYS THIS DISTANCE BETWEEN US.
I GUESS IF WE GOT TOO CLOSE...
...IT WOULD BE TOO MUCH TO BEAR WHEN WE LOSE SOMEONE.
BUT YOU KNOW WHAT?
I REALLY LIKE HOW WE ARE NOW.
I MEAN, SINCE YOU COULDN'T PARTICIPATE IN THE BASE-BALL GAME...
YOU WERE A PITCHING MACHINE FOR GOODNESS SAKE.
SO...
...I'D LIKE IT IF WE COULD GET TO KNOW EACH OTHER BETTER.

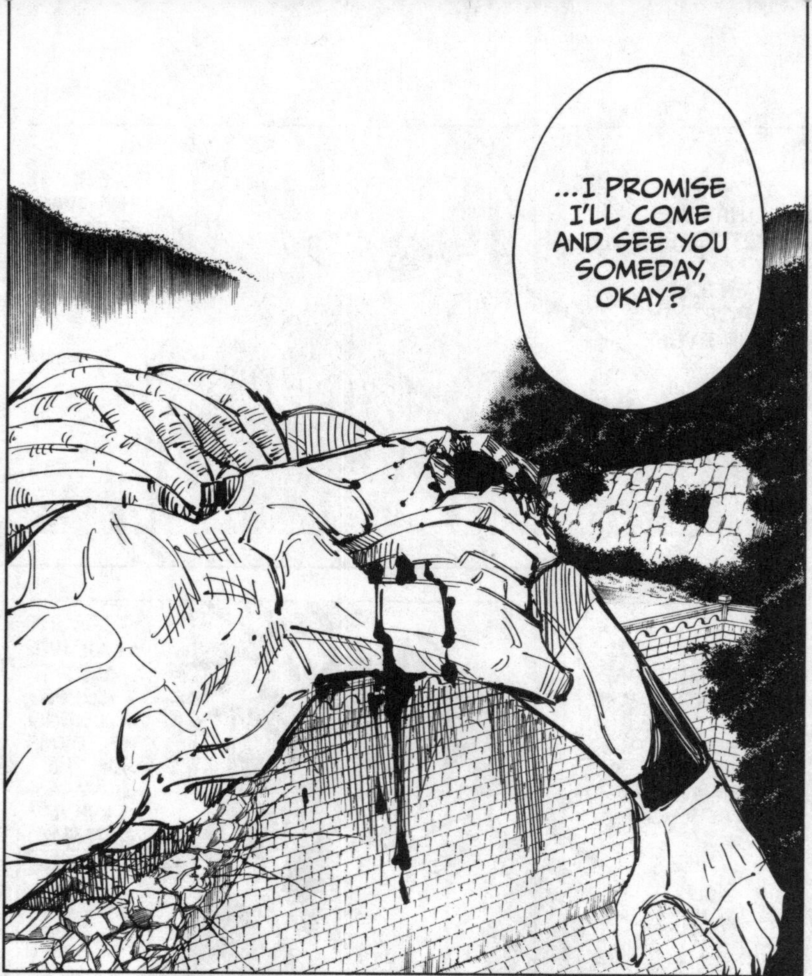
...I PROMISE I'LL COME AND SEE YOU SOMEDAY, OKAY?

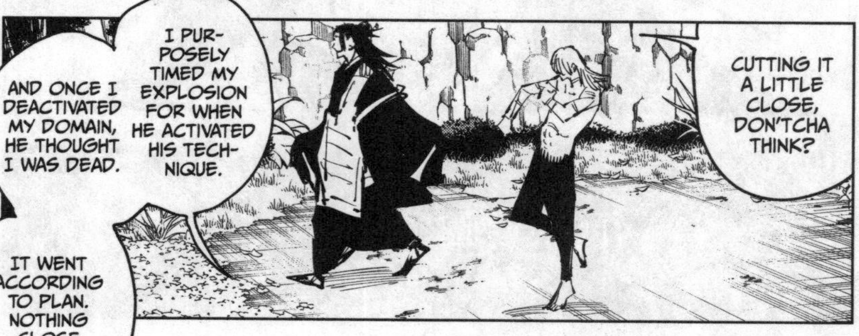
CUTTING IT A LITTLE CLOSE, DON'TCHA THINK?
I PURPOSELY TIMED MY EXPLOSION FOR WHEN HE ACTIVATED HIS TECHNIQUE.
AND ONCE I DEACTIVATED MY DOMAIN, HE THOUGHT I WAS DEAD.
IT WENT ACCORDING TO PLAN. NOTHING CLOSE ABOUT IT.

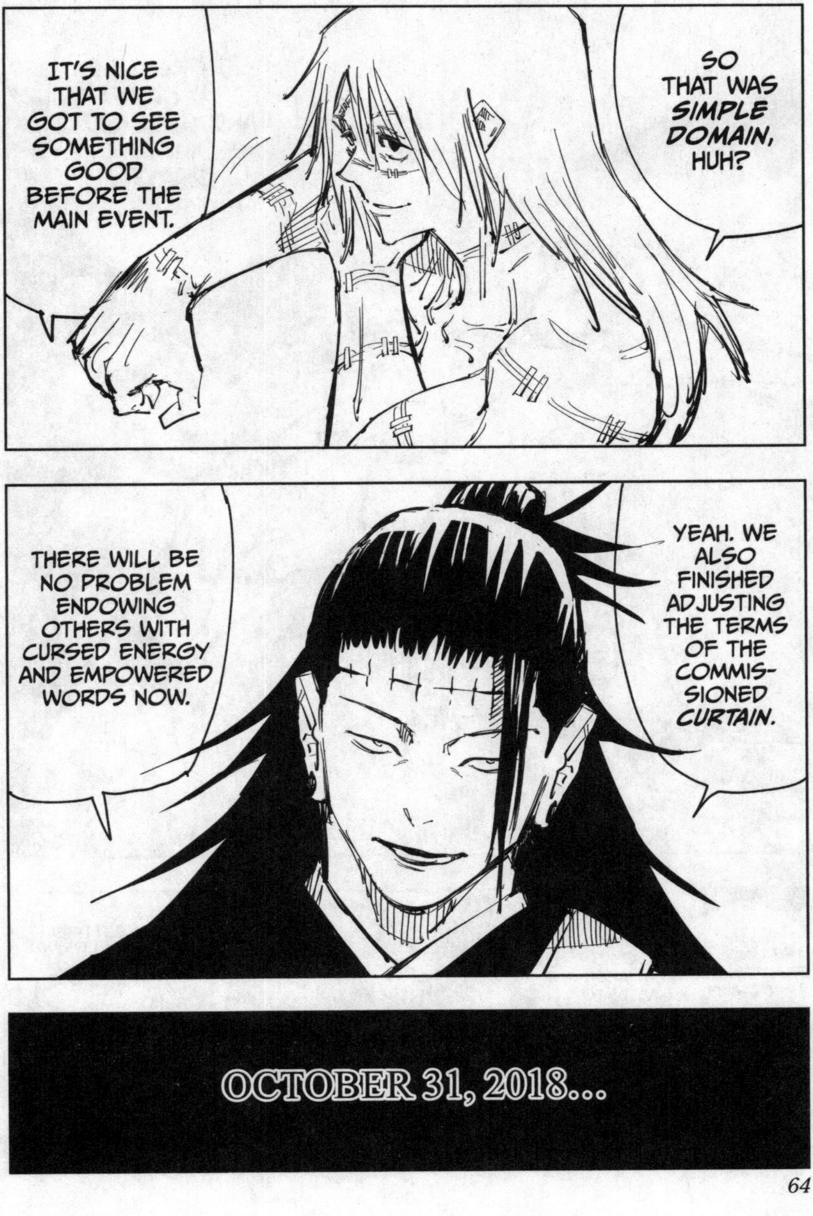
SO THAT WAS SIMPLE DOMAIN, HUH?
IT'S NICE THAT WE GOT TO SEE SOMETHING GOOD BEFORE THE MAIN EVENT.
YEAH. WE ALSO FINISHED ADJUSTING THE TERMS OF THE COMMISSIONED CURTAIN.
THERE WILL BE NO PROBLEM ENDOWING OTHERS WITH CURSED ENERGY AND EMPOWERED WORDS NOW.
OCTOBER 31, 2018...

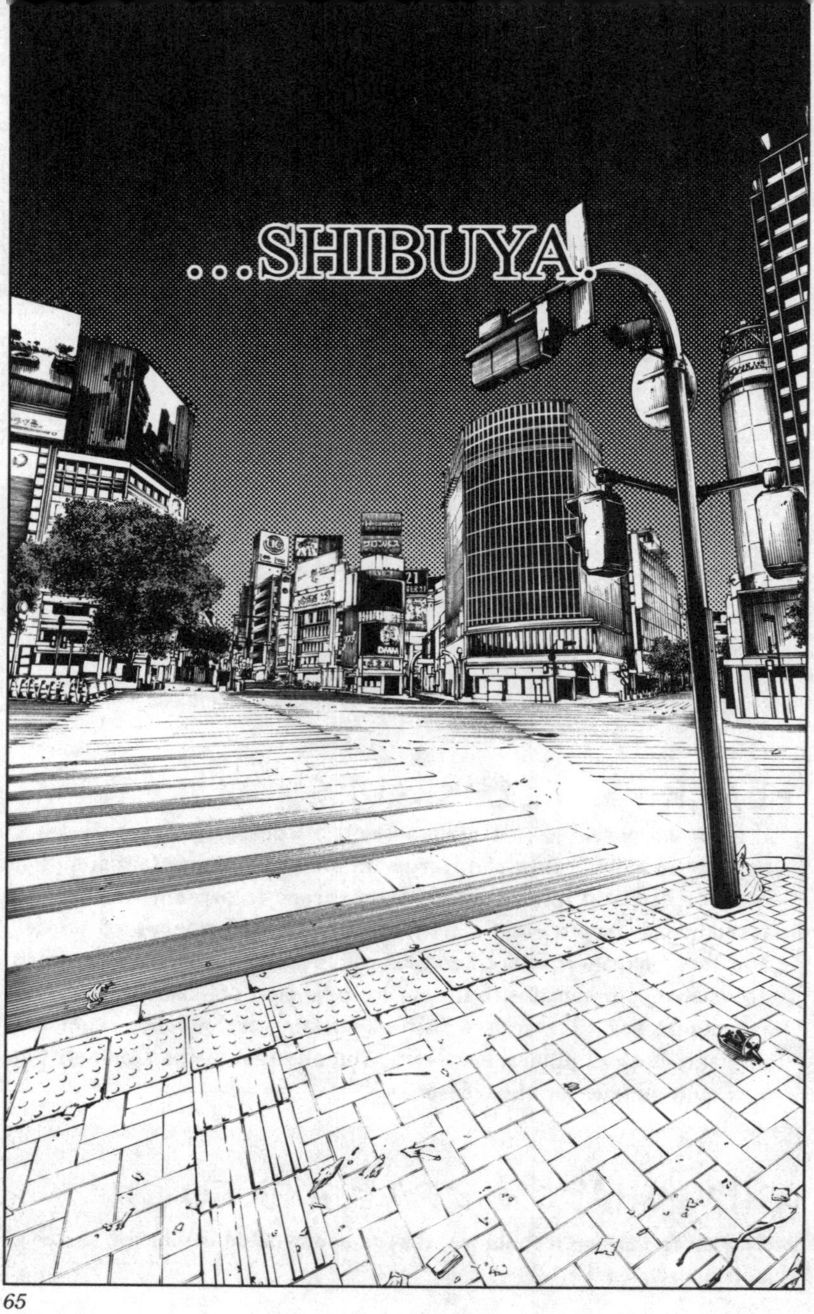
...SHIBUYA.

I DON'T REALLY UNDERSTAND WHAT YOU'RE SAYIN': CURSED TECHNIQUES

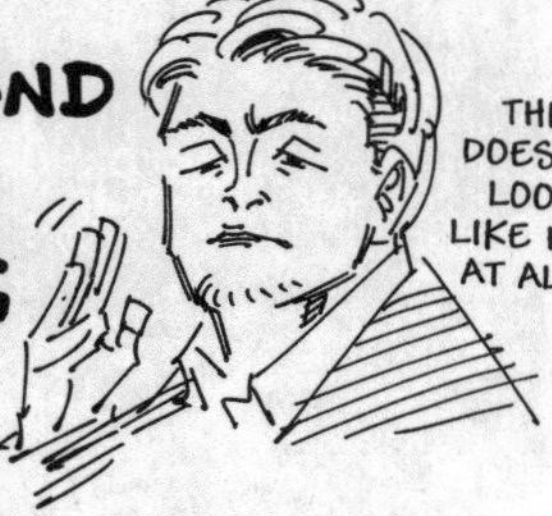

THIS DOESN'T LOOK LIKE HIM AT ALL.

• INNATE CURSED TECHNIQUE

A cursed technique that someone is born with. They're practically impossible for others to copy. When "cursed technique" is written in the manga, it's usually in reference to an innate cursed technique.

• BARRIER TECHNIQUES

If a person possesses a certain amount of cursed energy, barriers are actually something they can learn with enough training (although being good or bad at it differs greatly from person to person). For this technique, a person must start from scratch, add empowered words and then activate it with cursed energy. Barrier techniques are often associated with curtains, but domain expansion utilizes barrier techniques as well. Barriers such as curtains are effective against civilians, but not jujutsu sorcerers. The one cast at the Goodwill Event was quite unique for this reason.

• NEW SHADOW STYLE AND SO ON

Similar to barrier techniques, they're constructed within the caster and then activated.

CHAPTER 83: THE SHIBUYA INCIDENT, PART 1

RECORD OF THE INCIDENT ON OCTOBER 31, 2018 AT 7:00 P.M.

A CURTAIN WITH A 400-METER RADIUS WAS CAST WITH THE TOYOKO BRANCH OF THE TOKYU DEPARTMENT STORE AT ITS CENTER.

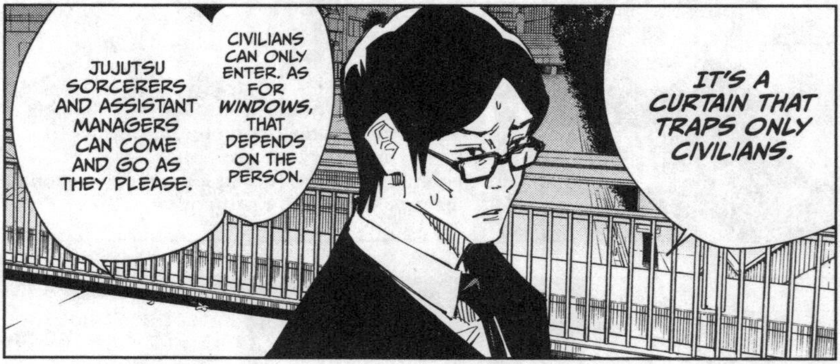

IT'S A CURTAIN THAT TRAPS ONLY CIVILIANS.
CIVILIANS CAN ONLY ENTER. AS FOR *WINDOWS*, THAT DEPENDS ON THE PERSON.
JUJUTSU SORCERERS AND ASSISTANT MANAGERS CAN COME AND GO AS THEY PLEASE.

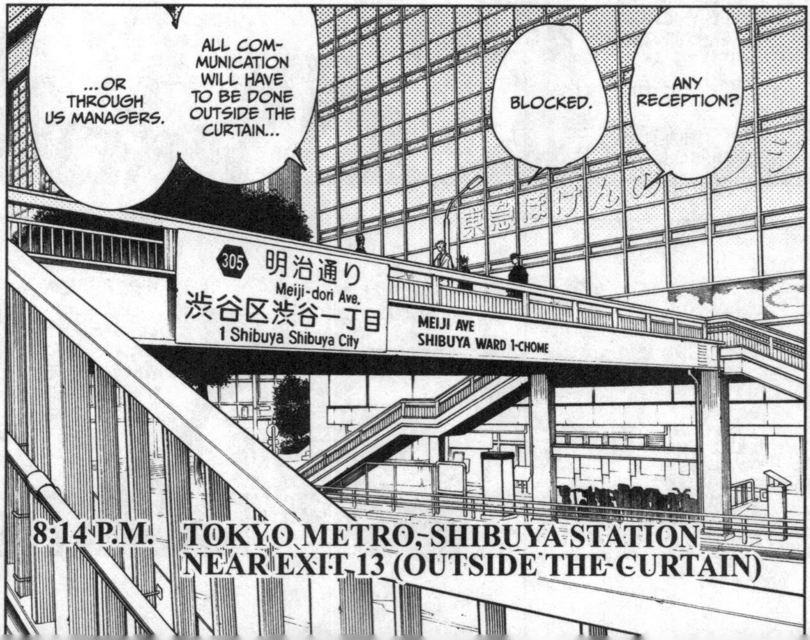

ANY RECEPTION?
BLOCKED.
ALL COMMUNICATION WILL HAVE TO BE DONE OUTSIDE THE CURTAIN...
...OR THROUGH US MANAGERS.
305 明治通り
Meiji-dori Ave.
渋谷区渋谷一丁目
1 Shibuya Shibuya City
MEIJI AVE
SHIBUYA WARD 1-CHOME
8:14 P.M. TOKYO METRO, SHIBUYA STATION NEAR EXIT 13 (OUTSIDE THE CURTAIN)

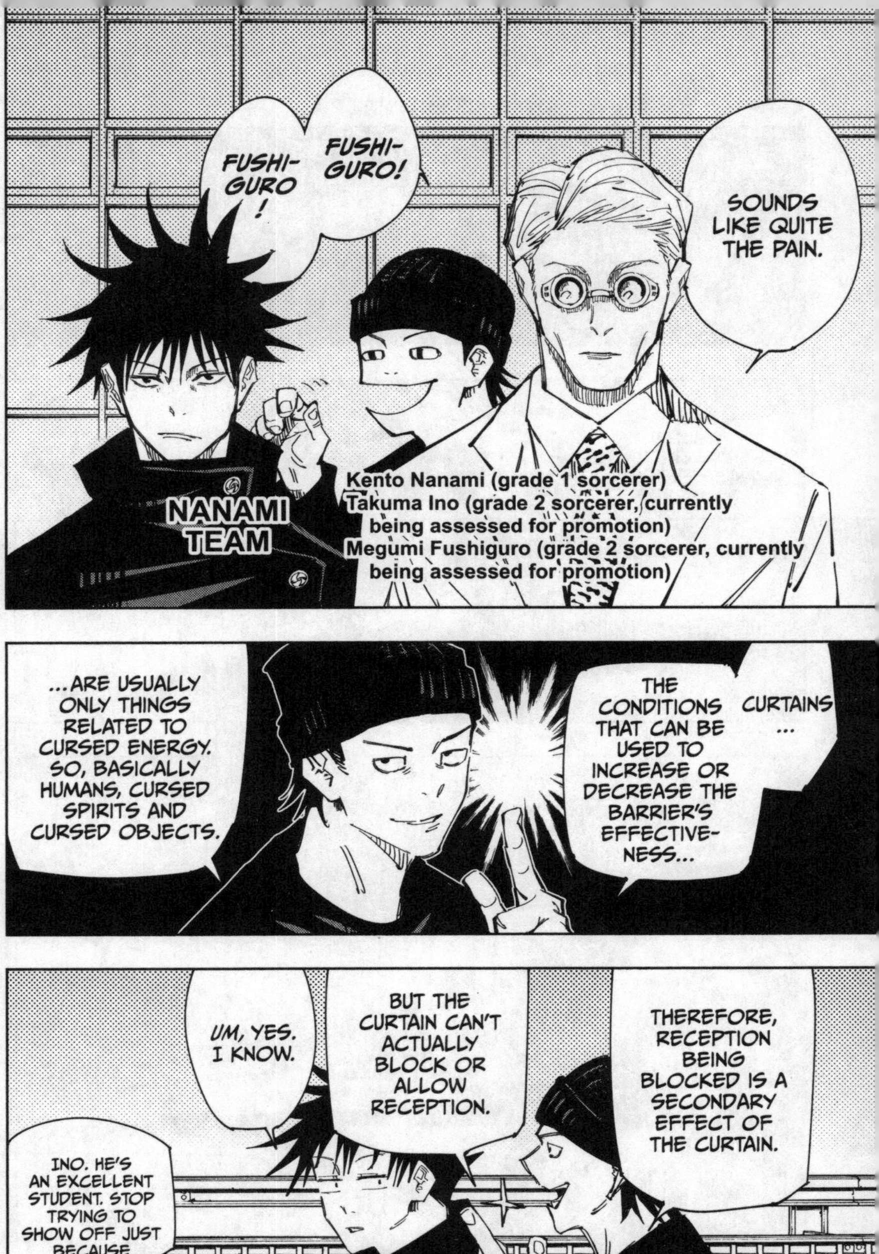
SOUNDS LIKE QUITE THE PAIN.
FUSHI-GURO!
FUSHI-GURO!
NANAMI TEAM
Kento Nanami (grade 1 sorcerer)
Takuma Ino (grade 2 sorcerer, currently being assessed for promotion)
Megumi Fushiguro (grade 2 sorcerer, currently being assessed for promotion)
CURTAINS...
THE CONDITIONS THAT CAN BE USED TO INCREASE OR DECREASE THE BARRIER'S EFFECTIVE-NESS...
...ARE USUALLY ONLY THINGS RELATED TO CURSED ENERGY. SO, BASICALLY HUMANS, CURSED SPIRITS AND CURSED OBJECTS.
THEREFORE, RECEPTION BEING BLOCKED IS A SECONDARY EFFECT OF THE CURTAIN.
BUT THE CURTAIN CAN'T ACTUALLY BLOCK OR ALLOW RECEPTION.
UM, YES. I KNOW.
INO. HE'S AN EXCELLENT STUDENT. STOP TRYING TO SHOW OFF JUST BECAUSE YOU'RE OLDER.

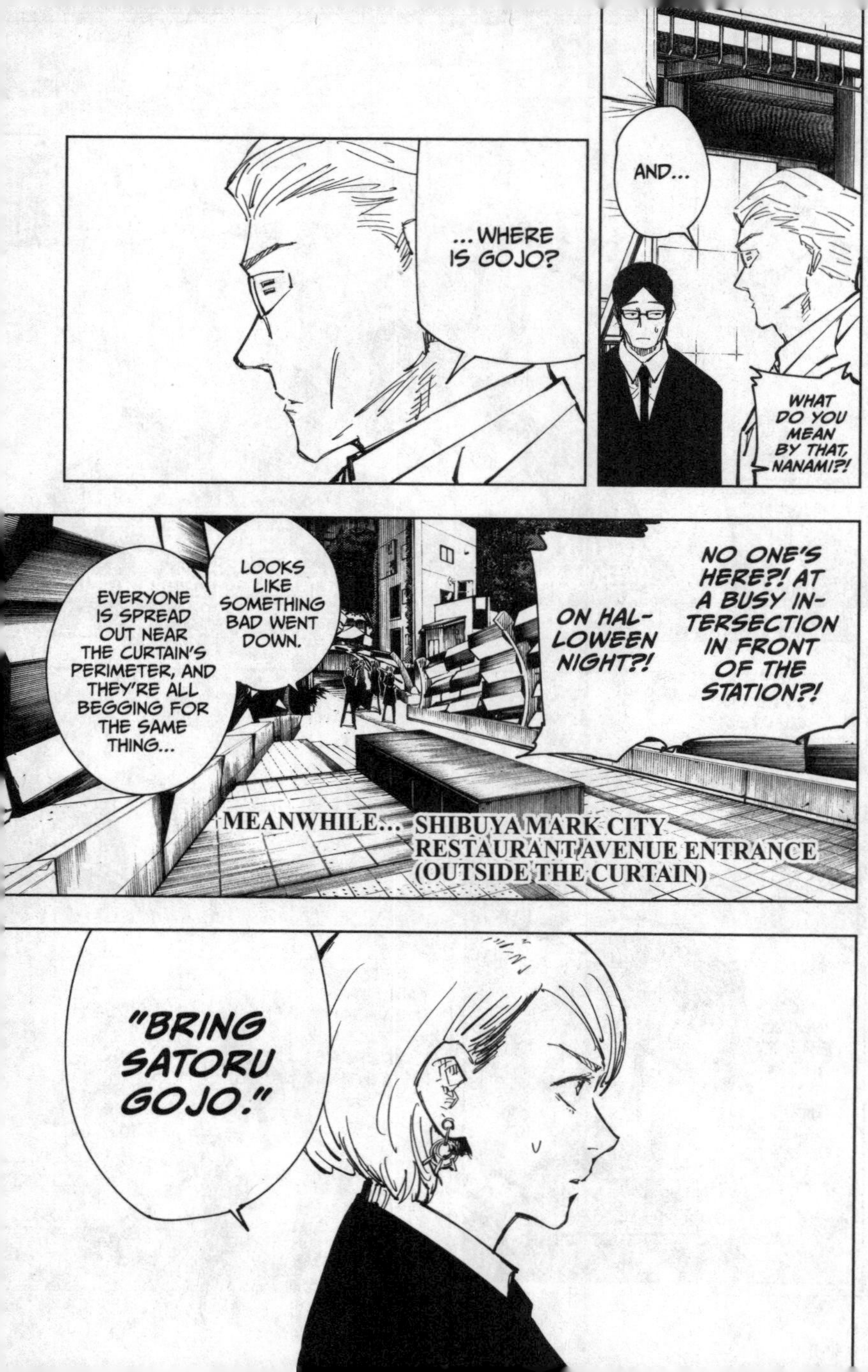
AND...
WHAT DO YOU MEAN BY THAT, NANAMI?!
...WHERE IS GOJO?
NO ONE'S HERE?! AT A BUSY IN-TERSECTION IN FRONT OF THE STATION?!
ON HAL-LOWEEN NIGHT?!
LOOKS LIKE SOMETHING BAD WENT DOWN.
EVERYONE IS SPREAD OUT NEAR THE CURTAIN'S PERIMETER, AND THEY'RE ALL BEGGING FOR THE SAME THING...
MEANWHILE...
SHIBUYA MARK CITY RESTAURANT AVENUE ENTRANCE (OUTSIDE THE CURTAIN)
"BRING SATORU GOJO."

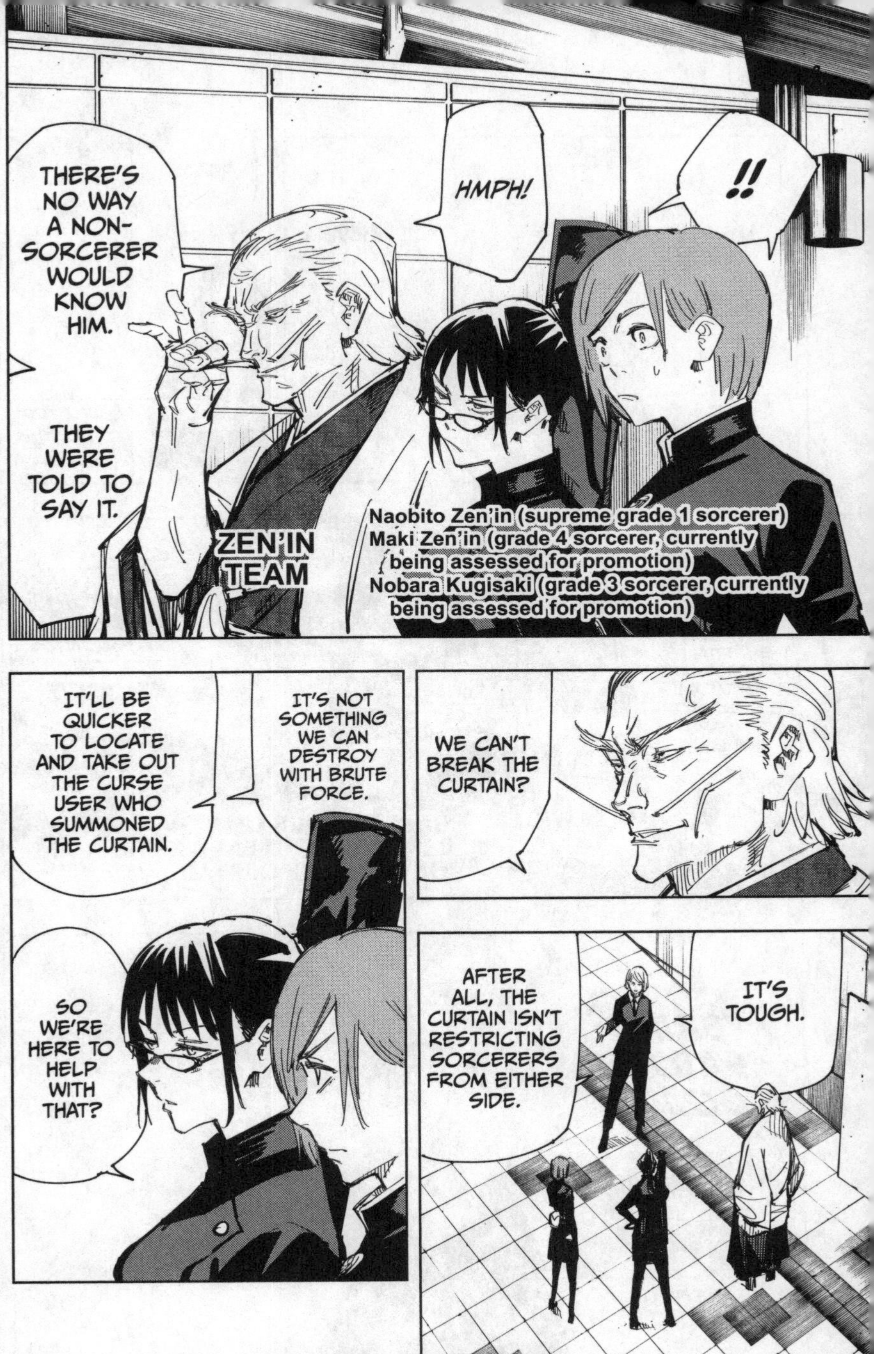
!!
HMPH!
THERE'S NO WAY A NON-SORCERER WOULD KNOW HIM.
THEY WERE TOLD TO SAY IT.
ZEN'IN TEAM
Naobito Zen'in (supreme grade 1 sorcerer)
Maki Zen'in (grade 4 sorcerer, currently being assessed for promotion)
Nobara Kugisaki (grade 3 sorcerer, currently being assessed for promotion)
WE CAN'T BREAK THE CURTAIN?
IT'S NOT SOMETHING WE CAN DESTROY WITH BRUTE FORCE.
IT'LL BE QUICKER TO LOCATE AND TAKE OUT THE CURSE USER WHO SUMMONED THE CURTAIN.
IT'S TOUGH.
AFTER ALL, THE CURTAIN ISN'T RESTRICTING SORCERERS FROM EITHER SIDE.
SO WE'RE HERE TO HELP WITH THAT?

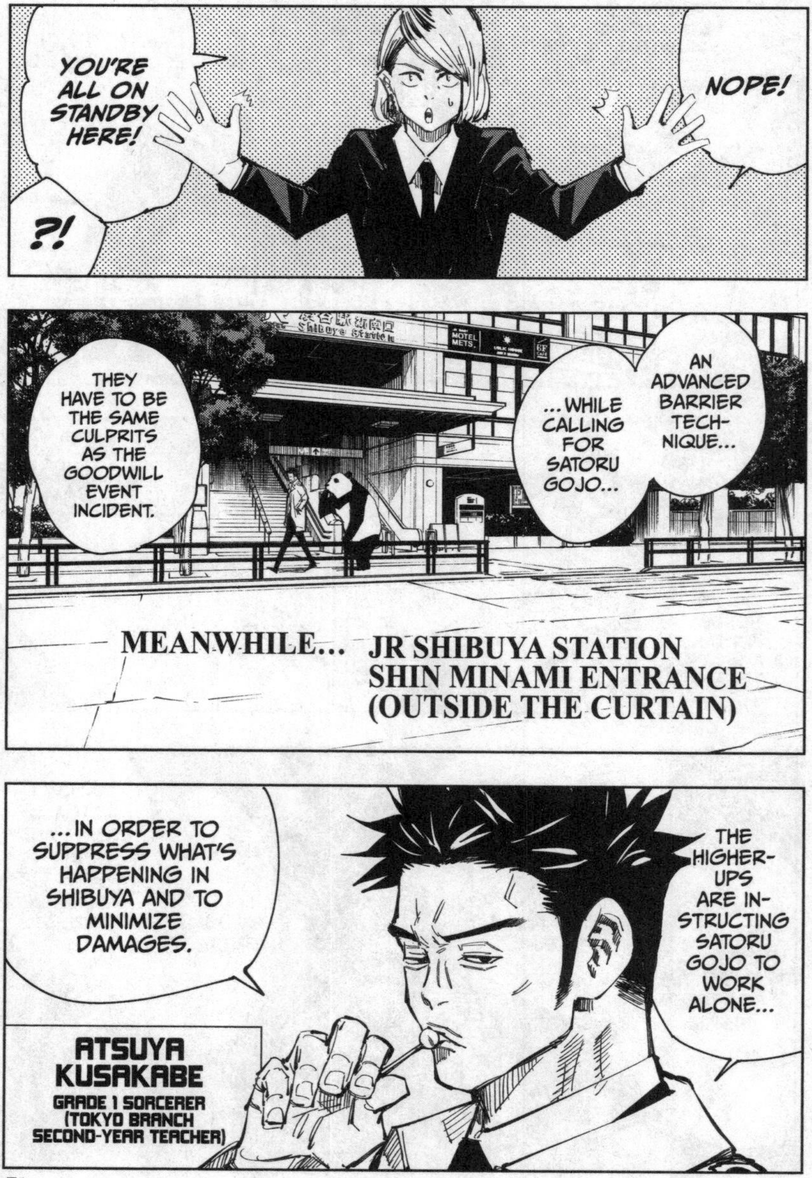
NOPE!
YOU'RE ALL ON STANDBY HERE!
?!
AN ADVANCED BARRIER TECHNIQUE...
...WHILE CALLING FOR SATORU GOJO...
THEY HAVE TO BE THE SAME CULPRITS AS THE GOODWILL EVENT INCIDENT.
MEANWHILE...
JR SHIBUYA STATION SHIN MINAMI ENTRANCE (OUTSIDE THE CURTAIN)
THE HIGHER-UPS ARE INSTRUCTING SATORU GOJO TO WORK ALONE...
...IN ORDER TO SUPPRESS WHAT'S HAPPENING IN SHIBUYA AND TO MINIMIZE DAMAGES.
ATSUYA KUSAKABE
GRADE 1 SORCERER (TOKYO BRANCH SECOND-YEAR TEACHER)

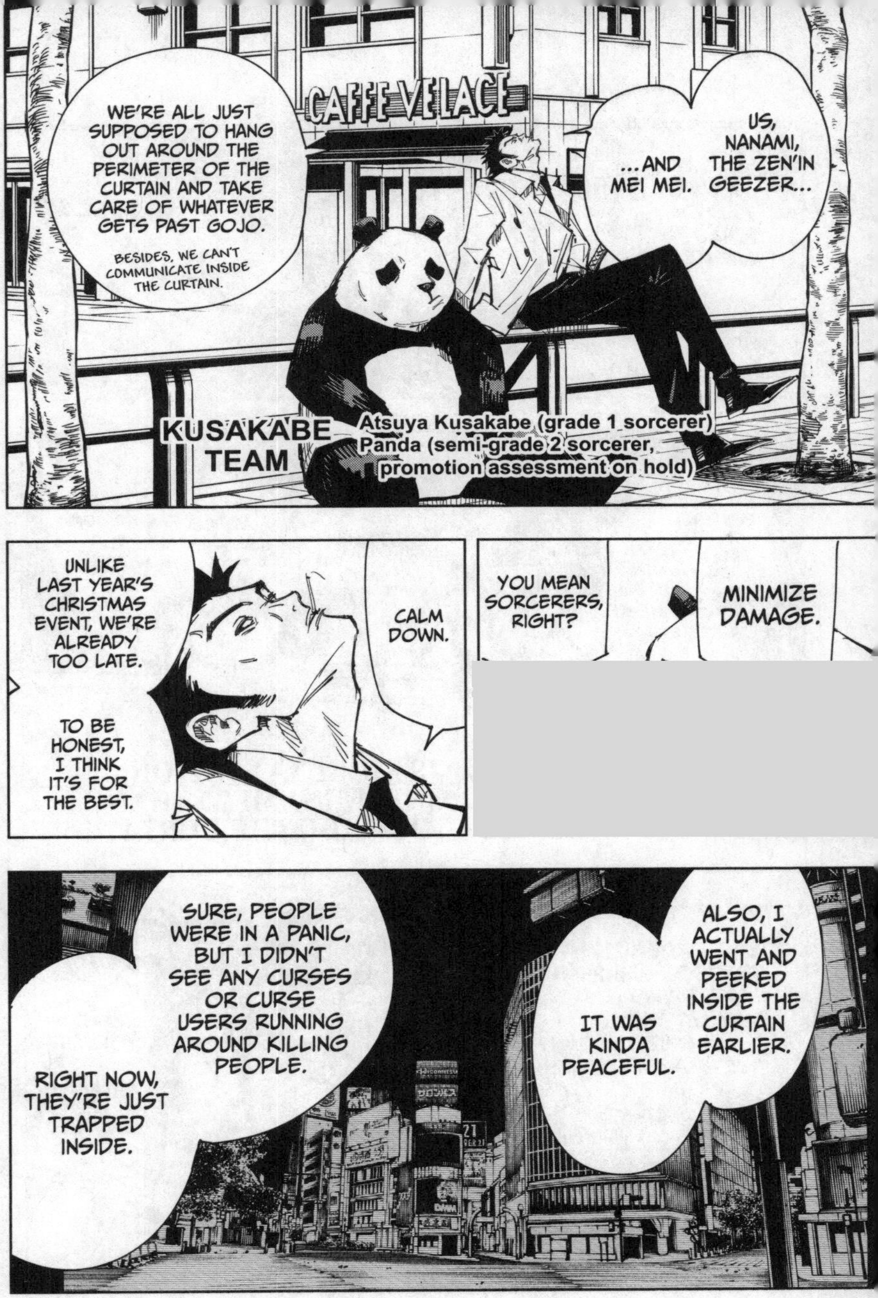

CAFFE VELACE
US, NANAMI, THE ZEN'IN GEEZER...
...AND MEI MEI.
WE'RE ALL JUST SUPPOSED TO HANG OUT AROUND THE PERIMETER OF THE CURTAIN AND TAKE CARE OF WHATEVER GETS PAST GOJO.
BESIDES, WE CAN'T COMMUNICATE INSIDE THE CURTAIN.
KUSAKABE TEAM
Atsuya Kusakabe (grade 1 sorcerer)
Panda (semi-grade 2 sorcerer, promotion assessment on hold)
MINIMIZE DAMAGE.
YOU MEAN SORCERERS, RIGHT?
CALM DOWN.
UNLIKE LAST YEAR'S CHRISTMAS EVENT, WE'RE ALREADY TOO LATE.
TO BE HONEST, I THINK IT'S FOR THE BEST.
ALSO, I ACTUALLY WENT AND PEEKED INSIDE THE CURTAIN EARLIER.
IT WAS KINDA PEACEFUL.
SURE, PEOPLE WERE IN A PANIC, BUT I DIDN'T SEE ANY CURSES OR CURSE USERS RUNNING AROUND KILLING PEOPLE.
RIGHT NOW, THEY'RE JUST TRAPPED INSIDE.

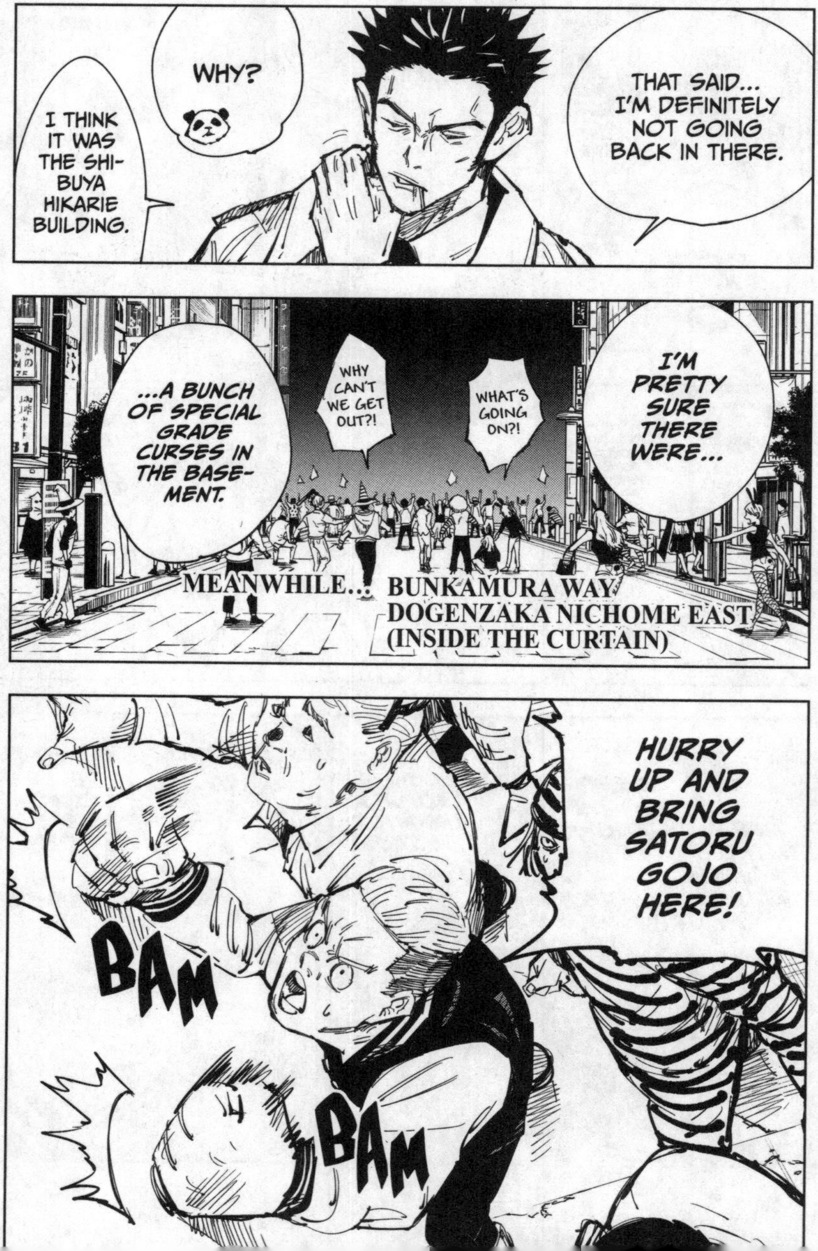
THAT SAID... I'M DEFINITELY NOT GOING BACK IN THERE.
WHY?
I THINK IT WAS THE SHIBUYA HIKARIE BUILDING.
I'M PRETTY SURE THERE WERE...
WHAT'S GOING ON?!
WHY CAN'T WE GET OUT?!
...A BUNCH OF SPECIAL GRADE CURSES IN THE BASEMENT.
MEANWHILE...
BUNKAMURA WAY DOGENZAKA NICHOME EAST (INSIDE THE CURTAIN)
HURRY UP AND BRING SATORU GOJO HERE!
BAM
BAM

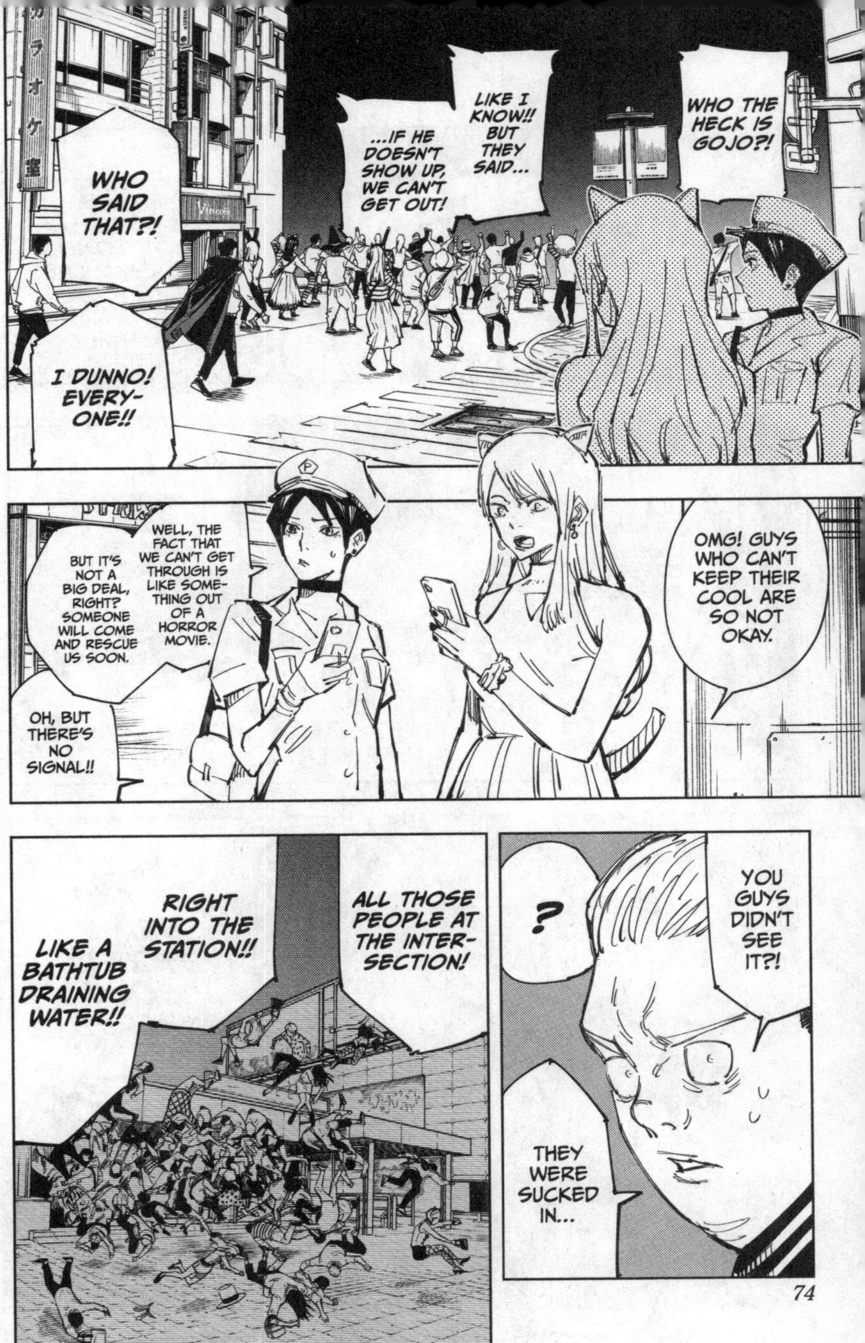
WHO THE HECK IS GOJO?!
LIKE I KNOW!! BUT THEY SAID...
...IF HE DOESN'T SHOW UP, WE CAN'T GET OUT!
WHO SAID THAT?!
I DUNNO! EVERY-ONE!!
OMG! GUYS WHO CAN'T KEEP THEIR COOL ARE SO NOT OKAY.
WELL, THE FACT THAT WE CAN'T GET THROUGH IS LIKE SOME-THING OUT OF A HORROR MOVIE.
BUT IT'S NOT A BIG DEAL, RIGHT? SOMEONE WILL COME AND RESCUE US SOON.
OH, BUT THERE'S NO SIGNAL!!
YOU GUYS DIDN'T SEE IT?!
?
THEY WERE SUCKED IN...
ALL THOSE PEOPLE AT THE INTER-SECTION!
RIGHT INTO THE STATION!!
LIKE A BATHTUB DRAINING WATER!!

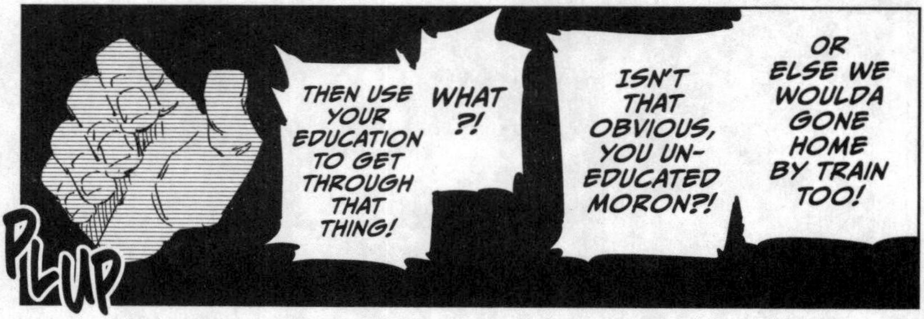
OR ELSE WE WOULDA GONE HOME BY TRAIN TOO!
ISN'T THAT OBVIOUS, YOU UN-EDUCATED MORON?!
WHAT ?!
THEN USE YOUR EDUCATION TO GET THROUGH THAT THING!
PLUP

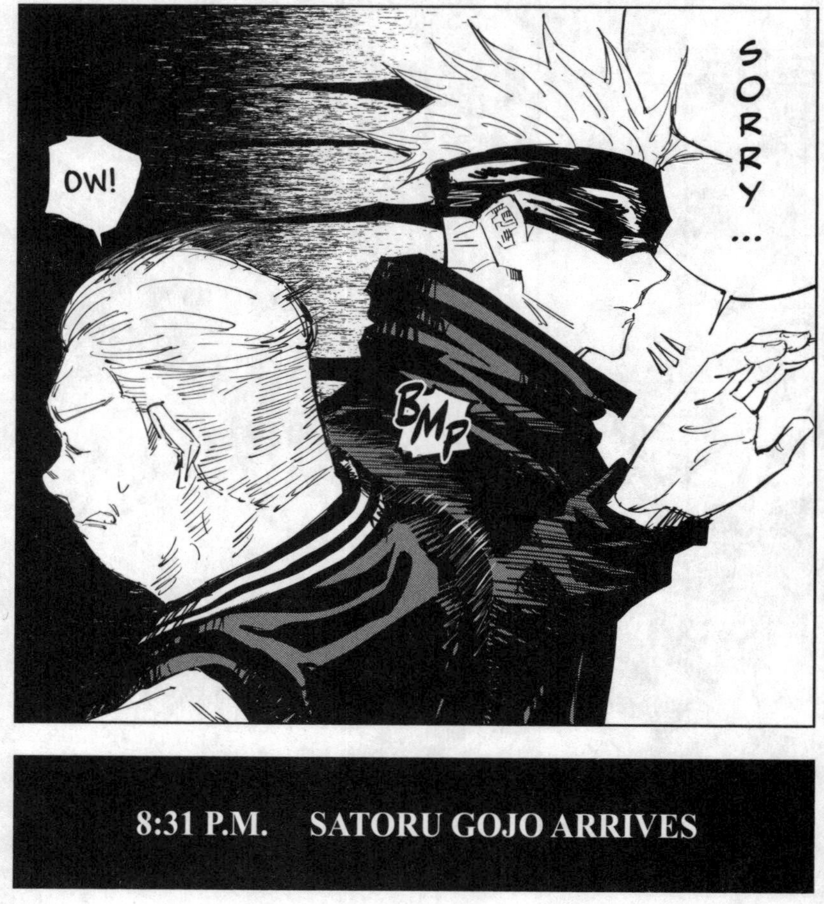
SORRY...
BMP
OW!

8:31 P.M. SATORU GOJO ARRIVES

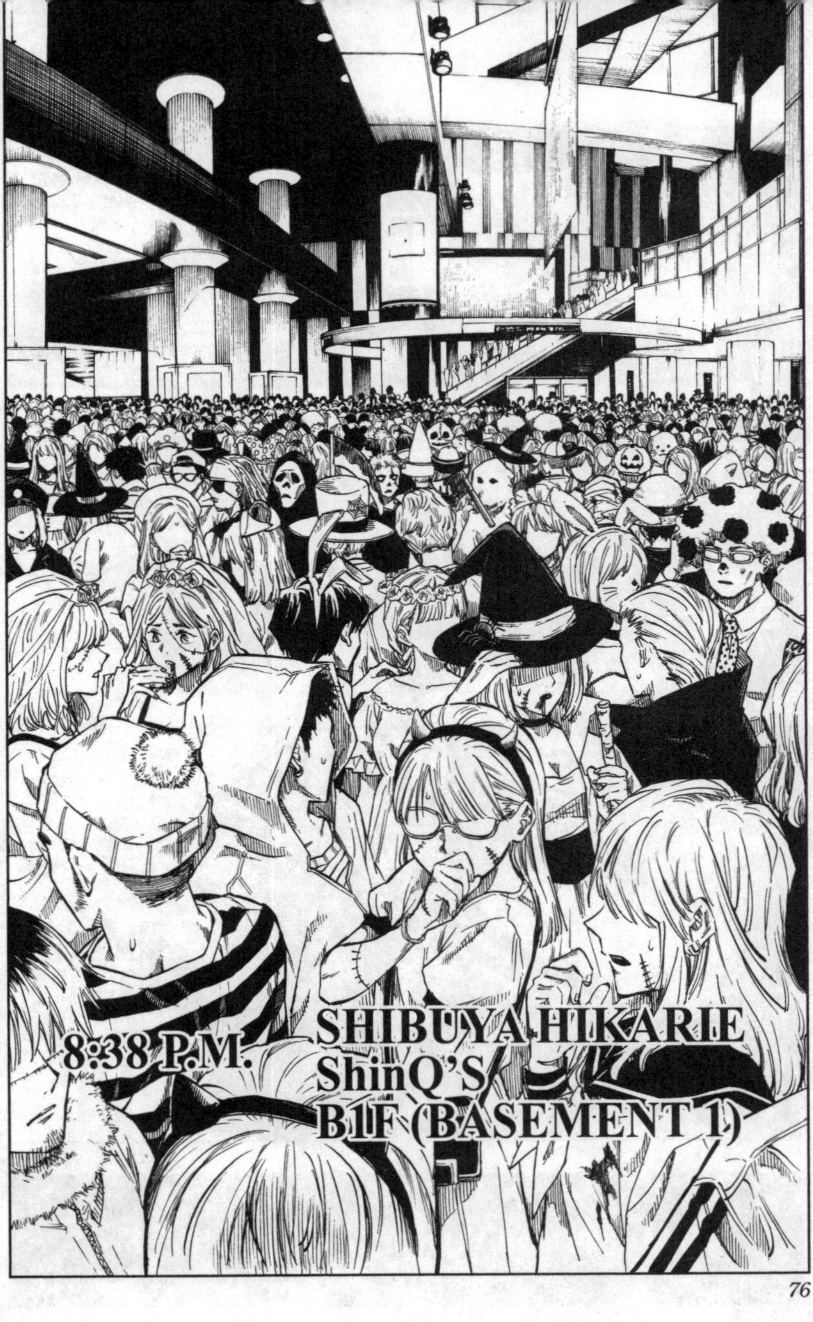
8:38 P.M.
SHIBUYA HIKARIE
ShinQ'S
B1F (BASEMENT 1)

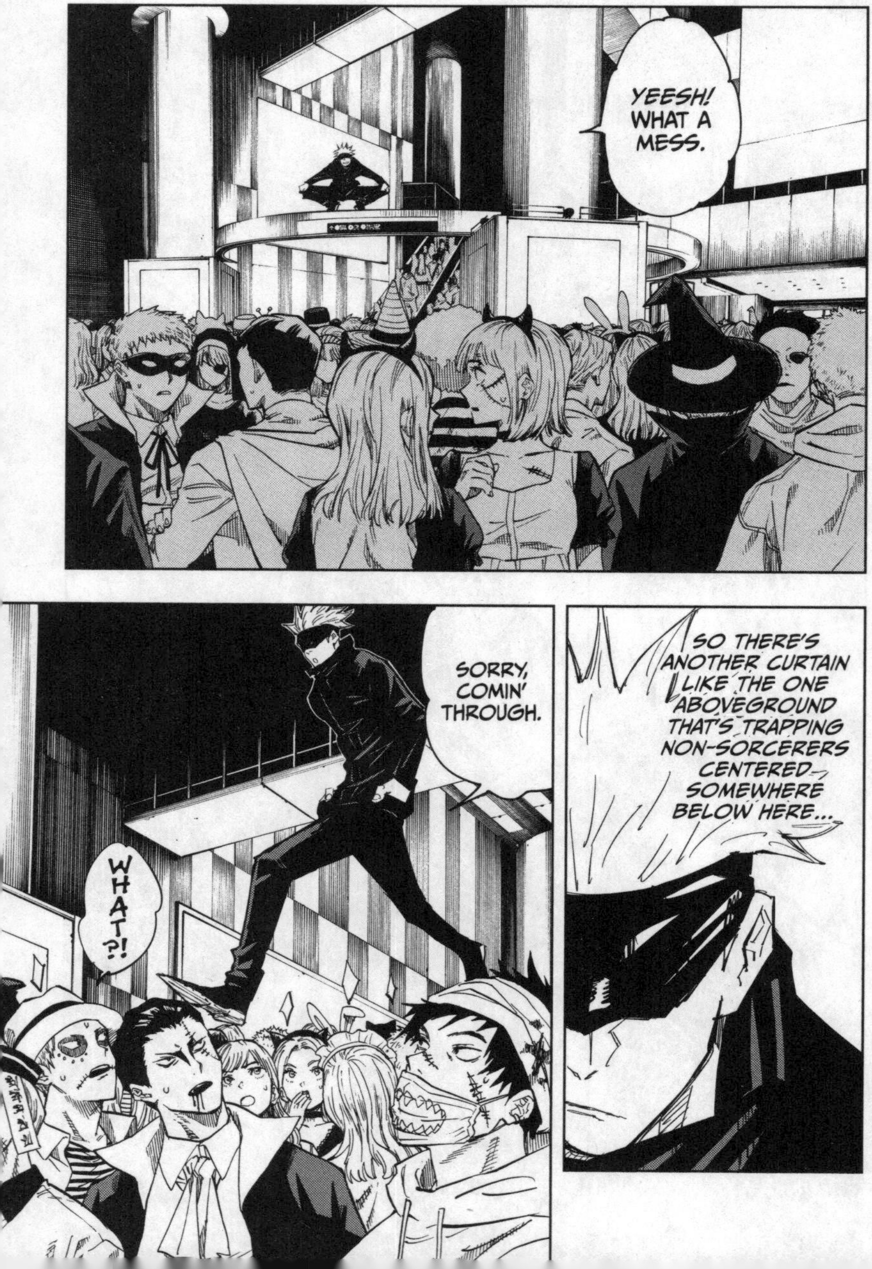
YEESH! WHAT A MESS.
SO THERE'S ANOTHER CURTAIN LIKE THE ONE ABOVEGROUND THAT'S TRAPPING NON-SORCERERS CENTERED SOMEWHERE BELOW HERE...
SORRY, COMIN' THROUGH.
WHAT?!

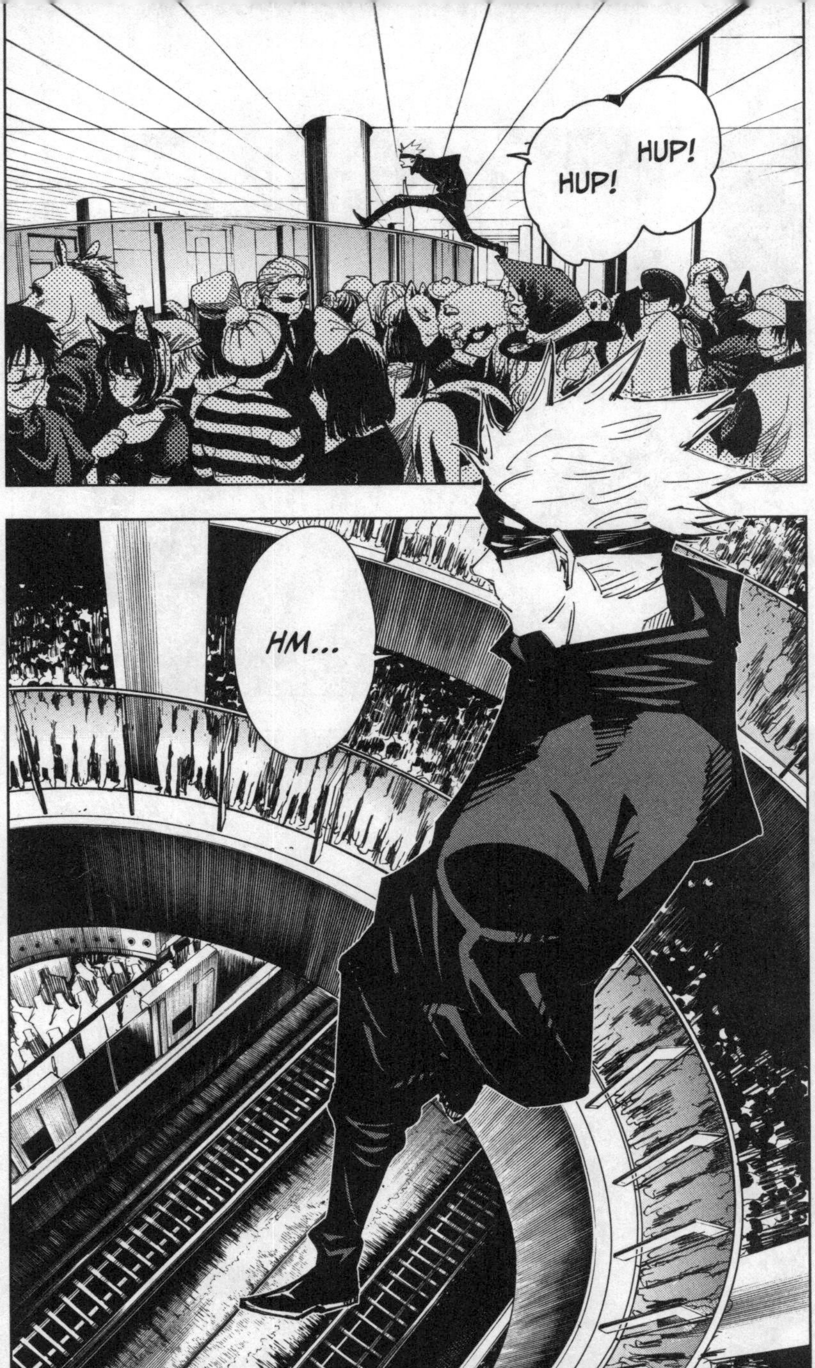
HUP! HUP!
HM...

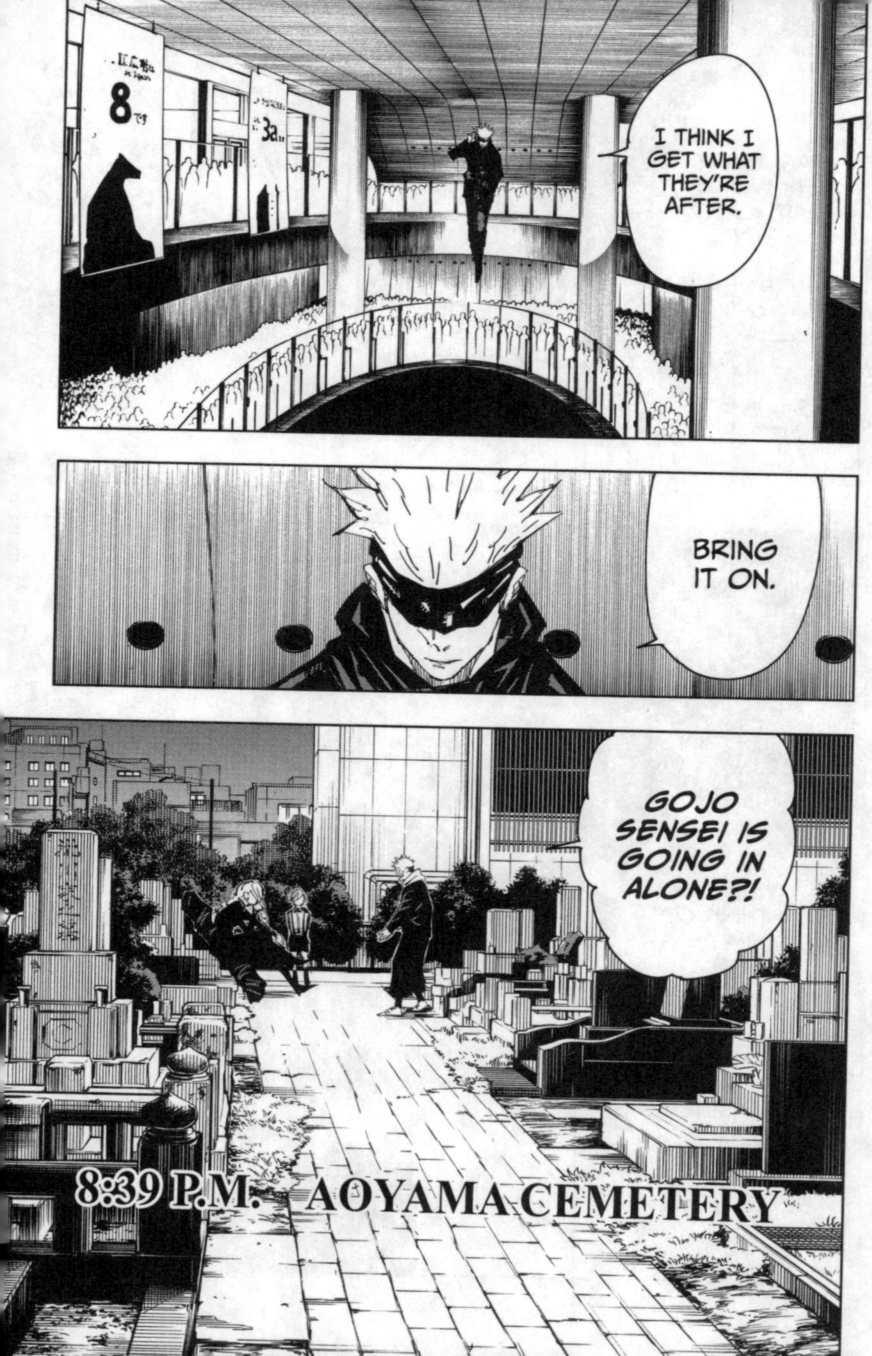
I THINK I GET WHAT THEY'RE AFTER.
BRING IT ON.
GOJO SENSEI IS GOING IN ALONE?!
8:39 P.M. AOYAMA CEMETERY

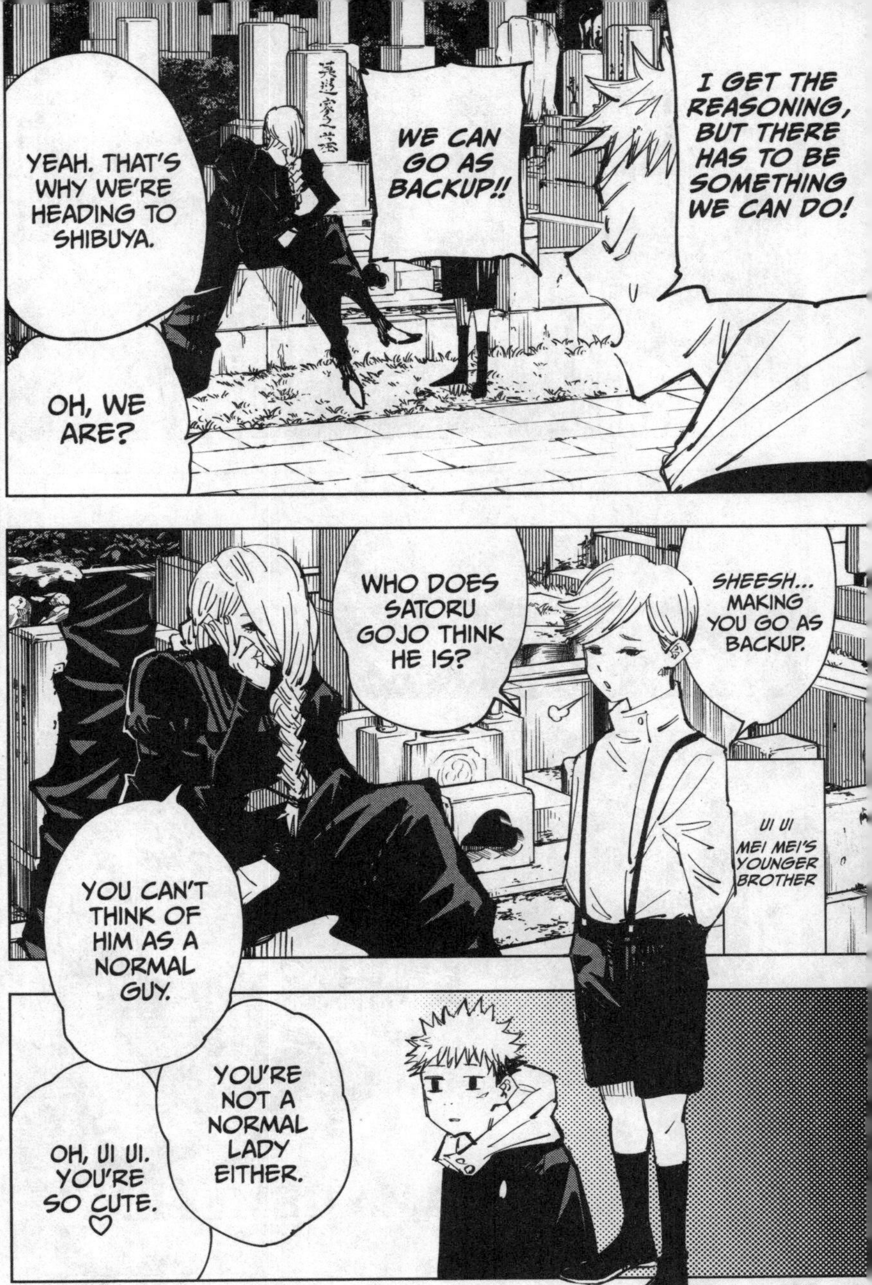
I GET THE REASONING, BUT THERE HAS TO BE SOMETHING WE CAN DO!
WE CAN GO AS BACKUP!!
YEAH. THAT'S WHY WE'RE HEADING TO SHIBUYA.
OH, WE ARE?
SHEESH... MAKING YOU GO AS BACKUP.
UI UI MEI MEI'S YOUNGER BROTHER
WHO DOES SATORU GOJO THINK HE IS?
YOU CAN'T THINK OF HIM AS A NORMAL GUY.
YOU'RE NOT A NORMAL LADY EITHER.
OH, UI UI. YOU'RE SO CUTE. ♡

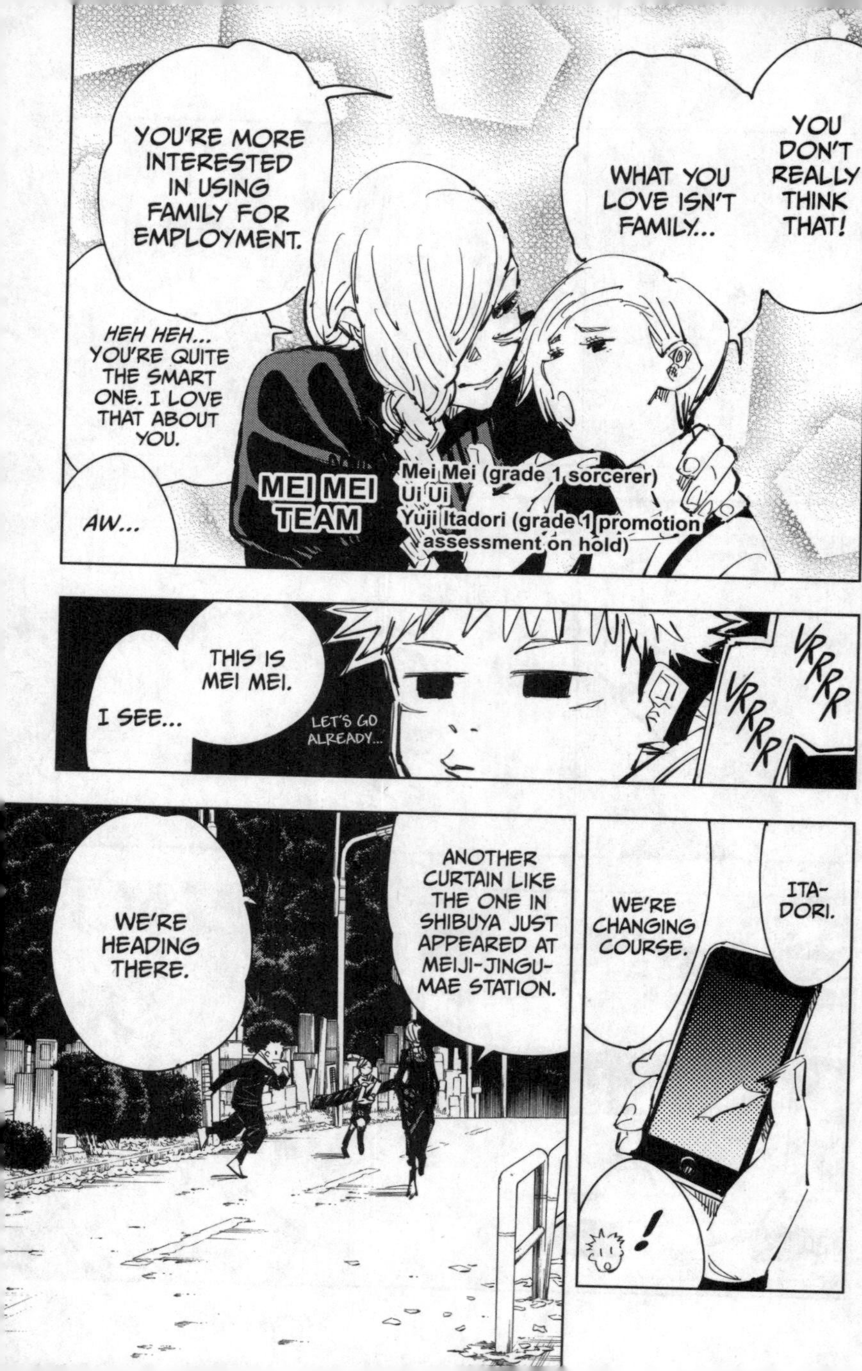
YOU DON'T REALLY THINK THAT!
WHAT YOU LOVE ISN'T FAMILY...
YOU'RE MORE INTERESTED IN USING FAMILY FOR EMPLOYMENT.
HEH HEH... YOU'RE QUITE THE SMART ONE. I LOVE THAT ABOUT YOU.
AW...
MEI MEI TEAM
Mei Mei (grade 1 sorcerer)
Ui Ui
Yuji Itadori (grade 1 promotion assessment on hold)
VRRRR
VRRRR
THIS IS MEI MEI.
LET'S GO ALREADY...
I SEE...
ITA-DORI.
WE'RE CHANGING COURSE.
!
ANOTHER CURTAIN LIKE THE ONE IN SHIBUYA JUST APPEARED AT MEIJI-JINGU-MAE STATION.
WE'RE HEADING THERE.

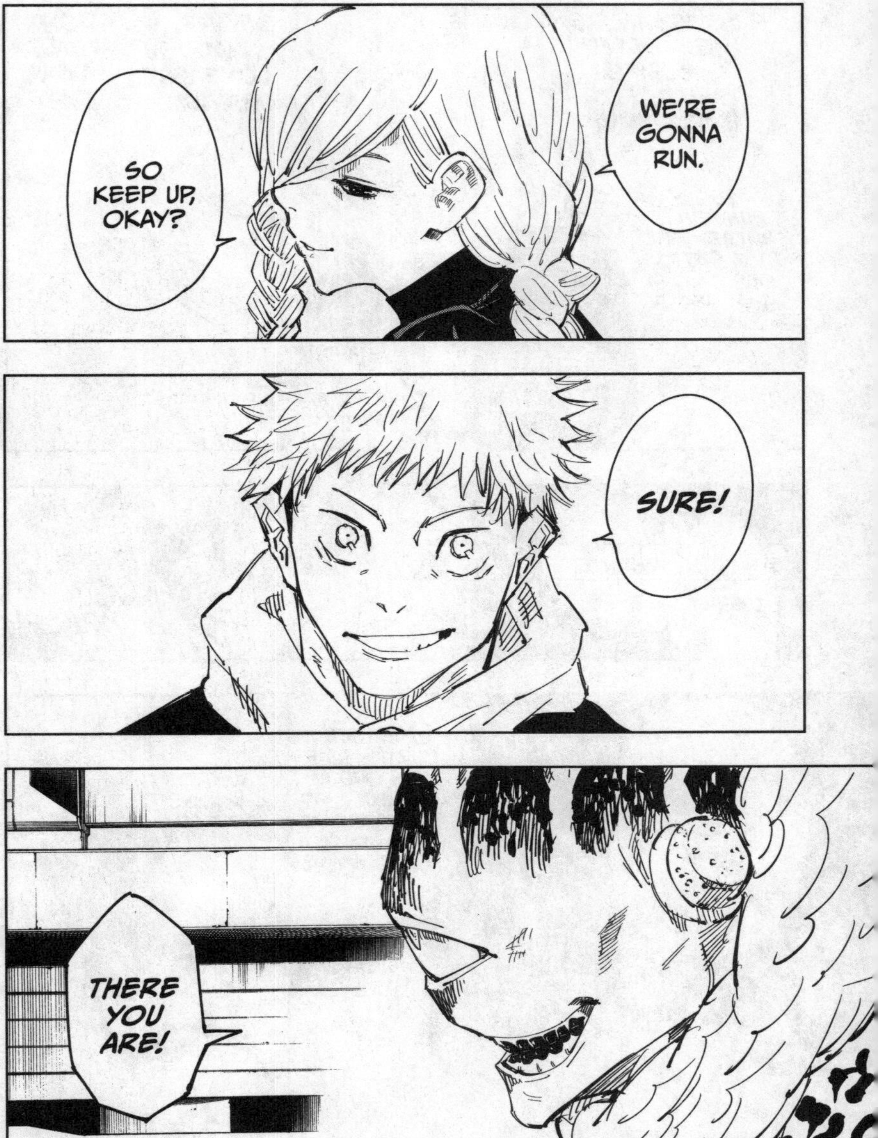
WE'RE GONNA RUN.
SO KEEP UP, OKAY?
SURE!
THERE YOU ARE!

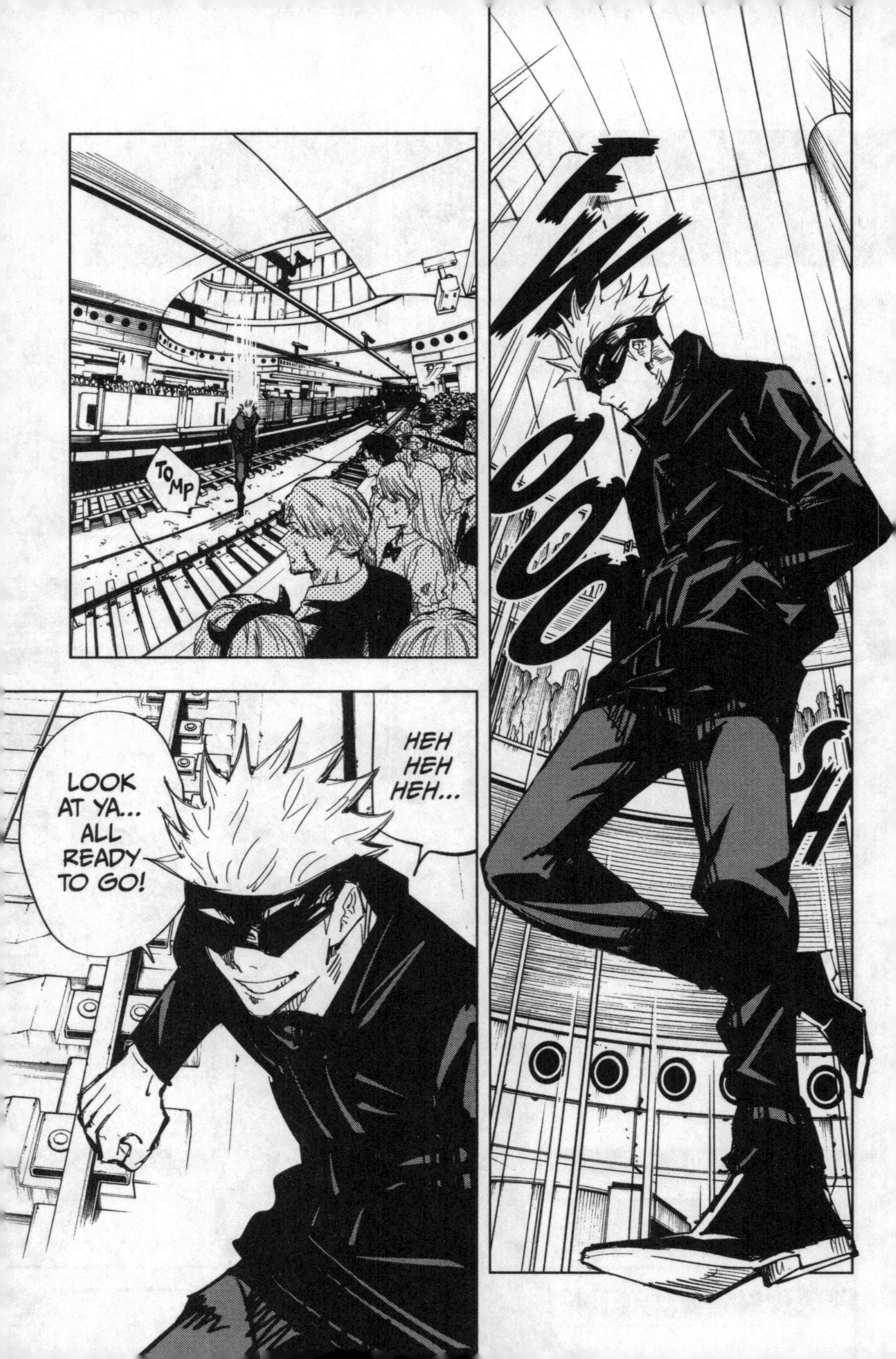
FWOOOOSH
...
TOMP
HEH HEH HEH...
LOOK AT YA... ALL READY TO GO!

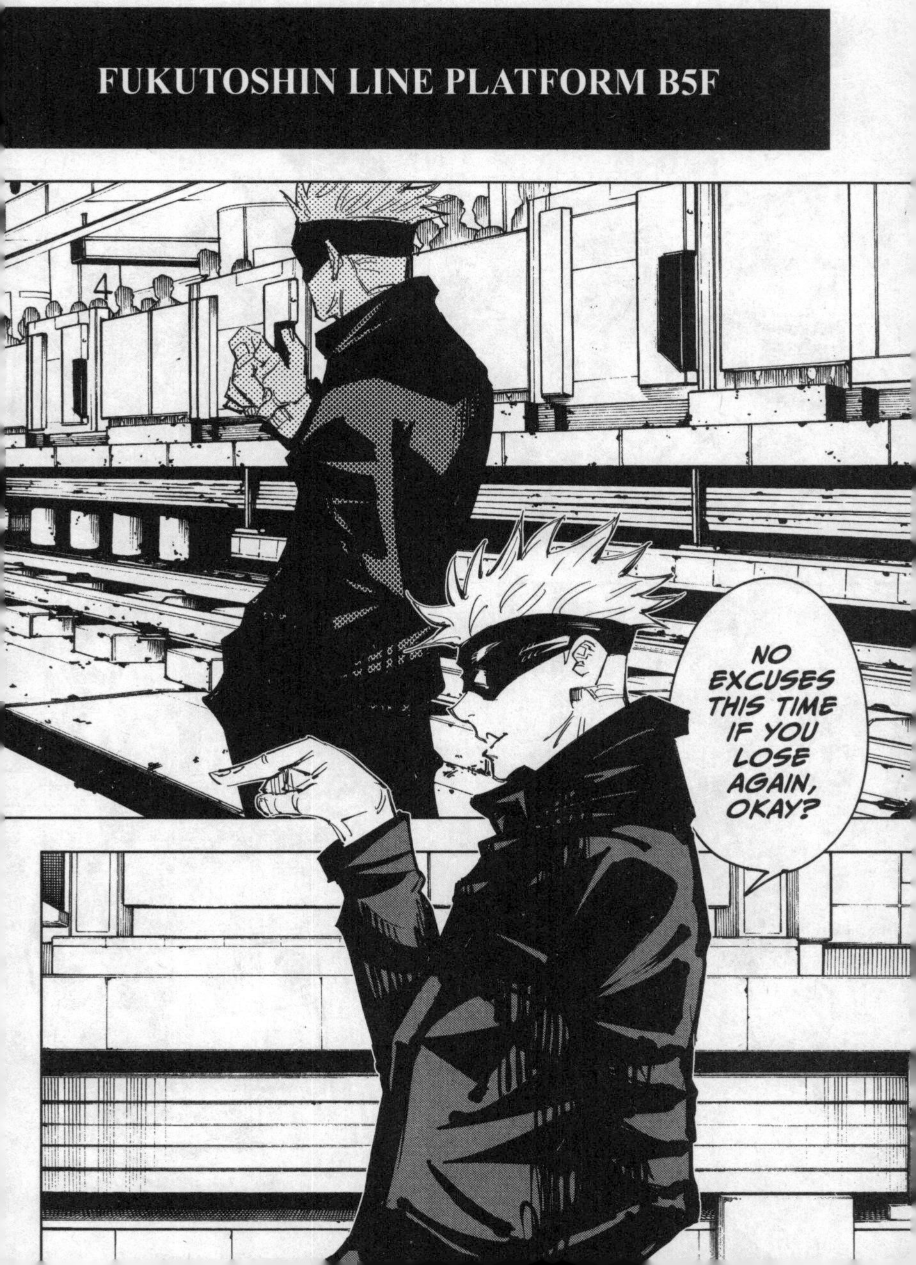
FUKUTOSHIN LINE PLATFORM B5F
NO EXCUSES THIS TIME IF YOU LOSE AGAIN, OKAY?

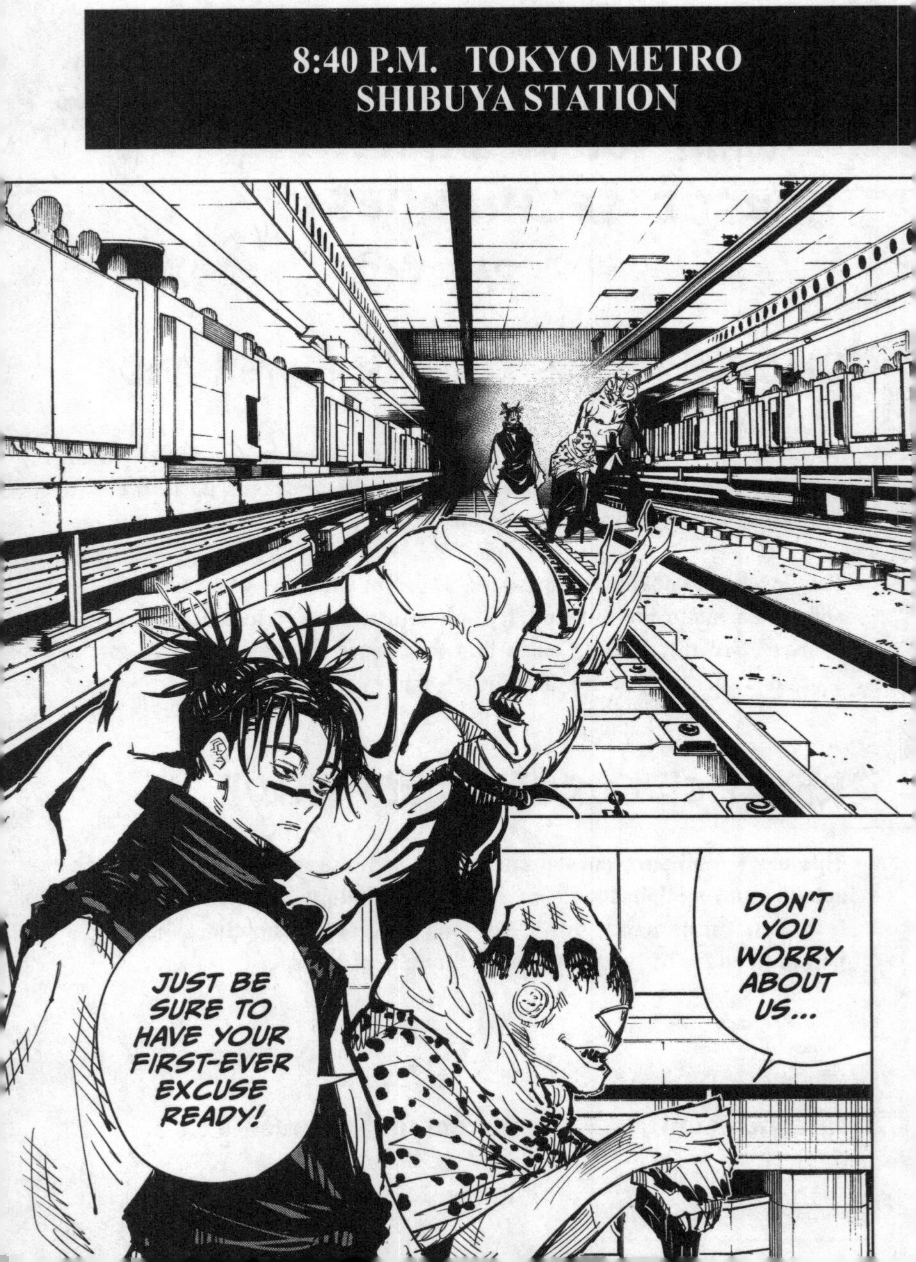
8:40 P.M. TOKYO METRO SHIBUYA STATION
DON'T YOU WORRY ABOUT US...
JUST BE SURE TO HAVE YOUR FIRST-EVER EXCUSE READY!

I DON'T REALLY UNDERSTAND WHAT YOU'RE SAYIN': CURSED TECHNIQUES PART ②

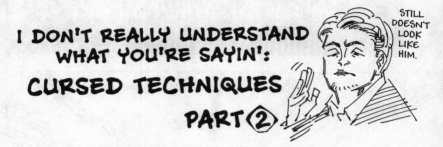

STILL DOESN'T LOOK LIKE HIM.

• DIVERGENT FIST, BLACK FLASH AND SO ON

These are not considered cursed techniques since they're actually using cursed energy to reinforce and strengthen the body. It's up to the individual to call them jujutsu or not.

This is what Fushiguro was talking about in volume 1 when he said something along the lines of "It's not jujutsu, you're just hurling cursed energy!" But this doesn't mean that Fushiguro doesn't accept Itadori as a jujutsu sorcerer, so it's all a little wishy-washy.

• REVERSE CURSED TECHNIQUE

This move multiplies cursed energy (-) with cursed energy (-), so it's actually just muliplication, not a cursed technique. It's got "cursed technique" in its name, but it still isn't a cursed technique. What the hell is wrong with the person who thought of this?

In conclusion...   It's so confuuuuusing!!

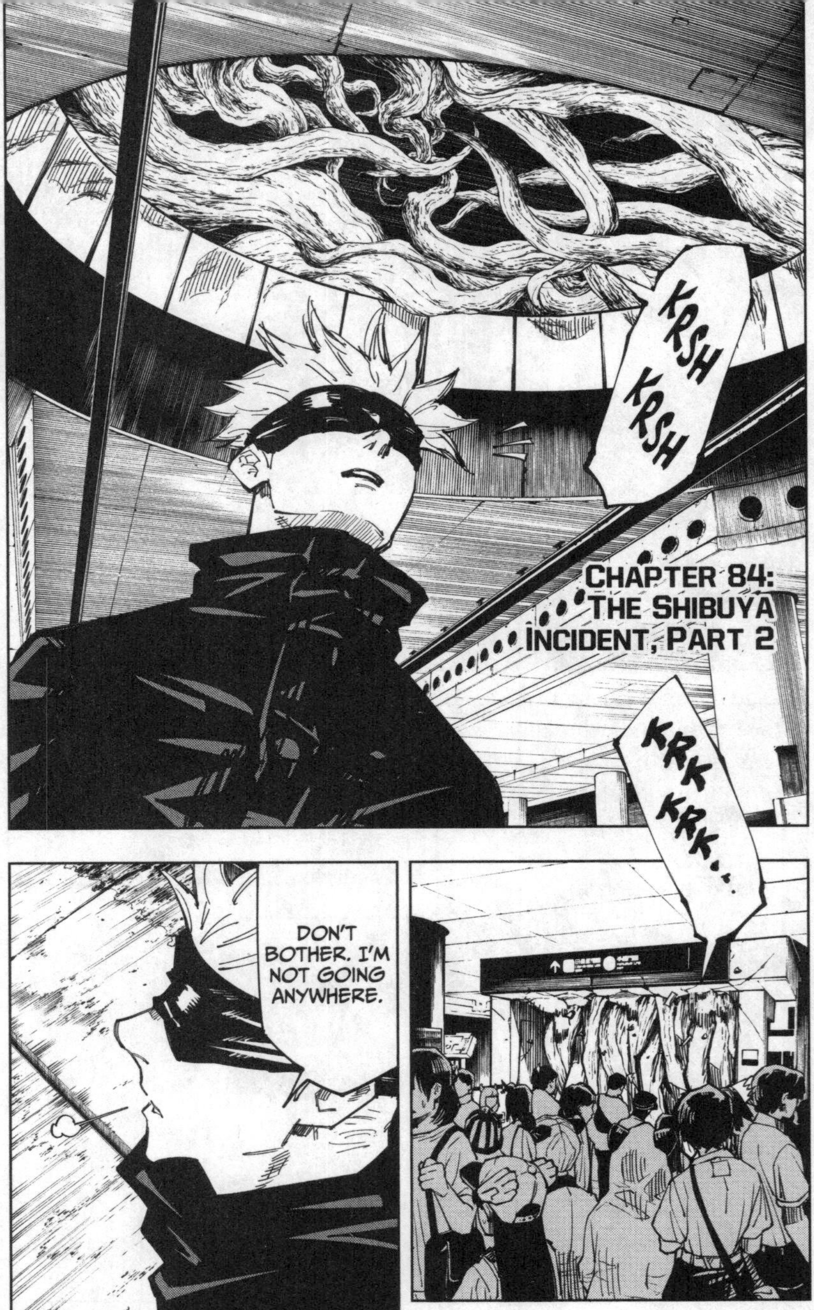
KRSH KRSH KRSH
CHAPTER 84: THE SHIBUYA INCIDENT, PART 2
KRK KRK...
DON'T BOTHER. I'M NOT GOING ANYWHERE.

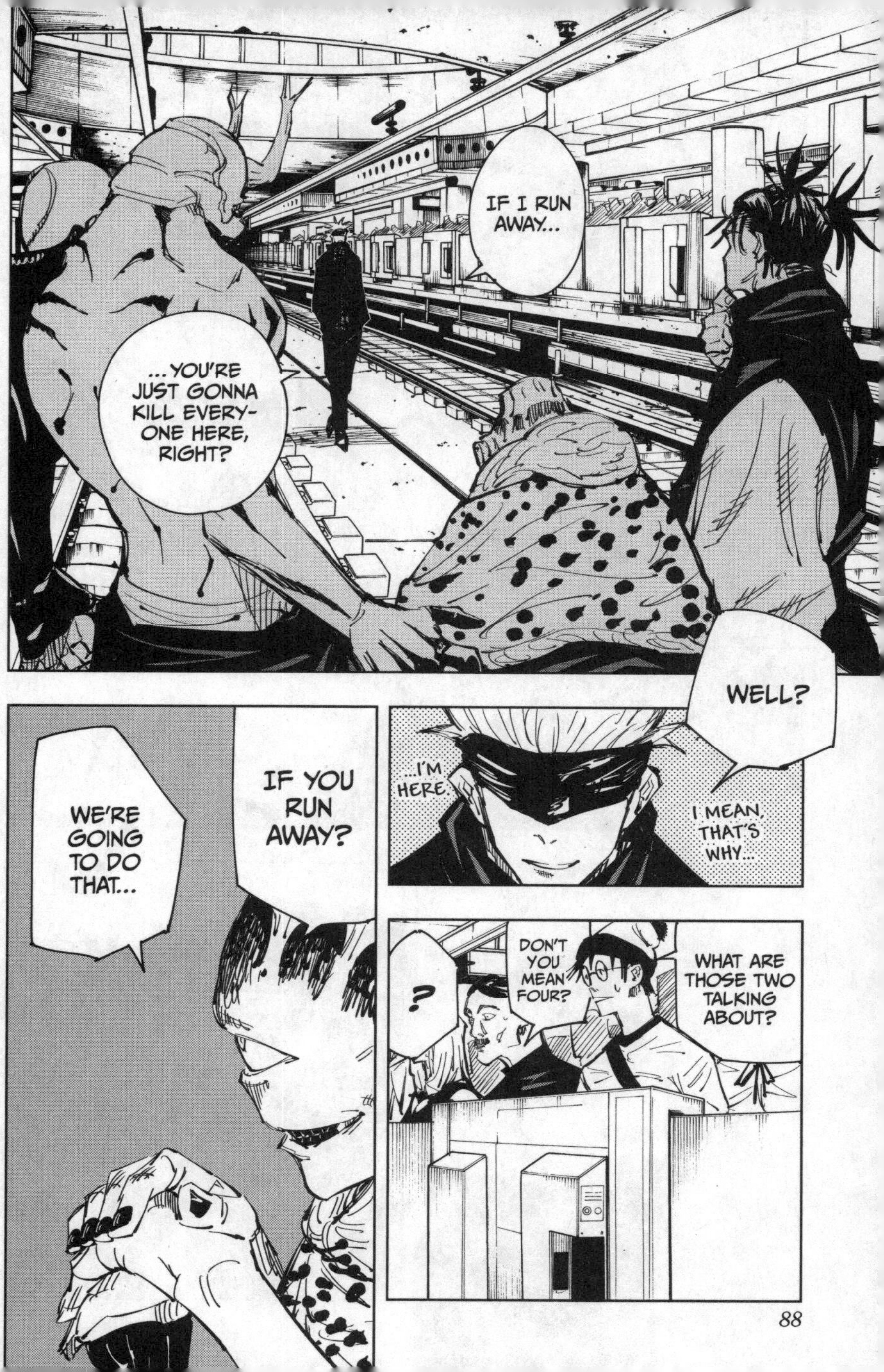
IF I RUN AWAY...
...YOU'RE JUST GONNA KILL EVERY-ONE HERE, RIGHT?
WELL?
I MEAN, THAT'S WHY...
...I'M HERE.
WHAT ARE THOSE TWO TALKING ABOUT?
DON'T YOU MEAN FOUR?
?
IF YOU RUN AWAY?
WE'RE GOING TO DO THAT...

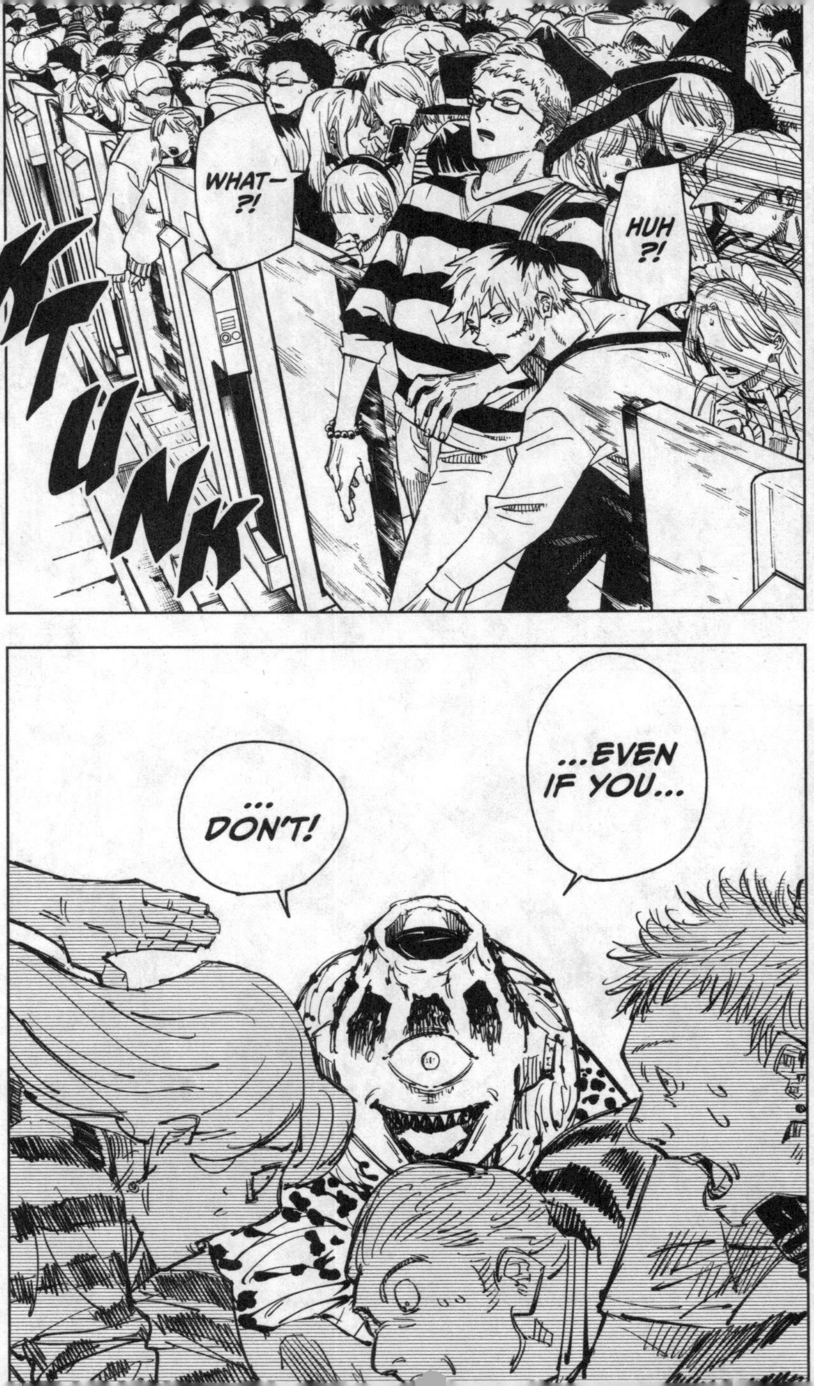
HUH ?!
WHAT— ?!
KTUNK
...EVEN IF YOU...
... DON'T!

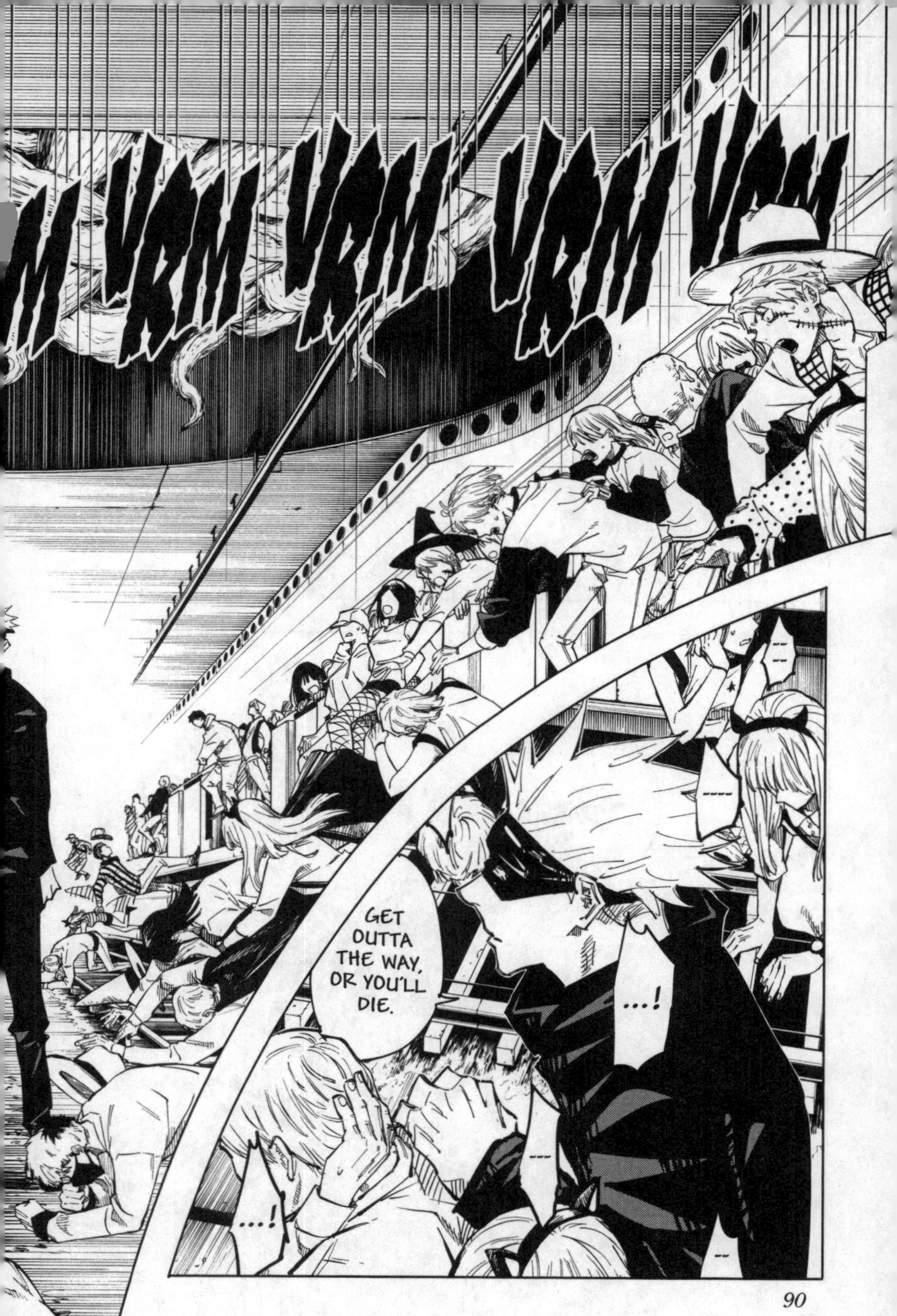
VRM VRM VRM VRM
...!
GET OUTTA THE WAY, OR YOU'LL DIE.
...!

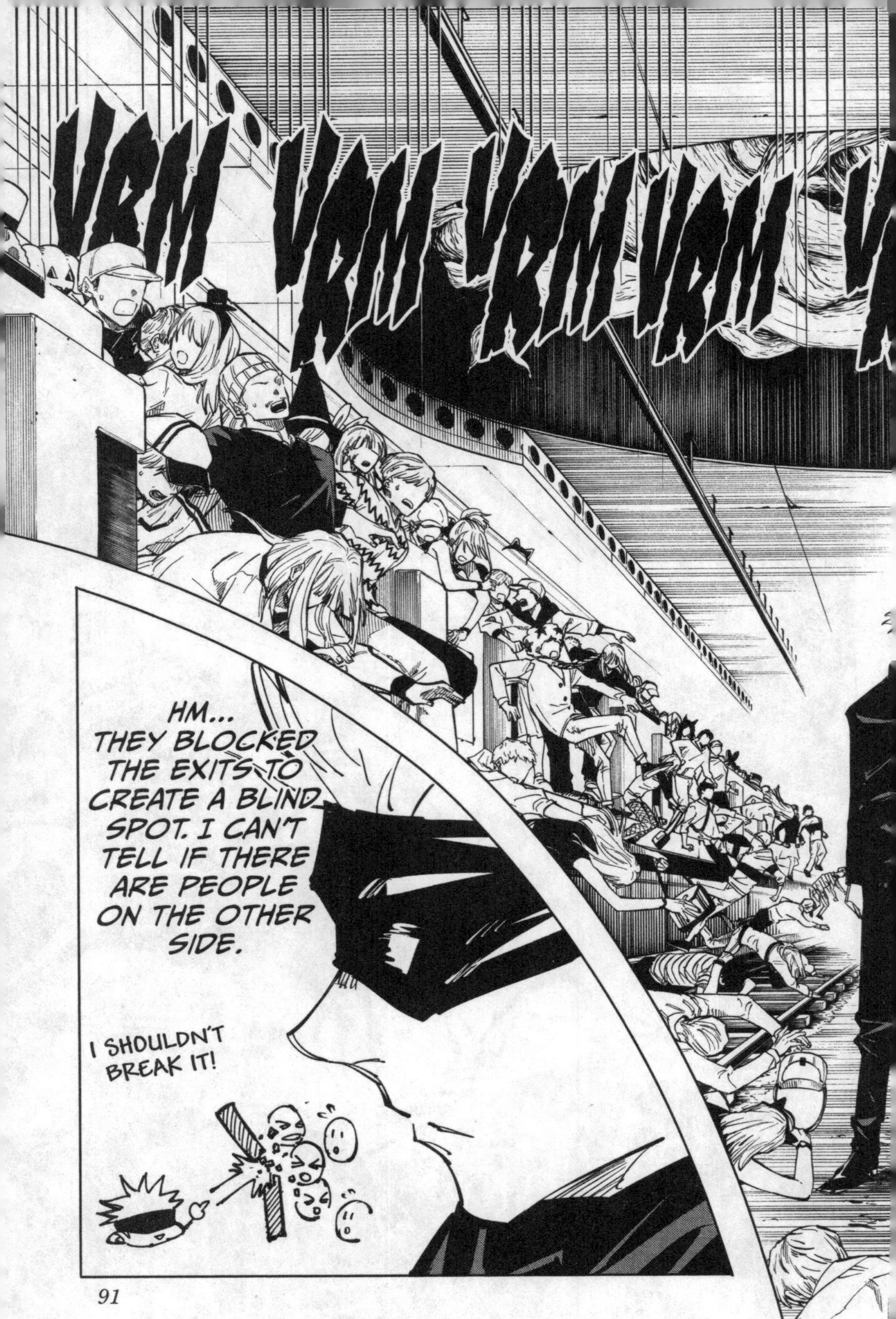
VRM VRM VRM VRM V
HM... THEY BLOCKED THE EXITS TO CREATE A BLIND SPOT. I CAN'T TELL IF THERE ARE PEOPLE ON THE OTHER SIDE.
I SHOULDN'T BREAK IT!

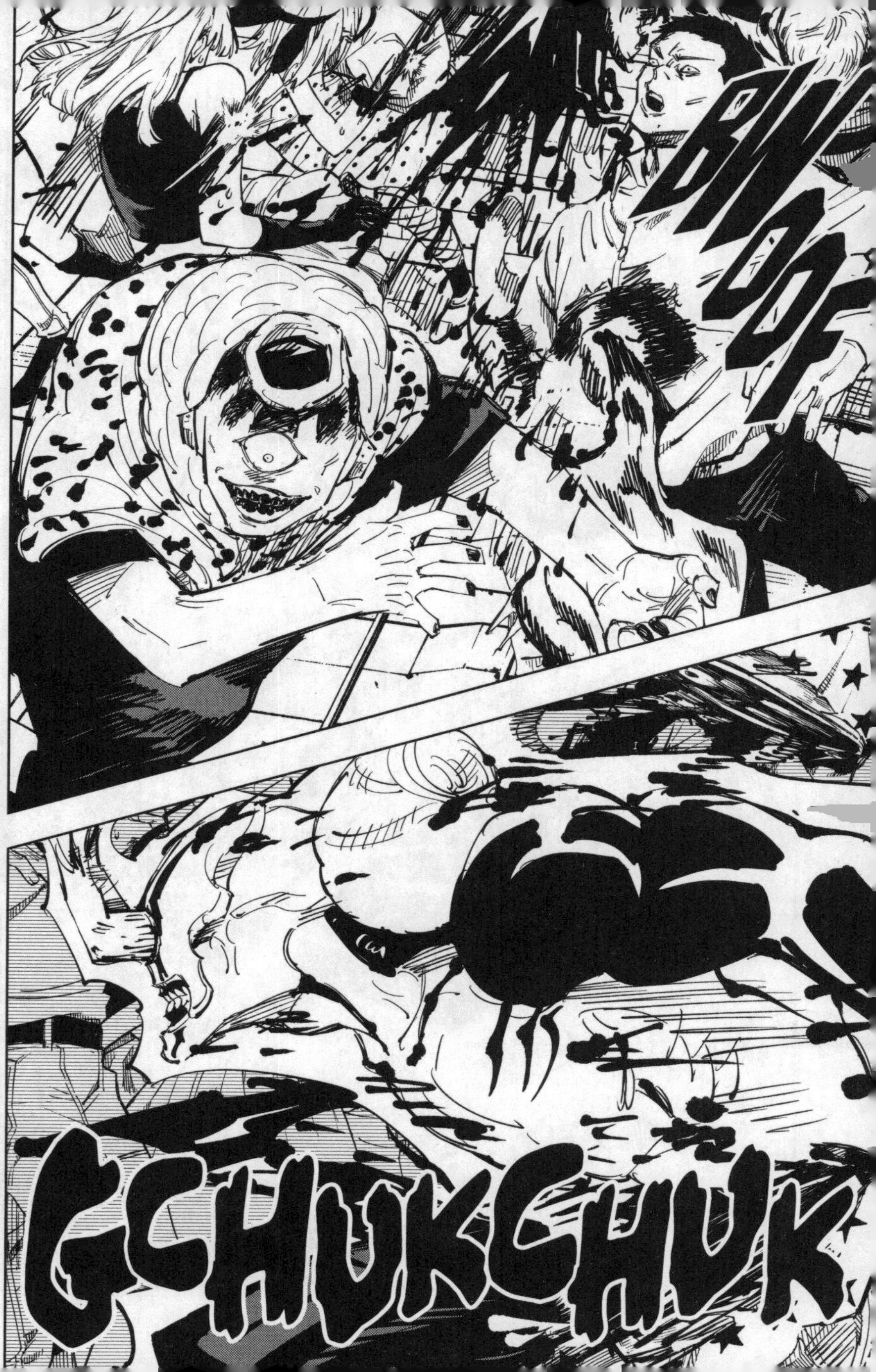
GCHUKCHUK

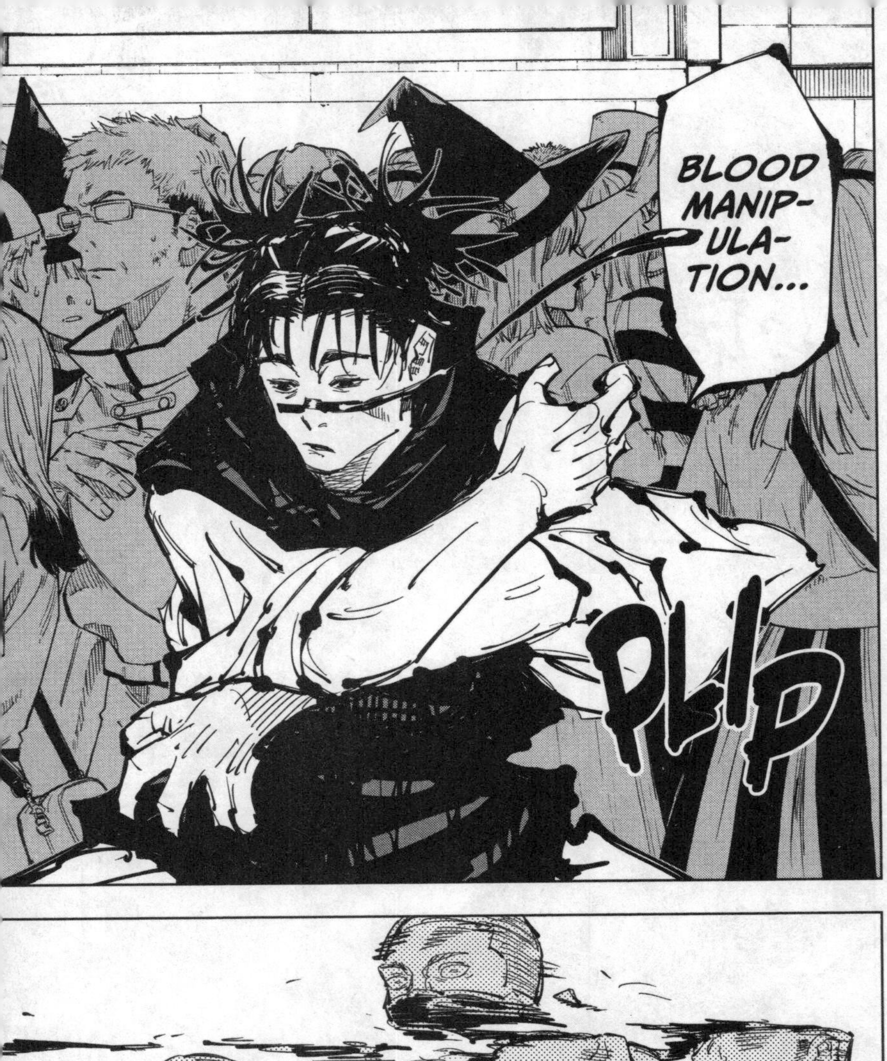
BLOOD MANIP-ULA-TION...
PLIP
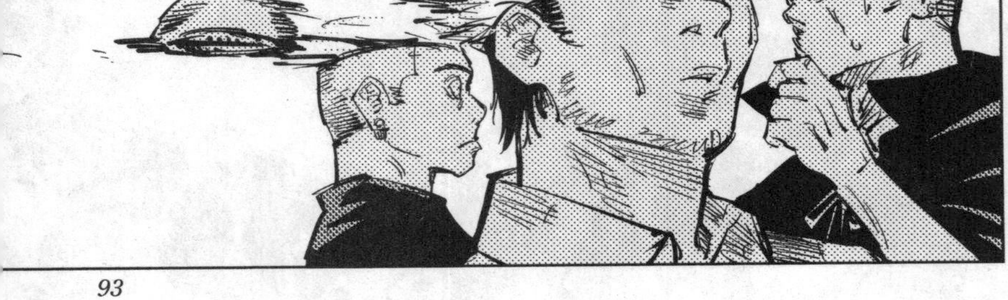

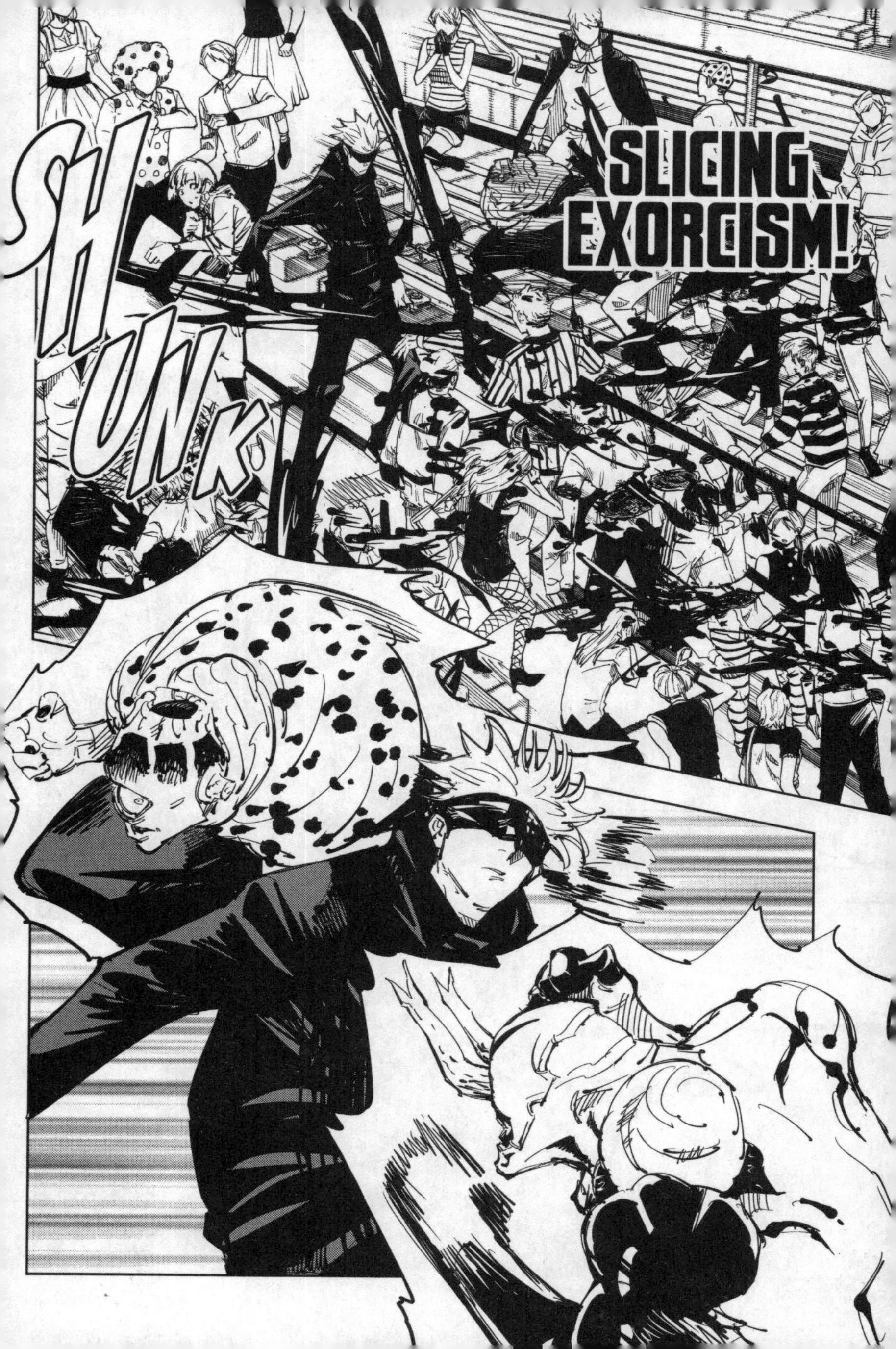
SLICING EXORCISM!
SHUNK

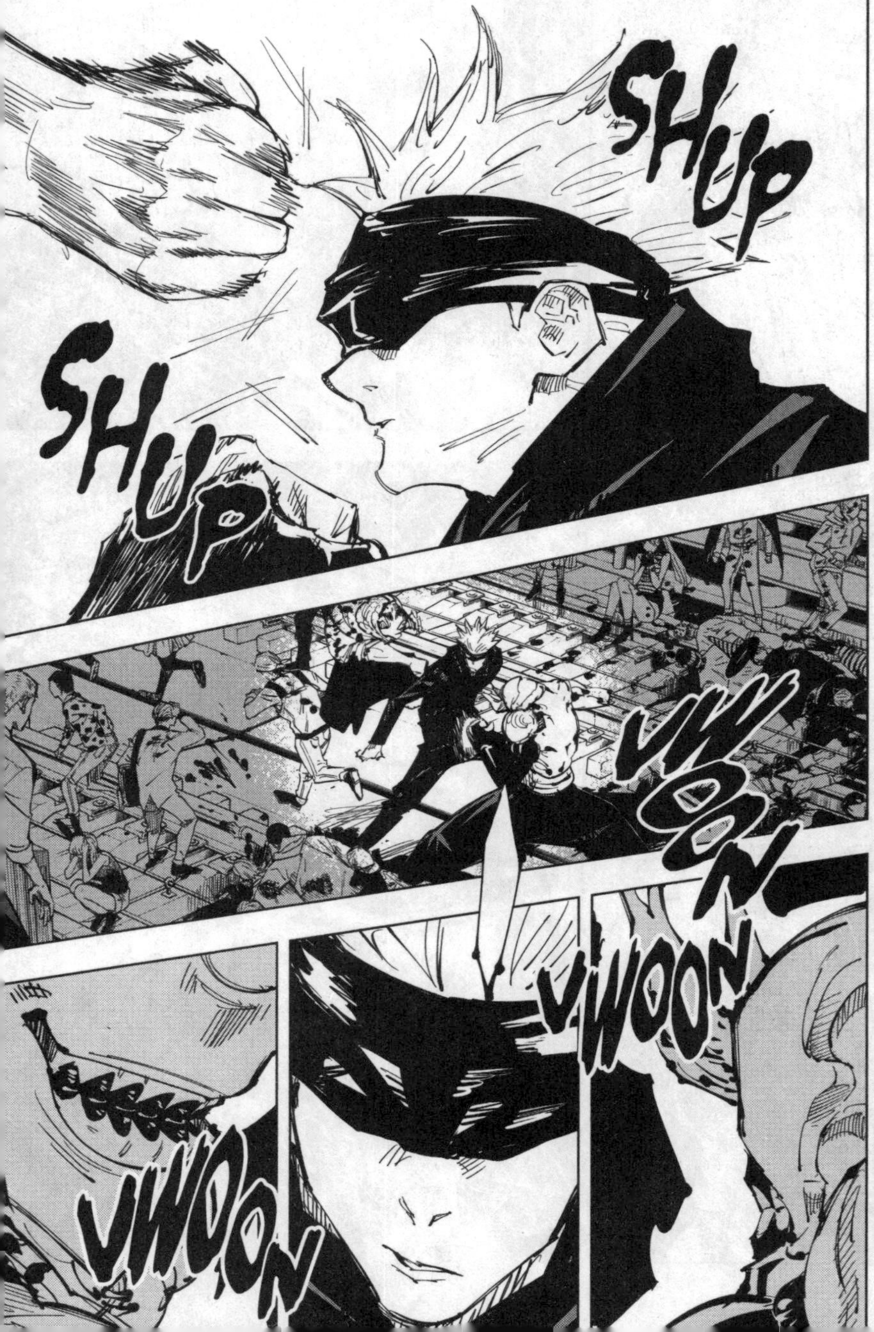
SHUP
SHUP
VWOON
VWOON
VWOON

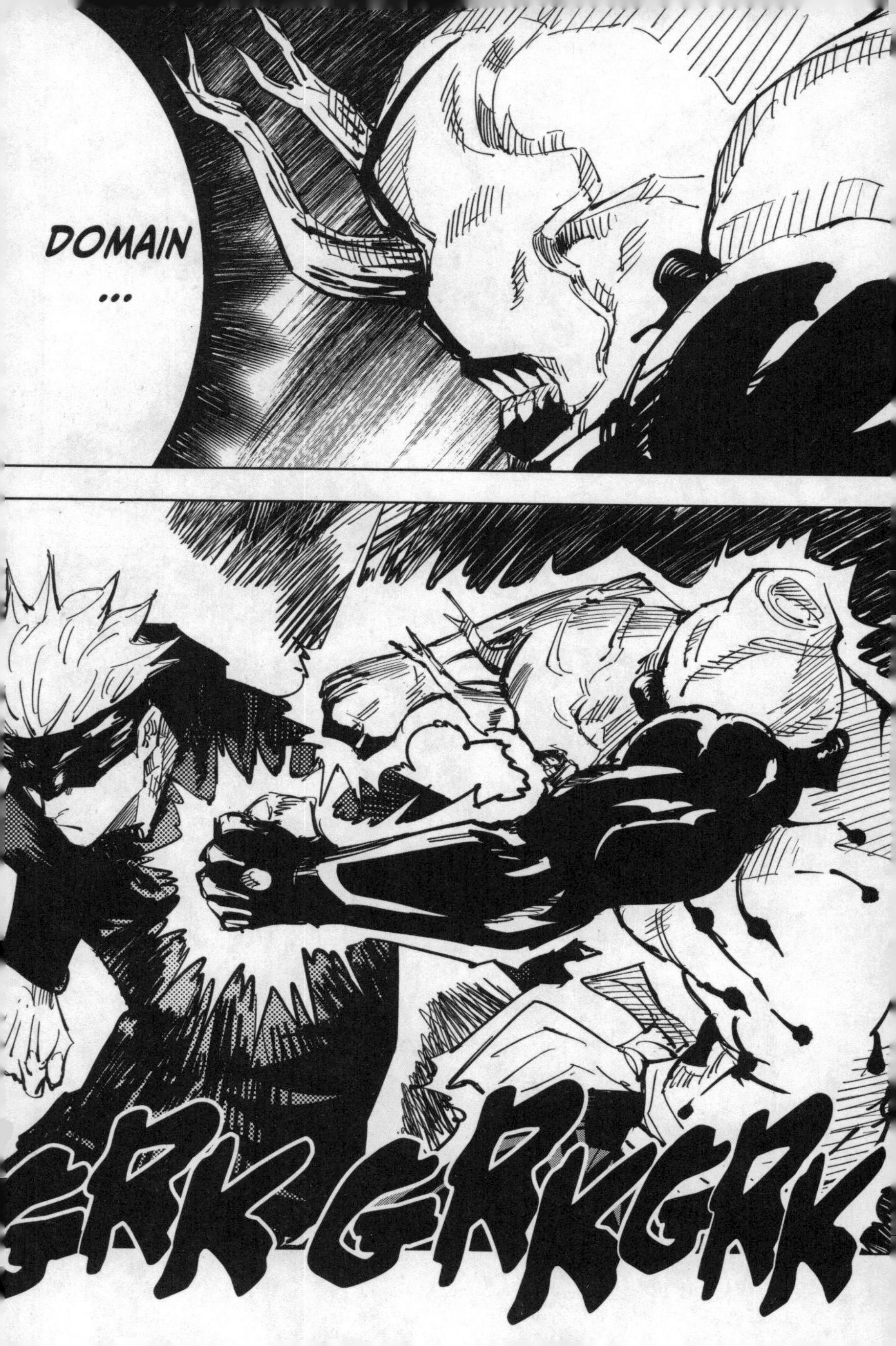
DOMAIN ...

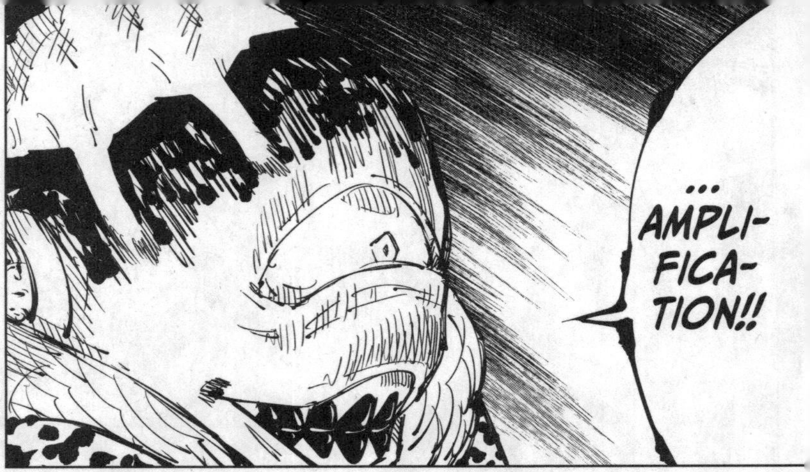
...AMPLI-FICA-TION!!
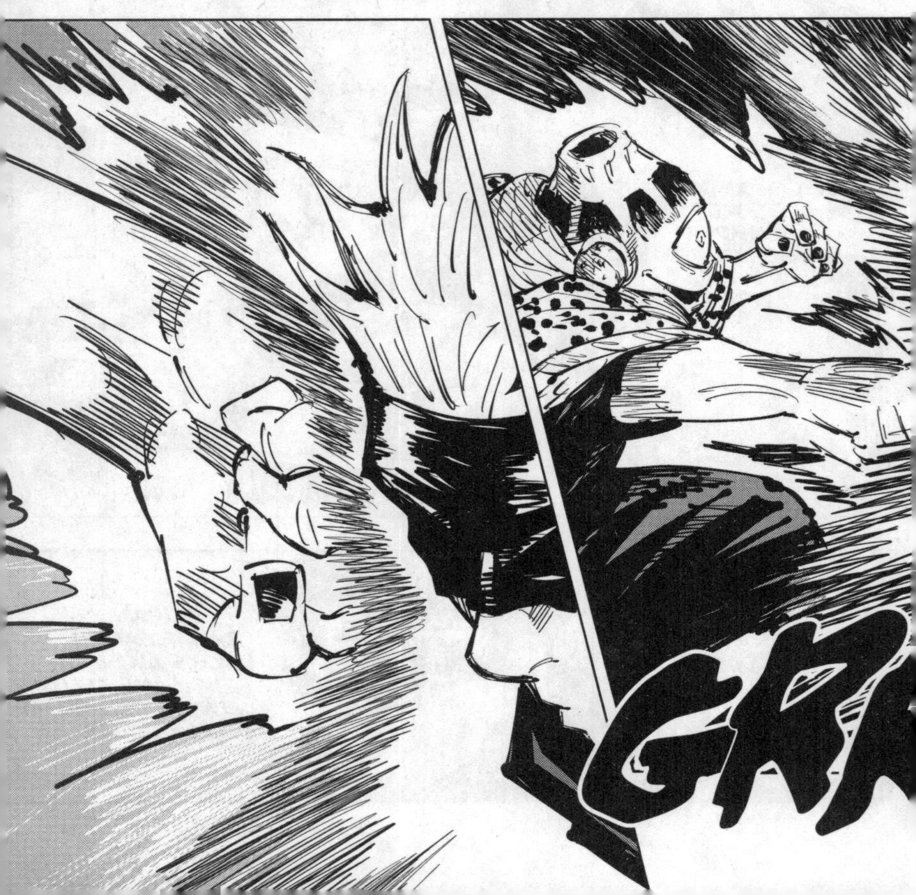
CRR

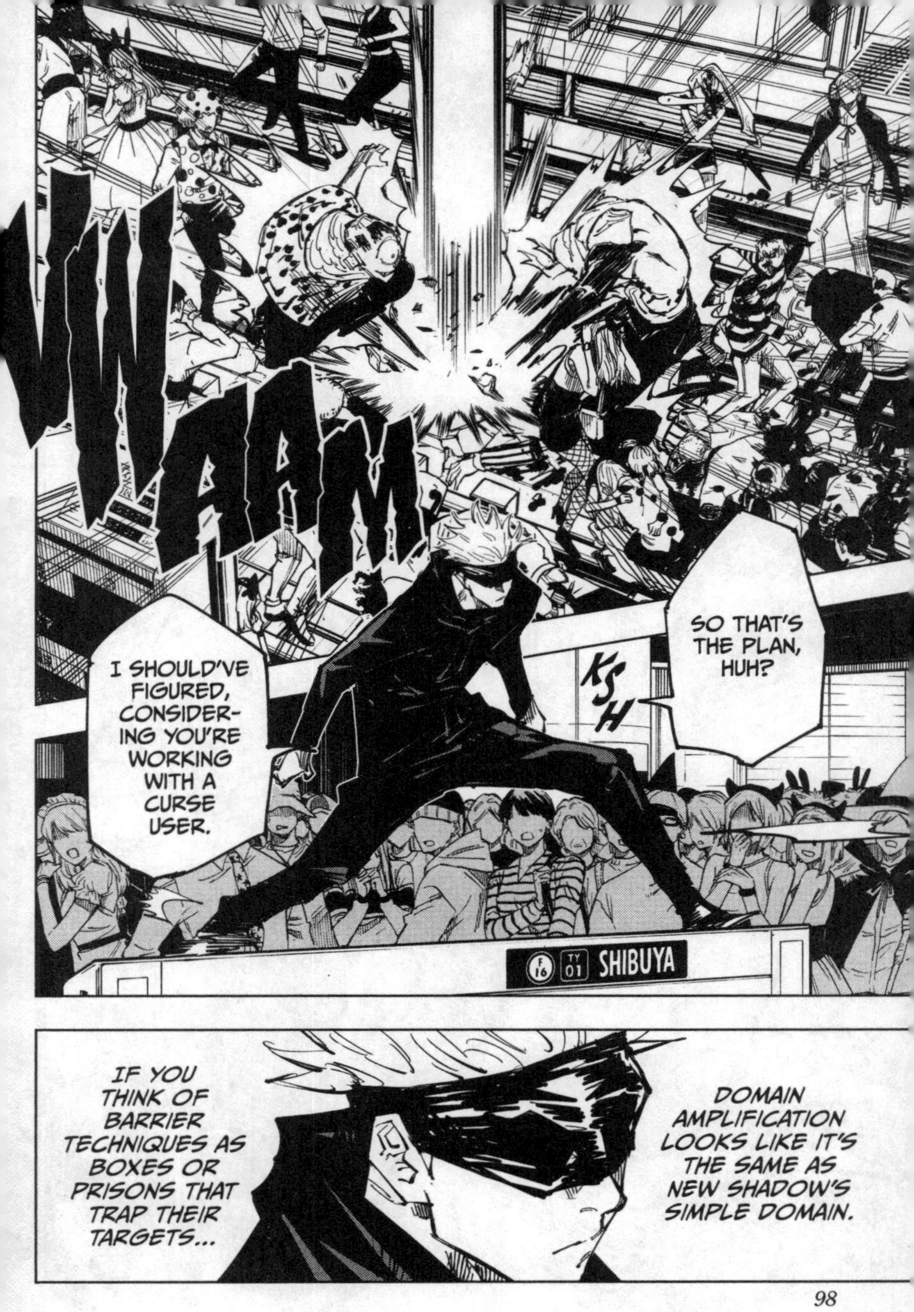
WHAM
KSH
SO THAT'S THE PLAN, HUH?
I SHOULD'VE FIGURED, CONSIDER-ING YOU'RE WORKING WITH A CURSE USER.
F 16 TY 01 SHIBUYA
DOMAIN AMPLIFICATION LOOKS LIKE IT'S THE SAME AS NEW SHADOW'S SIMPLE DOMAIN.
IF YOU THINK OF BARRIER TECHNIQUES AS BOXES OR PRISONS THAT TRAP THEIR TARGETS...

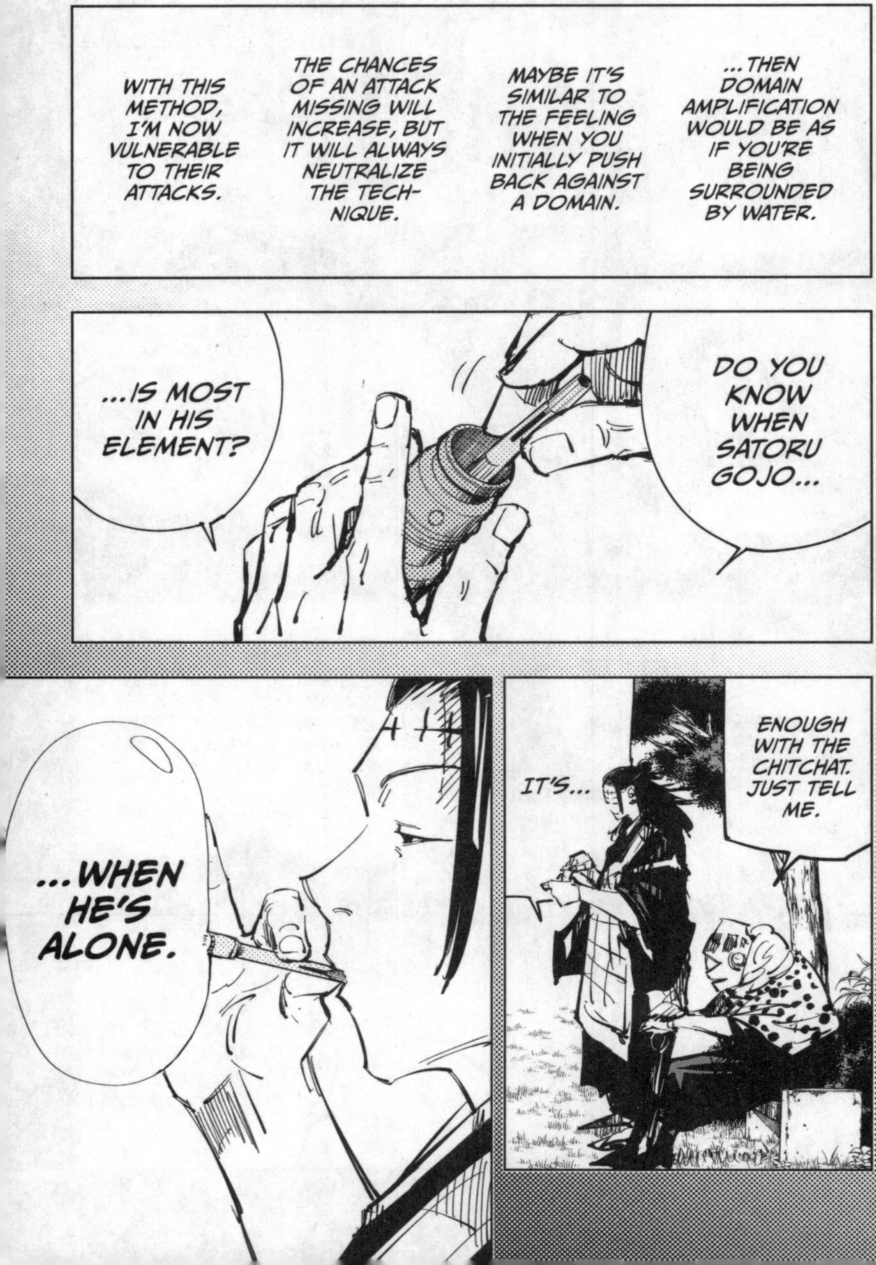
...THEN DOMAIN AMPLIFICATION WOULD BE AS IF YOU'RE BEING SURROUNDED BY WATER.
MAYBE IT'S SIMILAR TO THE FEELING WHEN YOU INITIALLY PUSH BACK AGAINST A DOMAIN.
THE CHANCES OF AN ATTACK MISSING WILL INCREASE, BUT IT WILL ALWAYS NEUTRALIZE THE TECH-NIQUE.
WITH THIS METHOD, I'M NOW VULNERABLE TO THEIR ATTACKS.
DO YOU KNOW WHEN SATORU GOJO...
...IS MOST IN HIS ELEMENT?
ENOUGH WITH THE CHITCHAT. JUST TELL ME.
IT'S...
...WHEN HE'S ALONE.

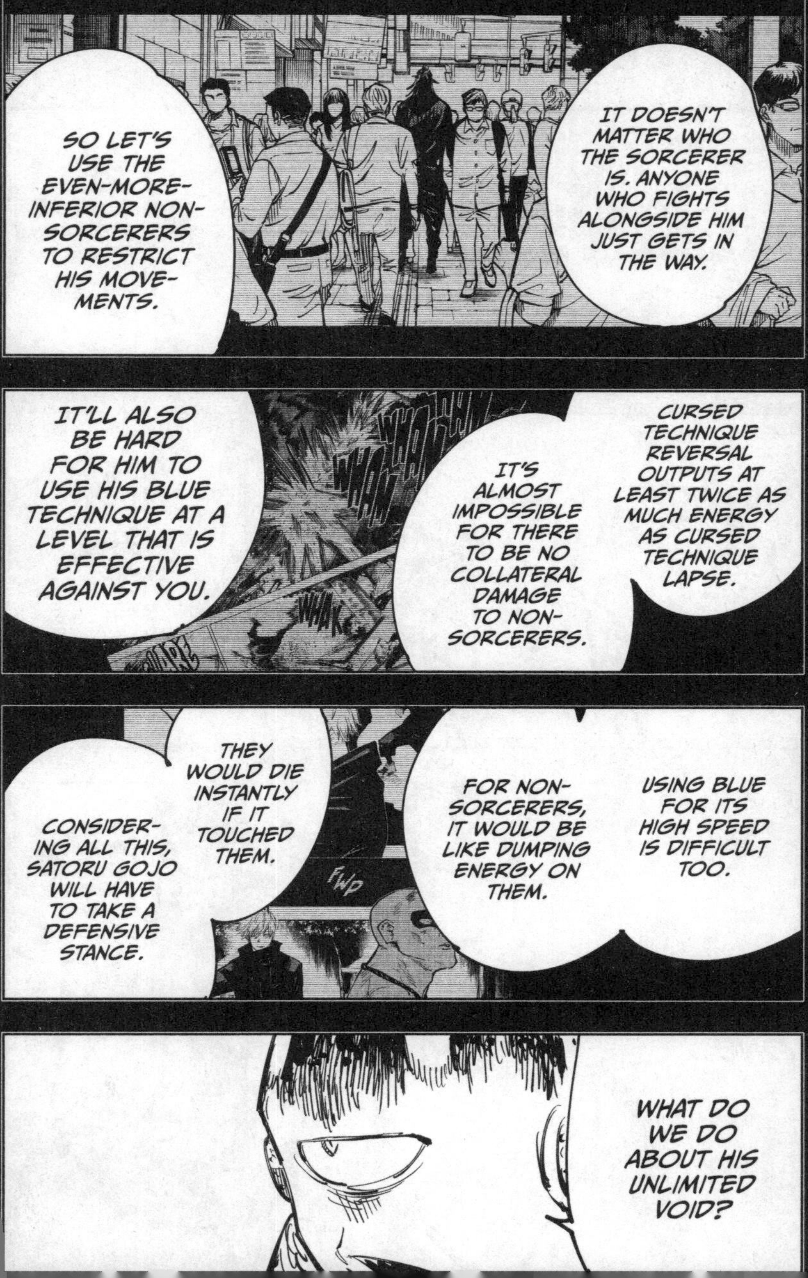
IT DOESN'T MATTER WHO THE SORCERER IS. ANYONE WHO FIGHTS ALONGSIDE HIM JUST GETS IN THE WAY.
SO LET'S USE THE EVEN-MORE-INFERIOR NON-SORCERERS TO RESTRICT HIS MOVEMENTS.
CURSED TECHNIQUE REVERSAL OUTPUTS AT LEAST TWICE AS MUCH ENERGY AS CURSED TECHNIQUE LAPSE.
IT'S ALMOST IMPOSSIBLE FOR THERE TO BE NO COLLATERAL DAMAGE TO NON-SORCERERS.
IT'LL ALSO BE HARD FOR HIM TO USE HIS BLUE TECHNIQUE AT A LEVEL THAT IS EFFECTIVE AGAINST YOU.
USING BLUE FOR ITS HIGH SPEED IS DIFFICULT TOO.
FOR NON-SORCERERS, IT WOULD BE LIKE DUMPING ENERGY ON THEM.
THEY WOULD DIE INSTANTLY IF IT TOUCHED THEM.
CONSIDERING ALL THIS, SATORU GOJO WILL HAVE TO TAKE A DEFENSIVE STANCE.
FWP
WHAT DO WE DO ABOUT HIS UNLIMITED VOID?

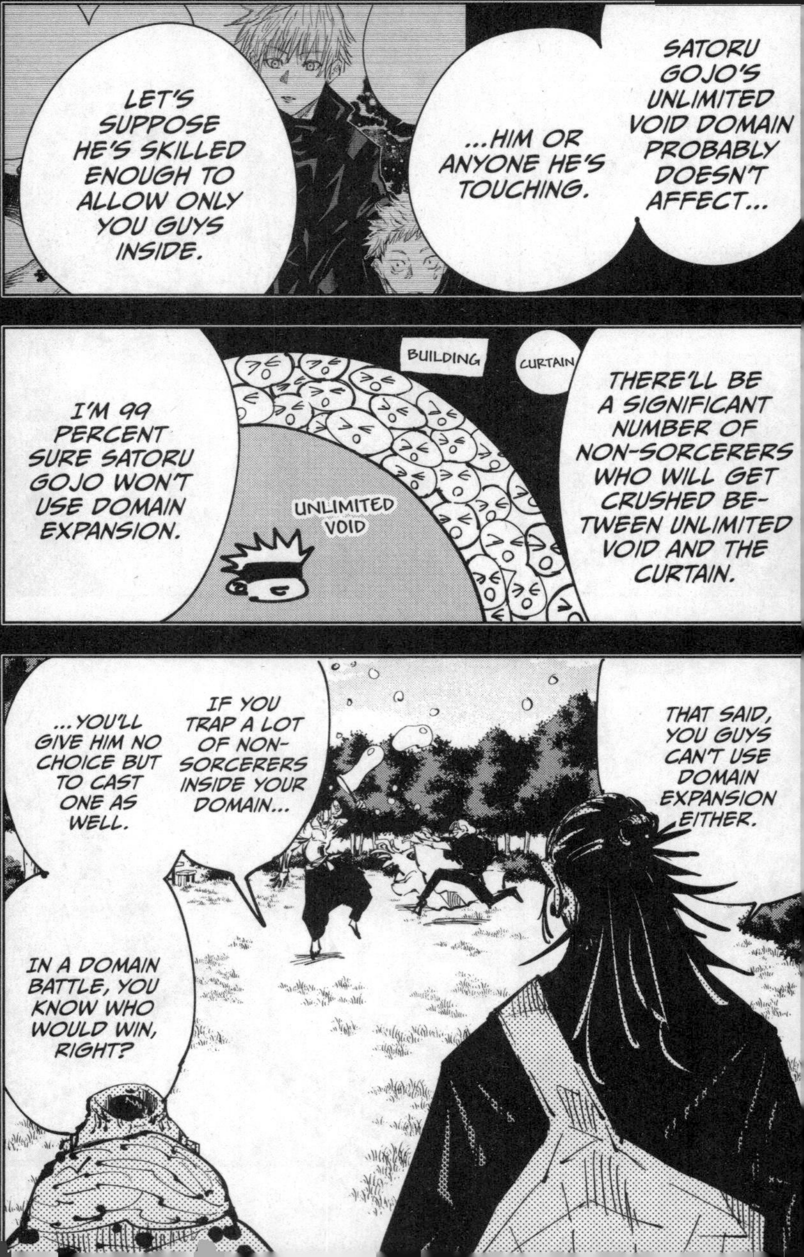
SATORU GOJO'S UNLIMITED VOID DOMAIN PROBABLY DOESN'T AFFECT...
...HIM OR ANYONE HE'S TOUCHING.
LET'S SUPPOSE HE'S SKILLED ENOUGH TO ALLOW ONLY YOU GUYS INSIDE.
THERE'LL BE A SIGNIFICANT NUMBER OF NON-SORCERERS WHO WILL GET CRUSHED BE- TWEEN UNLIMITED VOID AND THE CURTAIN.
CURTAIN
BUILDING
UNLIMITED VOID
I'M 99 PERCENT SURE SATORU GOJO WON'T USE DOMAIN EXPANSION.
THAT SAID, YOU GUYS CAN'T USE DOMAIN EXPANSION EITHER.
IF YOU TRAP A LOT OF NON- SORCERERS INSIDE YOUR DOMAIN...
...YOU'LL GIVE HIM NO CHOICE BUT TO CAST ONE AS WELL.
IN A DOMAIN BATTLE, YOU KNOW WHO WOULD WIN, RIGHT?

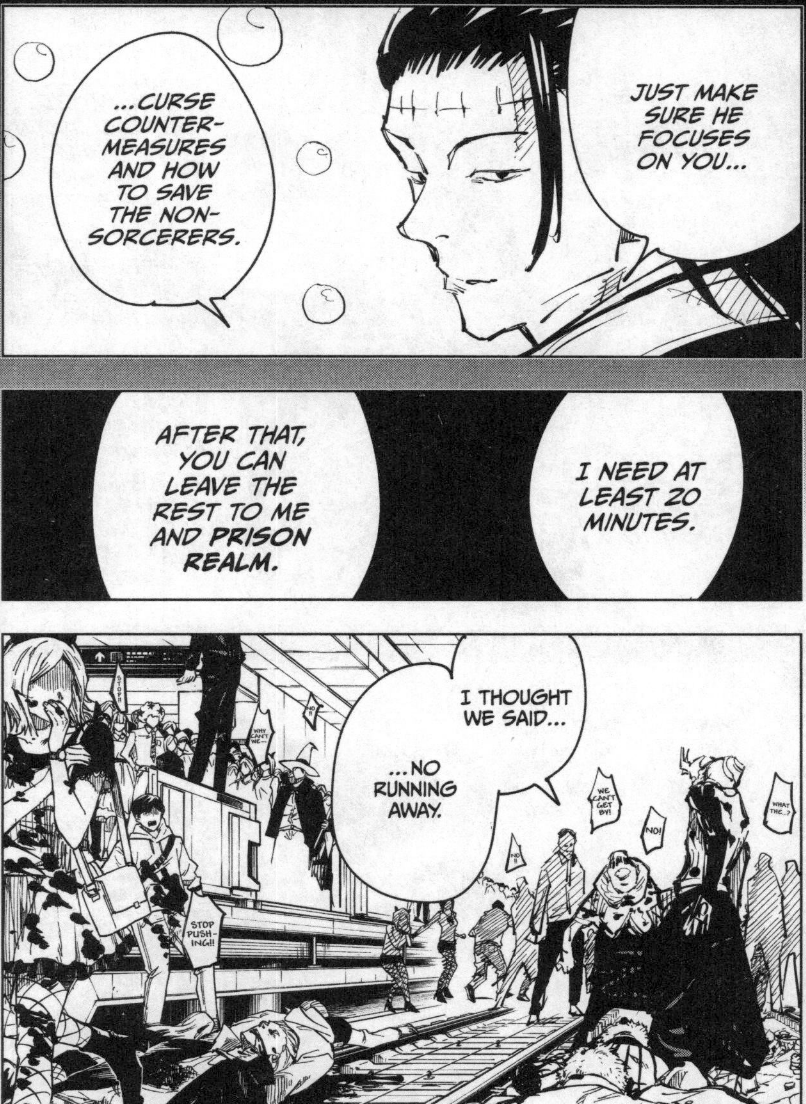
JUST MAKE SURE HE FOCUSES ON YOU...
...CURSE COUNTER-MEASURES AND HOW TO SAVE THE NON-SORCERERS.
I NEED AT LEAST 20 MINUTES.
AFTER THAT, YOU CAN LEAVE THE REST TO ME AND PRISON REALM.
WHAT THE...?
NO!
WE CAN'T GET BY!
NO!!
I THOUGHT WE SAID...
...NO RUNNING AWAY.
NO!!
WHY CAN'T WE—
STOP!!
STOP PUSHING!!

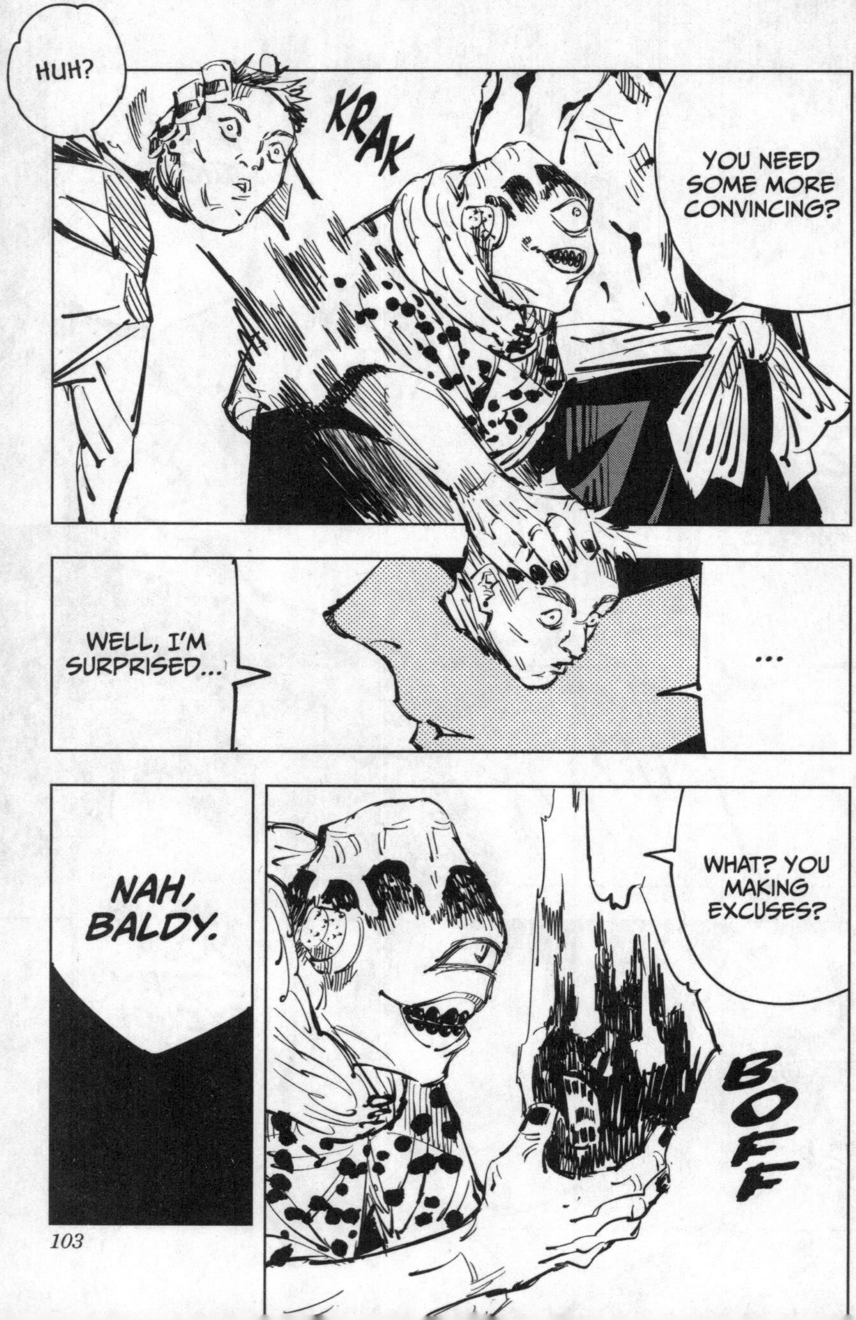
YOU NEED SOME MORE CONVINCING?
KRAK
HUH?
...
WELL, I'M SURPRISED...
WHAT? YOU MAKING EXCUSES?
BOFF
NAH, BALDY.

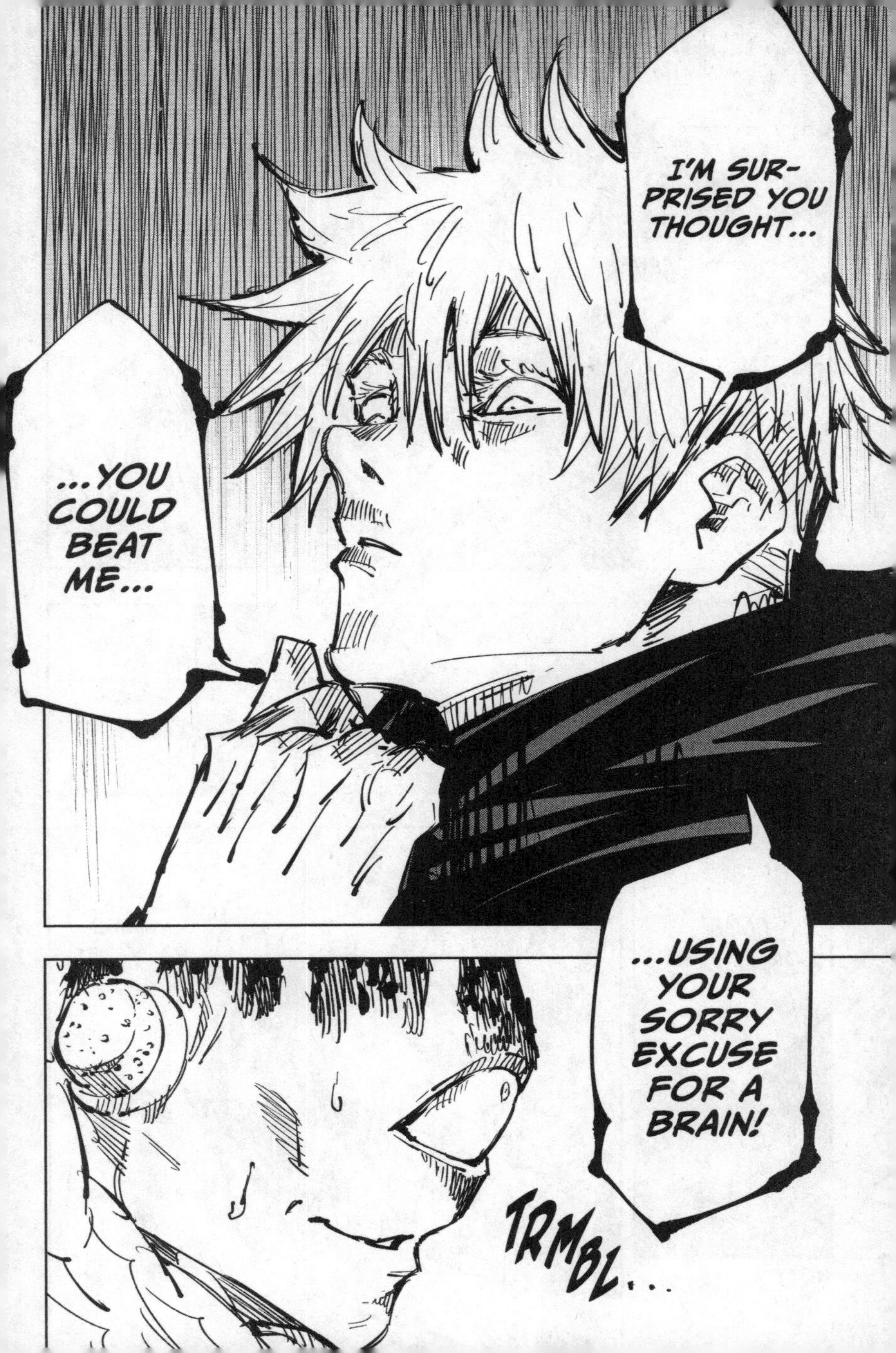
I'M SUR-PRISED YOU THOUGHT...
...YOU COULD BEAT ME...
...USING YOUR SORRY EXCUSE FOR A BRAIN!
TRMBL...

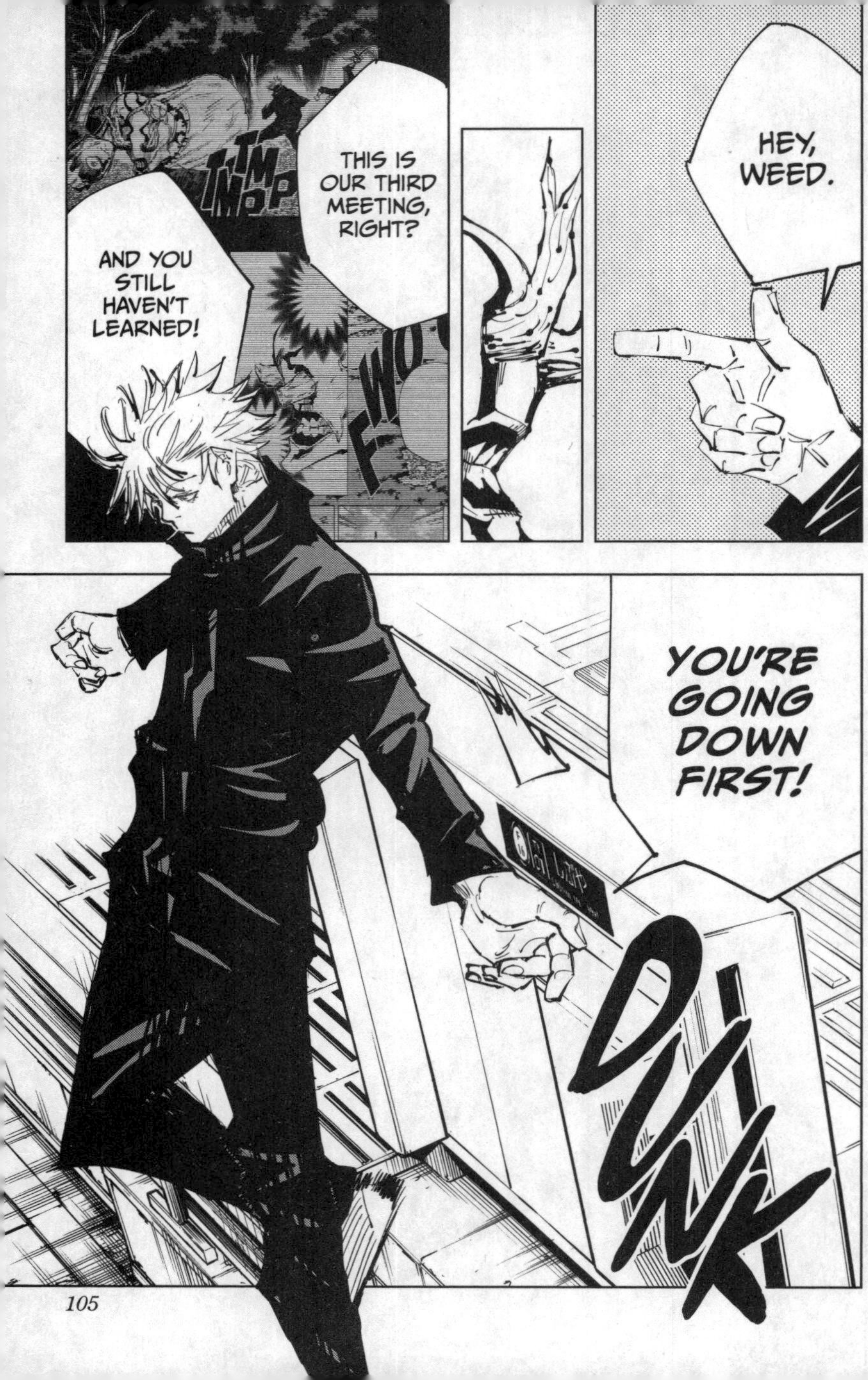
HEY, WEED.
THIS IS OUR THIRD MEETING, RIGHT?
AND YOU STILL HAVEN'T LEARNED!
YOU'RE GOING DOWN FIRST!

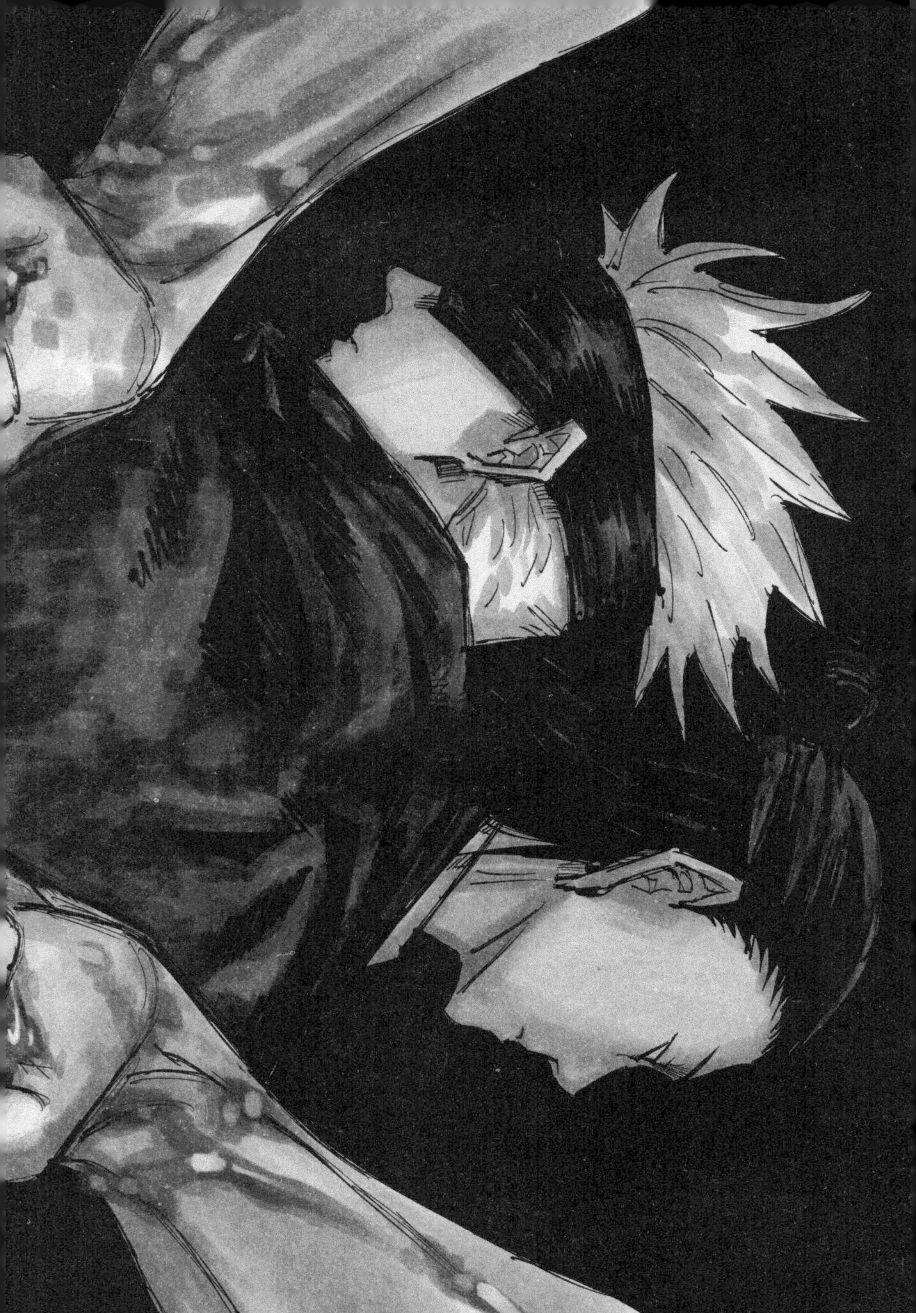

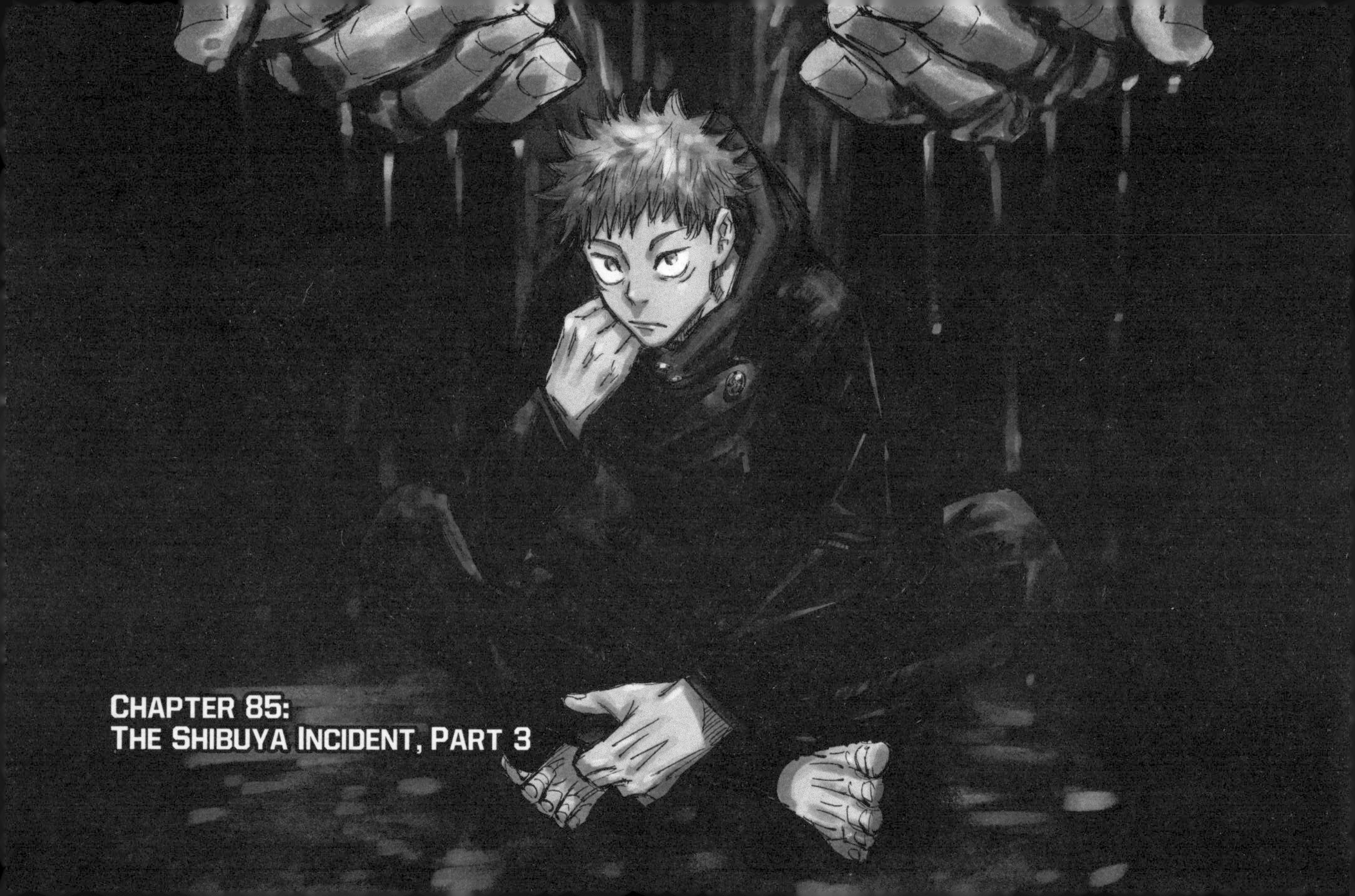
CHAPTER 85:
THE SHIBUYA INCIDENT, PART 3

JUJUTSU KAISEN

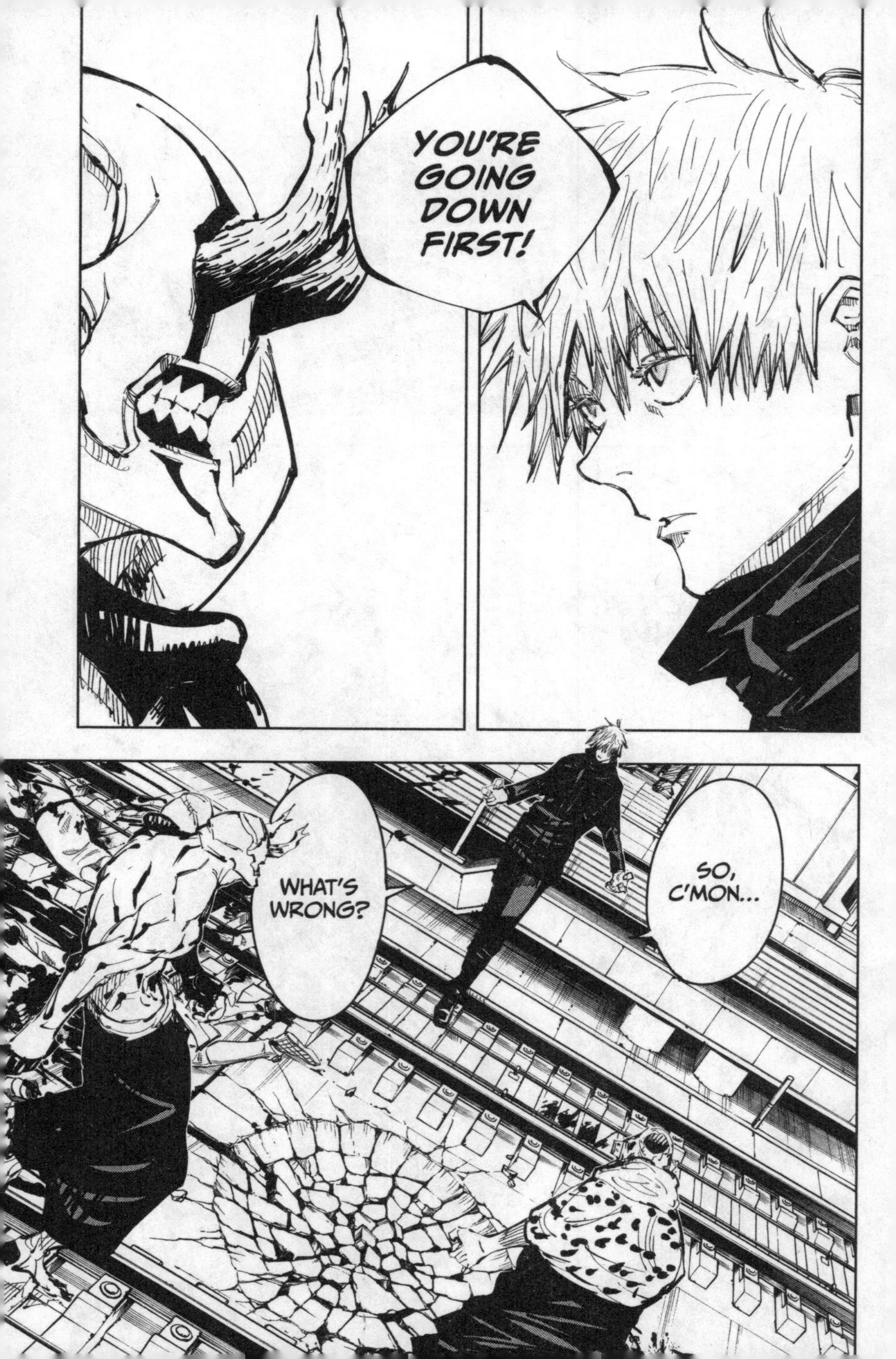
YOU'RE GOING DOWN FIRST!
SO, C'MON...
WHAT'S WRONG?

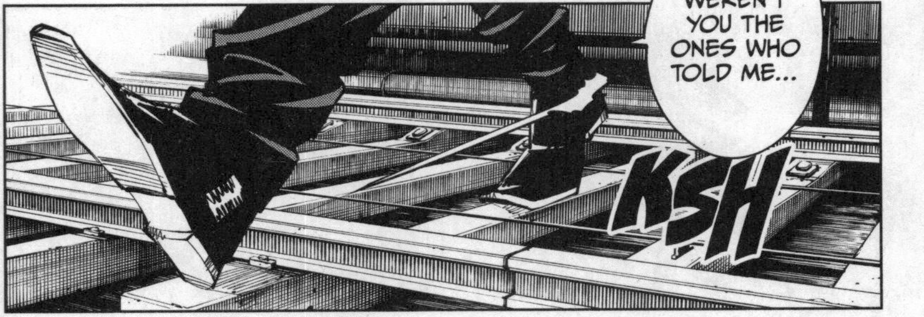
WEREN'T YOU THE ONES WHO TOLD ME...
KSH
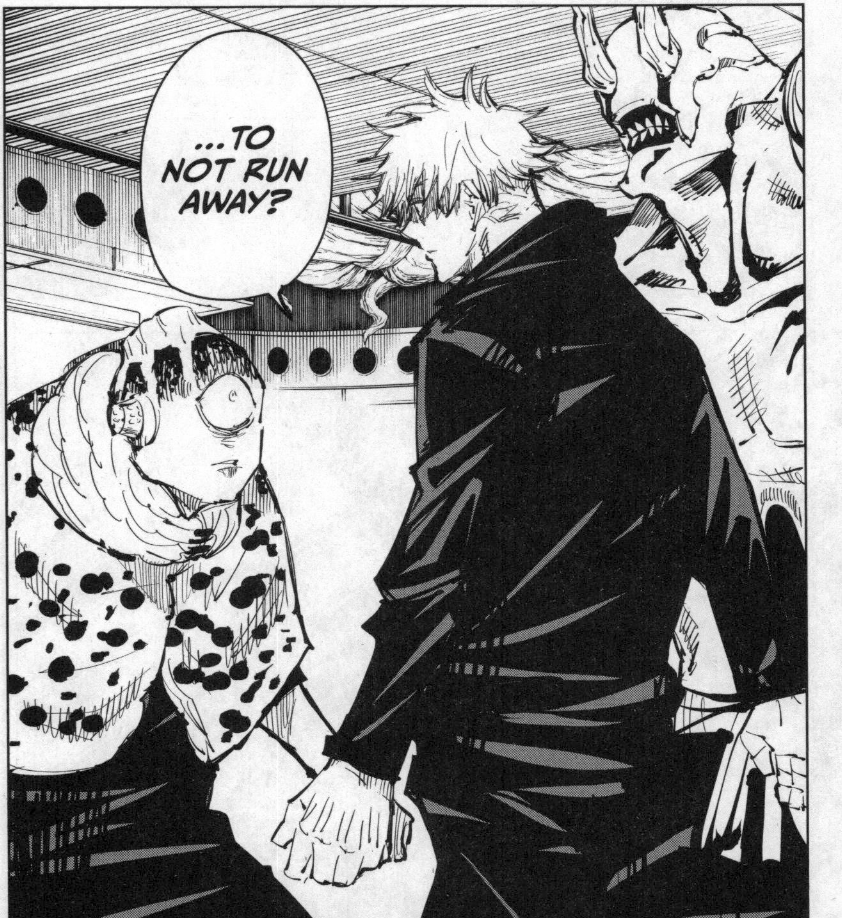
...TO NOT RUN AWAY?

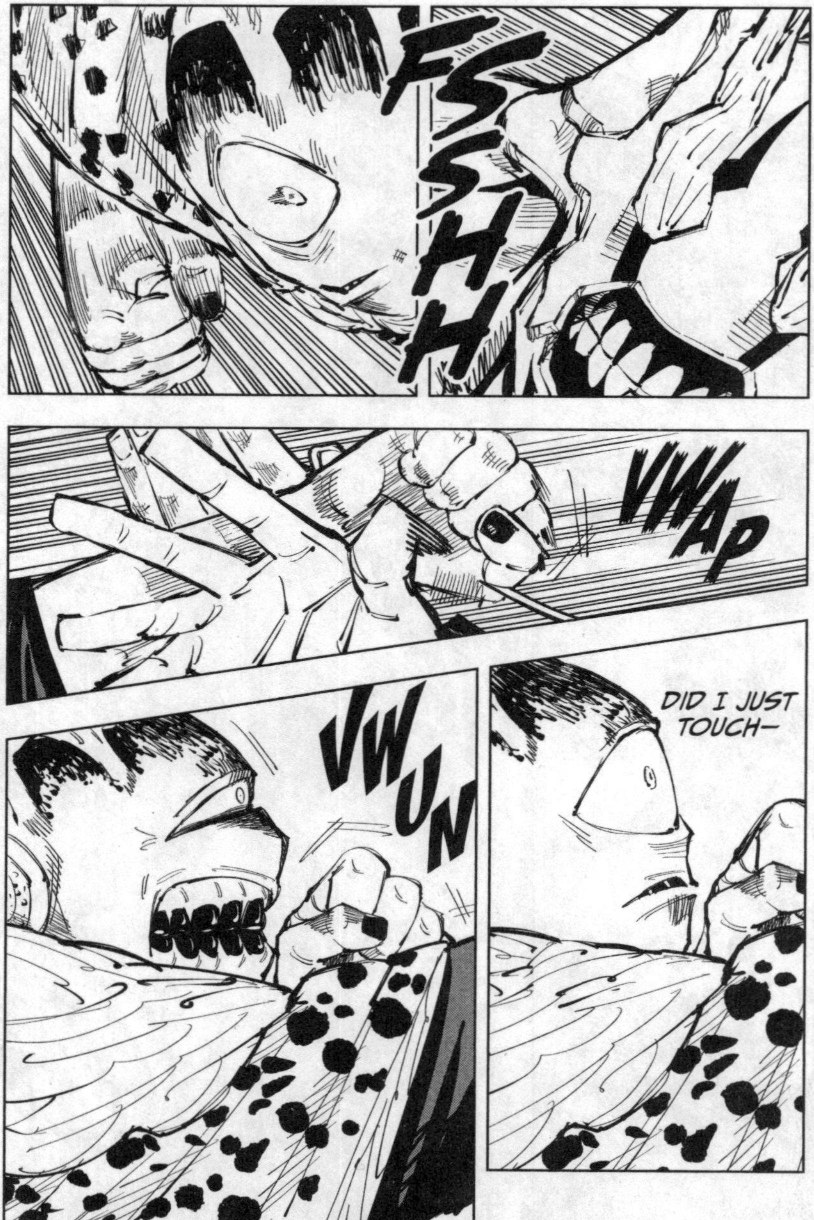
FSSHH
VWAP
DID I JUST TOUCH—
VWUN

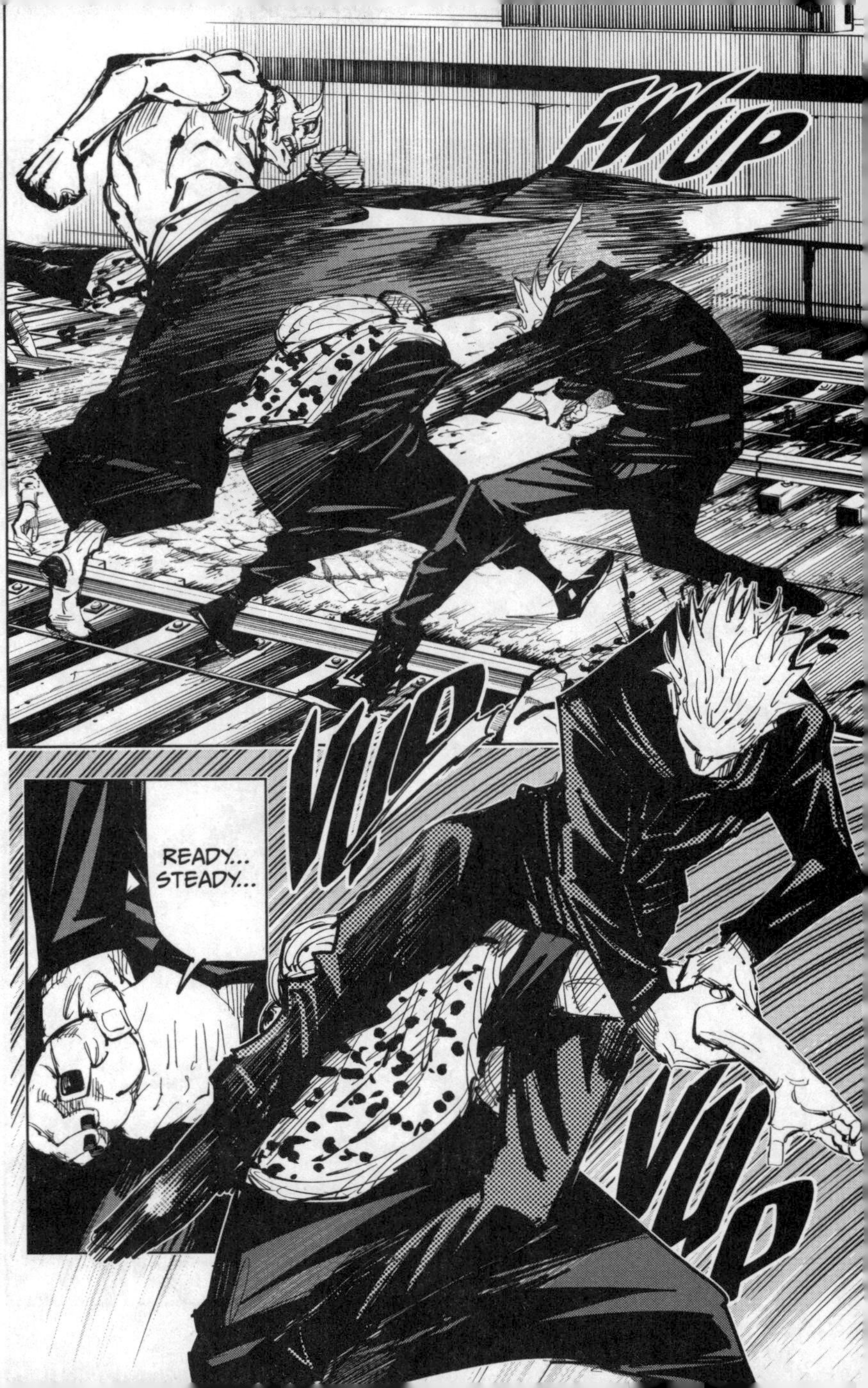
FWUP
READY... STEADY...

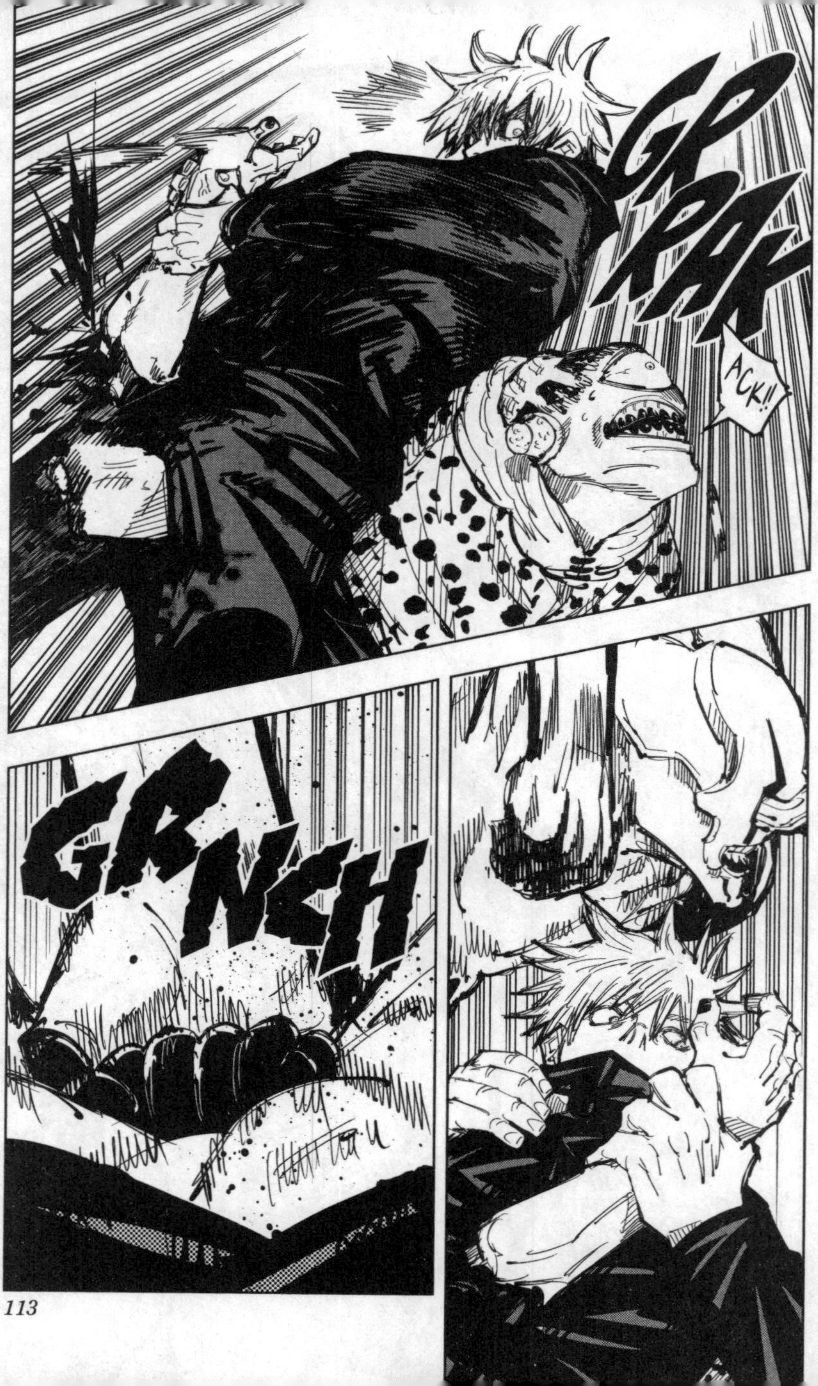
GRRAK
ACK!!
GRNCH

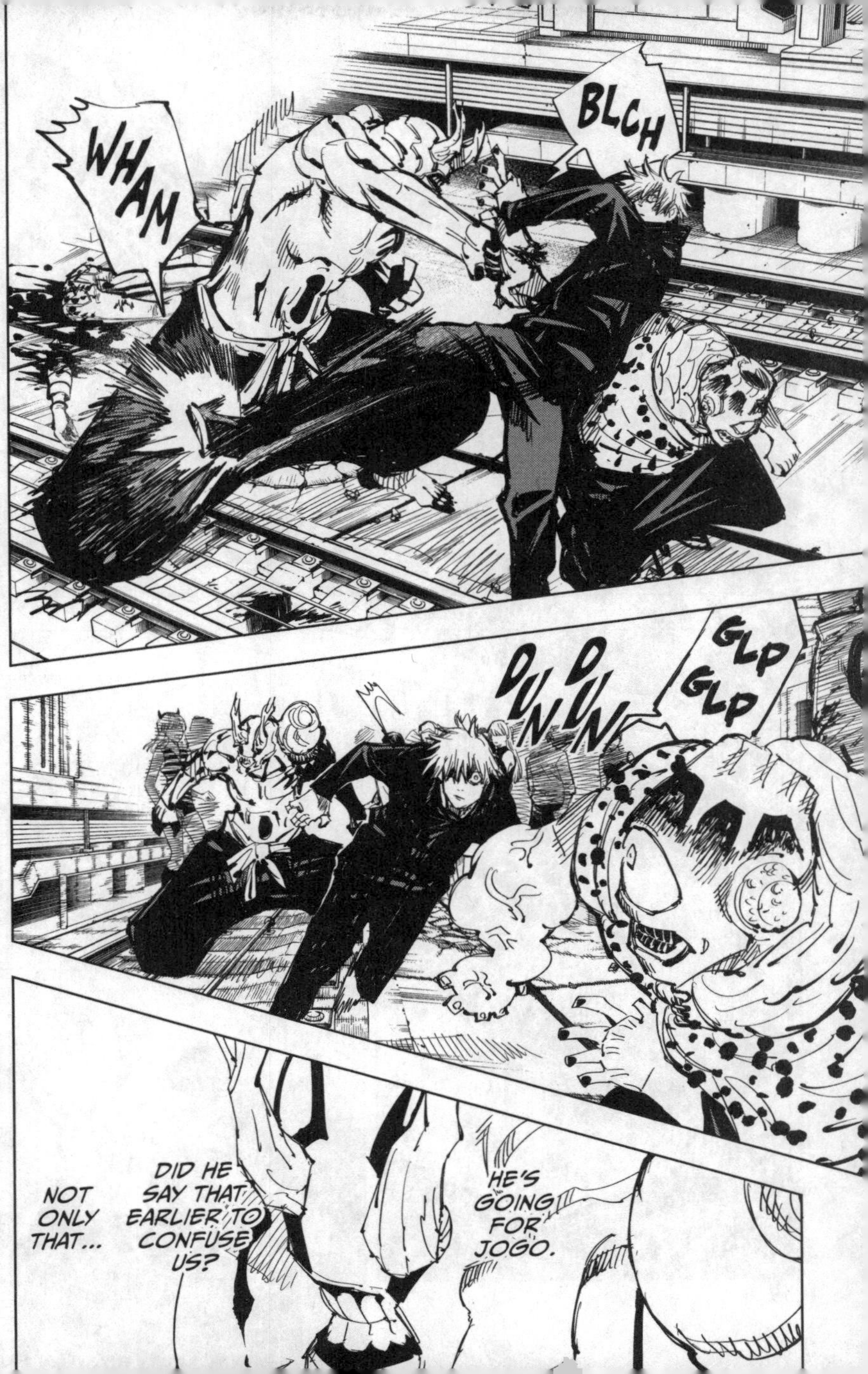
BLCH
WHAM
GLP GLP
DUN DUN
HE'S GOING FOR JOGO.
DID HE SAY THAT EARLIER TO CONFUSE US?
NOT ONLY THAT...

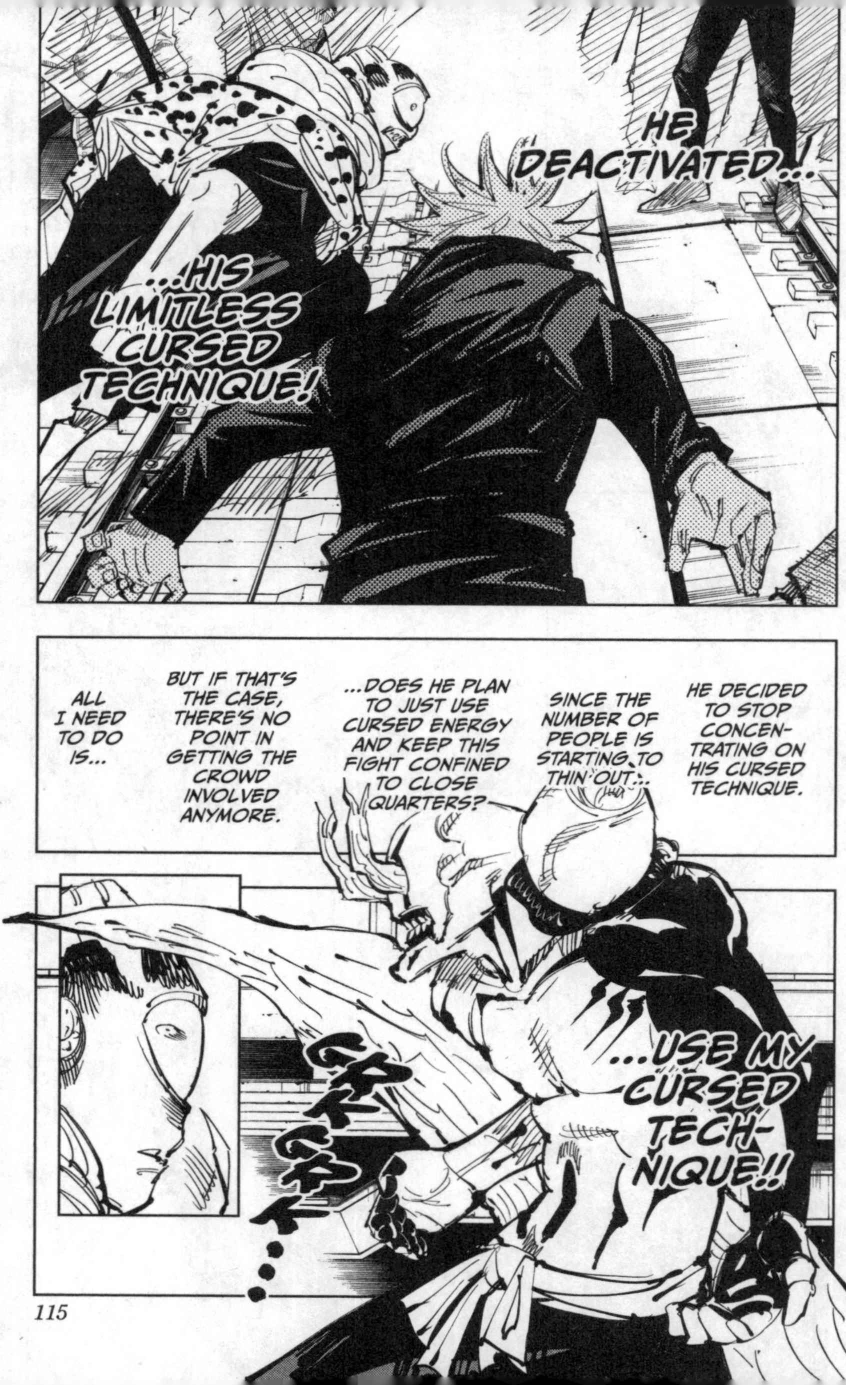
HE DEACTIVATED..!
...HIS LIMITLESS CURSED TECHNIQUE!
HE DECIDED TO STOP CONCEN-TRATING ON HIS CURSED TECHNIQUE.
SINCE THE NUMBER OF PEOPLE IS STARTING TO THIN OUT...
...DOES HE PLAN TO JUST USE CURSED ENERGY AND KEEP THIS FIGHT CONFINED TO CLOSE QUARTERS?
BUT IF THAT'S THE CASE, THERE'S NO POINT IN GETTING THE CROWD INVOLVED ANYMORE.
ALL I NEED TO DO IS...
...USE MY CURSED TECH-NIQUE!!
GRK GRK...

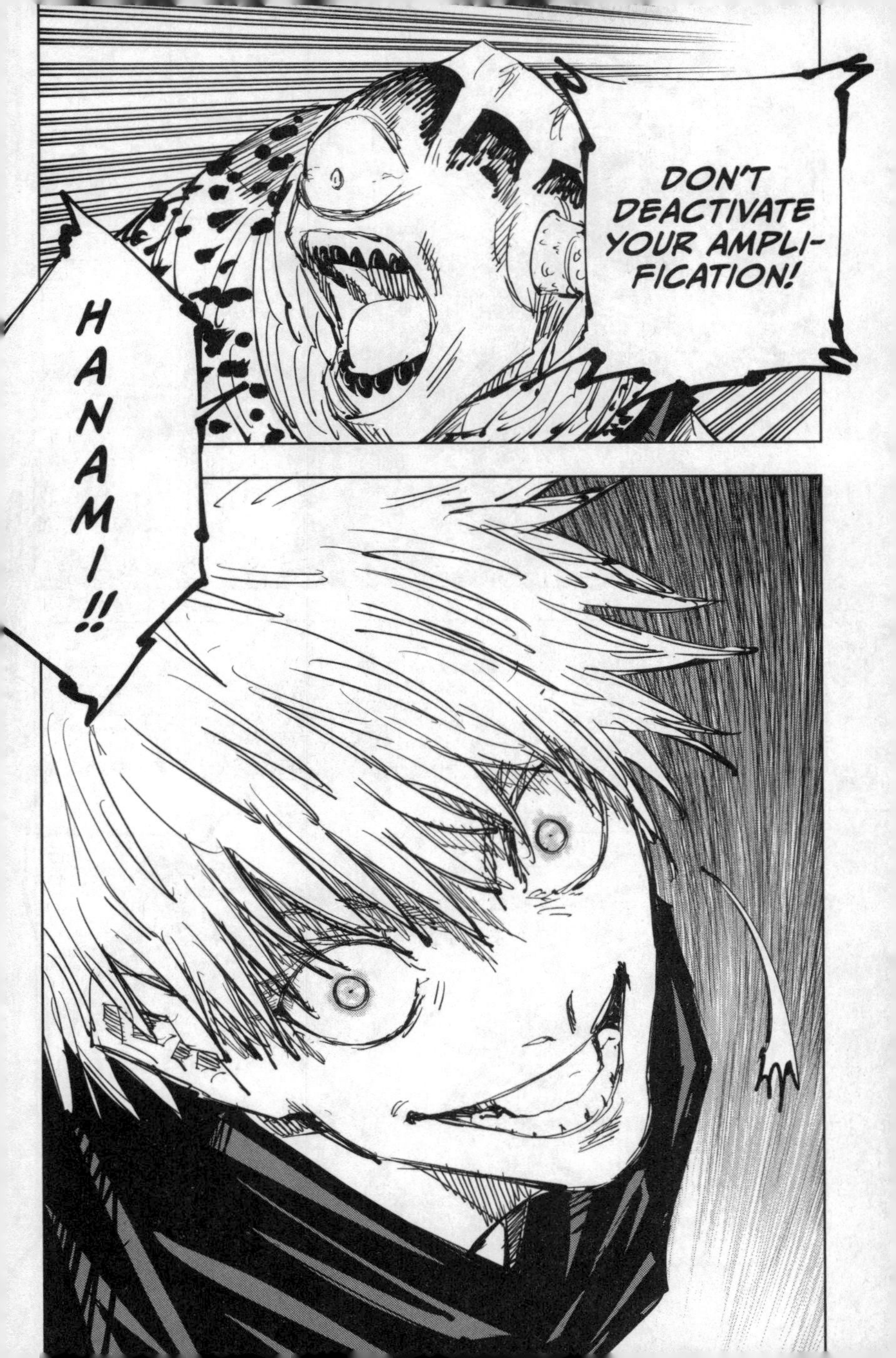
DON'T DEACTIVATE YOUR AMPLI-FICATION!
HANAMI!!

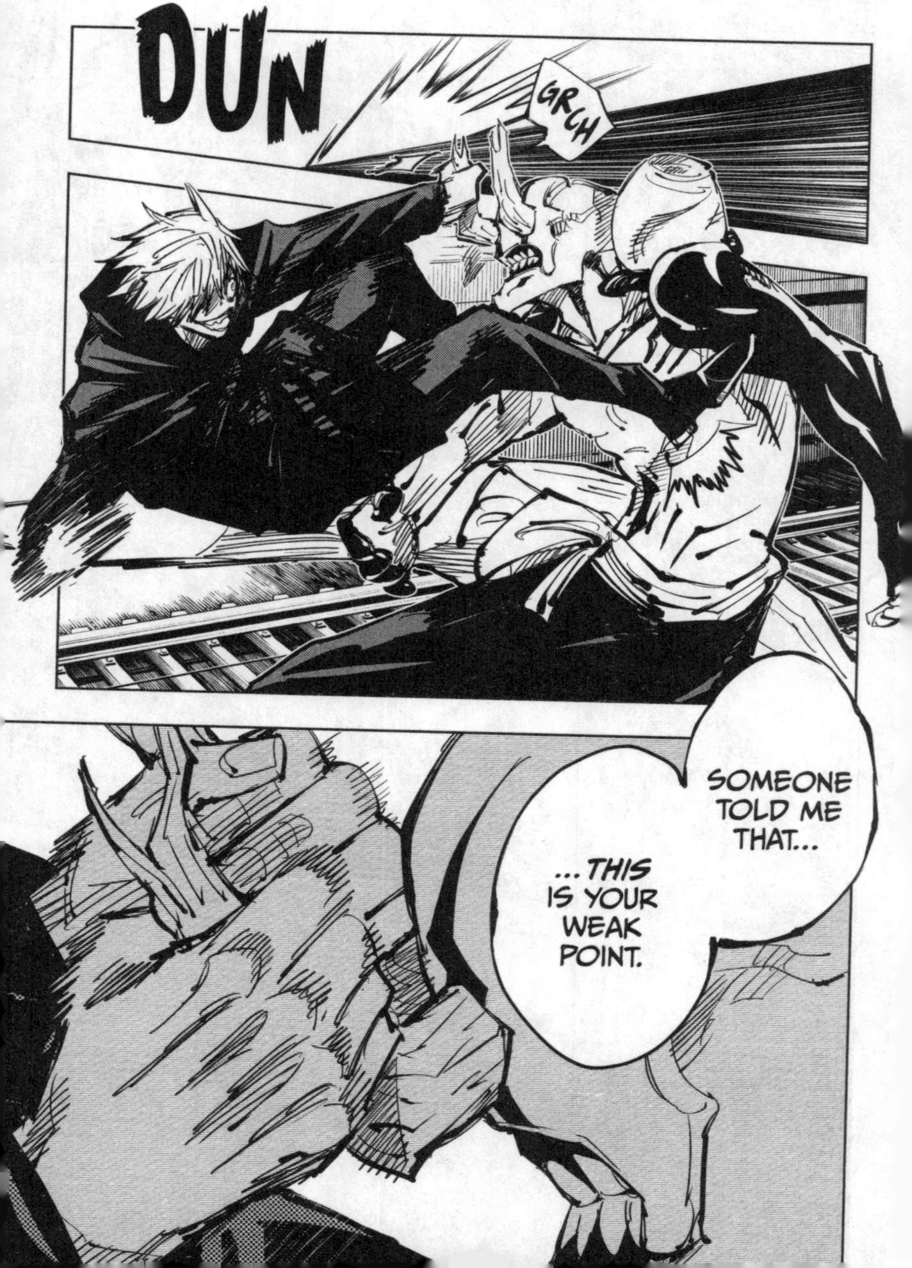
DUN
GRCH
SOMEONE TOLD ME THAT...
...THIS IS YOUR WEAK POINT.

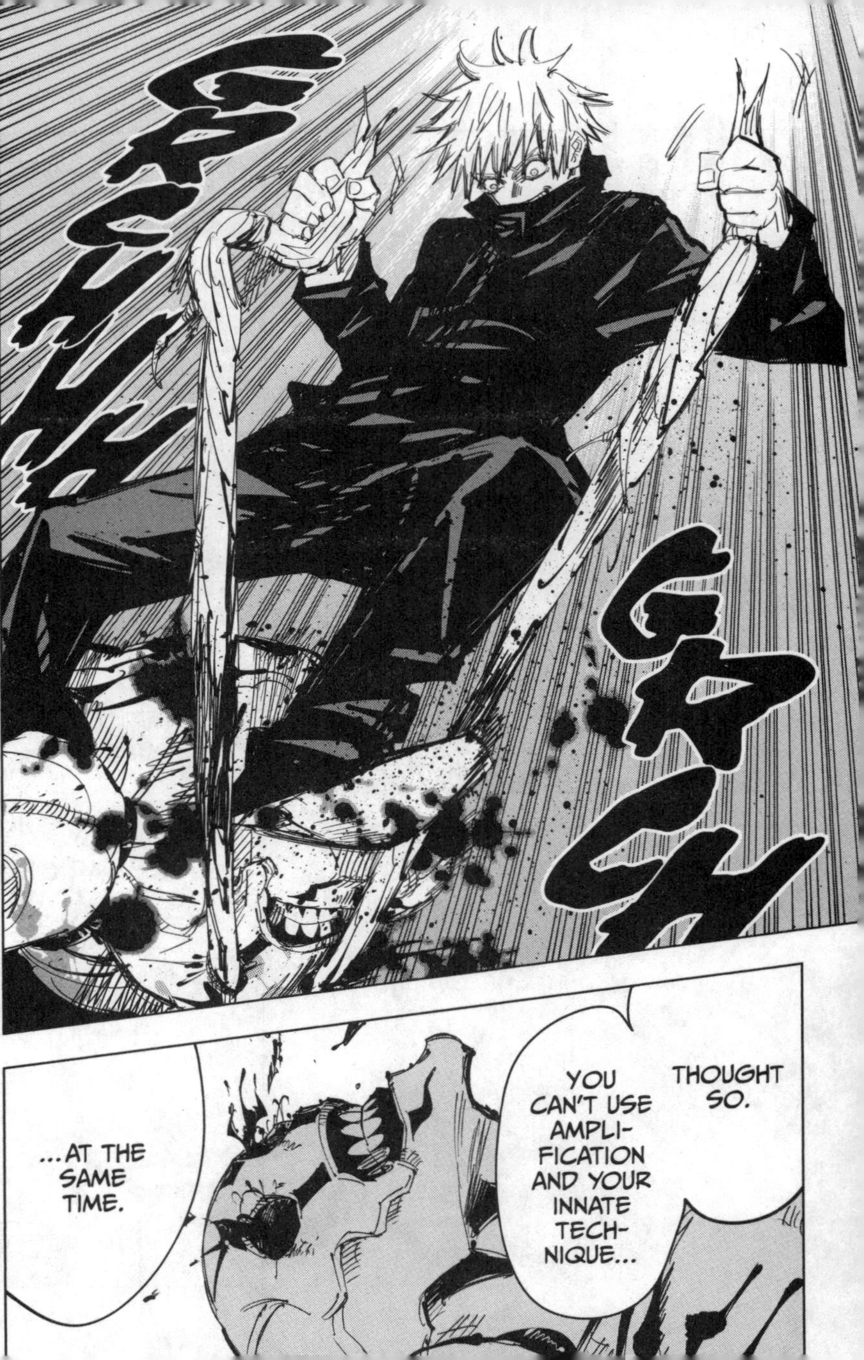
THOUGHT SO.
YOU CAN'T USE AMPLI- FICATION AND YOUR INNATE TECH- NIQUE...
...AT THE SAME TIME.

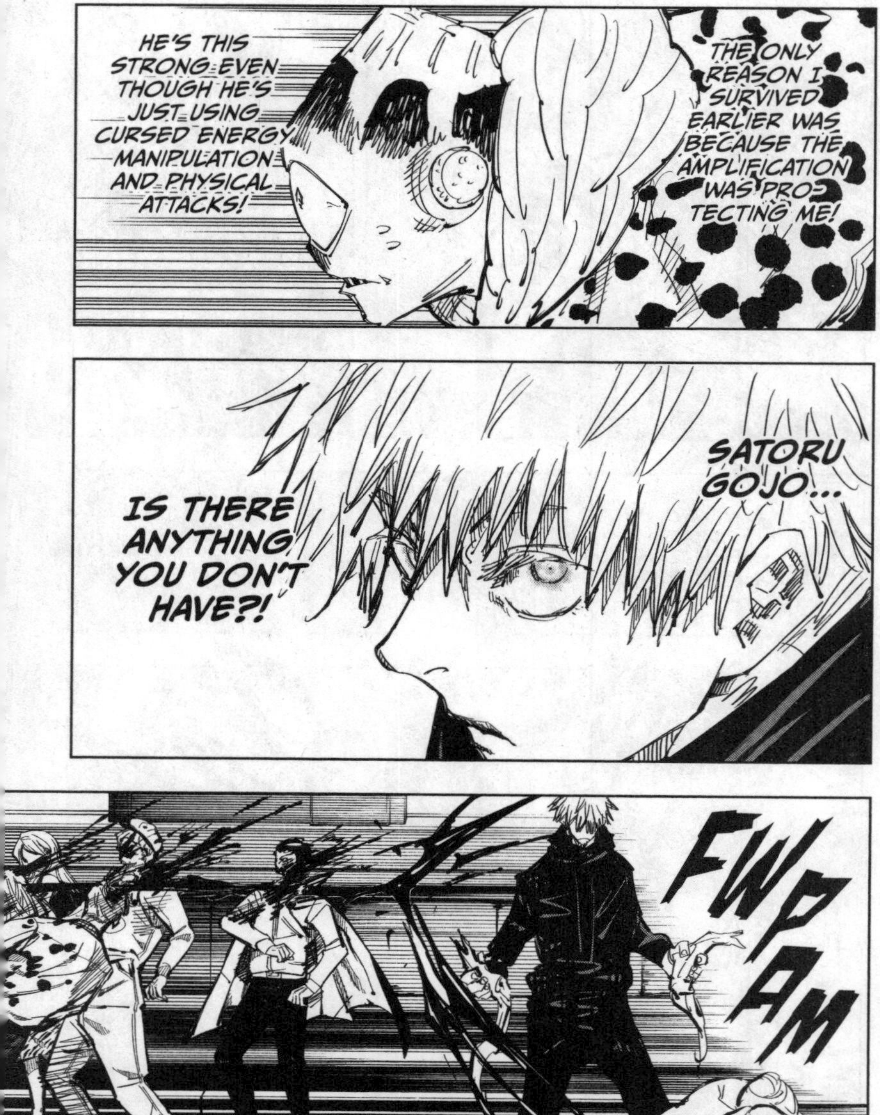
THE ONLY REASON I SURVIVED EARLIER WAS BECAUSE THE AMPLIFICATION WAS PRO-TECTING ME!
HE'S THIS STRONG EVEN THOUGH HE'S JUST USING CURSED ENERGY MANIPULATION AND PHYSICAL ATTACKS!
SATORU GOJO...
IS THERE ANYTHING YOU DON'T HAVE?!
FWPAM

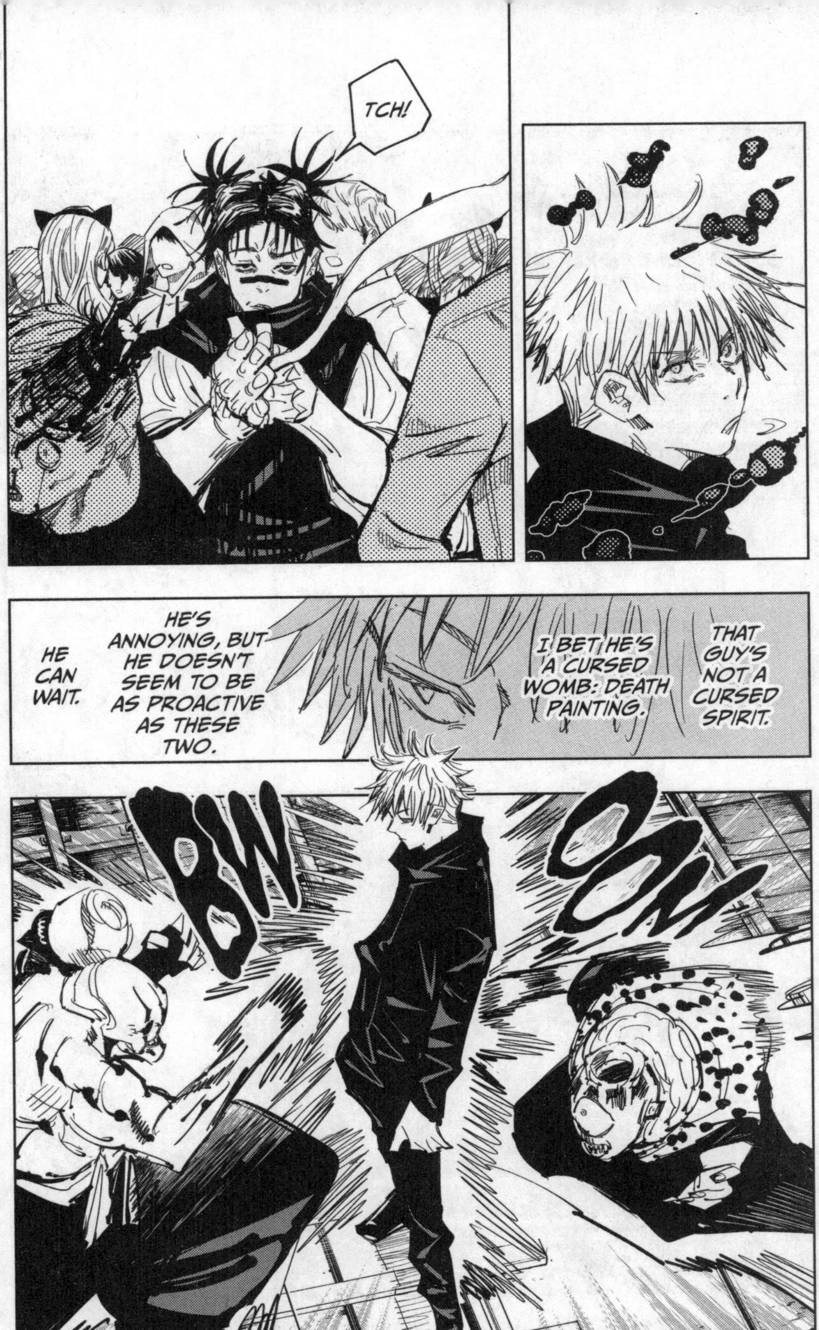
TCH!
THAT GUY'S NOT A CURSED SPIRIT.
I BET HE'S A CURSED WOMB: DEATH PAINTING.
HE'S ANNOYING, BUT HE DOESN'T SEEM TO BE AS PROACTIVE AS THESE TWO.
HE CAN WAIT.
BWOOM

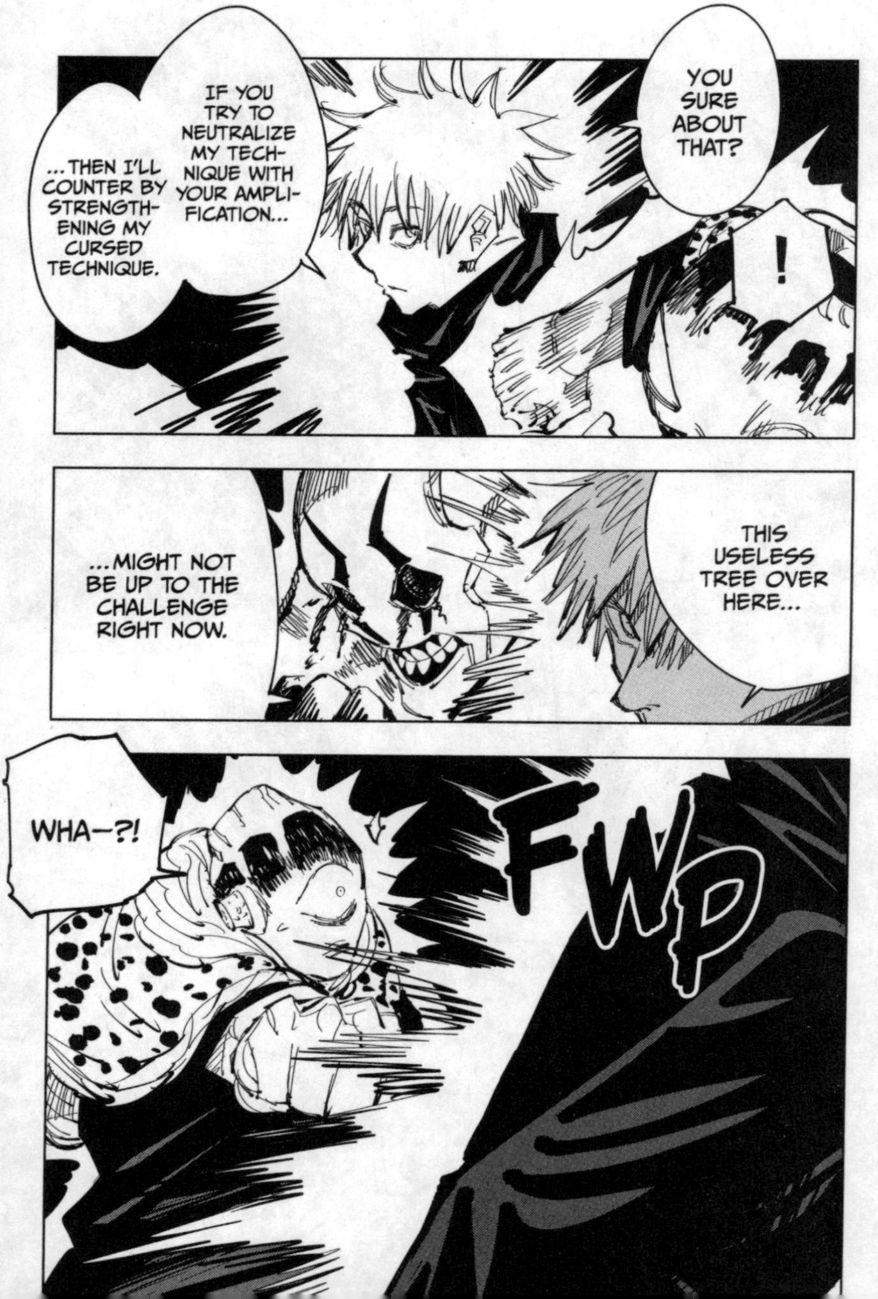
YOU SURE ABOUT THAT?
!
IF YOU TRY TO NEUTRALIZE MY TECH-NIQUE WITH YOUR AMPLI-FICATION...
...THEN I'LL COUNTER BY STRENGTH-ENING MY CURSED TECHNIQUE.
THIS USELESS TREE OVER HERE...
...MIGHT NOT BE UP TO THE CHALLENGE RIGHT NOW.
FWP
WHA-?!

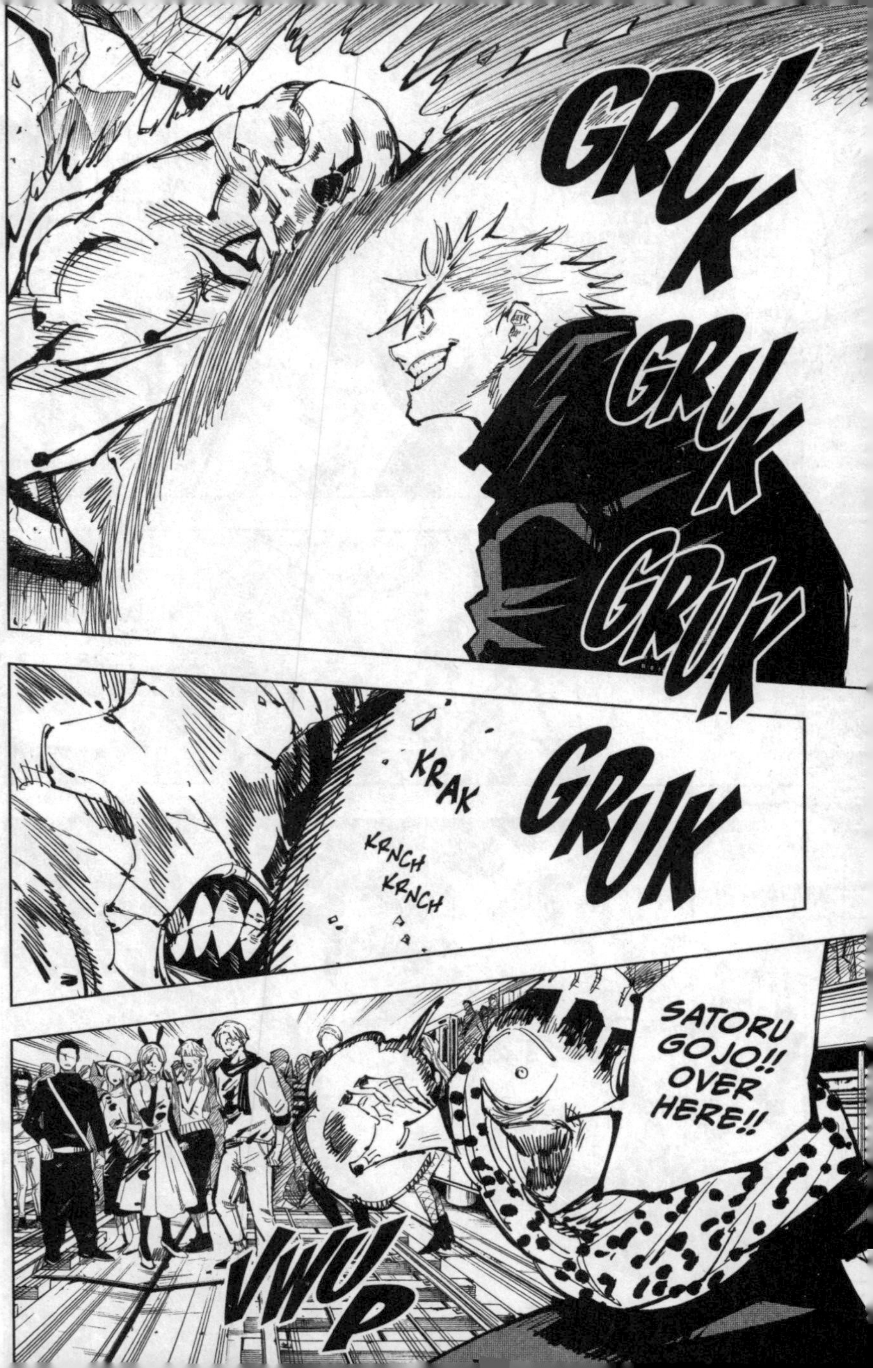
GRUK
GRUK
GRUK
GRUK
KRAK
KRNCH
KRNCH
SATORU GOJO!! OVER HERE!!
VWUP

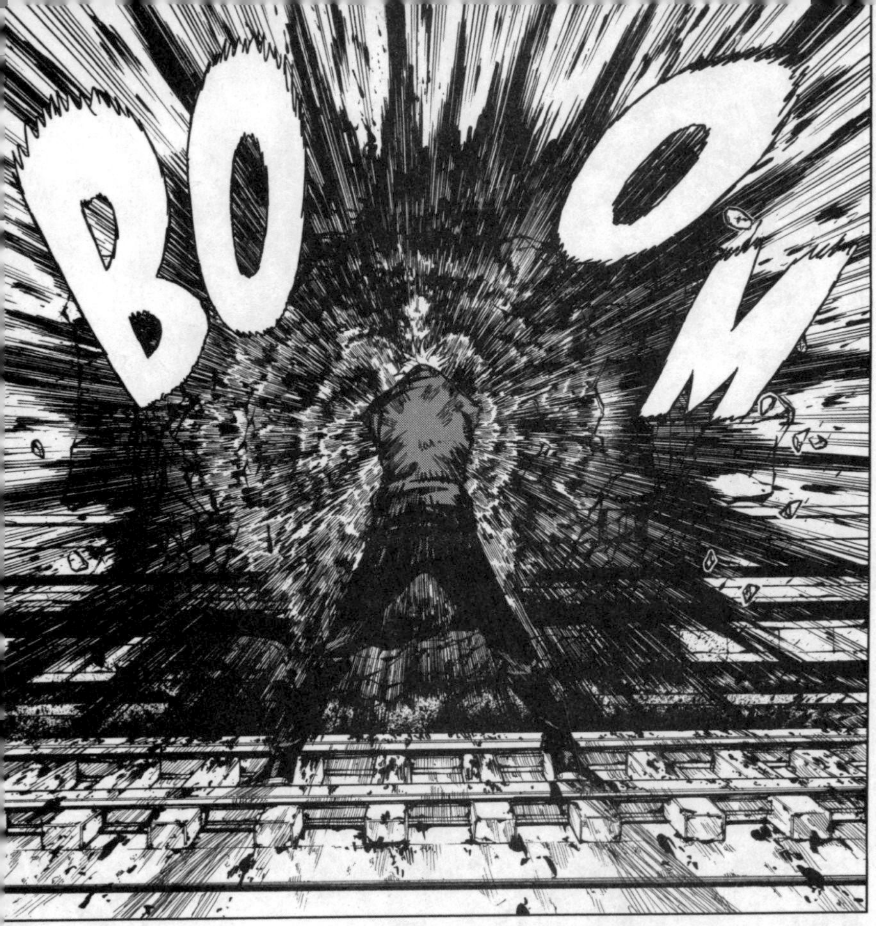
BOOM
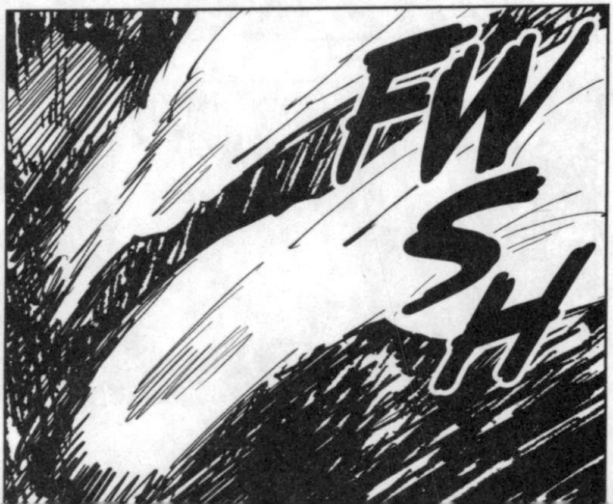
FWSH
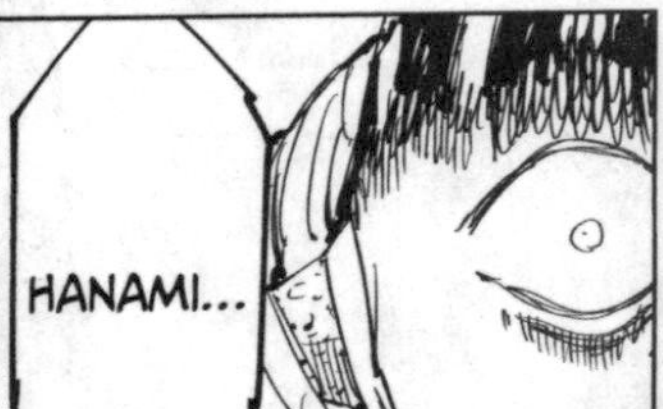
HANAMI...

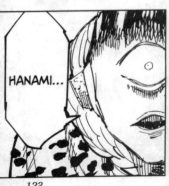

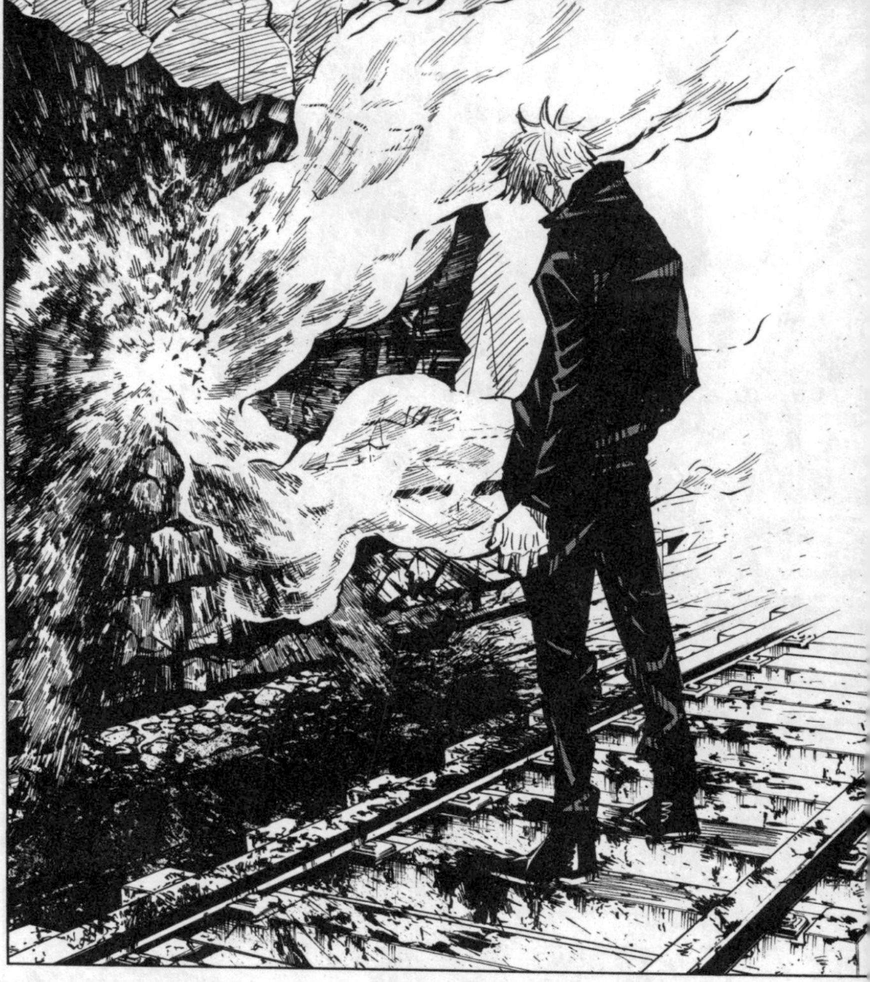
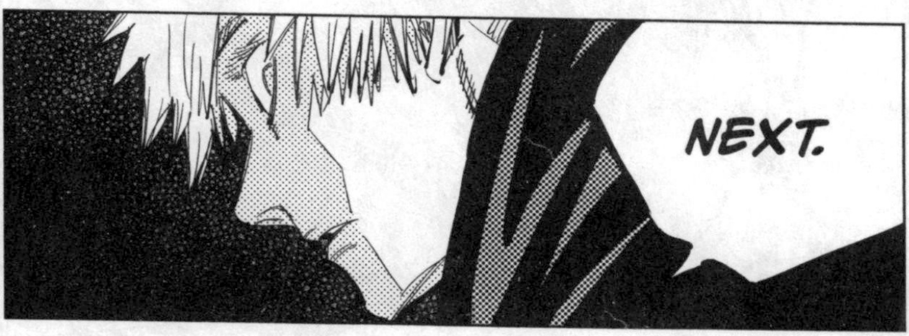
NEXT.

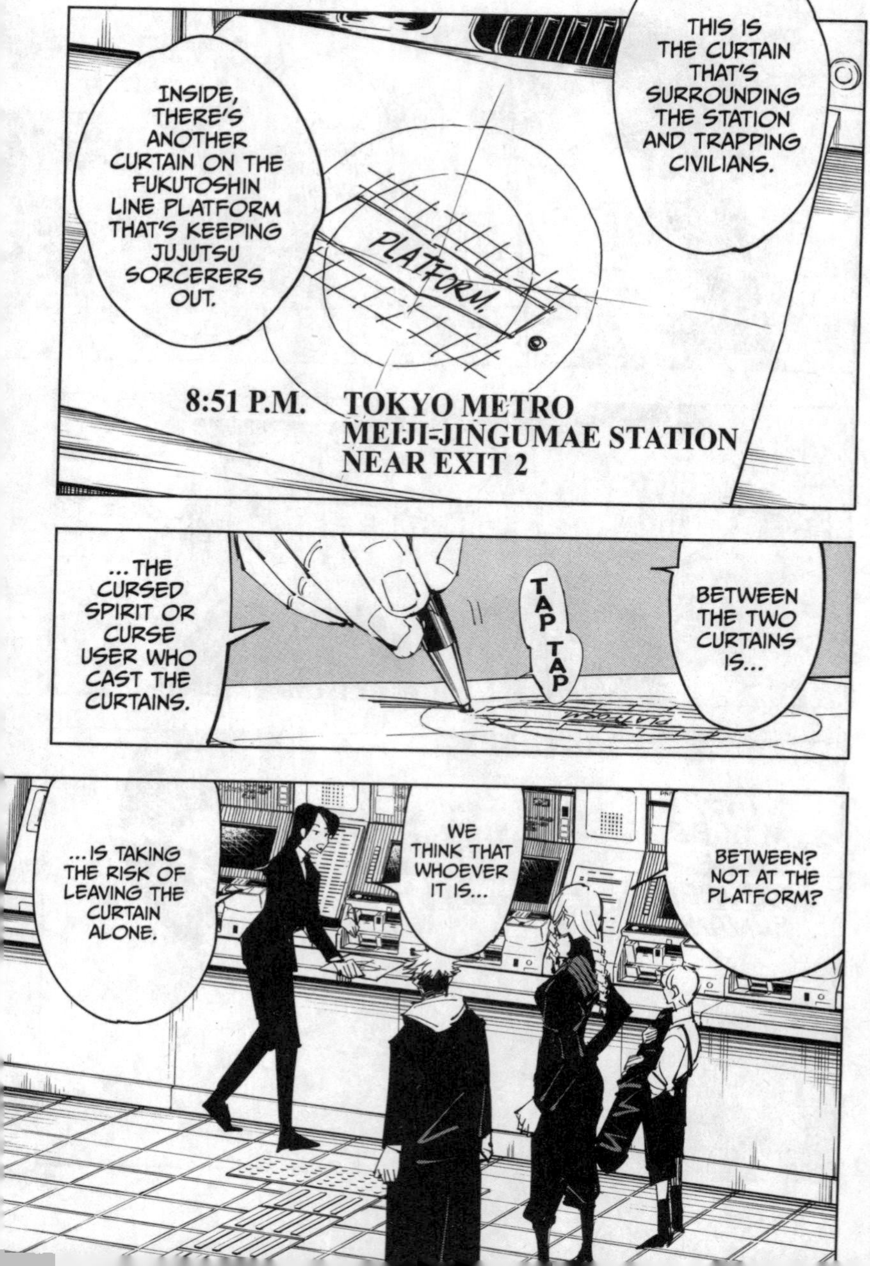
THIS IS THE CURTAIN THAT'S SURROUNDING THE STATION AND TRAPPING CIVILIANS.
INSIDE, THERE'S ANOTHER CURTAIN ON THE FUKUTOSHIN LINE PLATFORM THAT'S KEEPING JUJUTSU SORCERERS OUT.
PLATFORM
8:51 P.M. TOKYO METRO MEIJI-JINGUMAE STATION NEAR EXIT 2
BETWEEN THE TWO CURTAINS IS...
TAP TAP
...THE CURSED SPIRIT OR CURSE USER WHO CAST THE CURTAINS.
BETWEEN? NOT AT THE PLATFORM?
WE THINK THAT WHOEVER IT IS...
...IS TAKING THE RISK OF LEAVING THE CURTAIN ALONE.

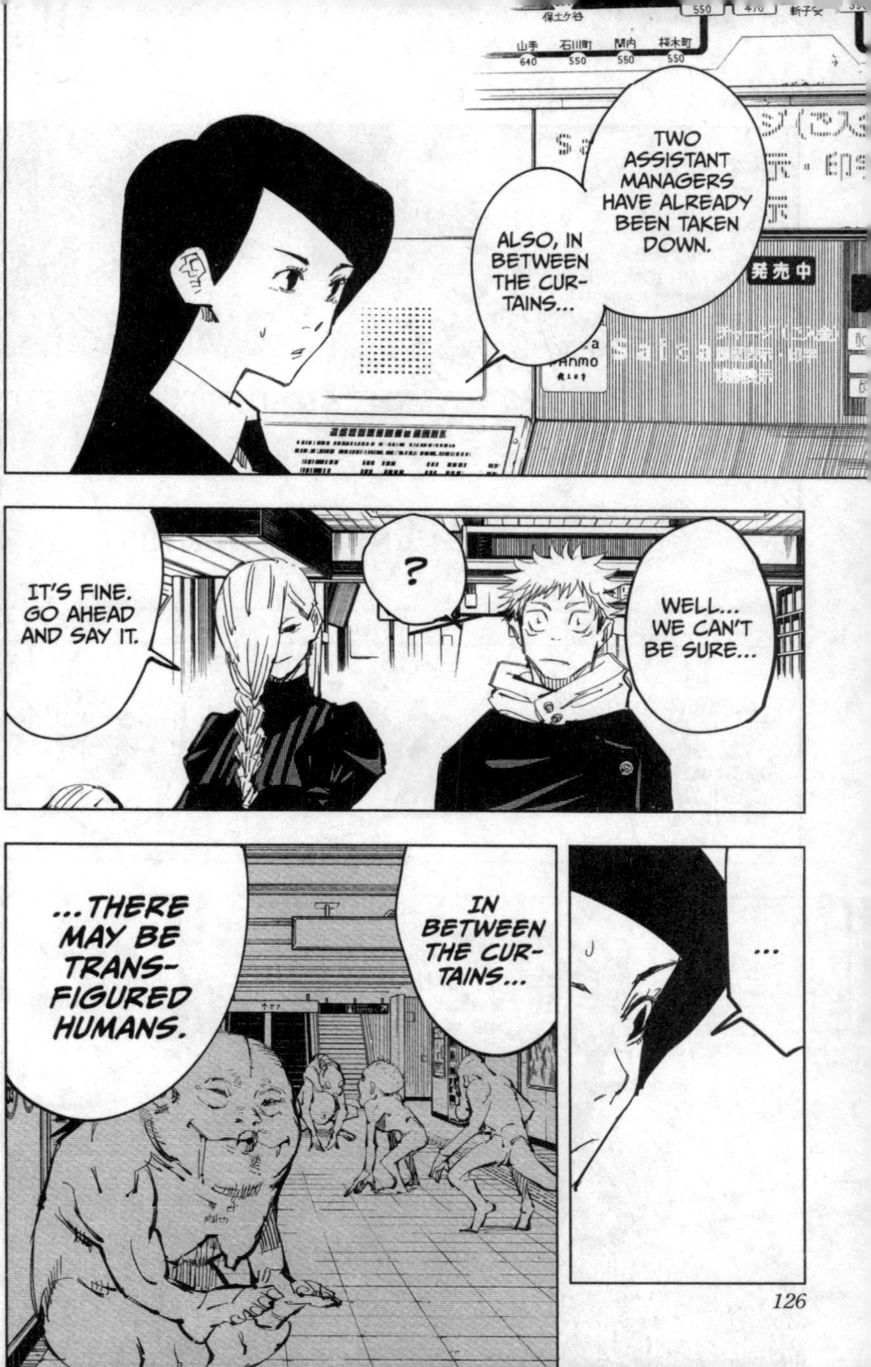
TWO ASSISTANT MANAGERS HAVE ALREADY BEEN TAKEN DOWN.
ALSO, IN BETWEEN THE CUR-TAINS...
発売中
WELL... WE CAN'T BE SURE...
?
IT'S FINE. GO AHEAD AND SAY IT.
...
IN BETWEEN THE CUR-TAINS...
...THERE MAY BE TRANS-FIGURED HUMANS.

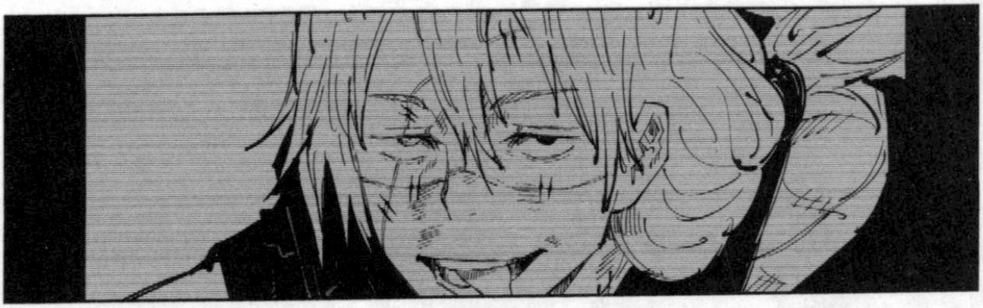
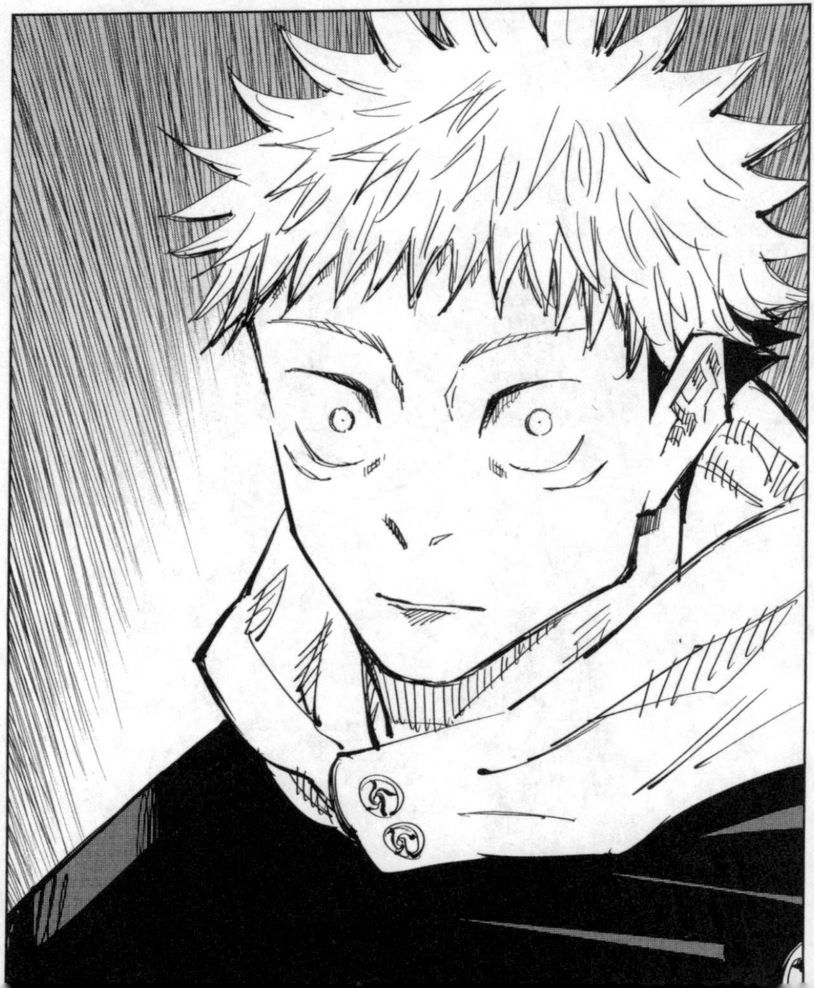

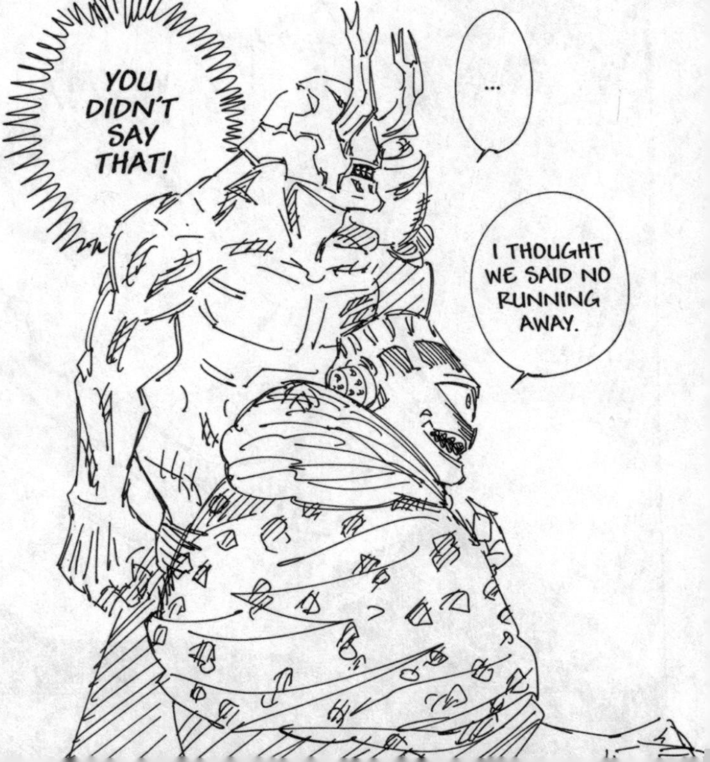
...
YOU DIDN'T SAY THAT!
I THOUGHT WE SAID NO RUNNING AWAY.

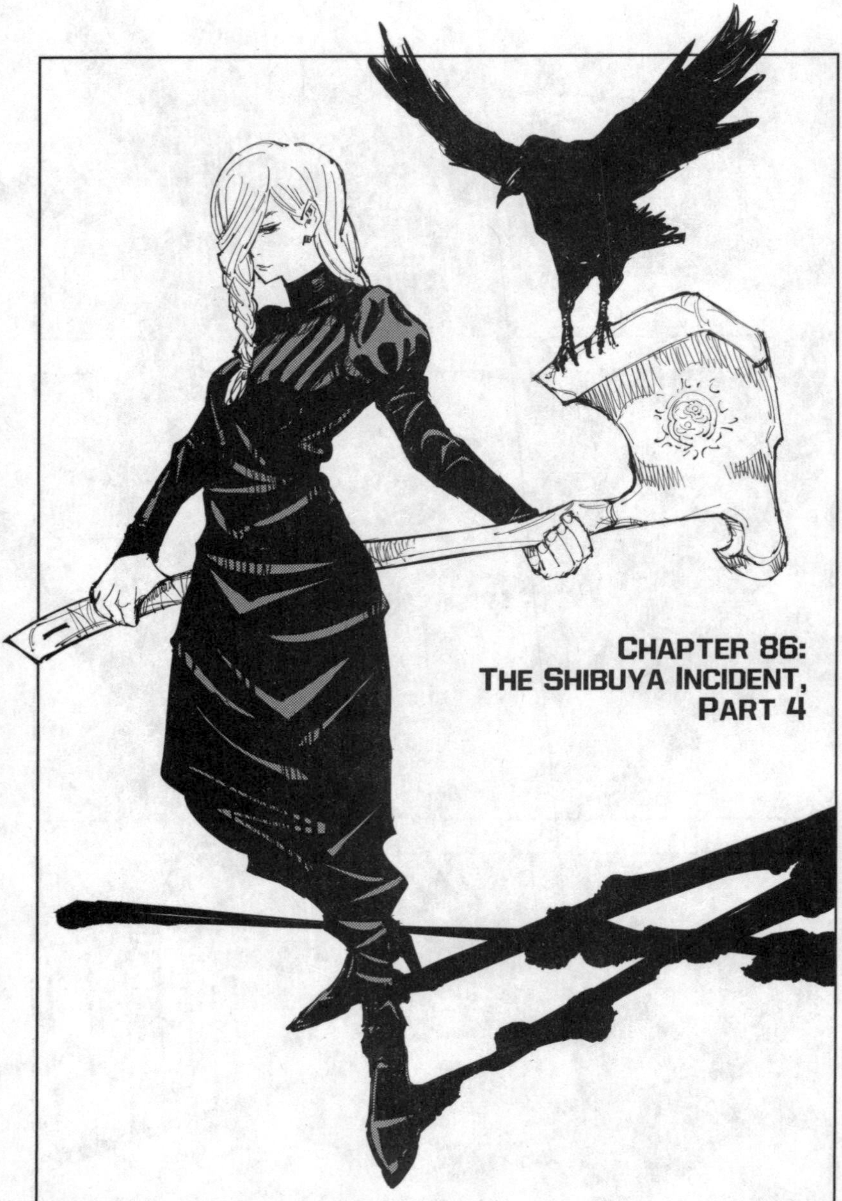
CHAPTER 86:
THE SHIBUYA INCIDENT,
PART 4

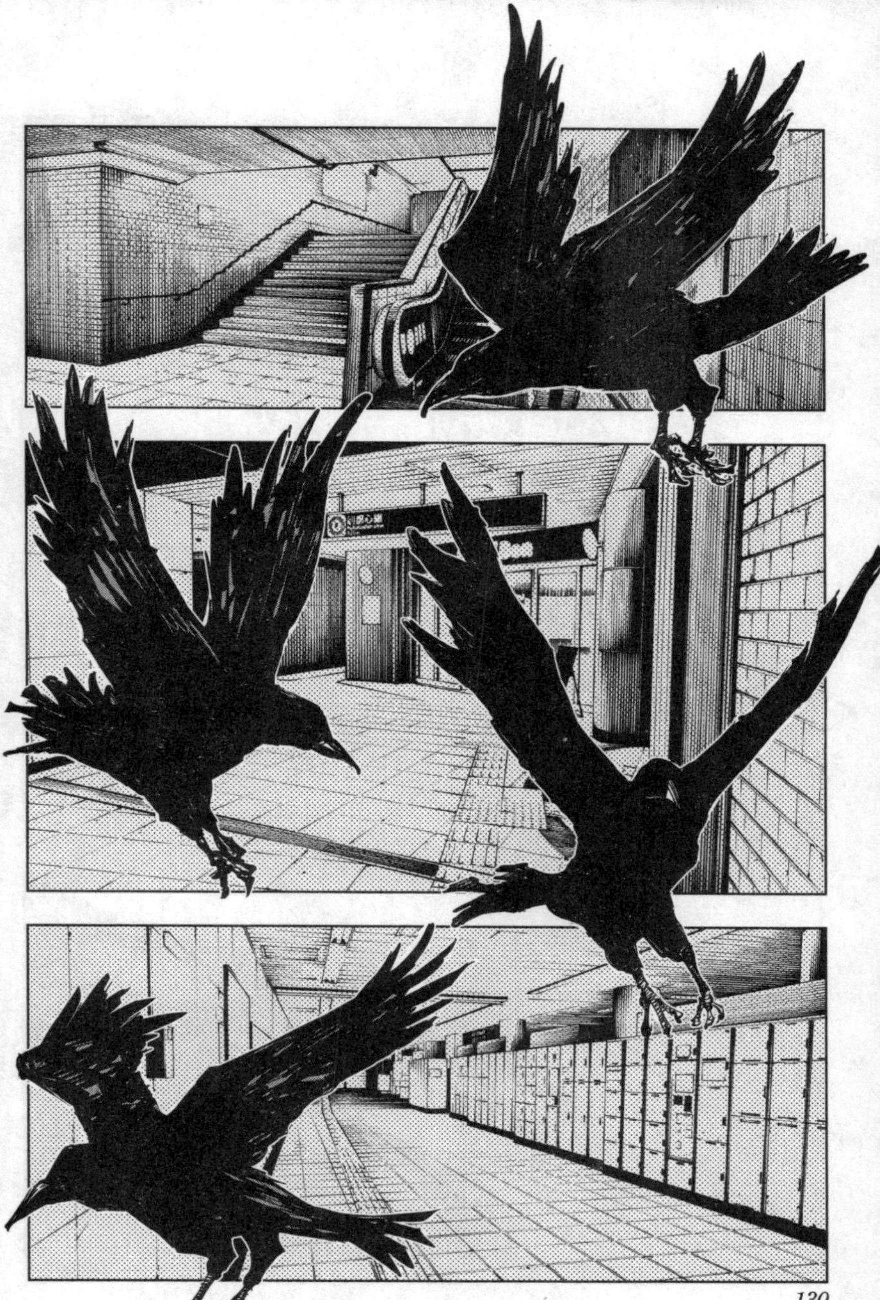

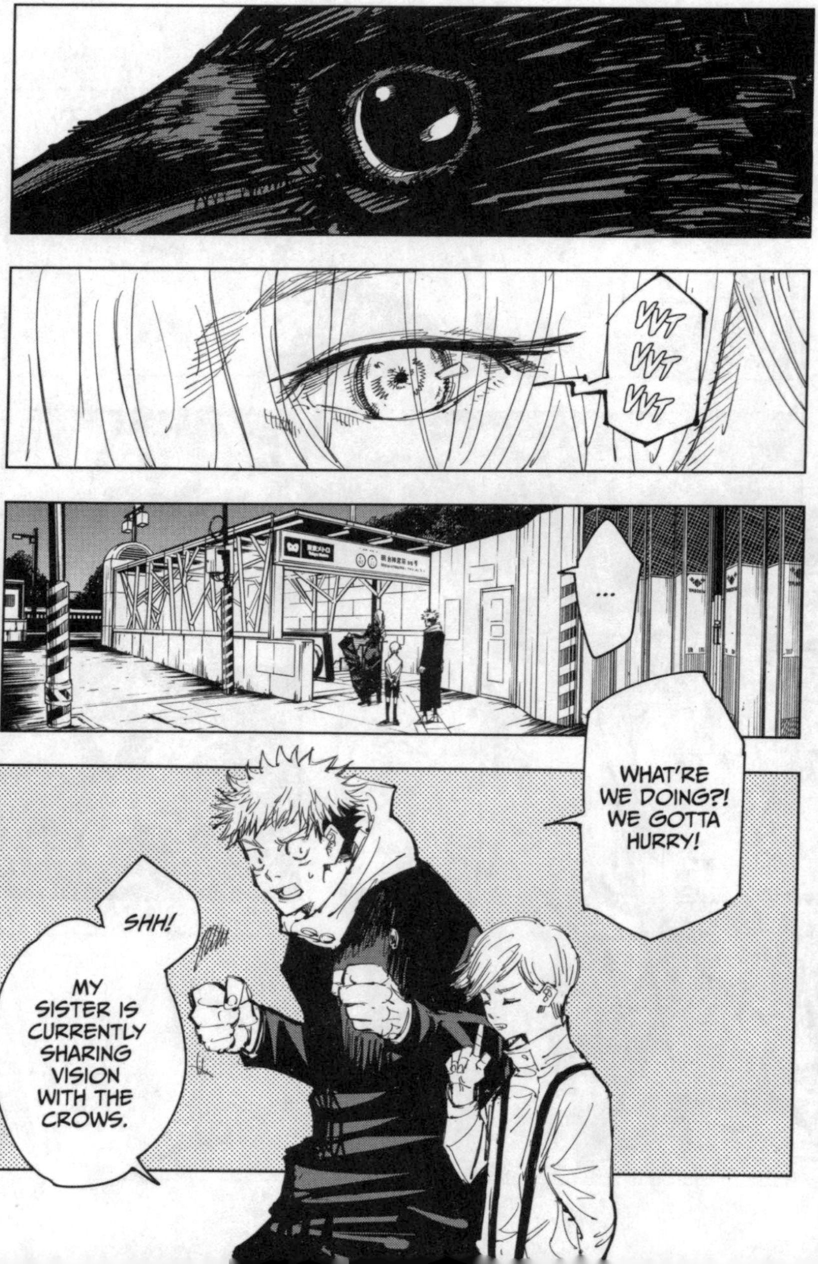
VVVT
VVVT
VVVT
...
WHAT'RE WE DOING?! WE GOTTA HURRY!
SHH!
MY SISTER IS CURRENTLY SHARING VISION WITH THE CROWS.

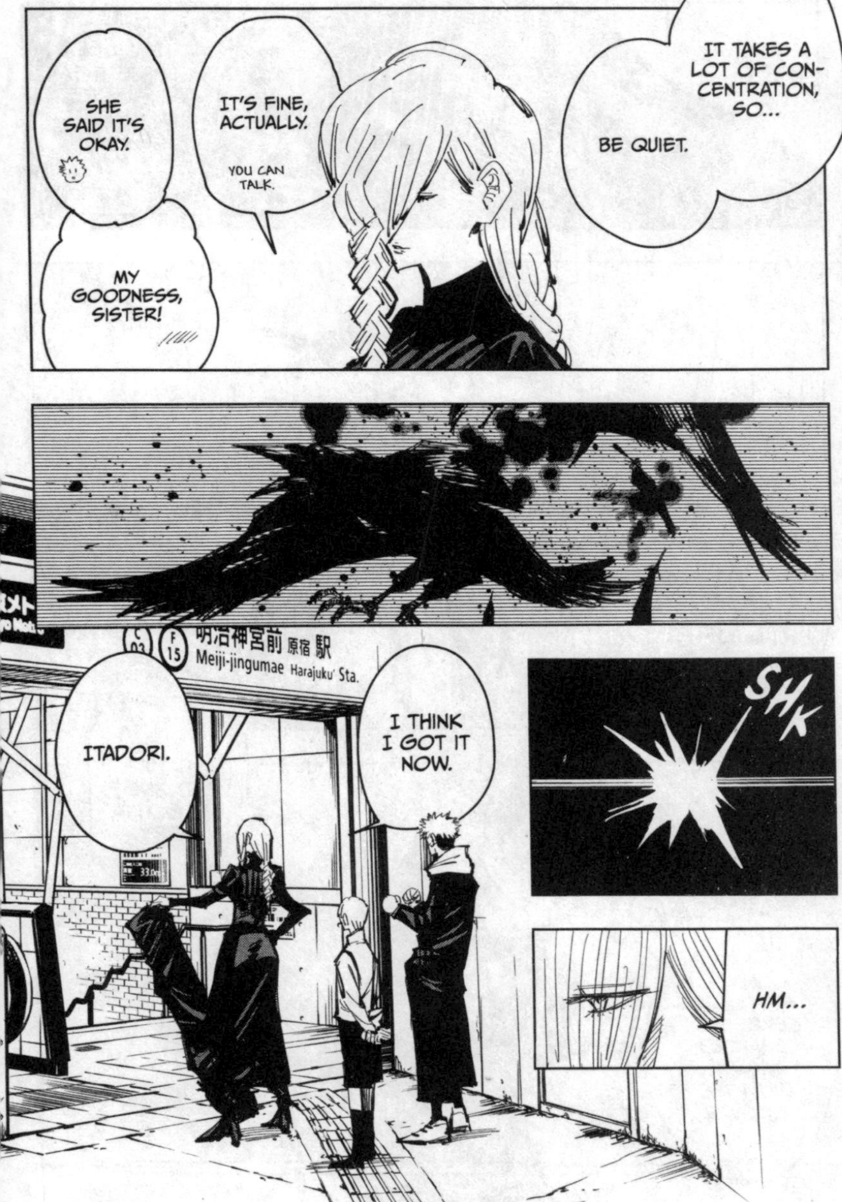
IT TAKES A LOT OF CON-CENTRATION, SO...
BE QUIET.
IT'S FINE, ACTUALLY.
YOU CAN TALK.
SHE SAID IT'S OKAY.
MY GOODNESS, SISTER!
SHK
HM...
明治神宮前 原宿 駅
Meiji-jingumae Harajuku' Sta.
I THINK I GOT IT NOW.
ITADORI.

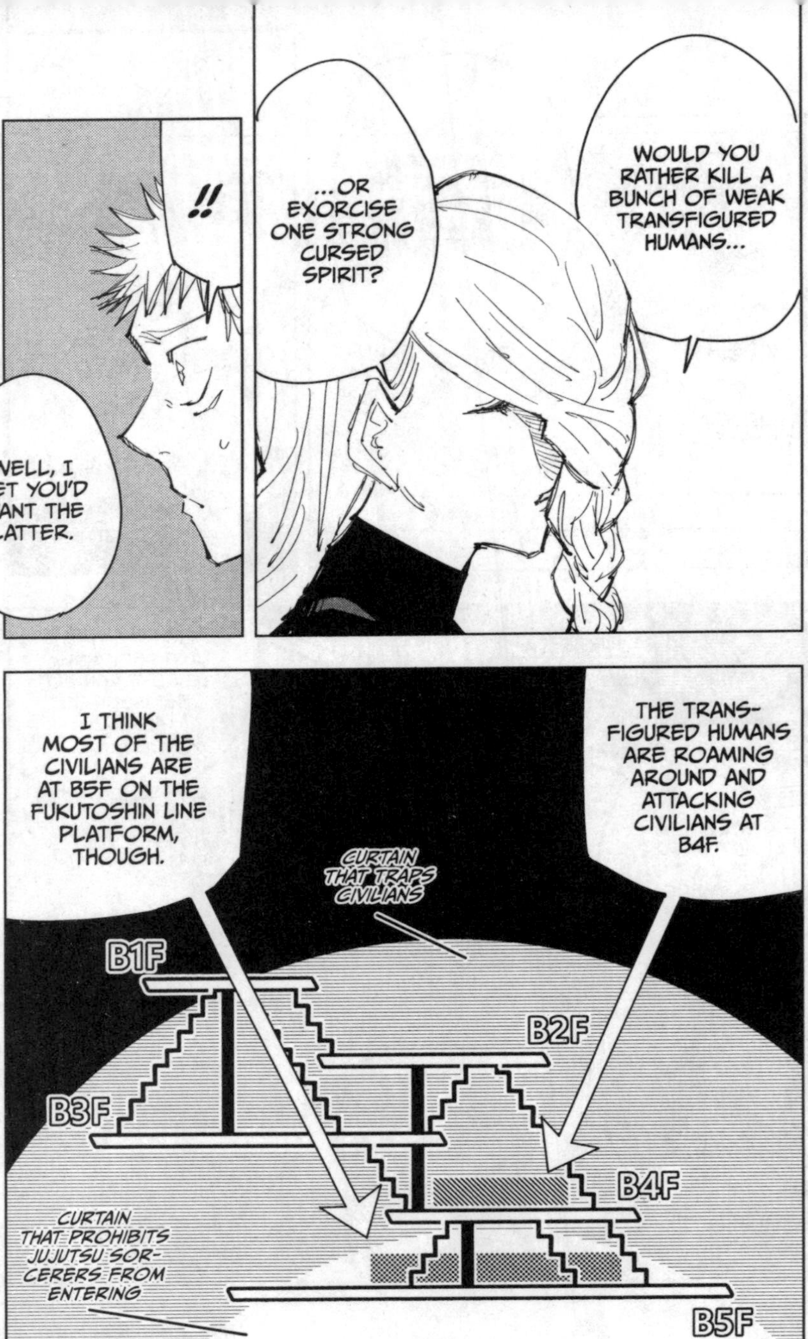
WOULD YOU RATHER KILL A BUNCH OF WEAK TRANSFIGURED HUMANS...
...OR EXORCISE ONE STRONG CURSED SPIRIT?
!!
WELL, I BET YOU'D WANT THE LATTER.
THE TRANS-FIGURED HUMANS ARE ROAMING AROUND AND ATTACKING CIVILIANS AT B4F.
I THINK MOST OF THE CIVILIANS ARE AT B5F ON THE FUKUTOSHIN LINE PLATFORM, THOUGH.
CURTAIN THAT TRAPS CIVILIANS
B1F
B2F
B3F
B4F
CURTAIN THAT PROHIBITS JUJUTSU SOR-CERERS FROM ENTERING
B5F

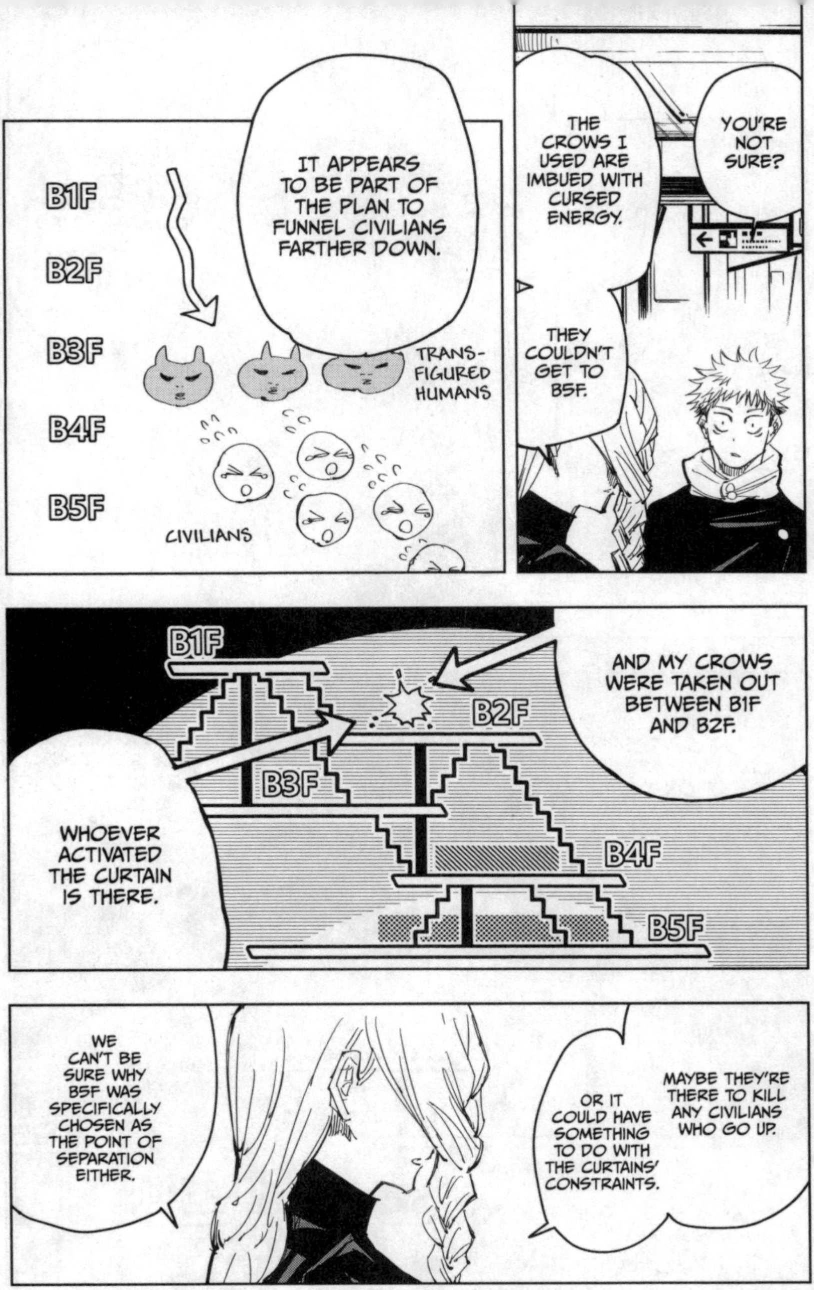
YOU'RE NOT SURE?
THE CROWS I USED ARE IMBUED WITH CURSED ENERGY.
THEY COULDN'T GET TO B5F.
IT APPEARS TO BE PART OF THE PLAN TO FUNNEL CIVILIANS FARTHER DOWN.
B1F
B2F
B3F
B4F
B5F
TRANS-FIGURED HUMANS
CIVILIANS
AND MY CROWS WERE TAKEN OUT BETWEEN B1F AND B2F.
WHOEVER ACTIVATED THE CURTAIN IS THERE.
B1F
B2F
B3F
B4F
B5F
MAYBE THEY'RE THERE TO KILL ANY CIVILIANS WHO GO UP.
OR IT COULD HAVE SOMETHING TO DO WITH THE CURTAINS' CONSTRAINTS.
WE CAN'T BE SURE WHY B5F WAS SPECIFICALLY CHOSEN AS THE POINT OF SEPARATION EITHER.

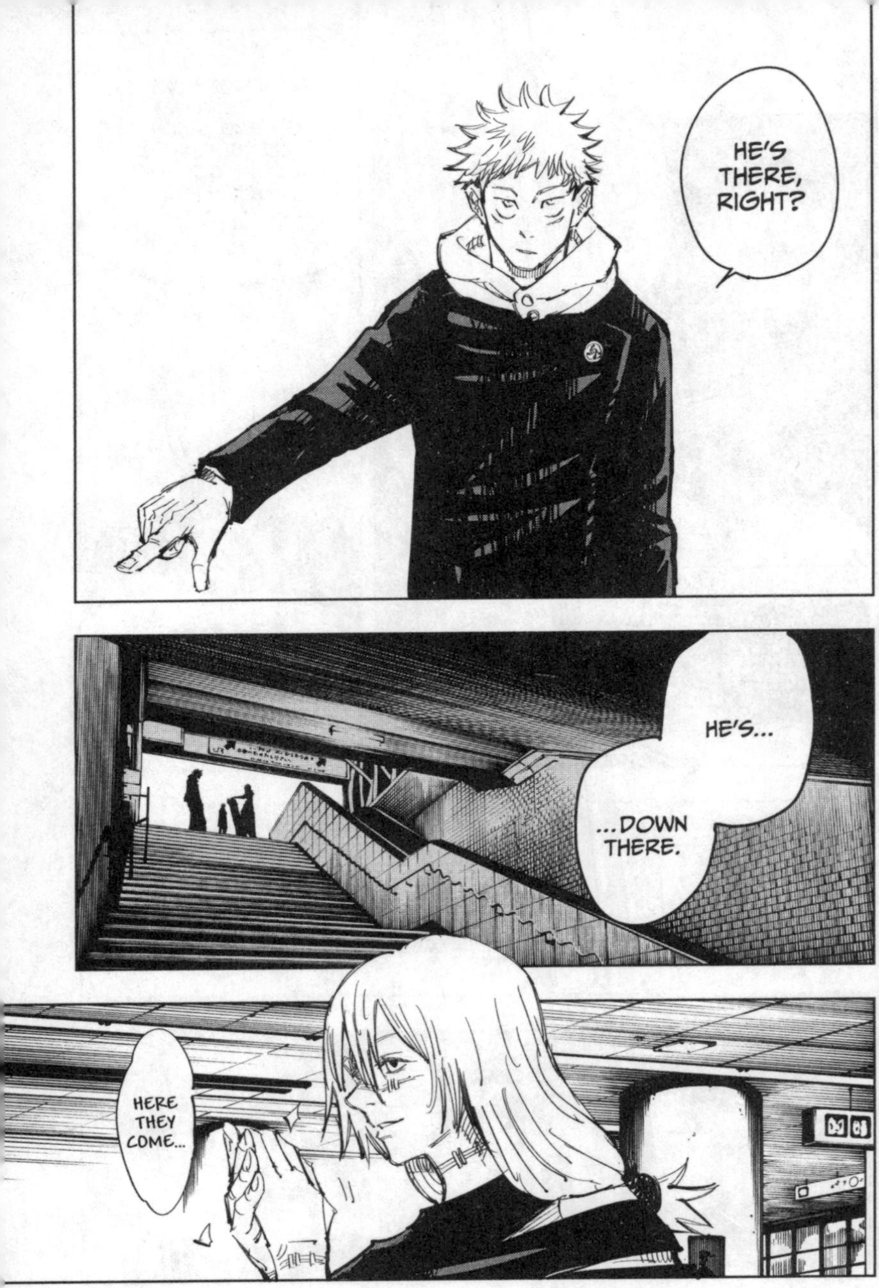
HE'S THERE, RIGHT?
HE'S...
...DOWN THERE.
HERE THEY COME...

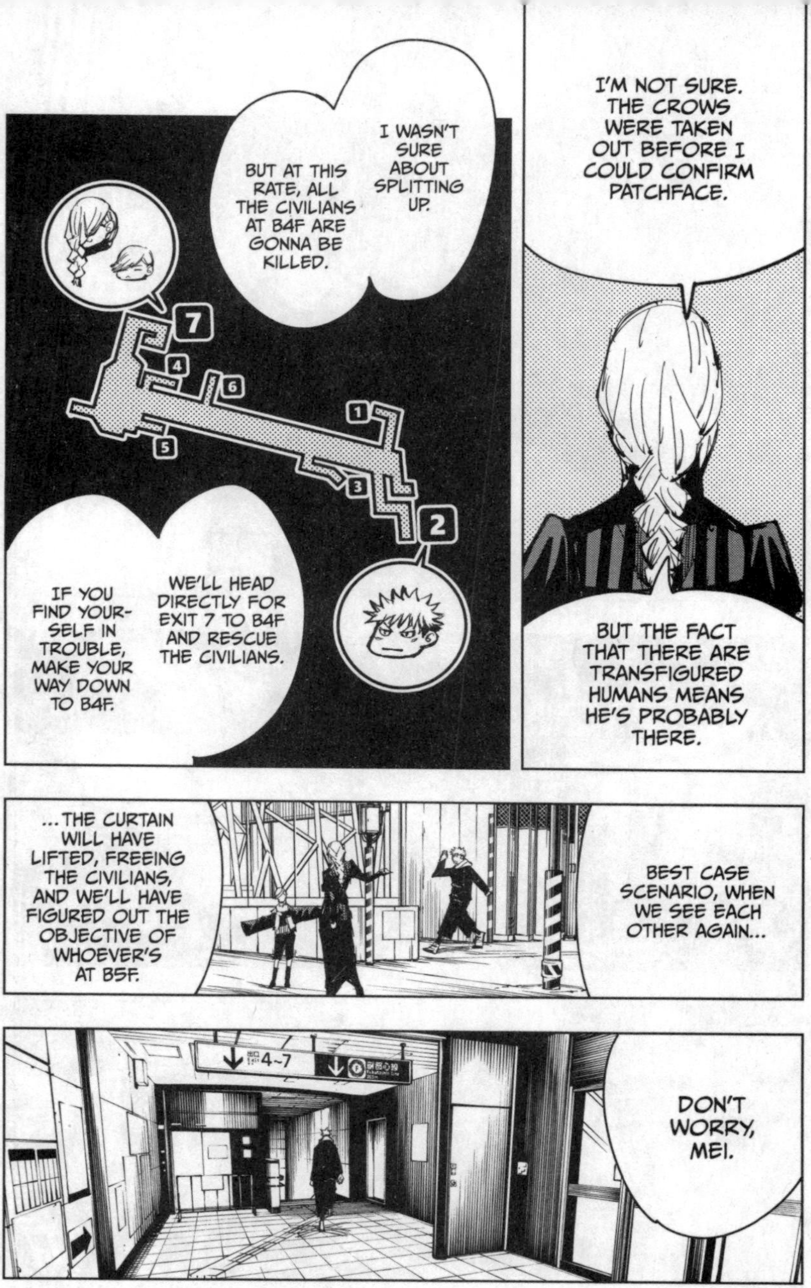
I'M NOT SURE. THE CROWS WERE TAKEN OUT BEFORE I COULD CONFIRM PATCHFACE.
BUT THE FACT THAT THERE ARE TRANSFIGURED HUMANS MEANS HE'S PROBABLY THERE.
I WASN'T SURE ABOUT SPLITTING UP.
BUT AT THIS RATE, ALL THE CIVILIANS AT B4F ARE GONNA BE KILLED.
7
4
6
1
5
3
2
WE'LL HEAD DIRECTLY FOR EXIT 7 TO B4F AND RESCUE THE CIVILIANS.
IF YOU FIND YOUR-SELF IN TROUBLE, MAKE YOUR WAY DOWN TO B4F.
BEST CASE SCENARIO, WHEN WE SEE EACH OTHER AGAIN...
...THE CURTAIN WILL HAVE LIFTED, FREEING THE CIVILIANS, AND WE'LL HAVE FIGURED OUT THE OBJECTIVE OF WHOEVER'S AT B5F.
4~7
DON'T WORRY, MEI.

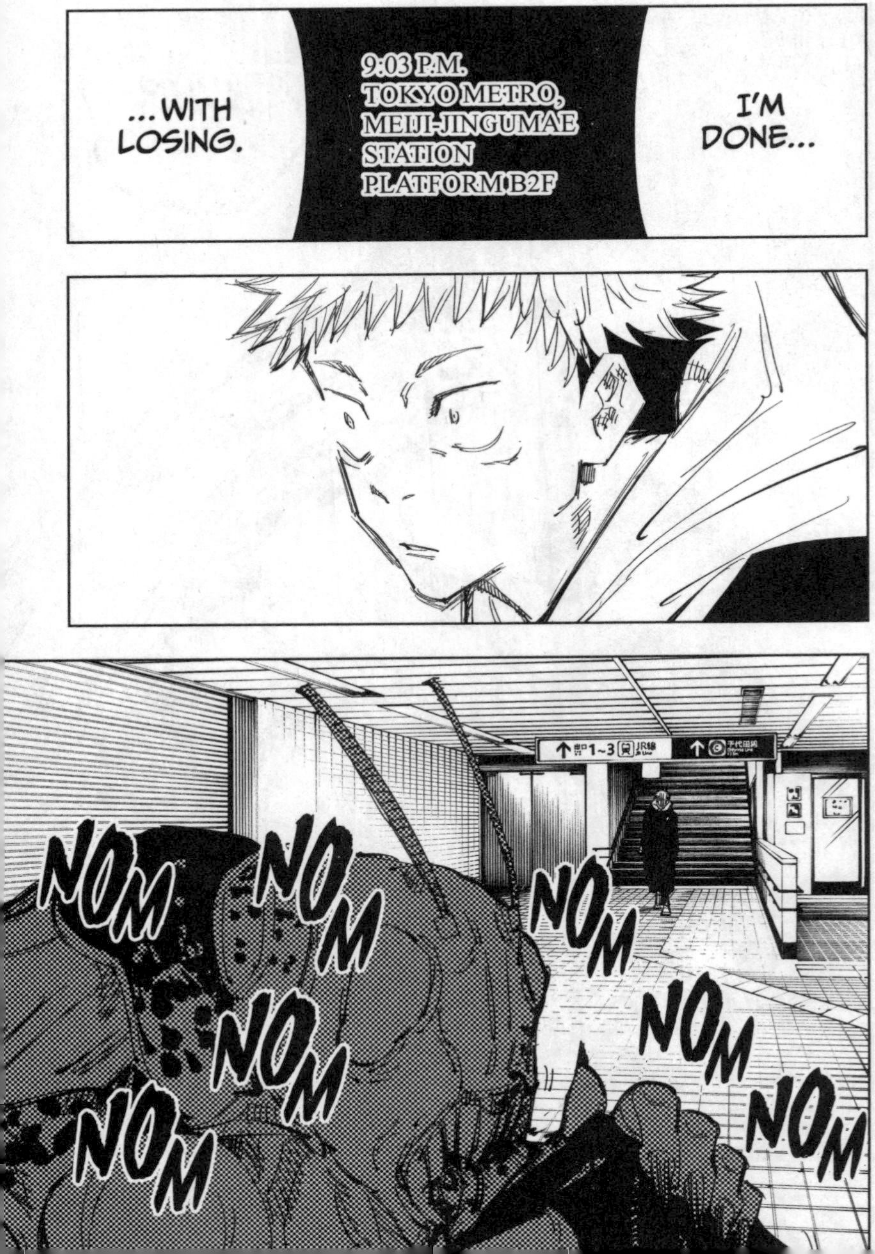
I'M DONE...
9:03 P.M.
TOKYO METRO, MEIJI-JINGUMAE STATION PLATFORM B2F
...WITH LOSING.
NOM
NOM
NOM
NOM
NOM
NOM
NOM

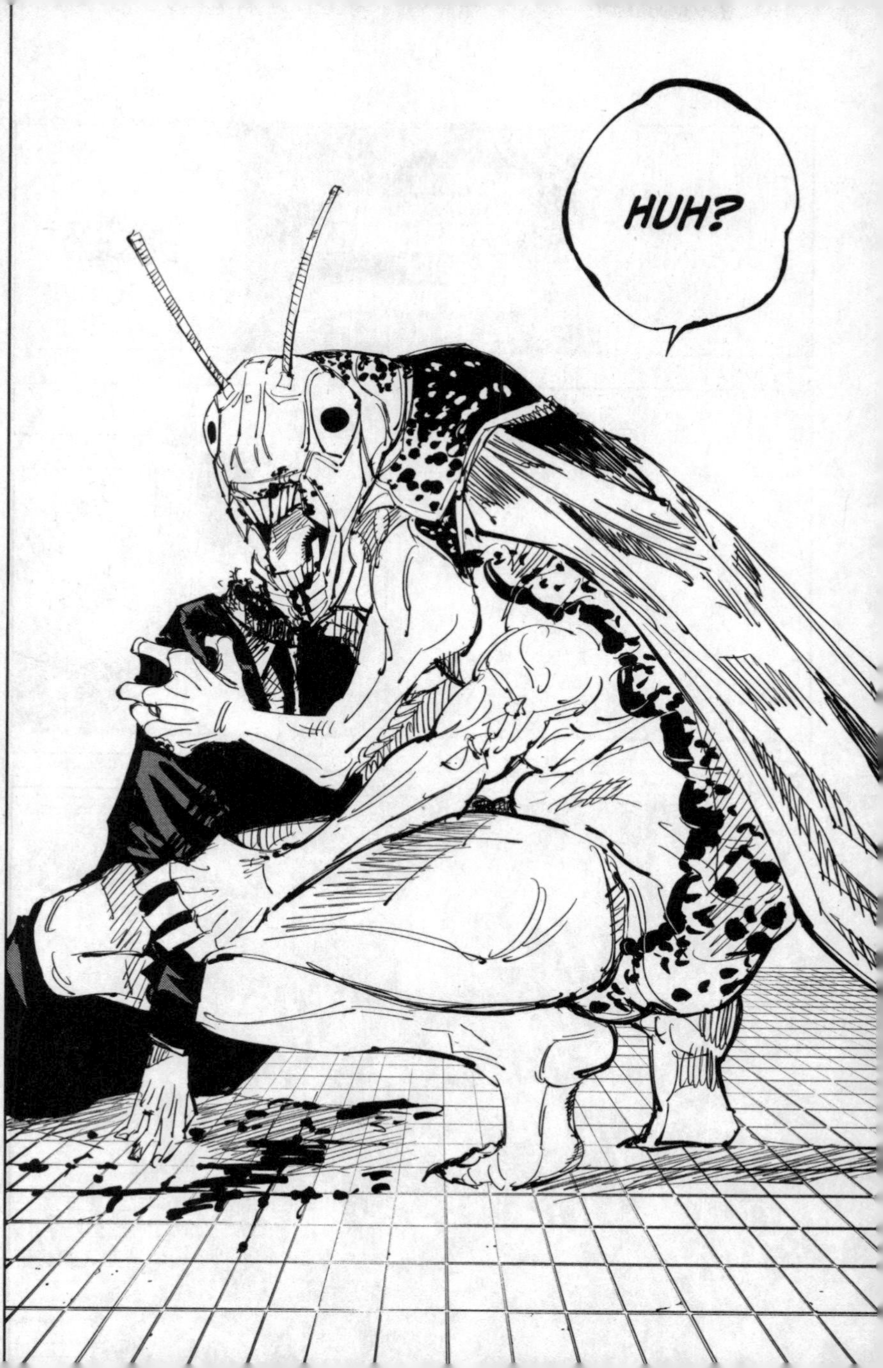
HUH?

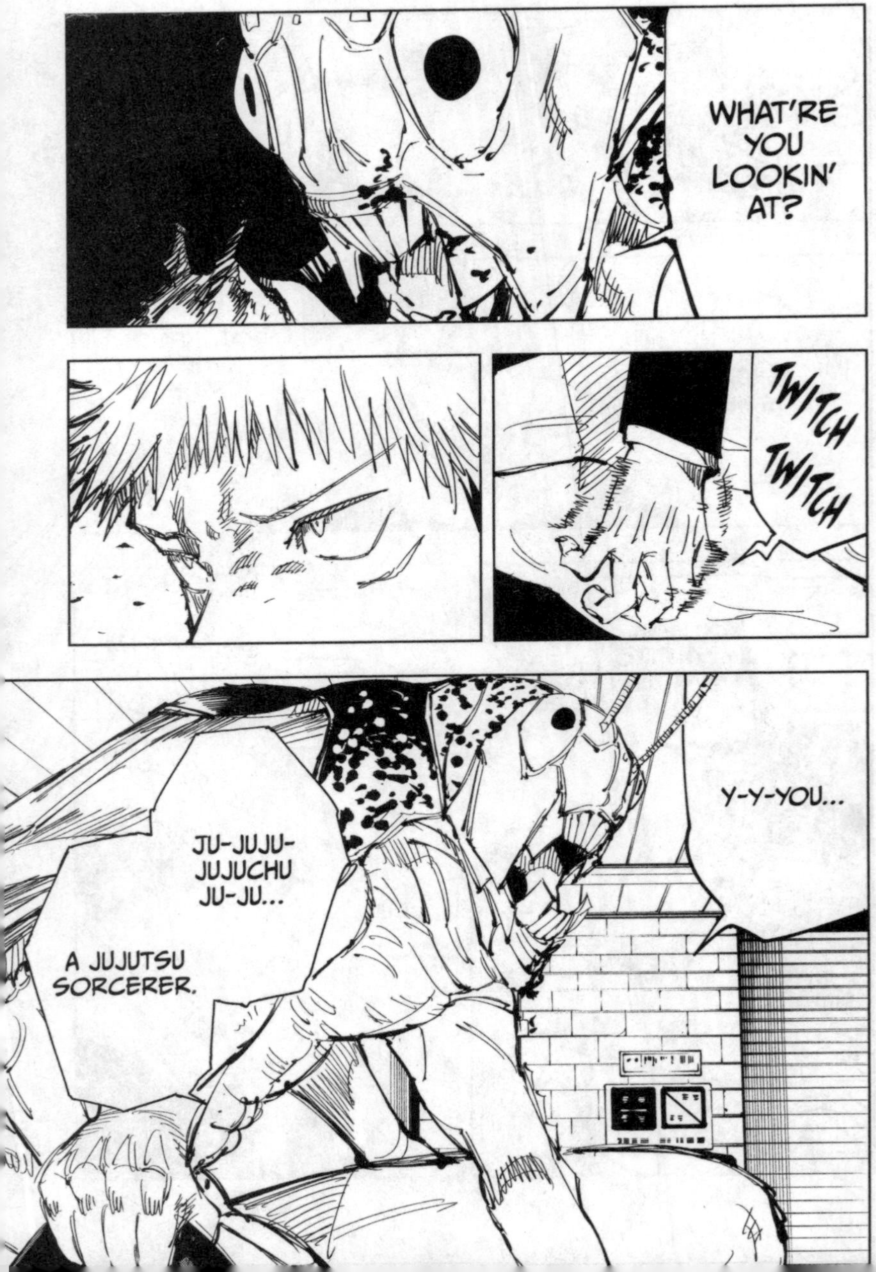
WHAT'RE YOU LOOKIN' AT?
TWITCH TWITCH
Y-Y-YOU...
JU-JUJU-JUJUCHU JU-JU...
A JUJUTSU SORCERER.

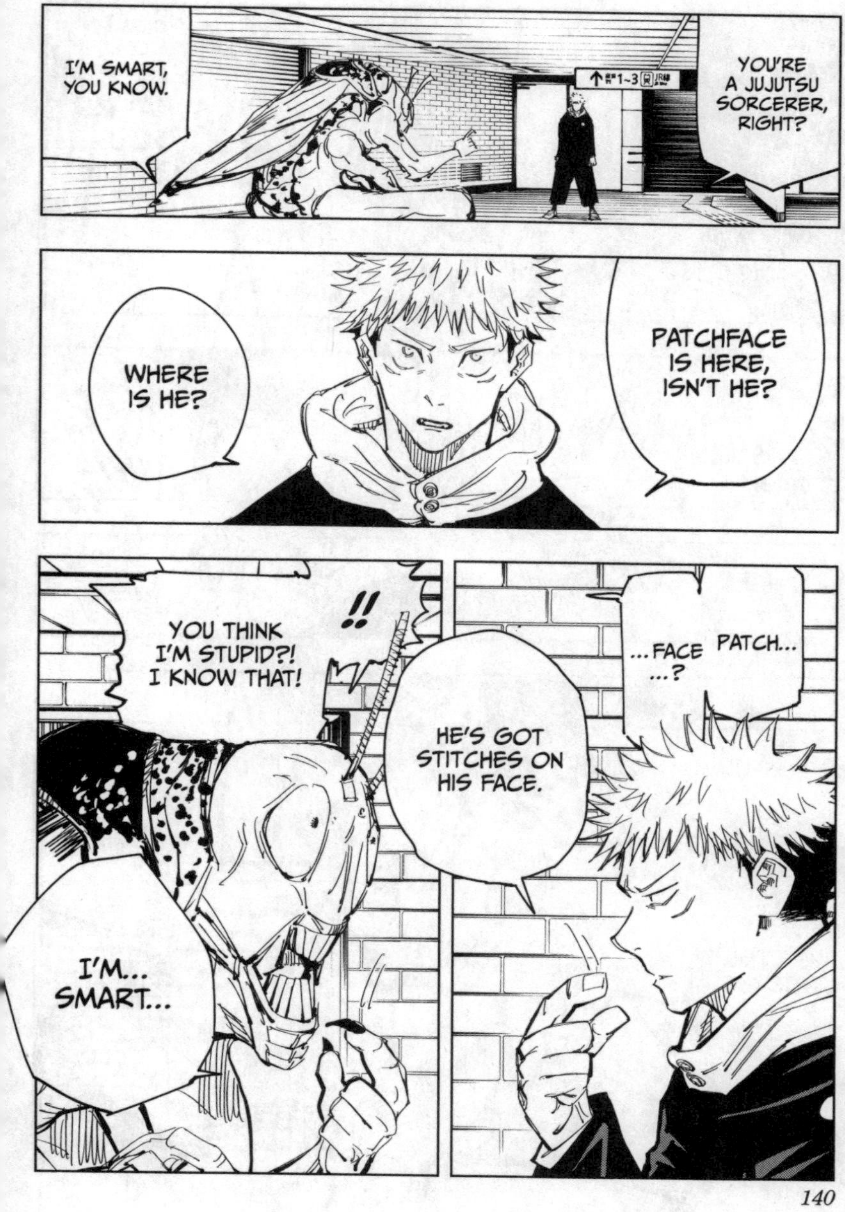
YOU'RE A JUJUTSU SORCERER, RIGHT?
I'M SMART, YOU KNOW.
PATCHFACE IS HERE, ISN'T HE?
WHERE IS HE?
PATCH...
...FACE ...?
HE'S GOT STITCHES ON HIS FACE.
!!
YOU THINK I'M STUPID?! I KNOW THAT!
I'M... SMART...

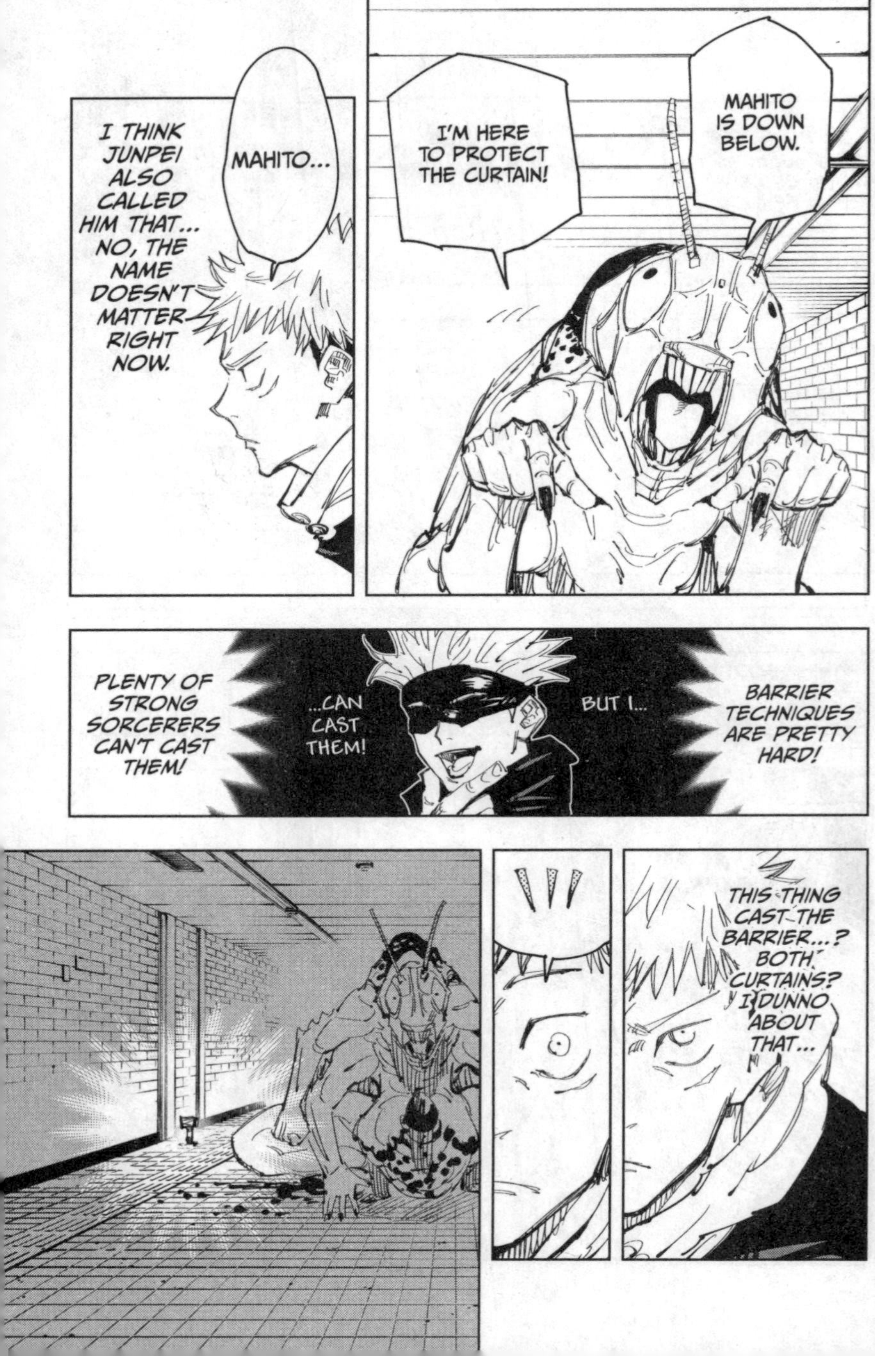

MAHITO IS DOWN BELOW.
I'M HERE TO PROTECT THE CURTAIN!
MAHITO...
I THINK JUNPEI ALSO CALLED HIM THAT... NO, THE NAME DOESN'T MATTER RIGHT NOW.
BARRIER TECHNIQUES ARE PRETTY HARD!
BUT I...
...CAN CAST THEM!
PLENTY OF STRONG SORCERERS CAN'T CAST THEM!
THIS THING CAST THE BARRIER...? BOTH CURTAINS? I DUNNO ABOUT THAT...

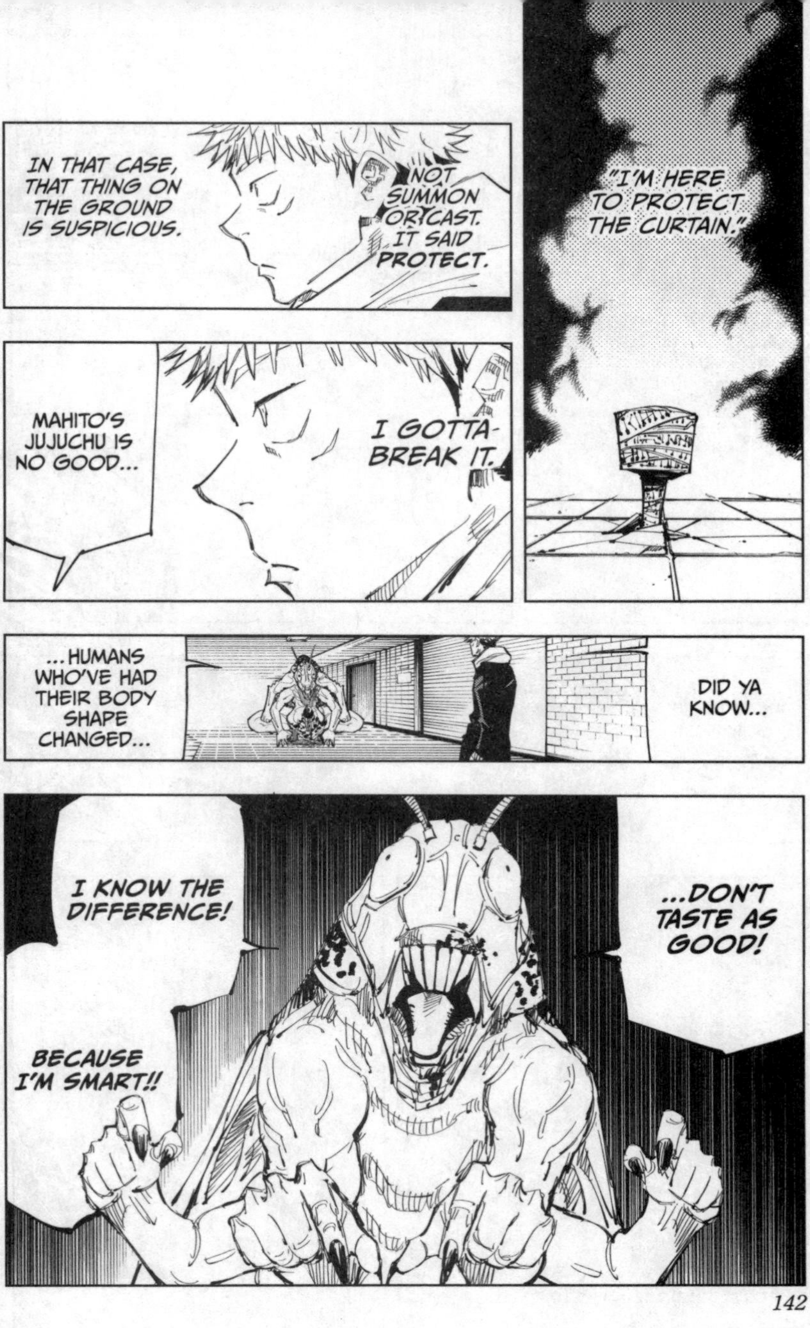
"I'M HERE TO PROTECT THE CURTAIN."
NOT SUMMON OR CAST. IT SAID PROTECT.
IN THAT CASE, THAT THING ON THE GROUND IS SUSPICIOUS.
I GOTTA-BREAK IT.
MAHITO'S JUJUCHU IS NO GOOD...
DID YA KNOW...
...HUMANS WHO'VE HAD THEIR BODY SHAPE CHANGED...
...DON'T TASTE AS GOOD!
I KNOW THE DIFFERENCE!
BECAUSE I'M SMART!!

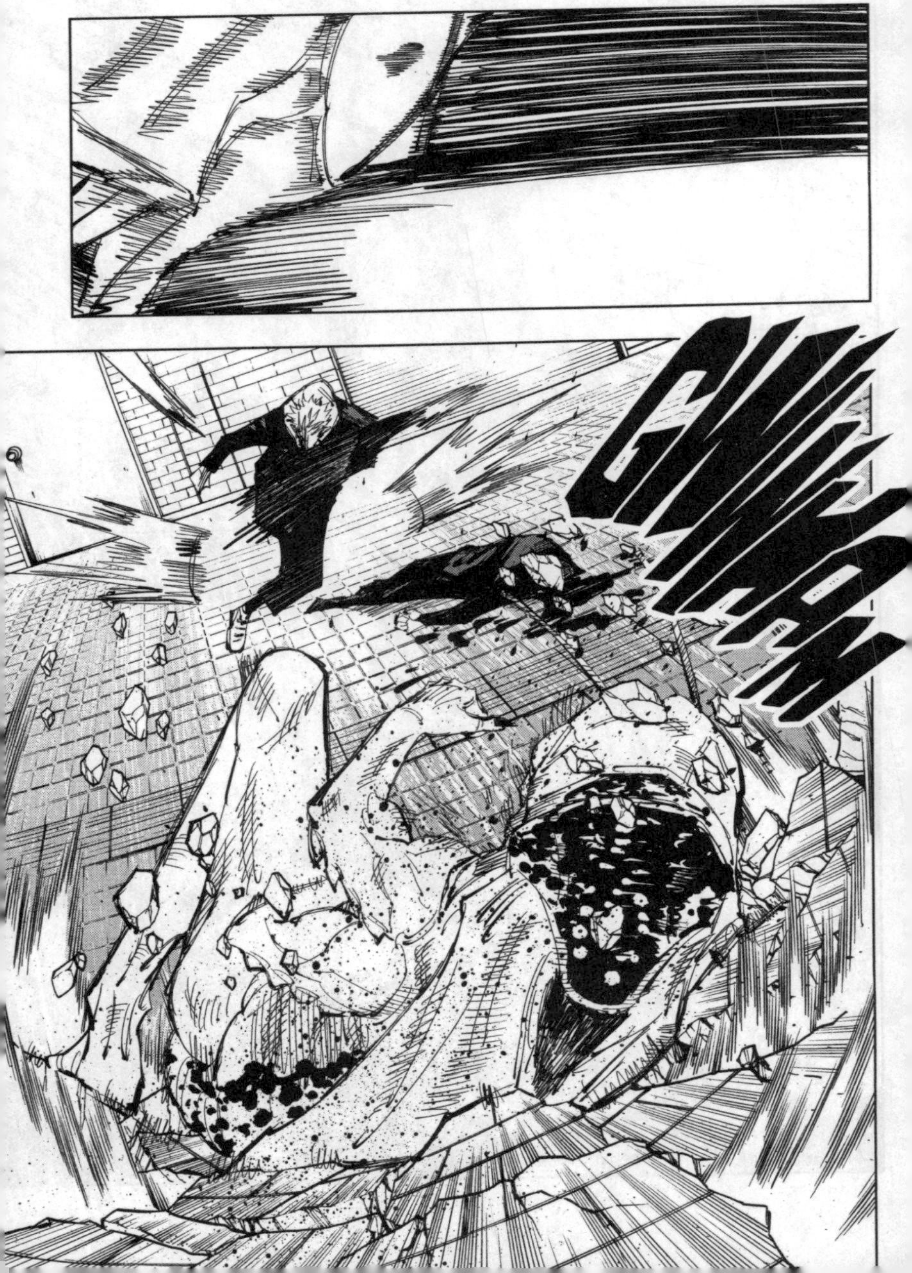

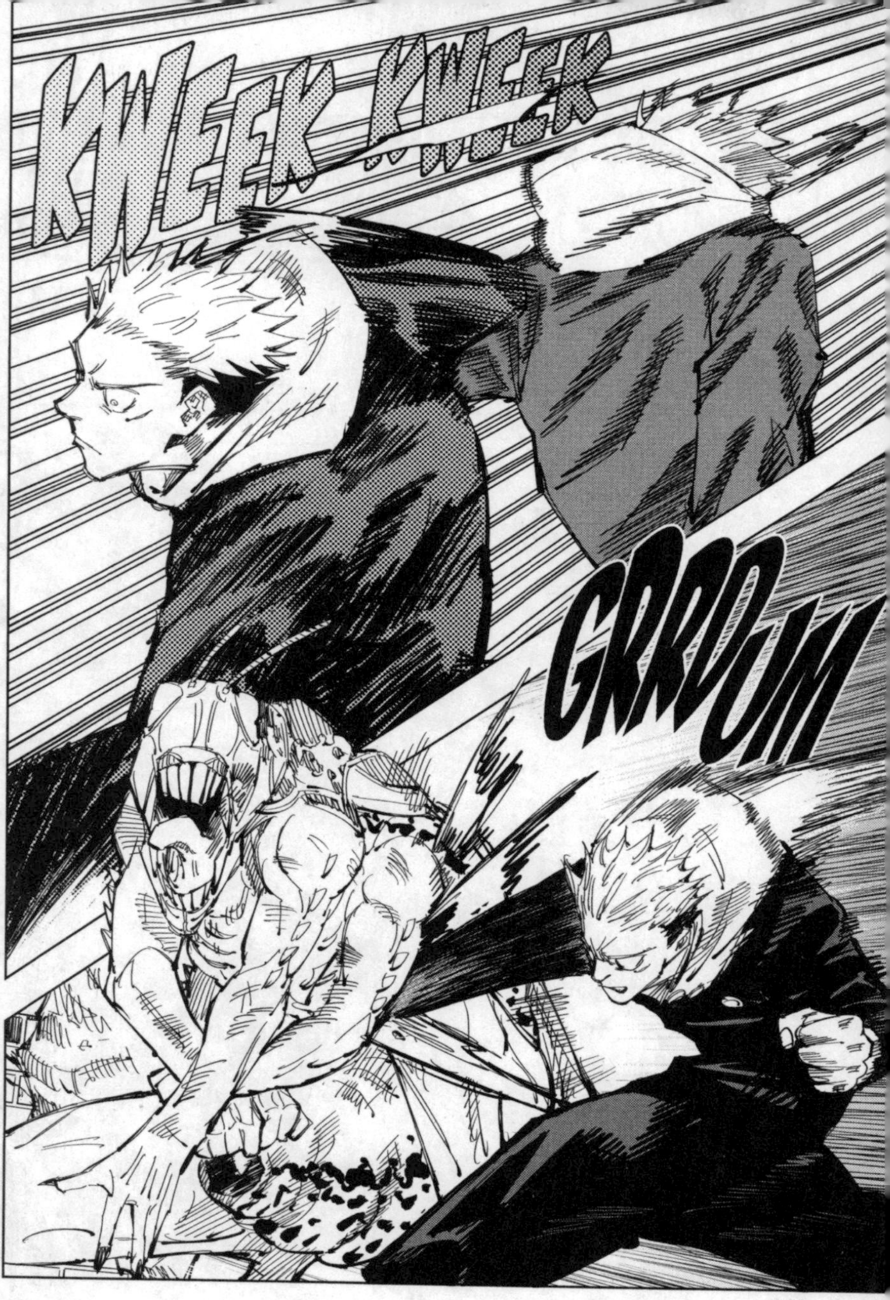
KWEEK KWEEK
GRROOM

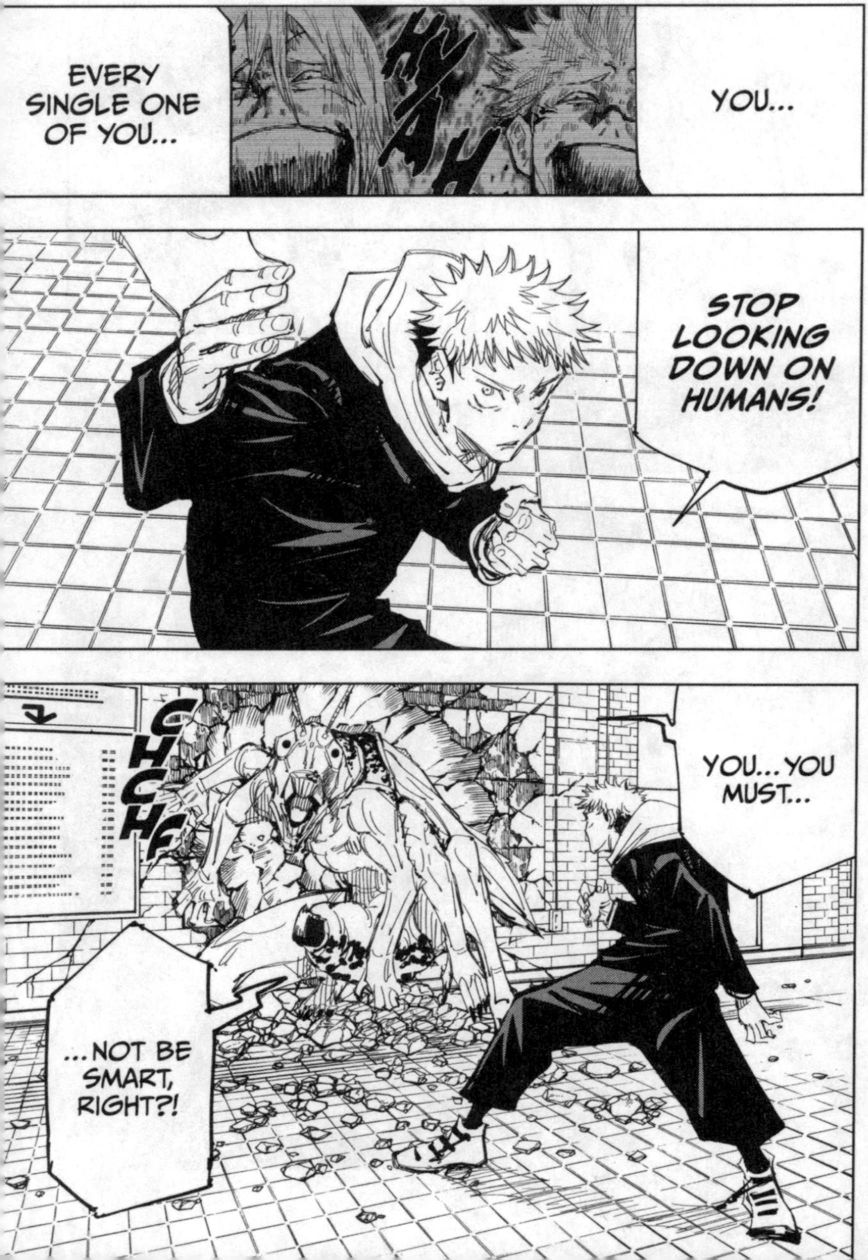
YOU...
EVERY SINGLE ONE OF YOU...
STOP LOOKING DOWN ON HUMANS!
YOU... YOU MUST...
...NOT BE SMART, RIGHT?!

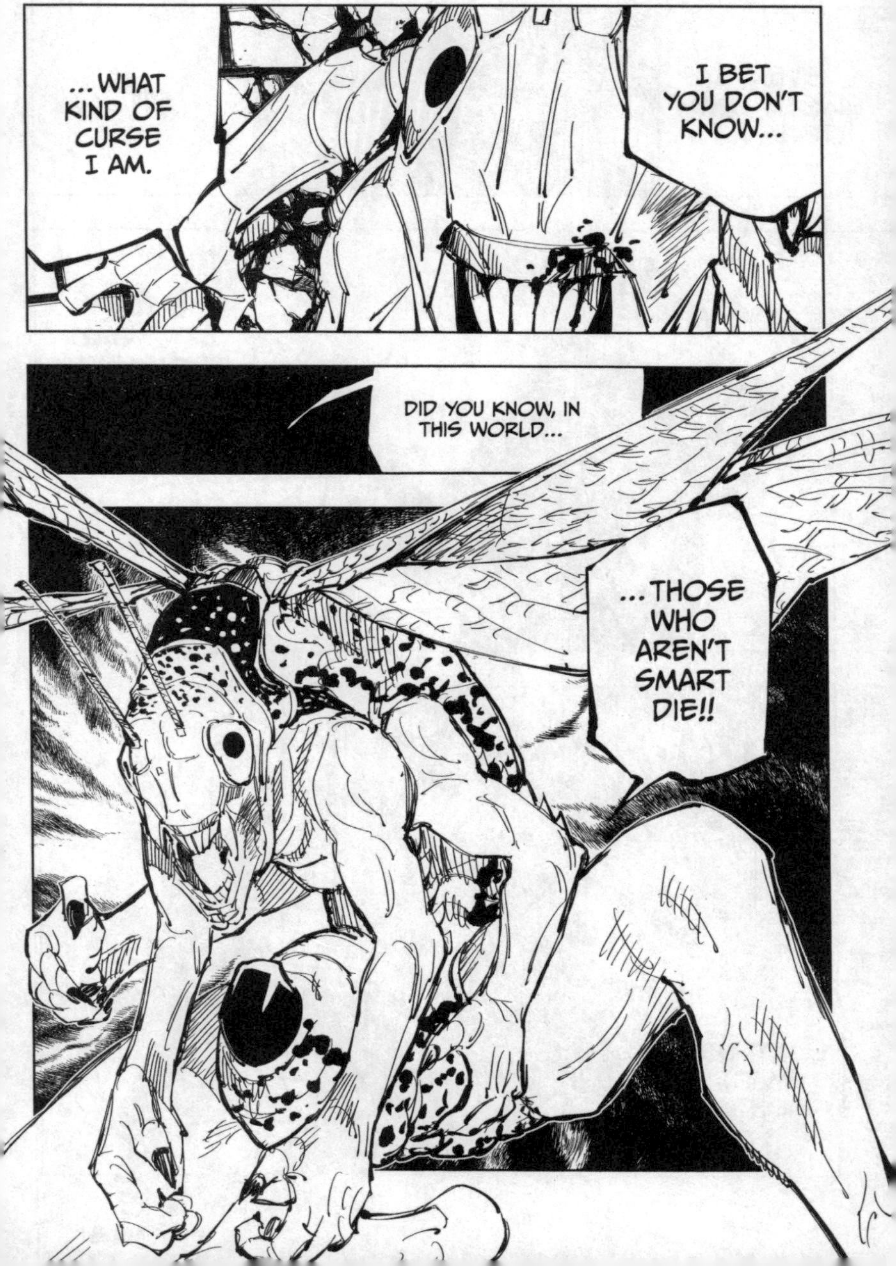
I BET YOU DON'T KNOW...
...WHAT KIND OF CURSE I AM.
DID YOU KNOW, IN THIS WORLD...
...THOSE WHO AREN'T SMART DIE!!

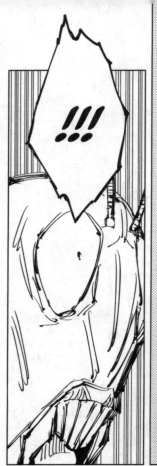

!!!
●●●

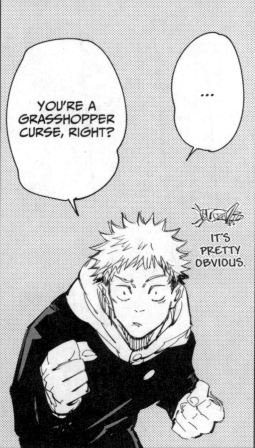

YOU'RE A GRASSHOPPER CURSE, RIGHT?

...

IT'S PRETTY OBVIOUS.

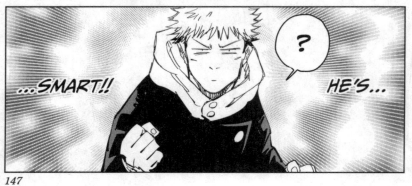

...SMART!!

?

HE'S...

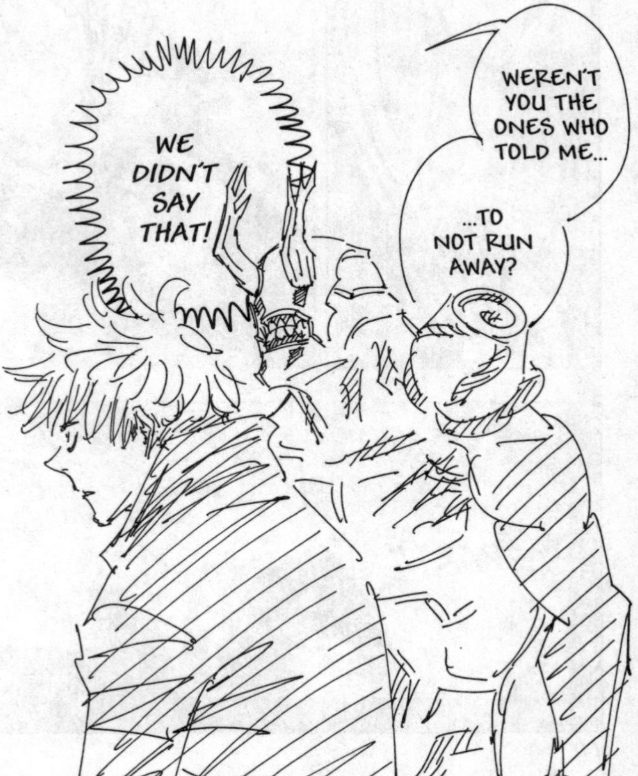
WEREN'T YOU THE ONES WHO TOLD ME...
...TO NOT RUN AWAY?
WE DIDN'T SAY THAT!

Chapter 87: The Shibuya Incident, Part 5

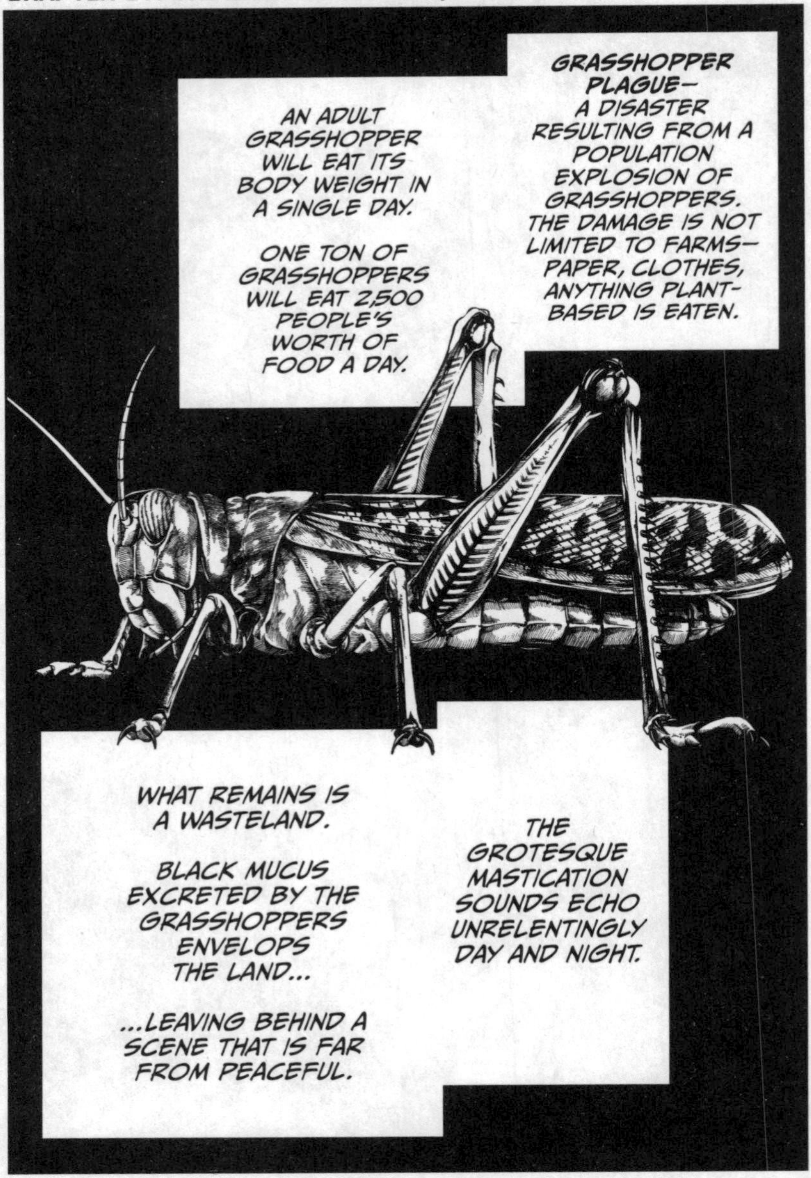
GRASSHOPPER PLAGUE— A DISASTER RESULTING FROM A POPULATION EXPLOSION OF GRASSHOPPERS. THE DAMAGE IS NOT LIMITED TO FARMS— PAPER, CLOTHES, ANYTHING PLANT-BASED IS EATEN.
AN ADULT GRASSHOPPER WILL EAT ITS BODY WEIGHT IN A SINGLE DAY.
ONE TON OF GRASSHOPPERS WILL EAT 2,500 PEOPLE'S WORTH OF FOOD A DAY.
THE GROTESQUE MASTICATION SOUNDS ECHO UNRELENTINGLY DAY AND NIGHT.
WHAT REMAINS IS A WASTELAND.
BLACK MUCUS EXCRETED BY THE GRASSHOPPERS ENVELOPS THE LAND...
...LEAVING BEHIND A SCENE THAT IS FAR FROM PEACEFUL.

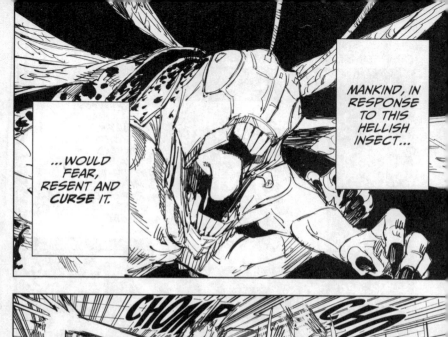

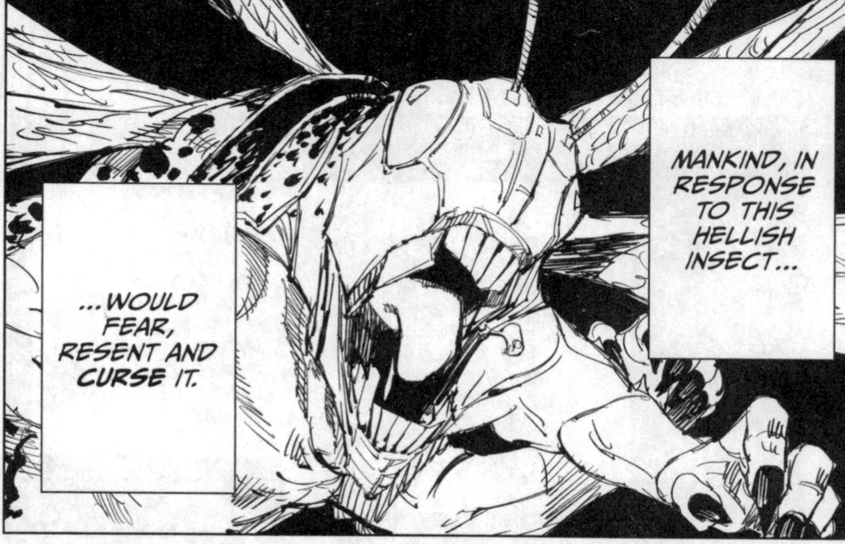
MANKIND, IN RESPONSE TO THIS HELLISH INSECT...
...WOULD FEAR, RESENT AND CURSE IT.

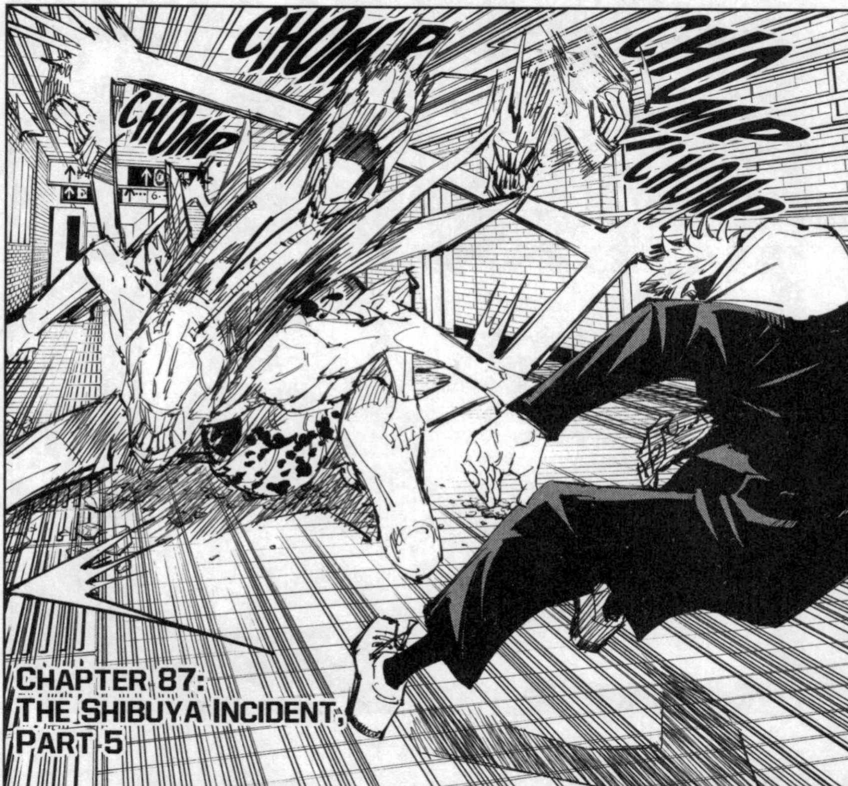
CHOMP CHOMP
CHOMP
CHOMP
CHOMP

**CHAPTER 87:
THE SHIBUYA INCIDENT,
PART 5**

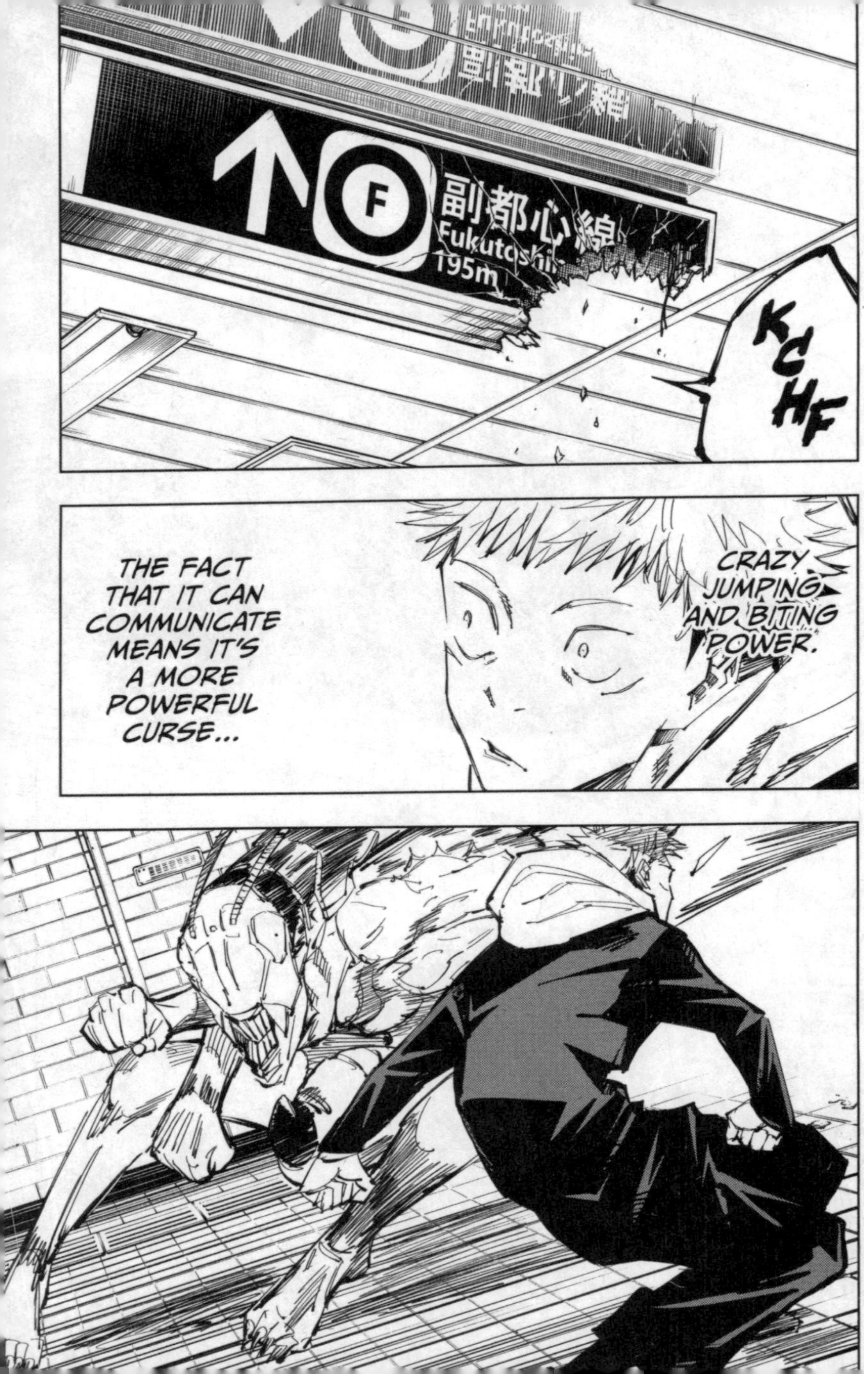
副都心線
Fukutoshi
195m
KCHF
CRAZY JUMPING AND BITING POWER.
THE FACT THAT IT CAN COMMUNICATE MEANS IT'S A MORE POWERFUL CURSE...

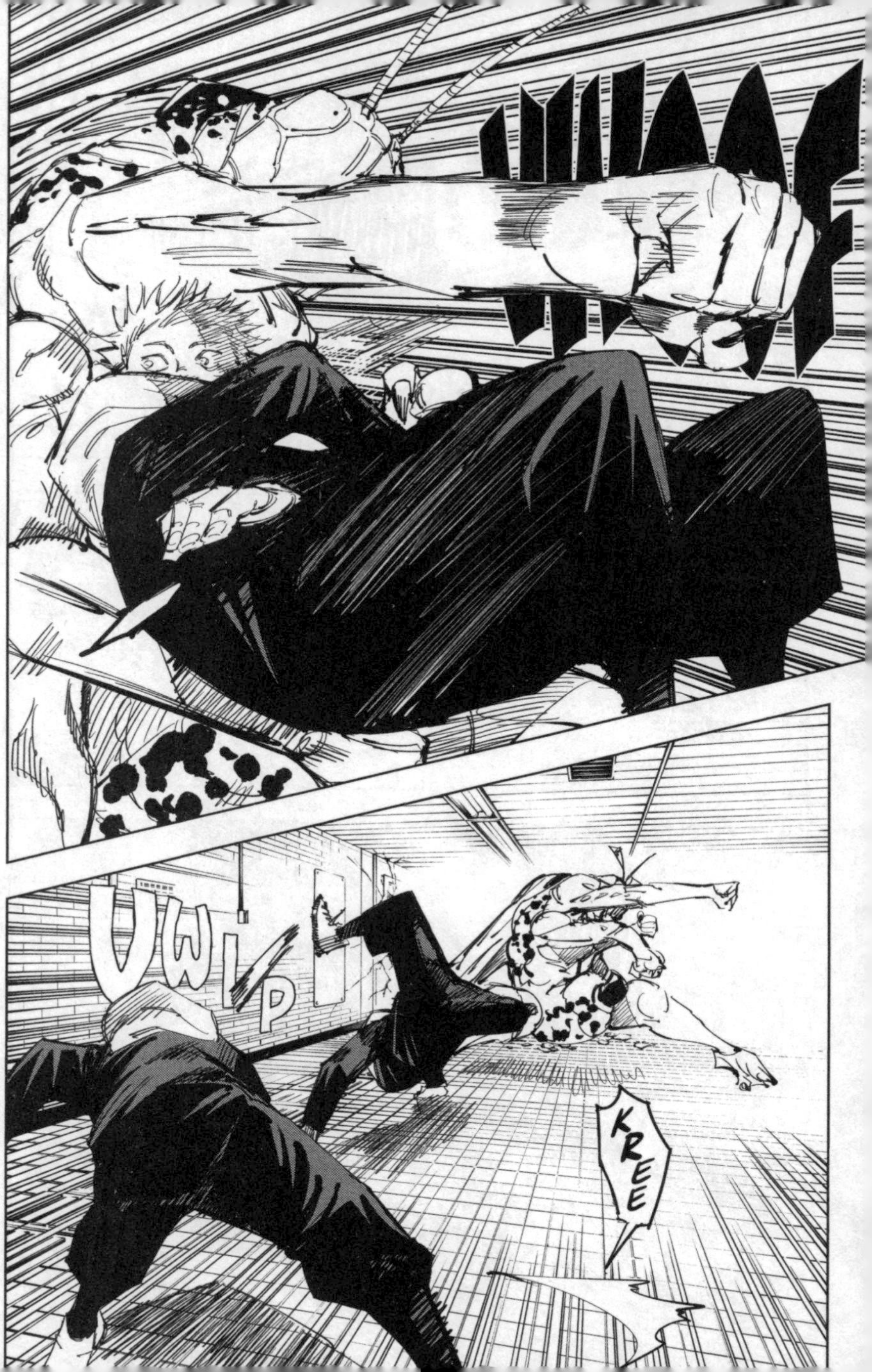
KREE

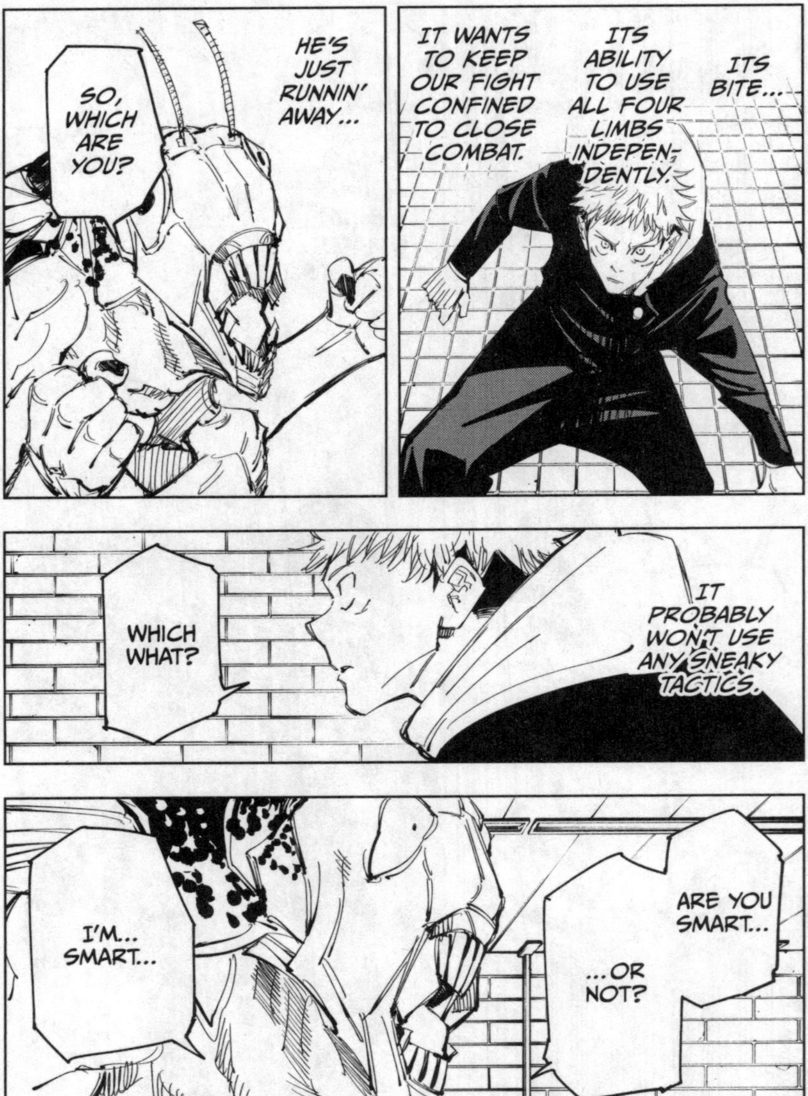
ITS BITE...
ITS ABILITY TO USE ALL FOUR LIMBS INDEPENDENTLY.
IT WANTS TO KEEP OUR FIGHT CONFINED TO CLOSE COMBAT.
HE'S JUST RUNNIN' AWAY...
SO, WHICH ARE YOU?
IT PROBABLY WON'T USE ANY SNEAKY TACTICS.
WHICH WHAT?
ARE YOU SMART...
...OR NOT?
I'M... SMART...

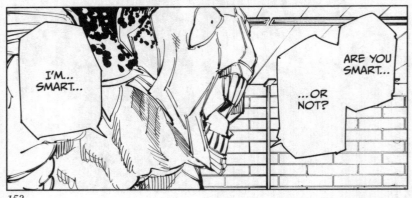

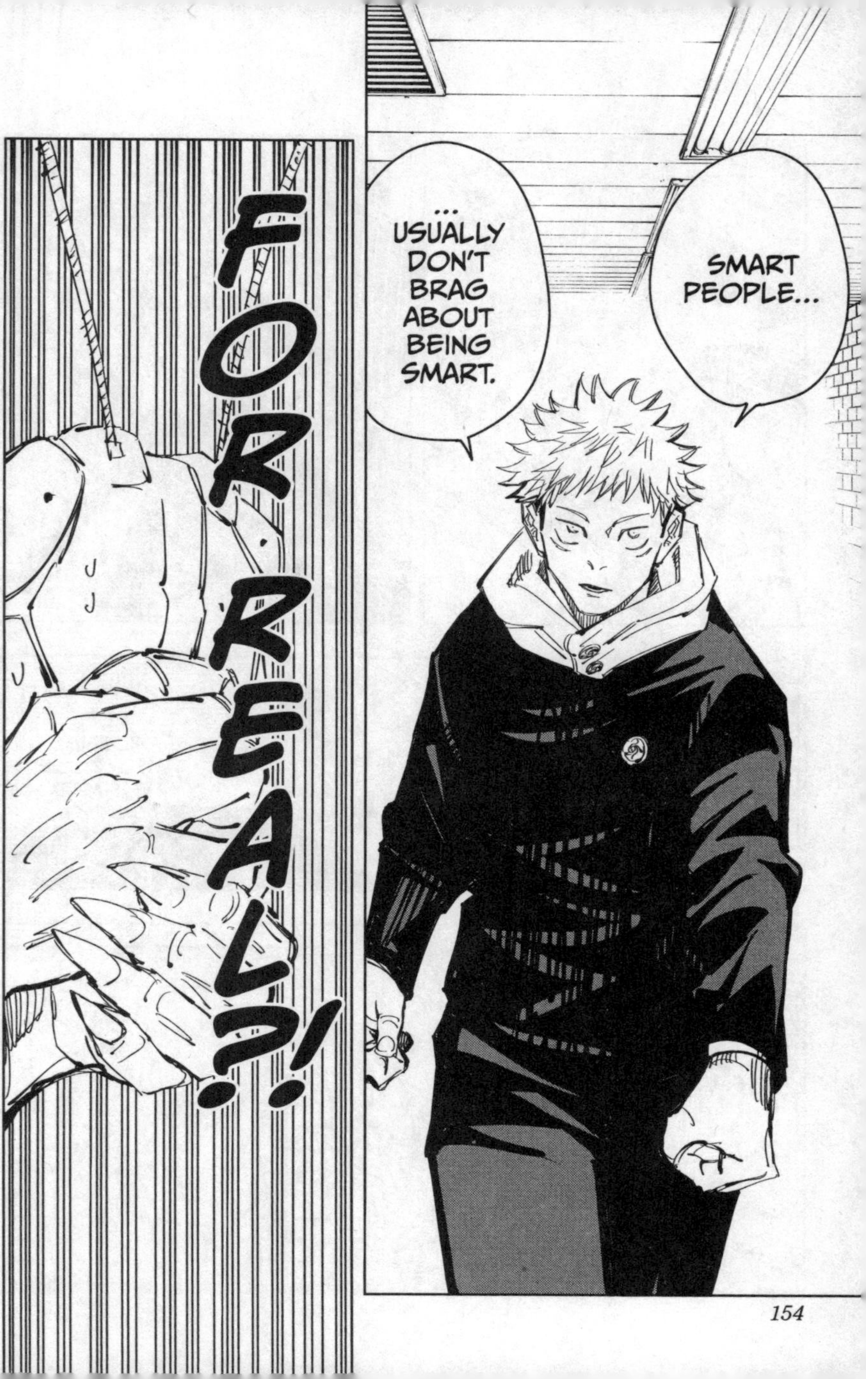
SMART PEOPLE...
...USUALLY DON'T BRAG ABOUT BEING SMART.
FOR REAL?!

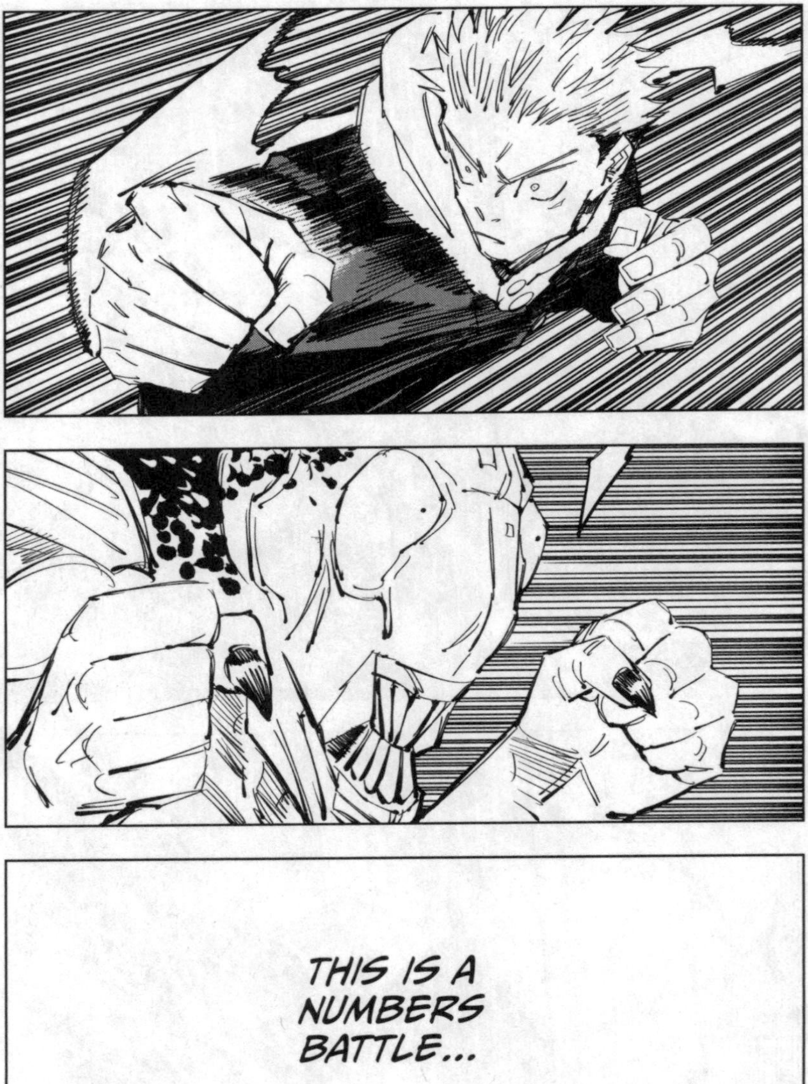
THIS IS A NUMBERS BATTLE...

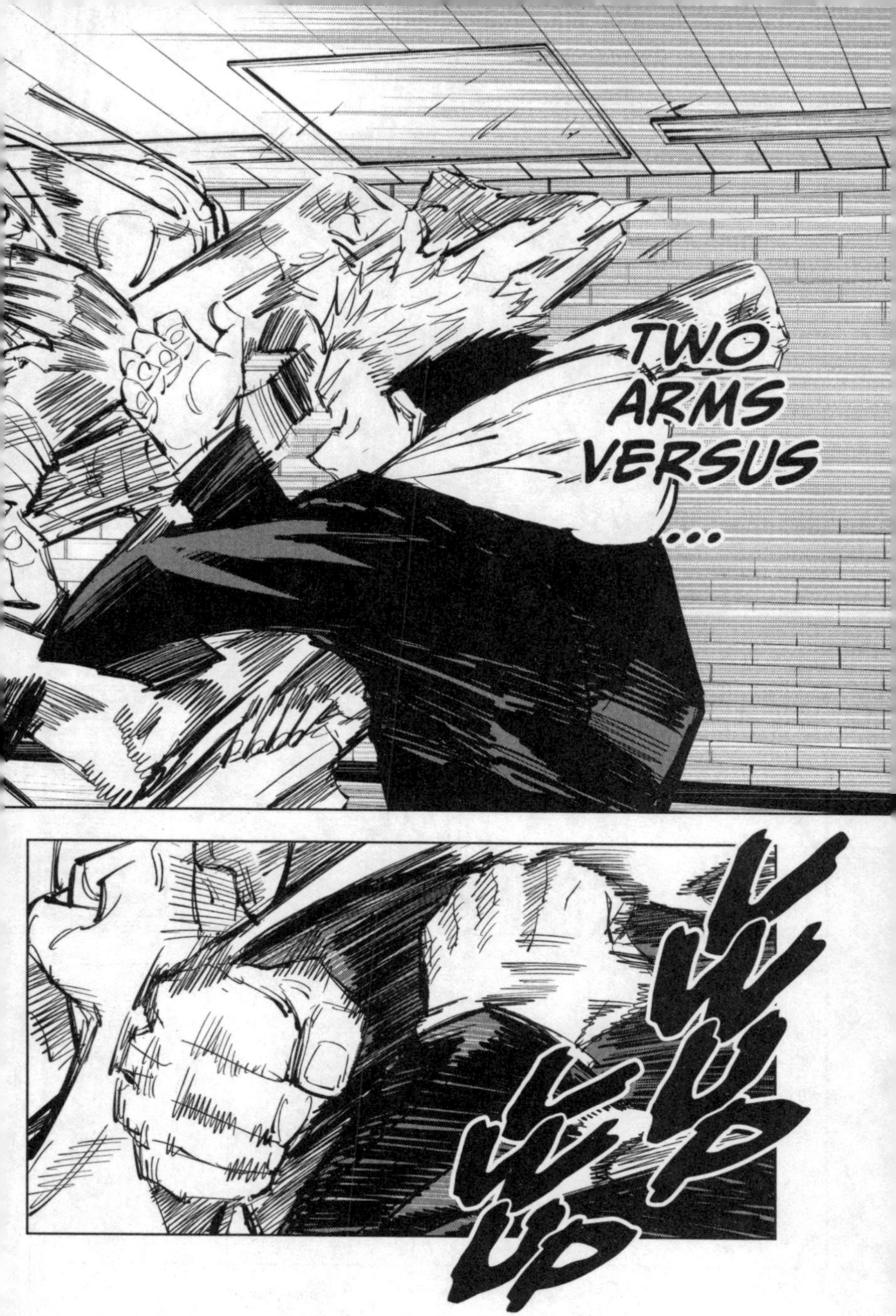
TWO ARMS VERSUS ...
ZUP ZUP ZUP ZUP

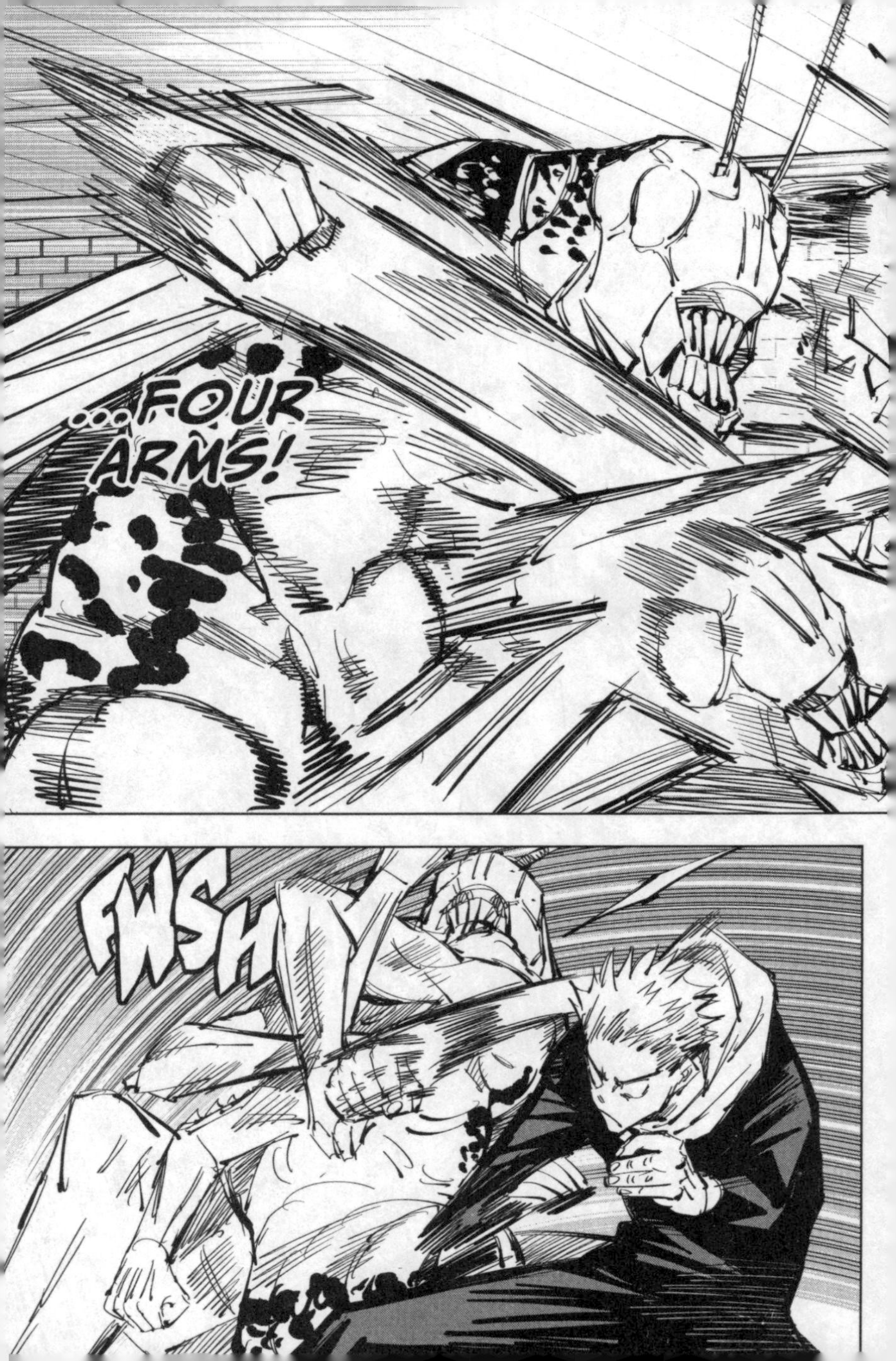
...FOUR ARMS!
FWSH

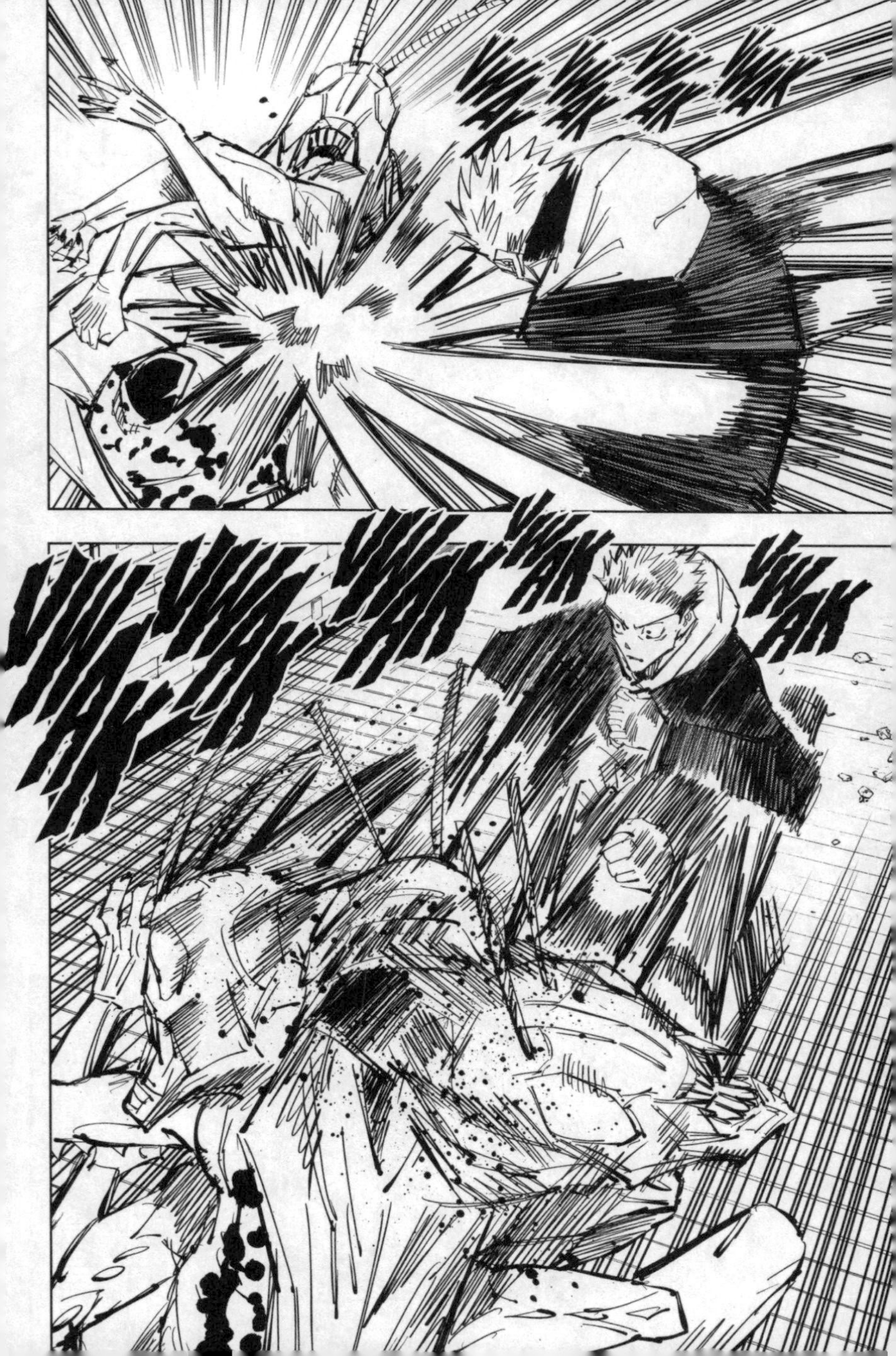
WAK WAK WAK WAK
WHAK WHAK WHAK WHAK WHAK

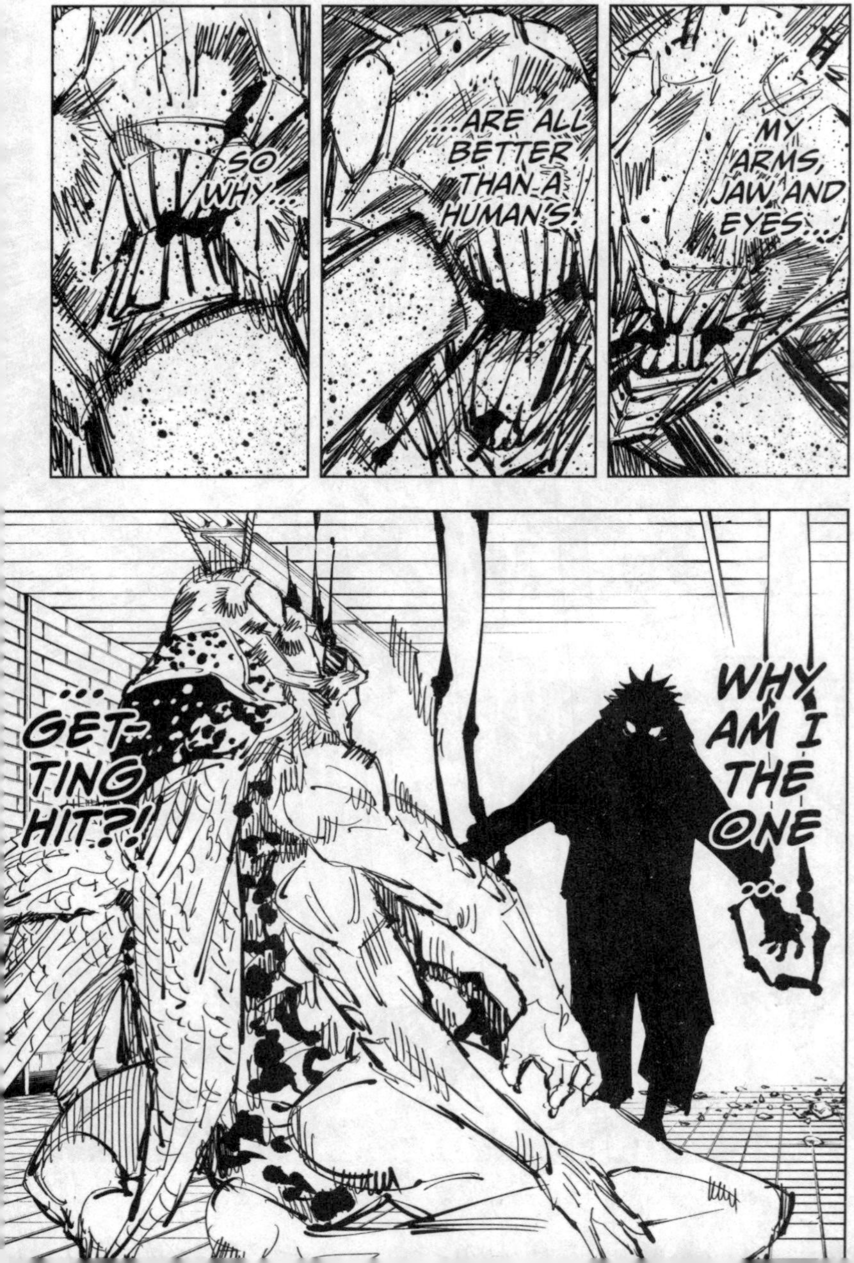
MY ARMS, JAW AND EYES...
...ARE ALL BETTER THAN A HUMAN'S.
SO WHY...
WHY AM I THE ONE...
...GETTING HIT?!

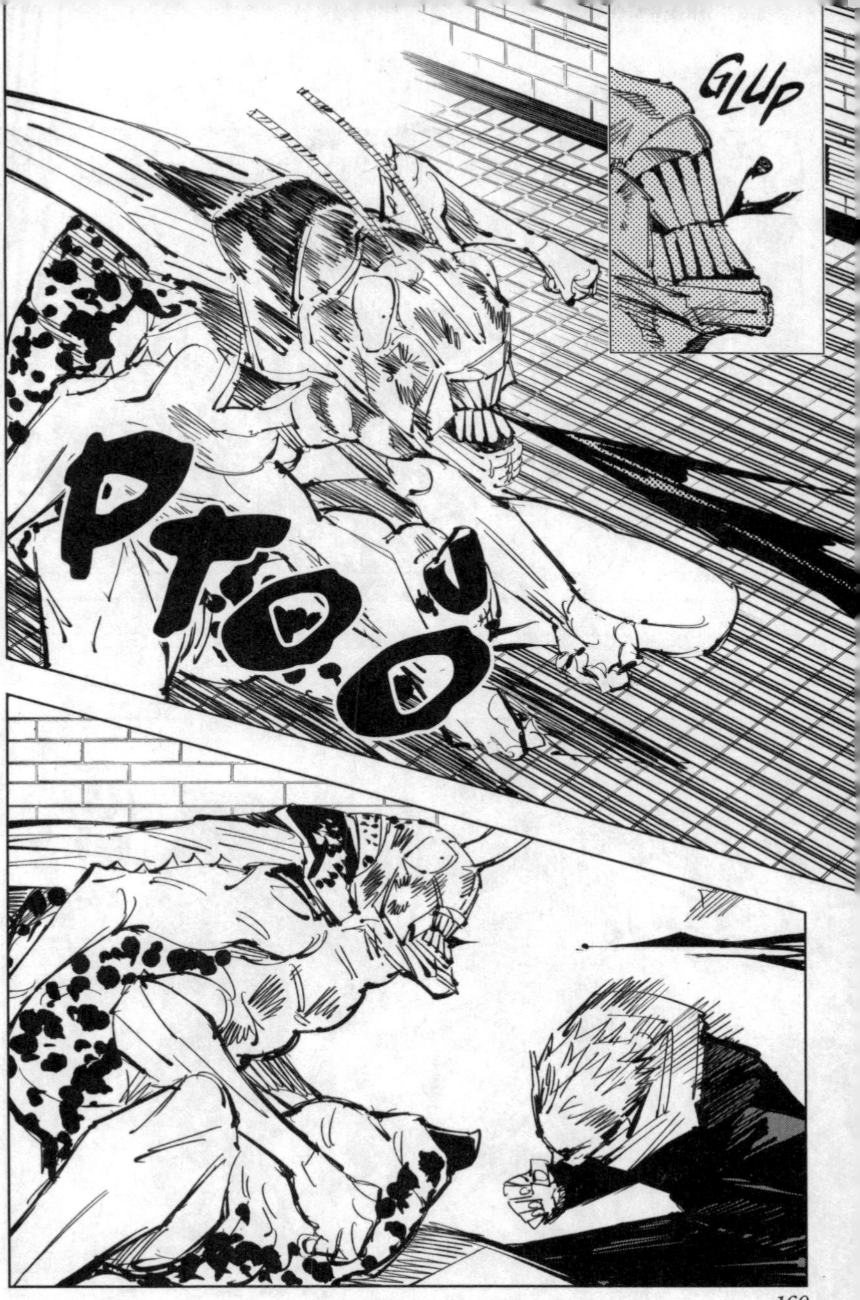
GLUP
PTOO

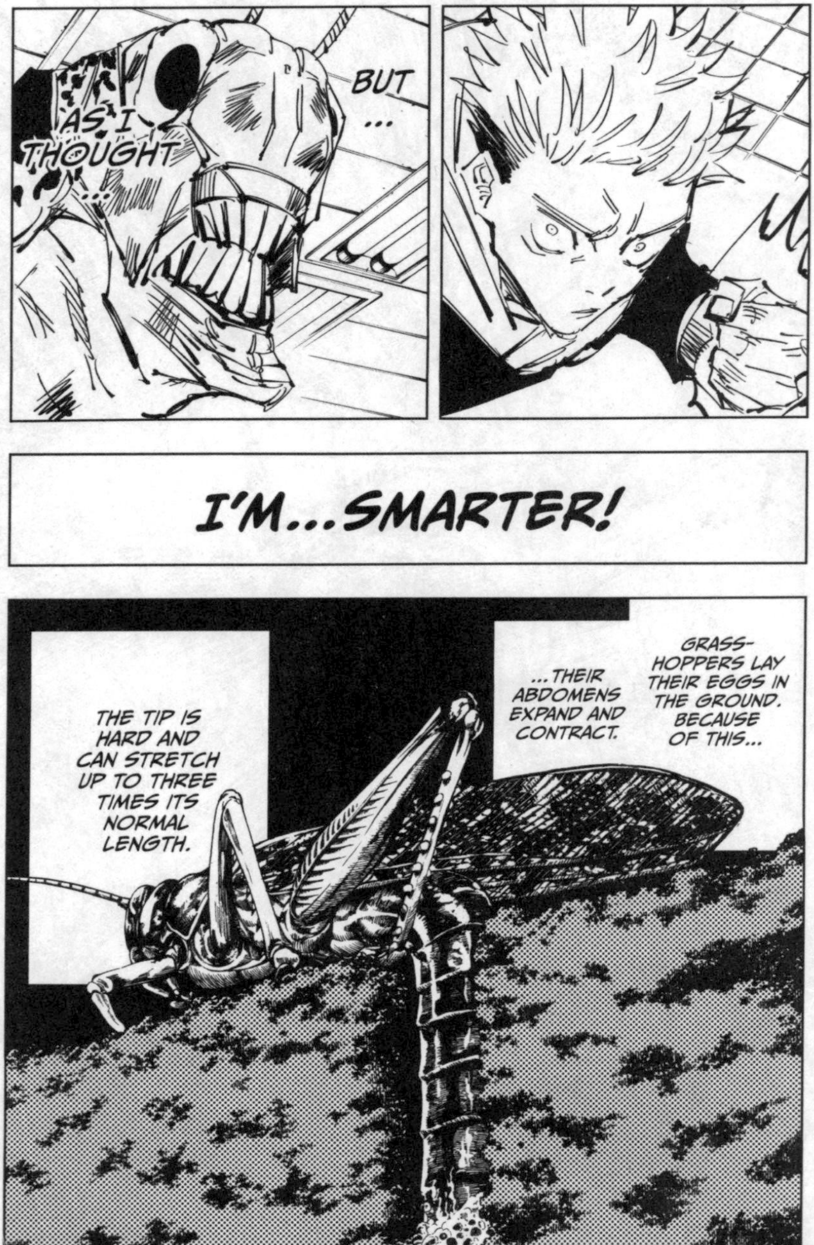
AS I THOUGHT...
BUT...
I'M...SMARTER!
GRASS-HOPPERS LAY THEIR EGGS IN THE GROUND. BECAUSE OF THIS...
...THEIR ABDOMENS EXPAND AND CONTRACT.
THE TIP IS HARD AND CAN STRETCH UP TO THREE TIMES ITS NORMAL LENGTH.

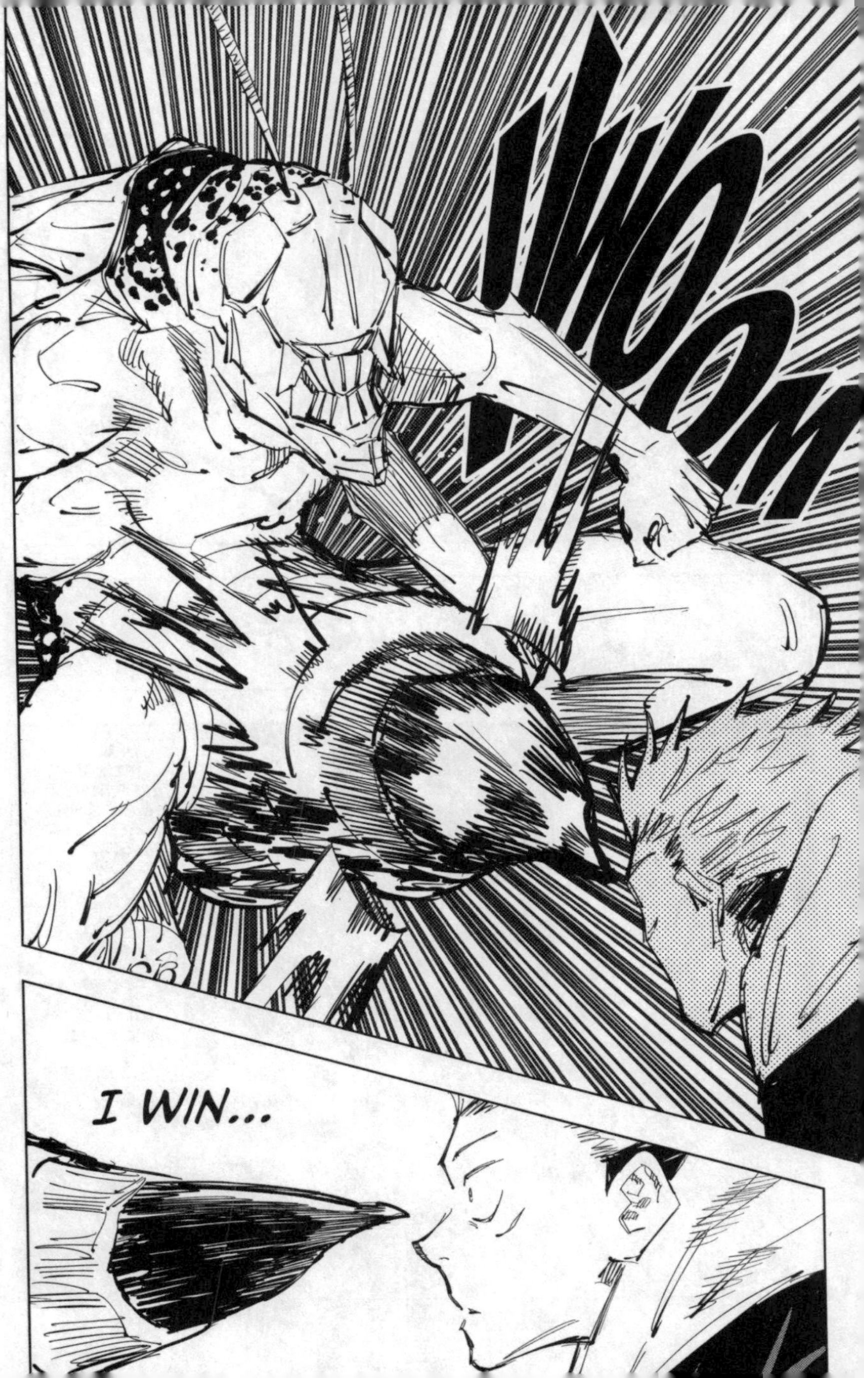
WHOOM
I WIN...

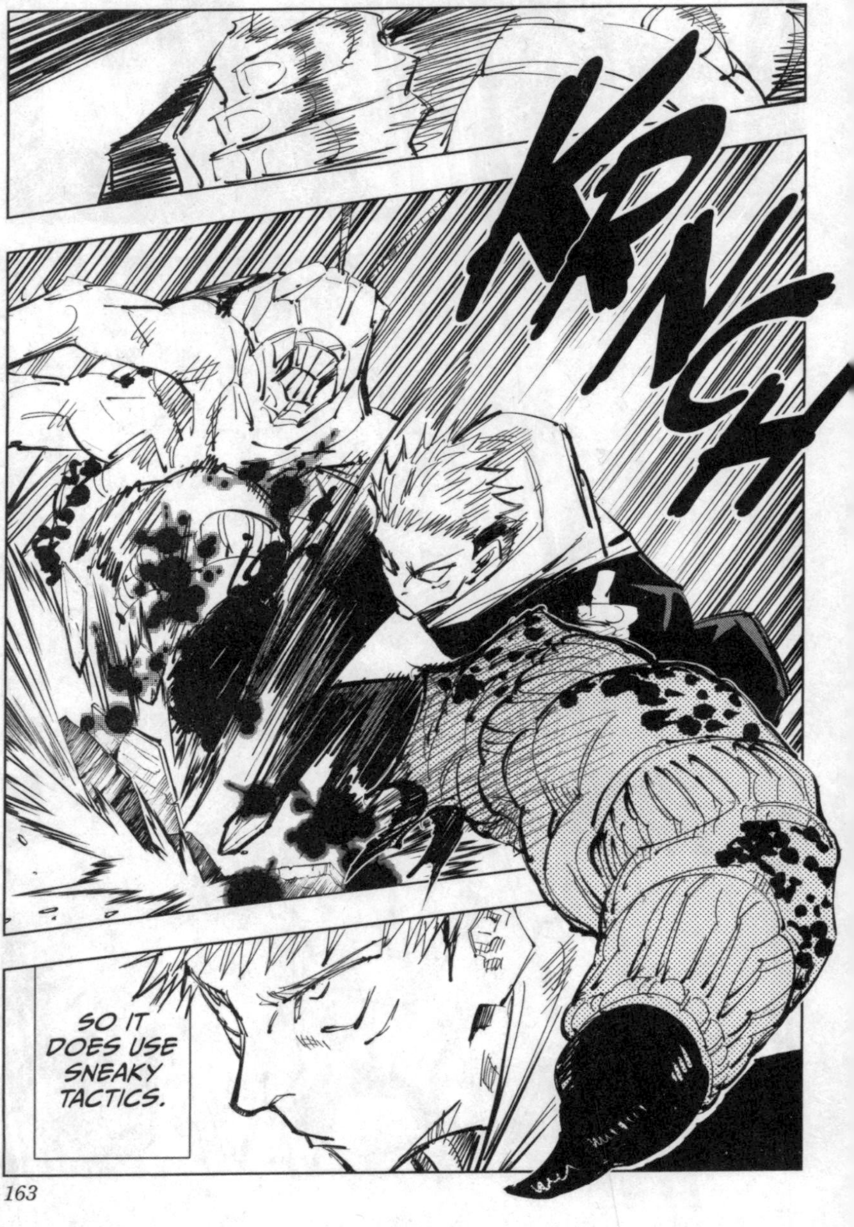
KRNCH
SO IT DOES USE SNEAKY TACTICS.

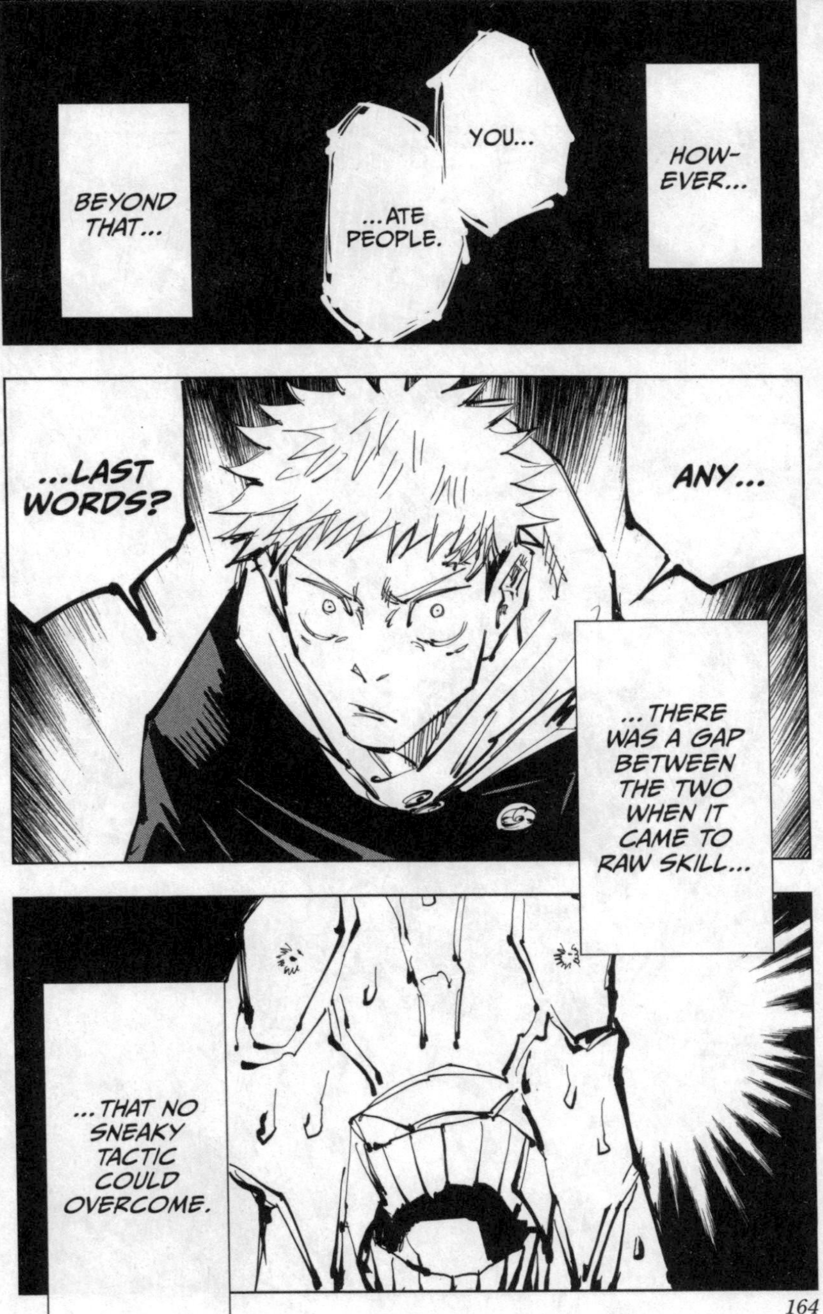
HOW-EVER...
YOU...
...ATE PEOPLE.
BEYOND THAT...
ANY...
...LAST WORDS?
...THERE WAS A GAP BETWEEN THE TWO WHEN IT CAME TO RAW SKILL...
...THAT NO SNEAKY TACTIC COULD OVERCOME.

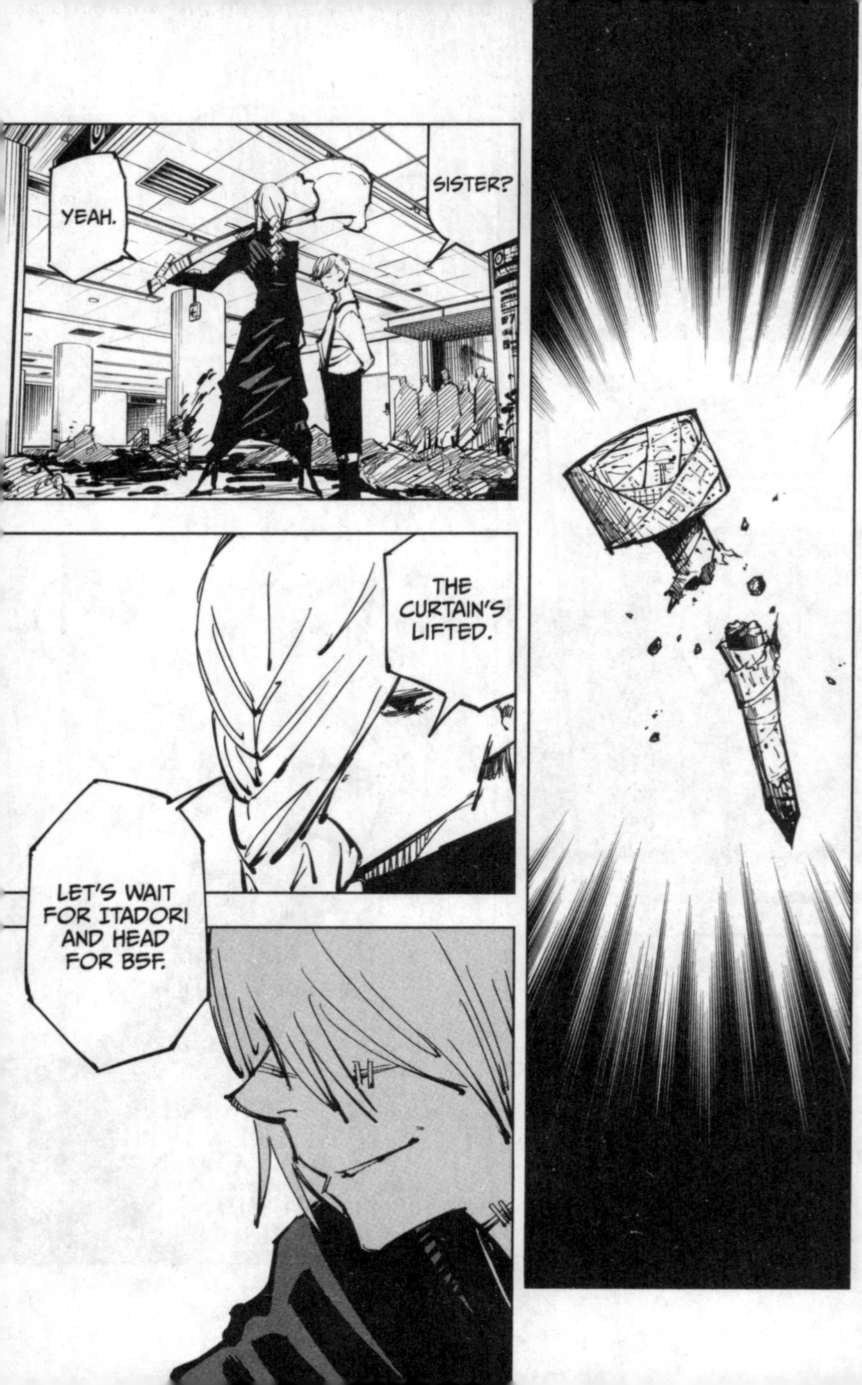
SISTER?
YEAH.
THE CURTAIN'S LIFTED.
LET'S WAIT FOR ITADORI AND HEAD FOR B5F.

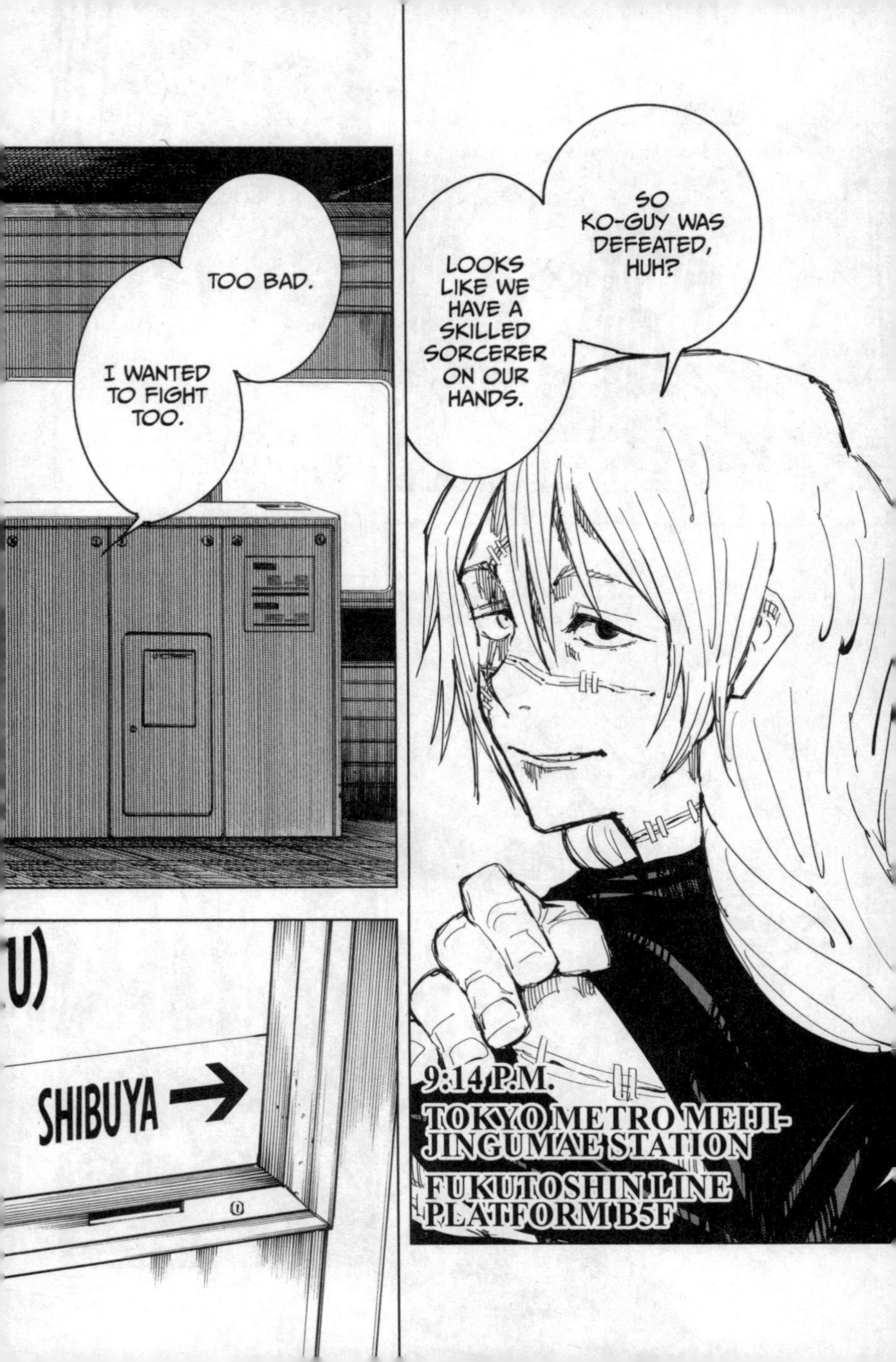
SO KO-GUY WAS DEFEATED, HUH?
LOOKS LIKE WE HAVE A SKILLED SORCERER ON OUR HANDS.
9:14 P.M.
TOKYO METRO MEIJI-JINGUMAE STATION
FUKUTOSHIN LINE PLATFORM B5F
TOO BAD.
I WANTED TO FIGHT TOO.
SHIBUYA

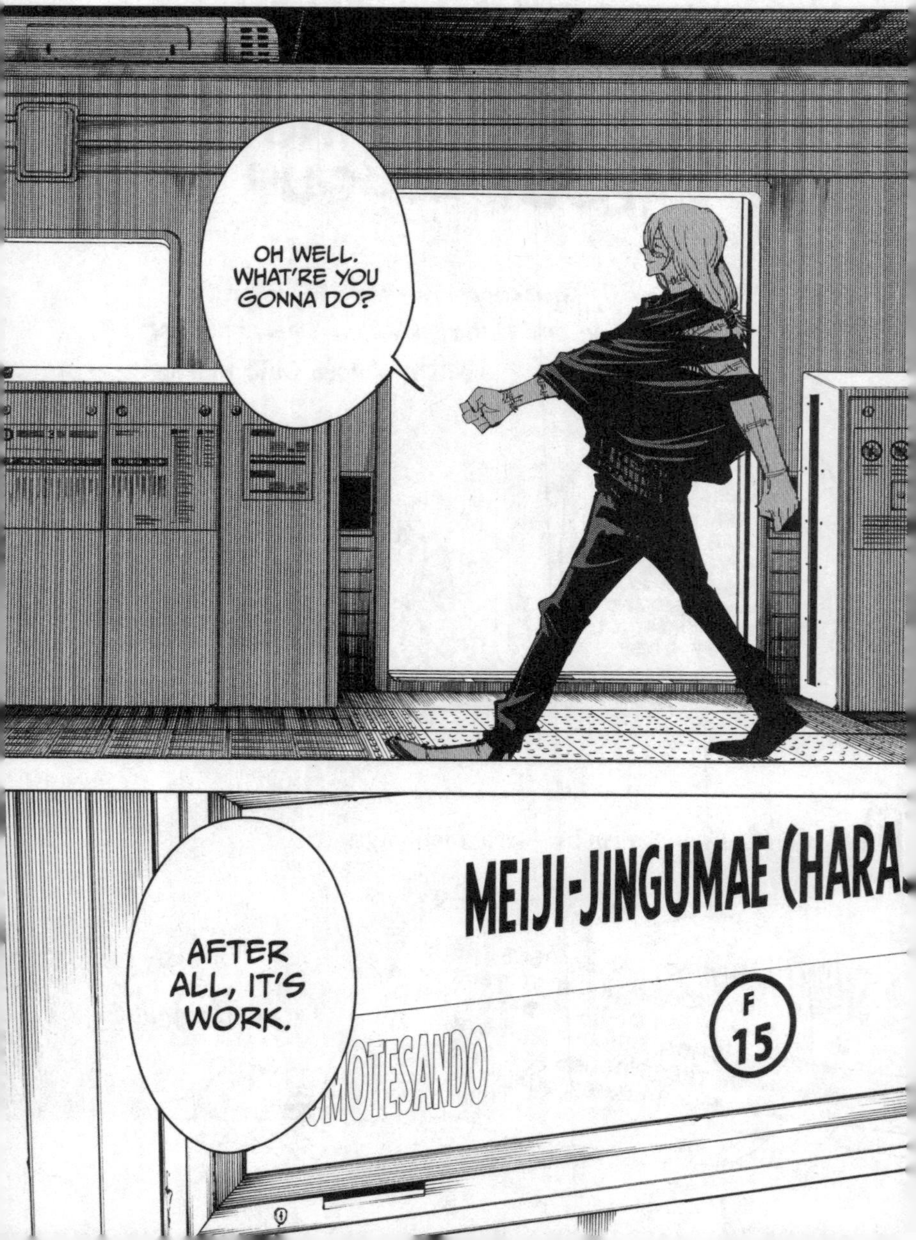
OH WELL. WHAT'RE YOU GONNA DO?
MEIJI-JINGUMAE (HARA
F 15
AFTER ALL, IT'S WORK.
OMOTESANDO

BOOKS I USED FOR INSPIRATION WHEN WRITING ABOUT KO-GUY

- *When Lonely Grasshoppers Flock Together: The Mutation and Outbreak of the Desert Locust* by Dr. Kotaro Ould Maeno

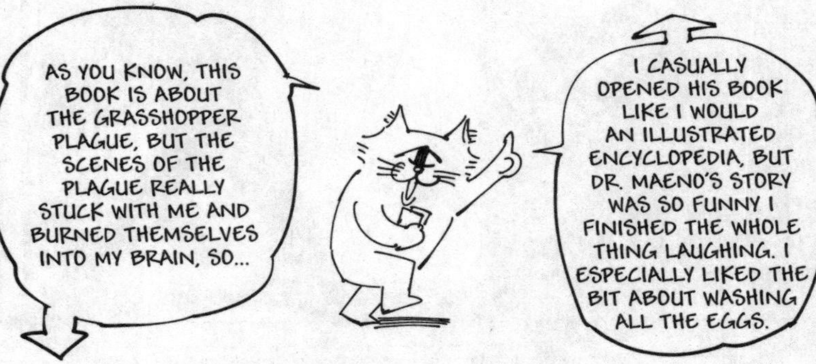
I CASUALLY OPENED HIS BOOK LIKE I WOULD AN ILLUSTRATED ENCYCLOPEDIA, BUT DR. MAENO'S STORY WAS SO FUNNY I FINISHED THE WHOLE THING LAUGHING. I ESPECIALLY LIKED THE BIT ABOUT WASHING ALL THE EGGS.
AS YOU KNOW, THIS BOOK IS ABOUT THE GRASSHOPPER PLAGUE, BUT THE SCENES OF THE PLAGUE REALLY STUCK WITH ME AND BURNED THEMSELVES INTO MY BRAIN, SO...

- *Bear Storm* by Akira Yoshimura

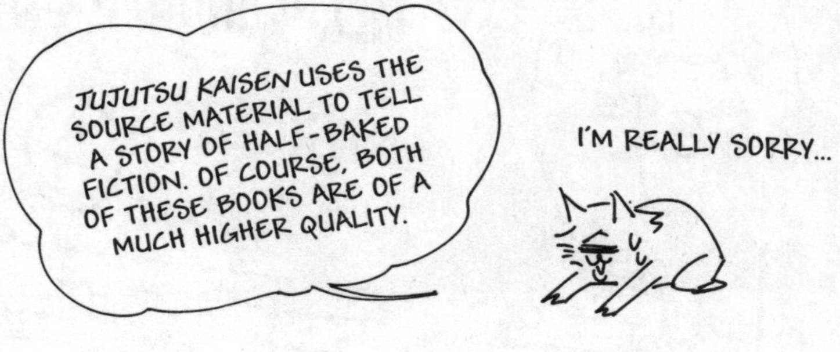
I'M REALLY SORRY...
JUJUTSU KAISEN USES THE SOURCE MATERIAL TO TELL A STORY OF HALF-BAKED FICTION. OF COURSE, BOTH OF THESE BOOKS ARE OF A MUCH HIGHER QUALITY.

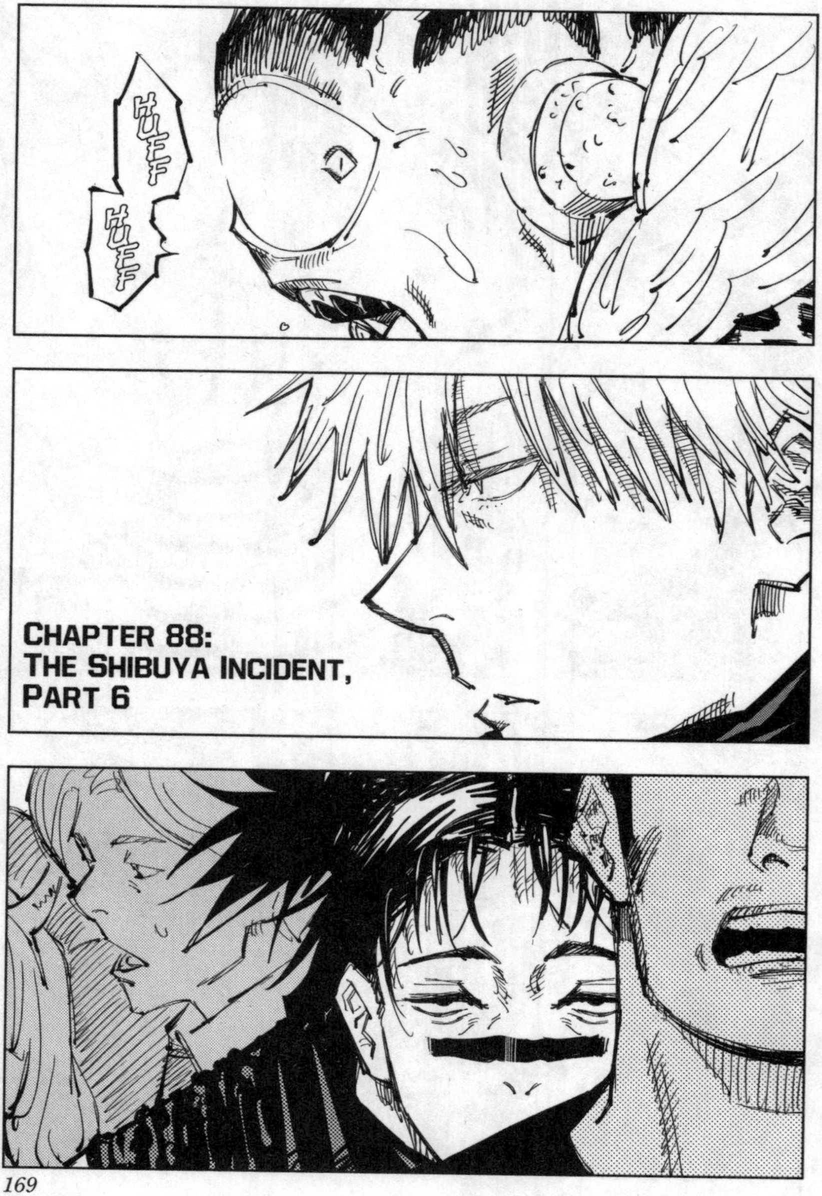
HUFF
HUFF
CHAPTER 88:
THE SHIBUYA INCIDENT,
PART 6

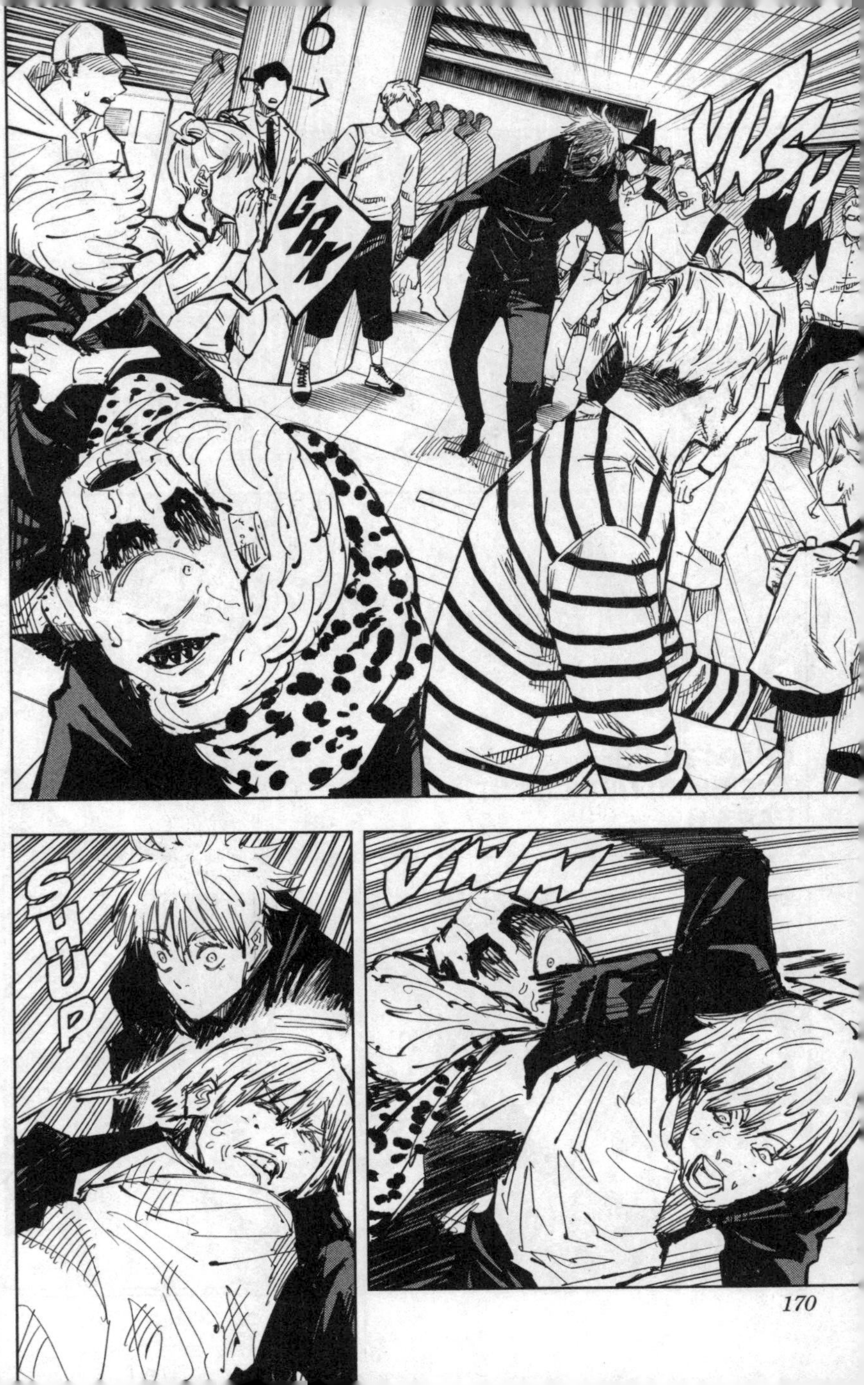
VRSH
6
GRK
VWM
SHUP

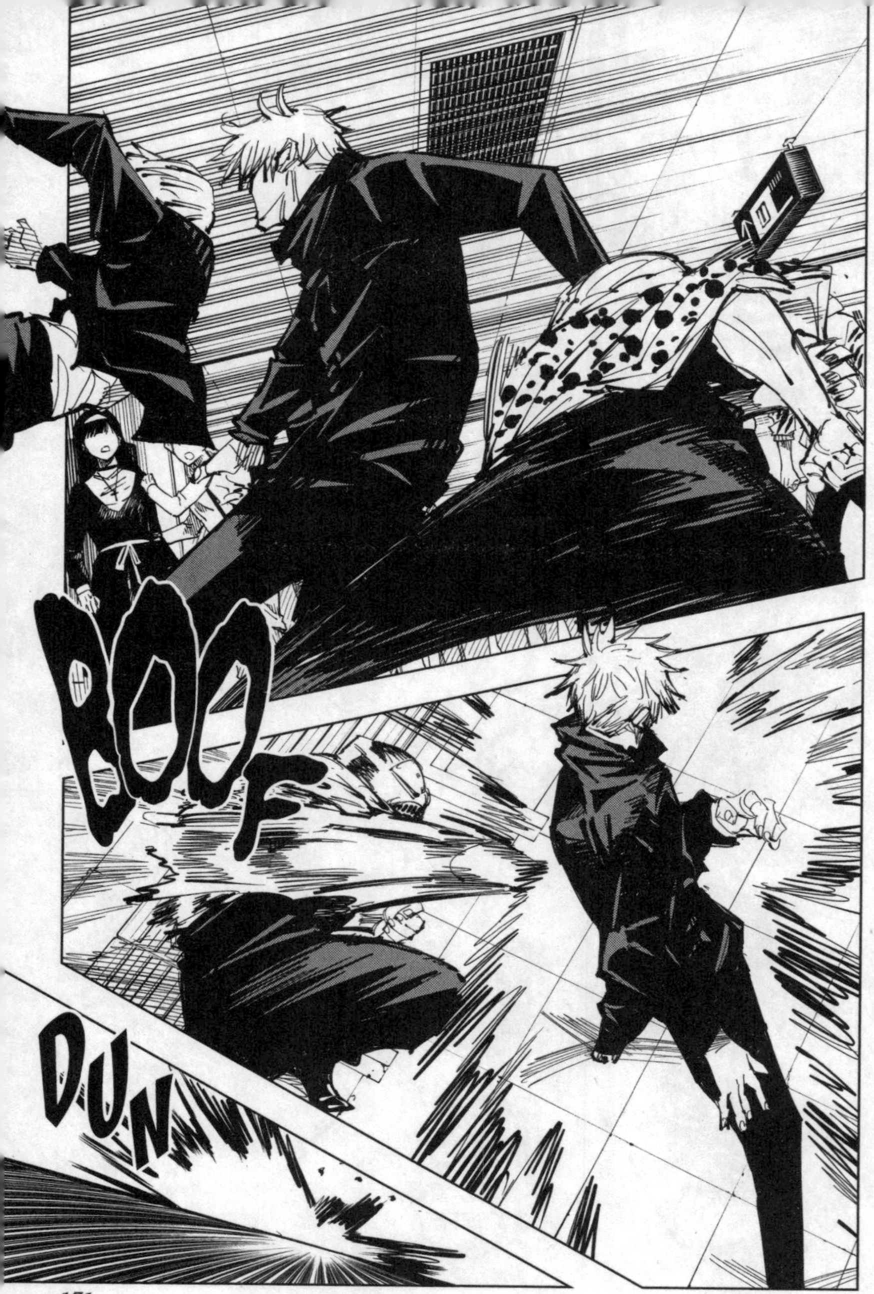
BOOF
DUN

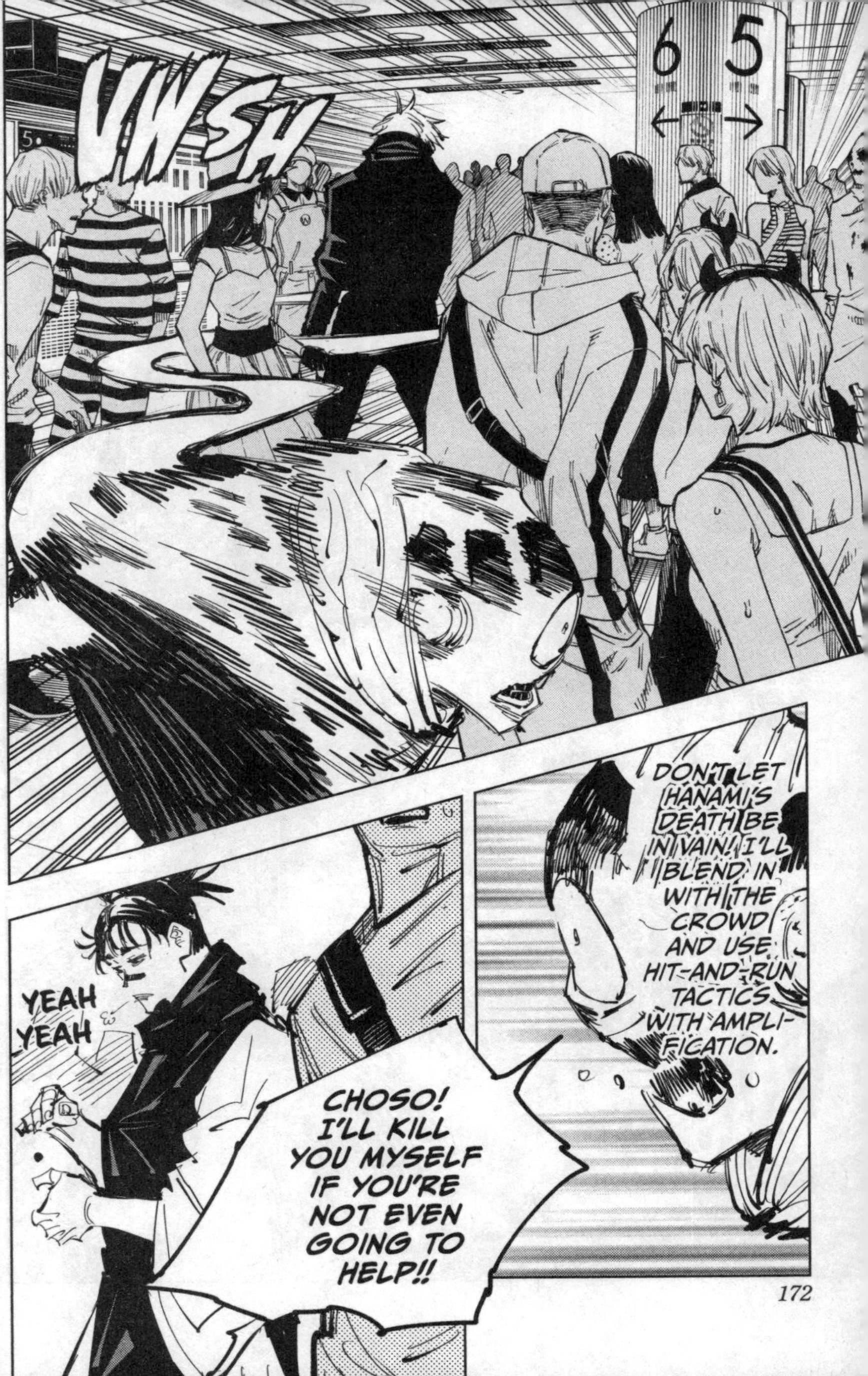
VWSH
DON'T LET HANAMI'S DEATH BE IN VAIN! I'LL BLEND IN WITH THE CROWD AND USE HIT-AND-RUN TACTICS WITH AMPLIFICATION.
CHOSO! I'LL KILL YOU MYSELF IF YOU'RE NOT EVEN GOING TO HELP!!
YEAH YEAH

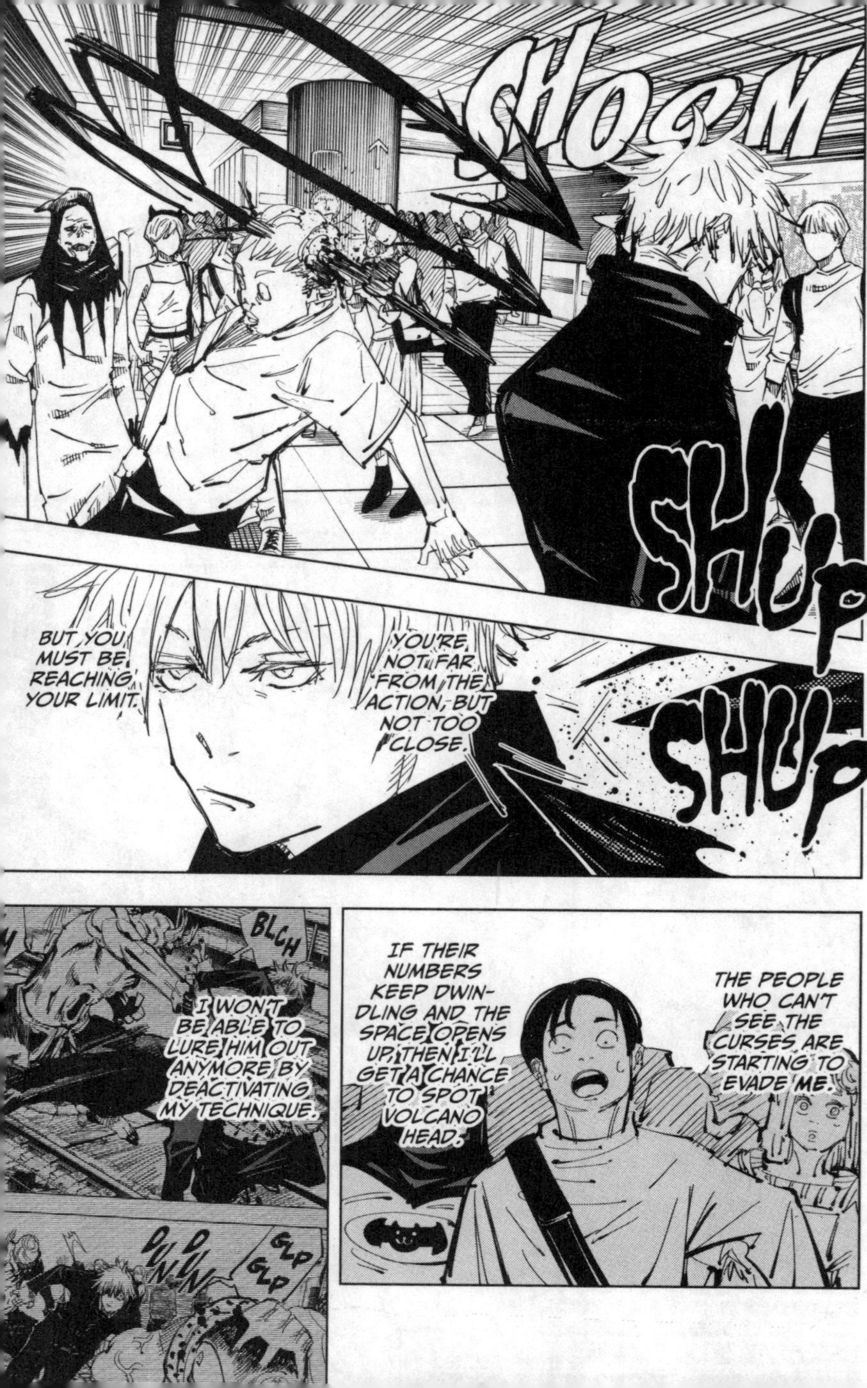
CHOOM
SHUP
SHUP
YOU'RE NOT FAR FROM THE ACTION, BUT NOT TOO CLOSE.
BUT YOU MUST BE REACHING YOUR LIMIT.
THE PEOPLE WHO CAN'T SEE THE CURSES ARE STARTING TO EVADE ME.
IF THEIR NUMBERS KEEP DWIN-DLING AND THE SPACE OPENS UP, THEN I'LL GET A CHANCE TO SPOT VOLCANO HEAD.
BLCH
I WON'T BE ABLE TO LURE HIM OUT ANYMORE BY DEACTIVATING MY TECHNIQUE.
GLP GLP
DUN DUN

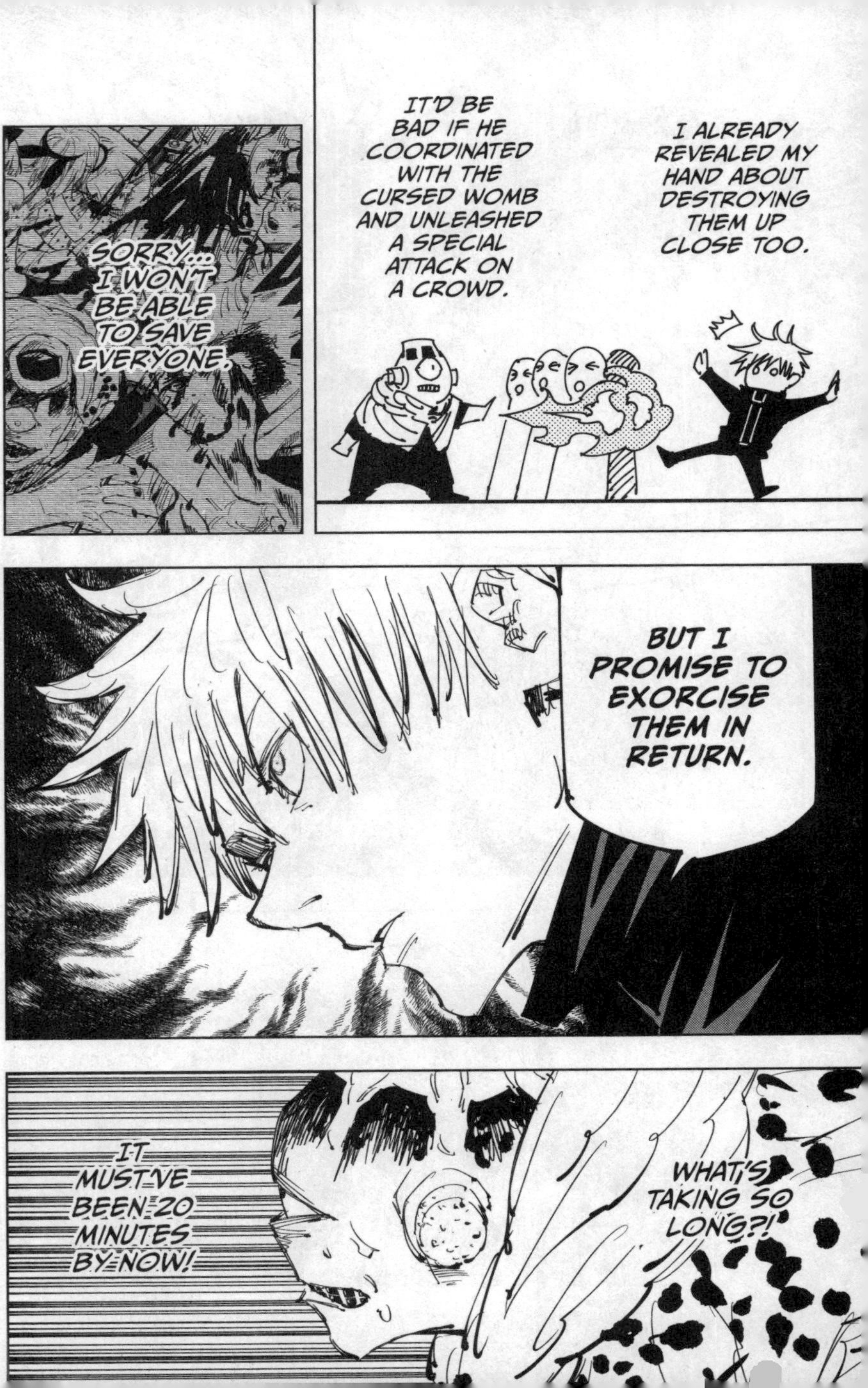

IT'D BE BAD IF HE COORDINATED WITH THE CURSED WOMB AND UNLEASHED A SPECIAL ATTACK ON A CROWD.
I ALREADY REVEALED MY HAND ABOUT DESTROYING THEM UP CLOSE TOO.
SORRY... I WON'T BE ABLE TO SAVE EVERYONE.
BUT I PROMISE TO EXORCISE THEM IN RETURN.
WHAT'S TAKING SO LONG?!
IT MUST'VE BEEN 20 MINUTES BY NOW!

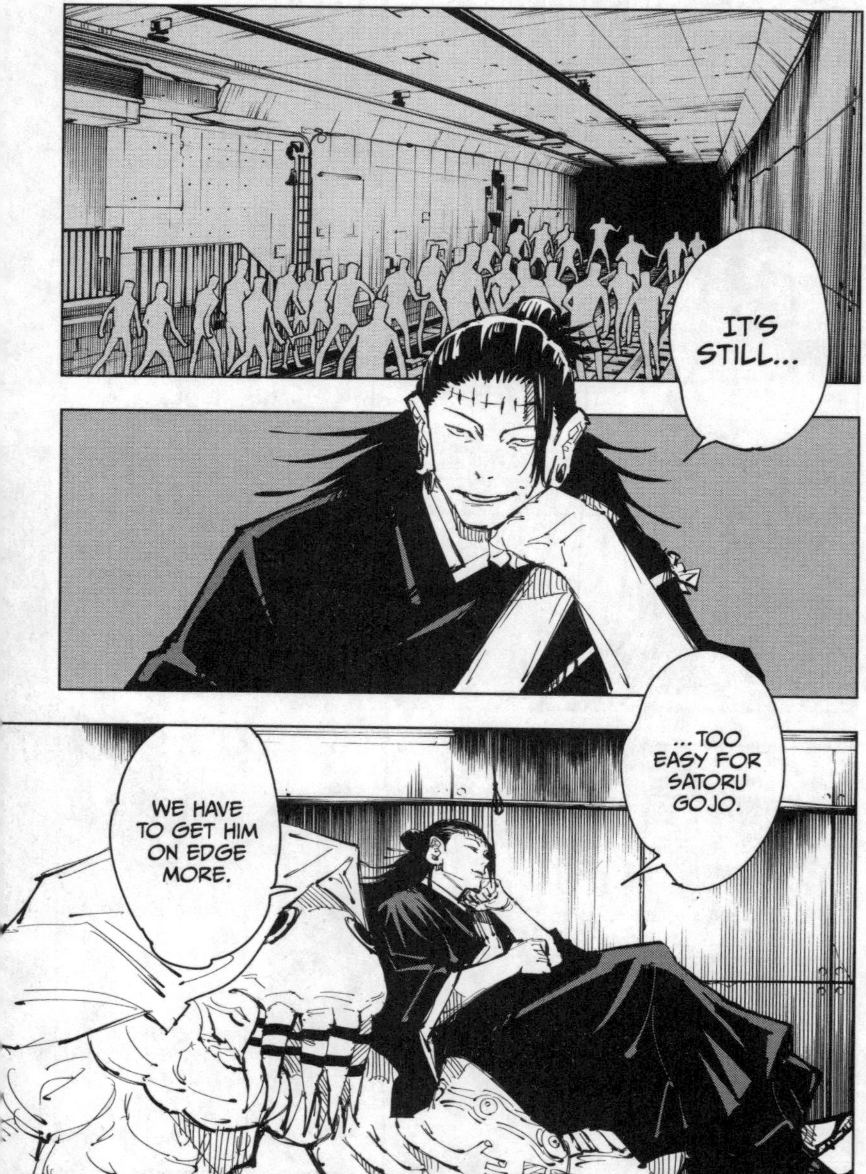
IT'S STILL...
...TOO EASY FOR SATORU GOJO.
WE HAVE TO GET HIM ON EDGE MORE.

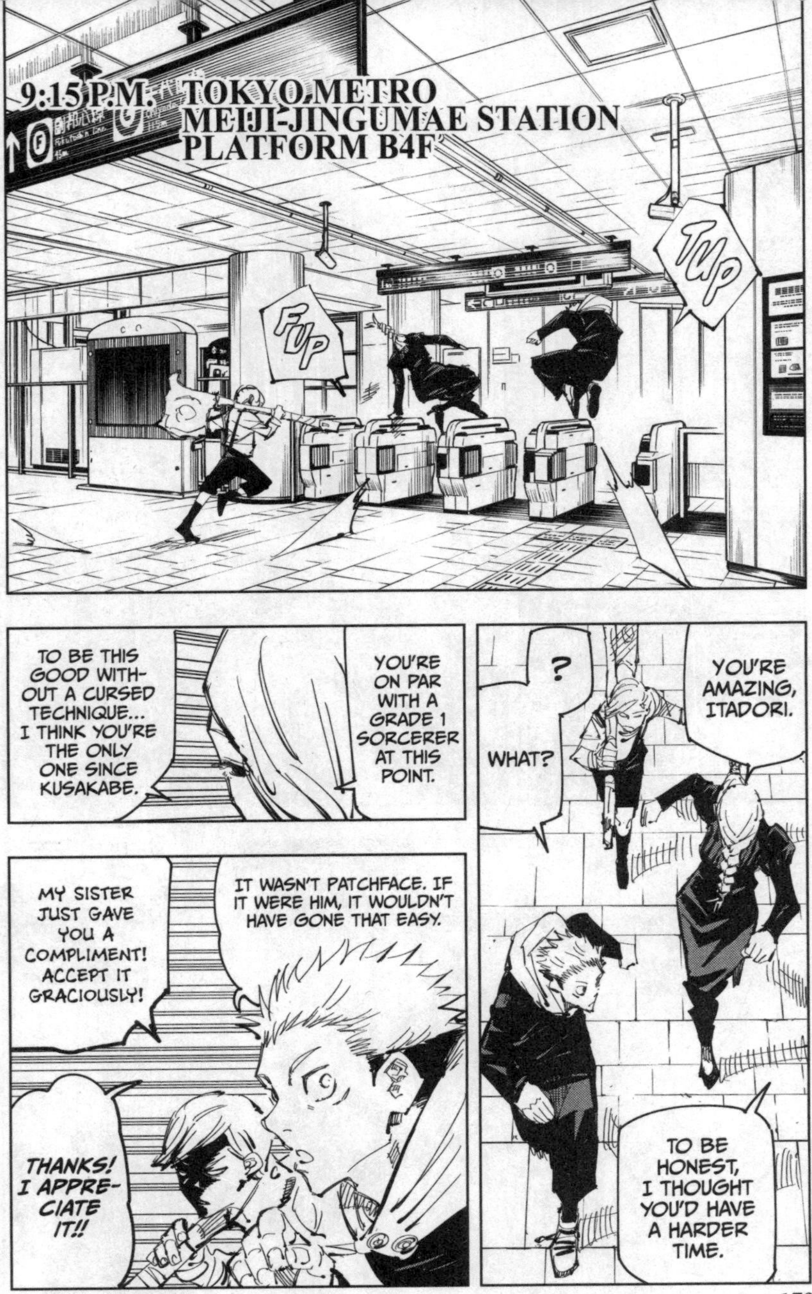
9:15 P.M. TOKYO METRO MEIJI-JINGUMAE STATION PLATFORM B4F
TUP
FUP
YOU'RE AMAZING, ITADORI.
?
WHAT?
TO BE HONEST, I THOUGHT YOU'D HAVE A HARDER TIME.
YOU'RE ON PAR WITH A GRADE 1 SORCERER AT THIS POINT.
TO BE THIS GOOD WITHOUT A CURSED TECHNIQUE... I THINK YOU'RE THE ONLY ONE SINCE KUSAKABE.
IT WASN'T PATCHFACE. IF IT WERE HIM, IT WOULDN'T HAVE GONE THAT EASY.
MY SISTER JUST GAVE YOU A COMPLIMENT! ACCEPT IT GRACIOUSLY!
THANKS! I APPRECIATE IT!!

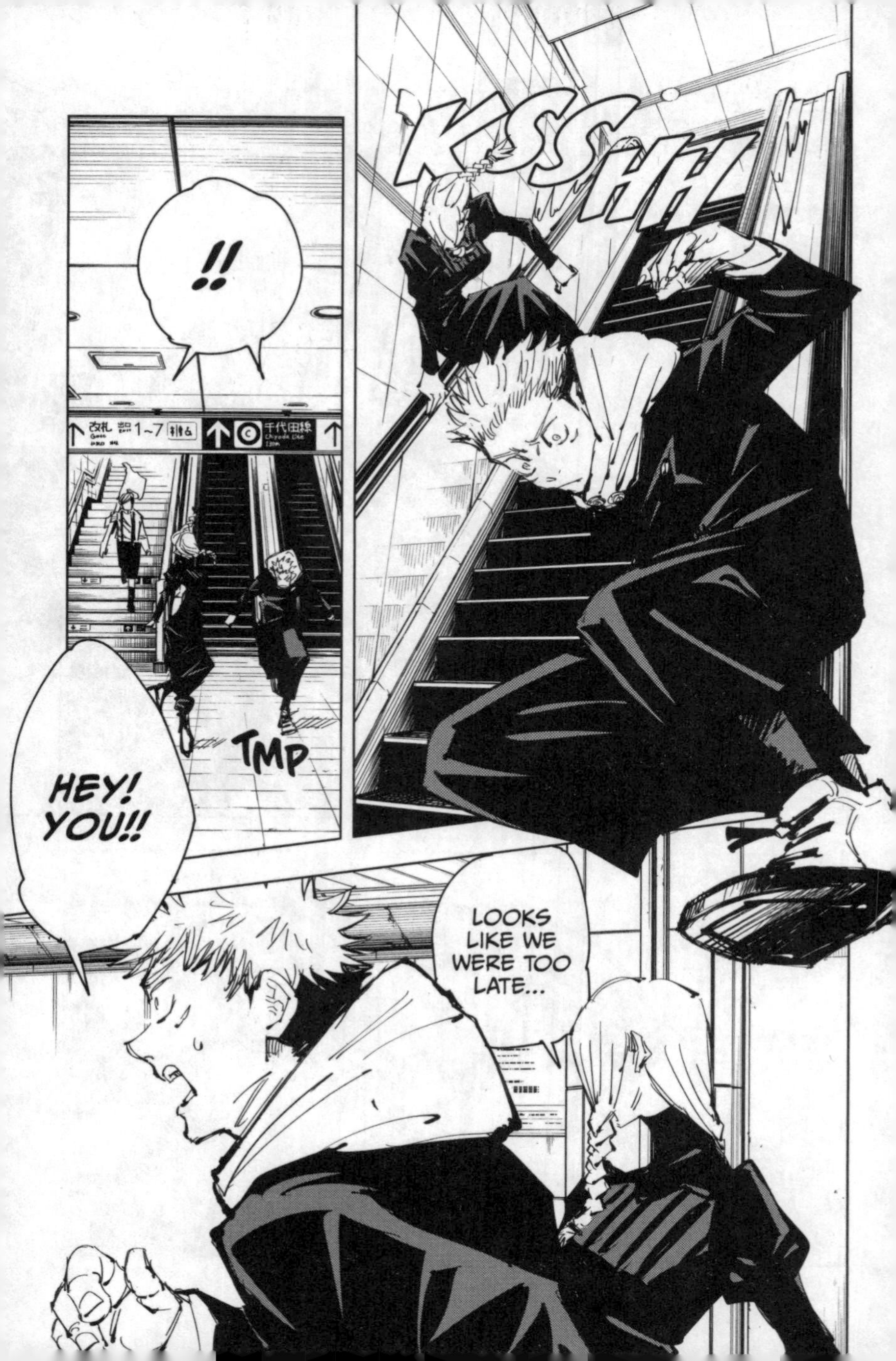
KSSHH
!!
改札
千代田線
TMP
HEY! YOU!!
LOOKS LIKE WE WERE TOO LATE...

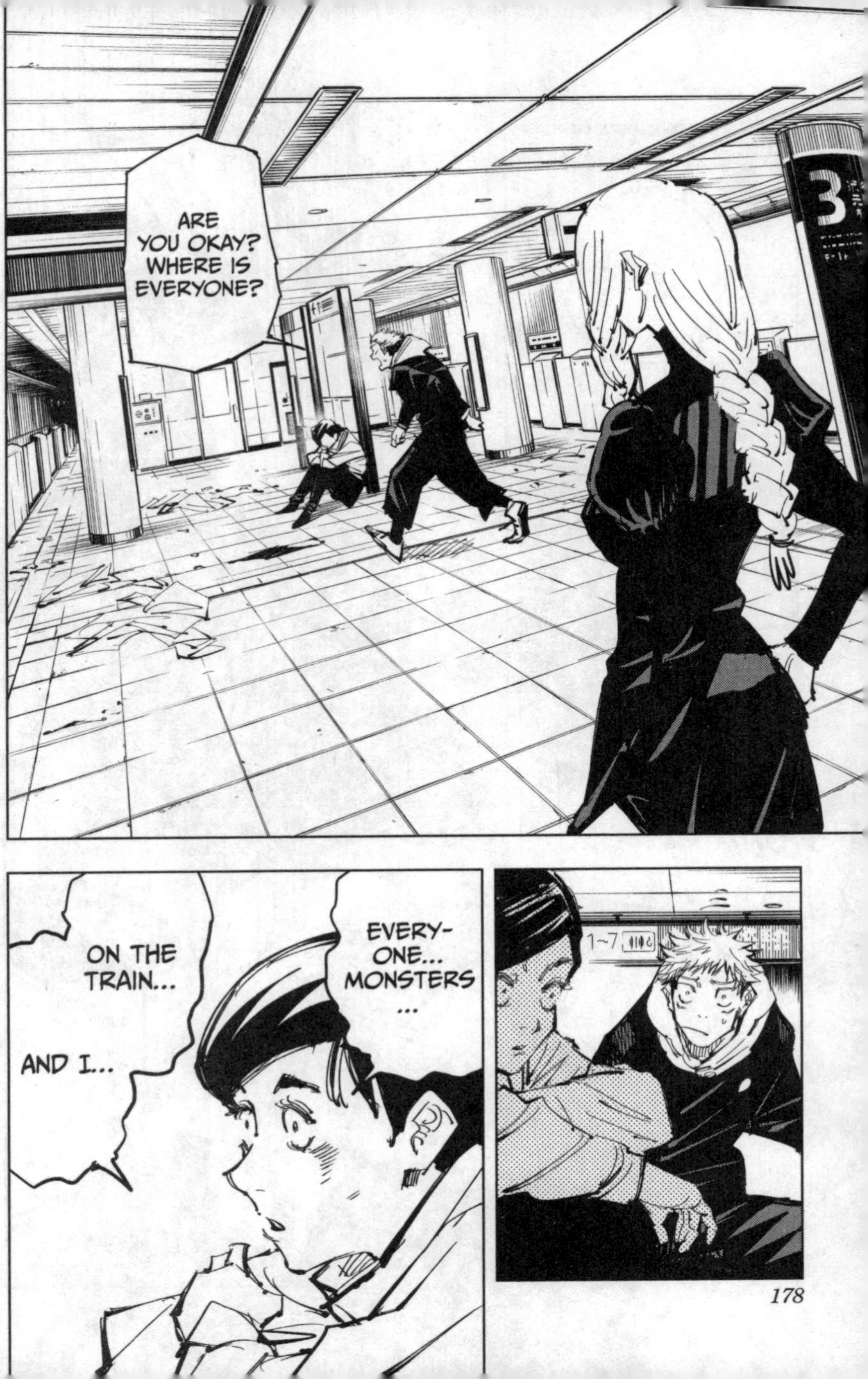
ARE YOU OKAY? WHERE IS EVERYONE?
EVERY-ONE... MONSTERS ...
ON THE TRAIN...
AND I...

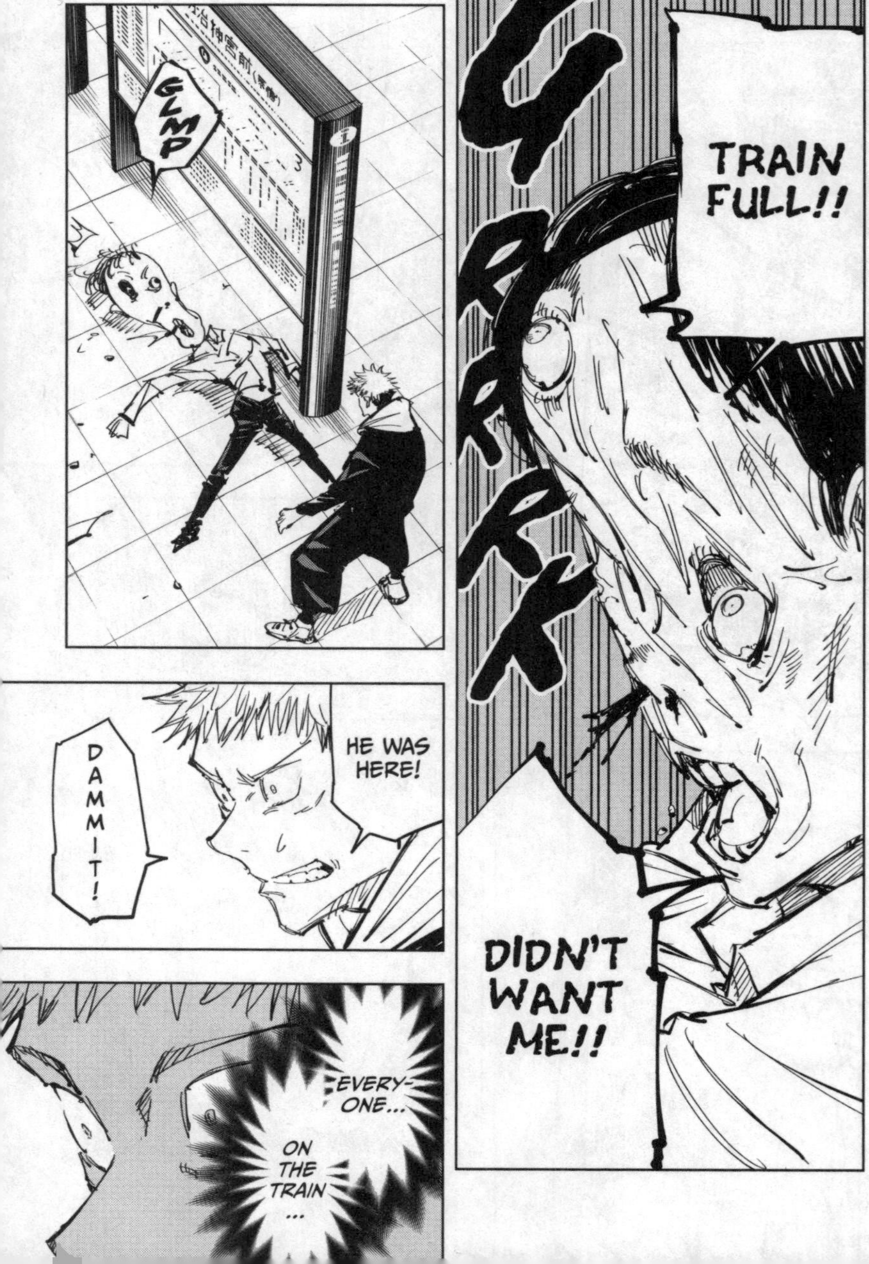
GRRRK
TRAIN FULL!!
DIDN'T WANT ME!!
GLMP
HE WAS HERE!
DAMMIT!
EVERY-ONE...
ON THE TRAIN...

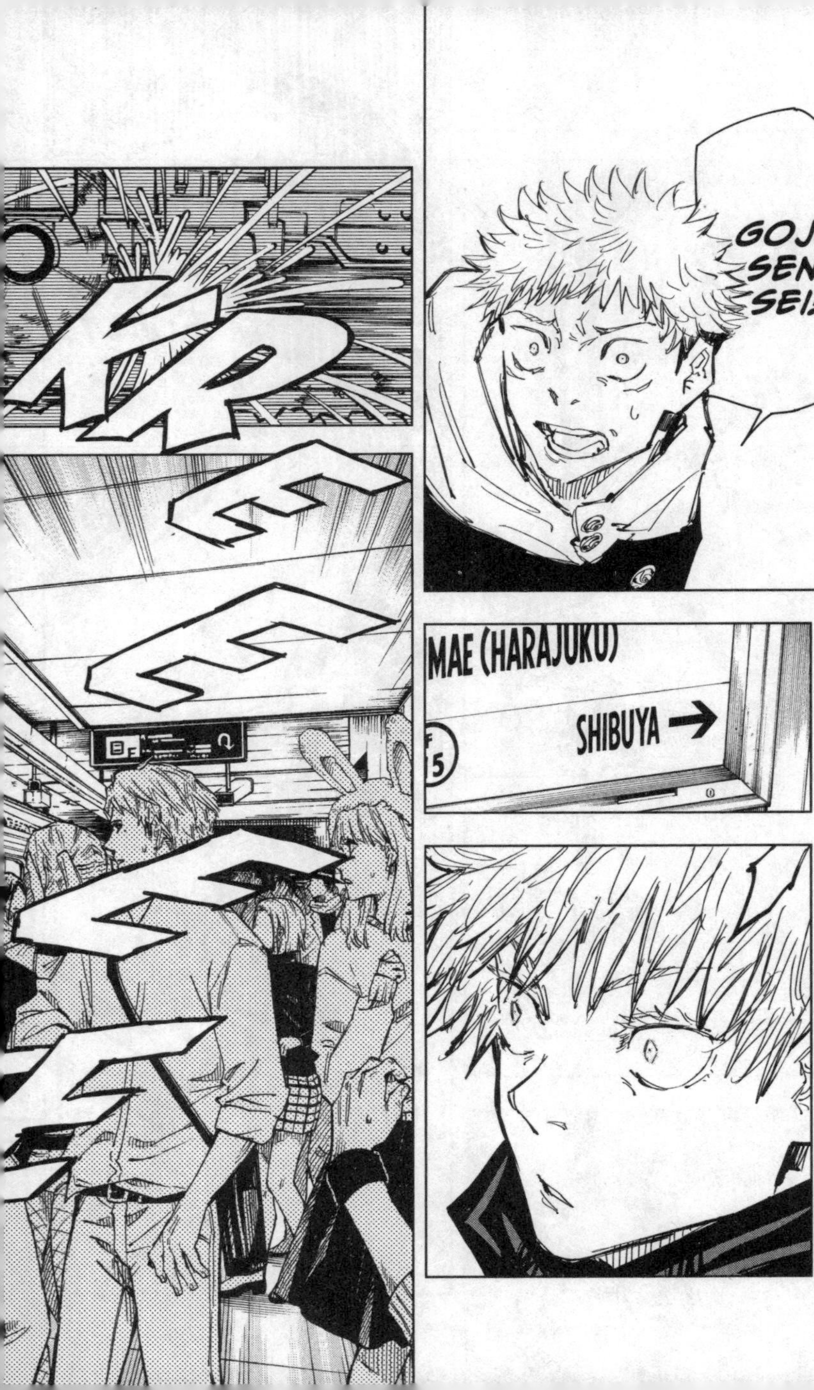
GOJO SEN-SEI!!
MAE (HARAJUKU)
SHIBUYA →

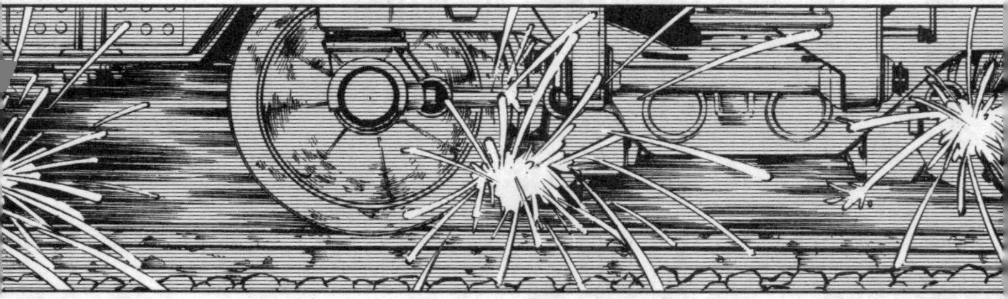

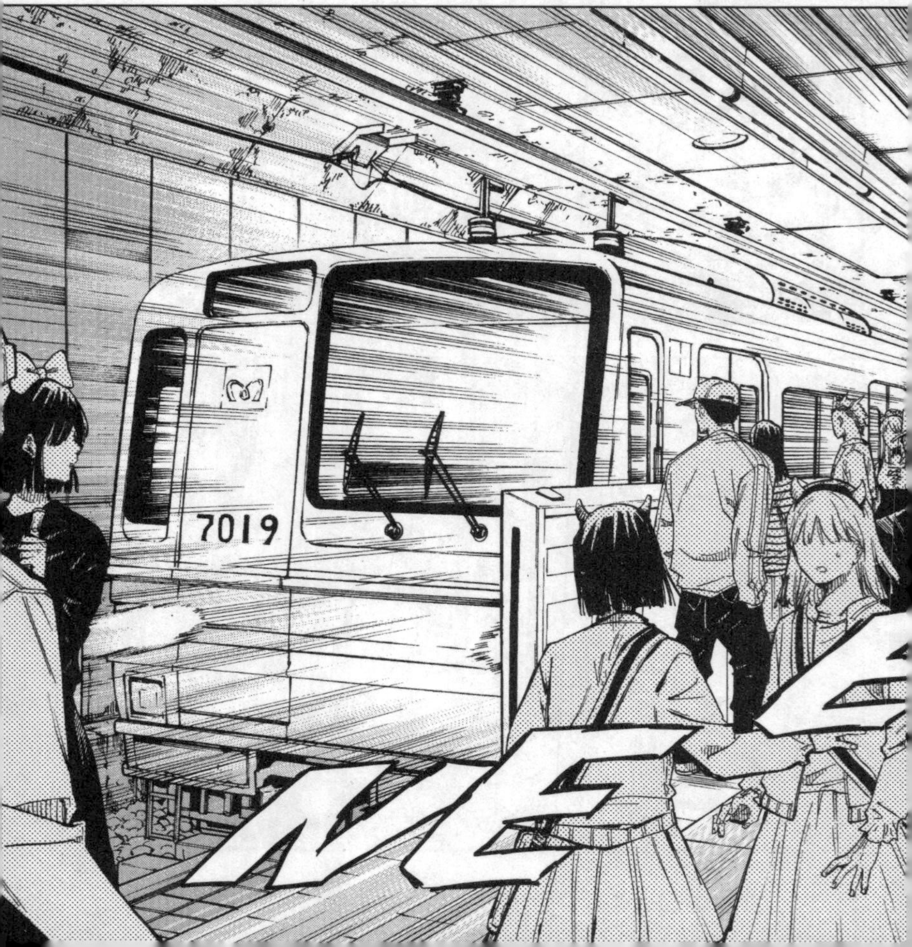
7019

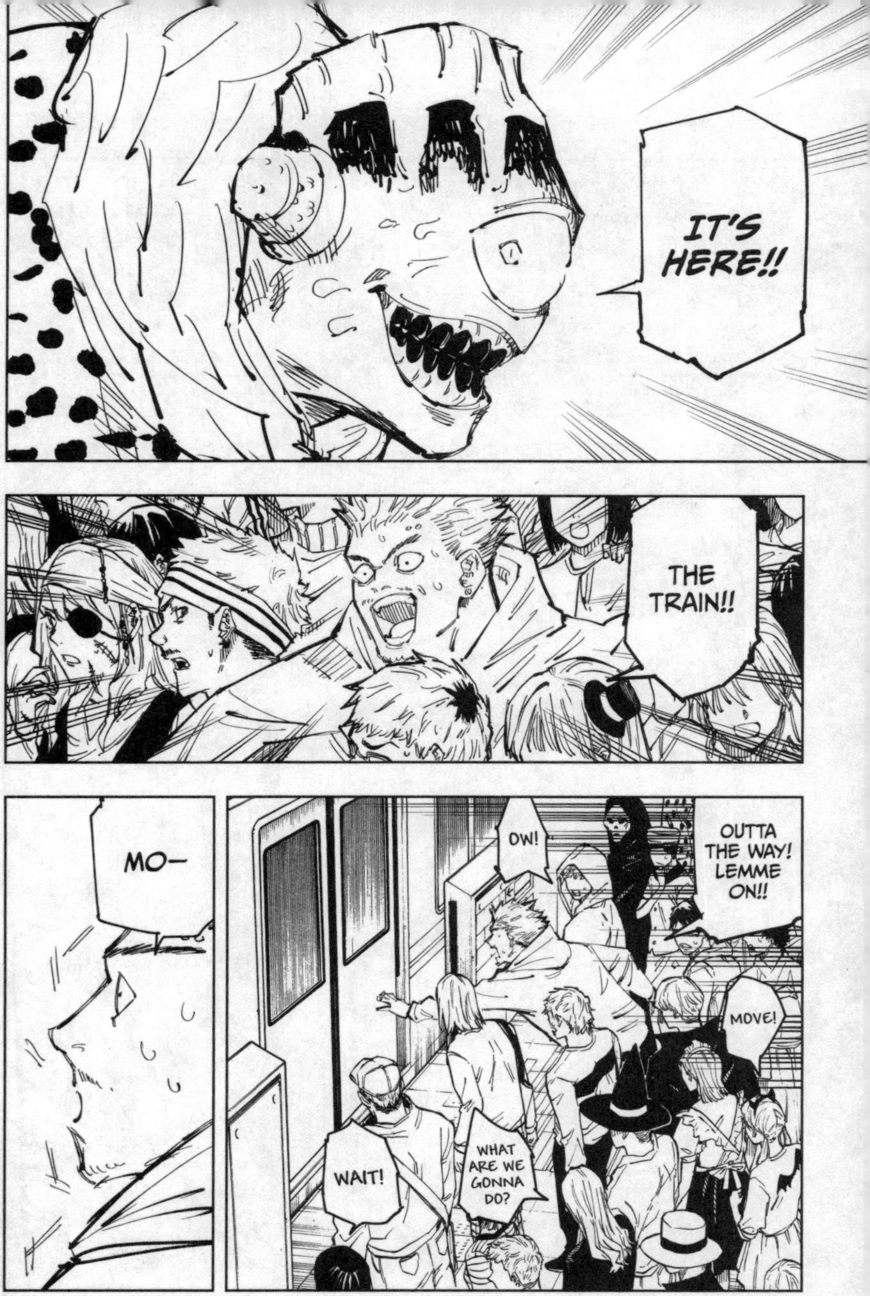
IT'S HERE!!
THE TRAIN!!
OUTTA THE WAY! LEMME ON!!
OW!
MOVE!
WHAT ARE WE GONNA DO?
WAIT!
MO-

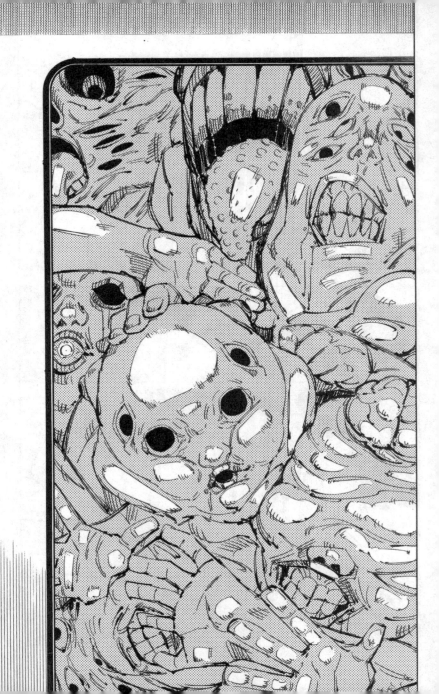

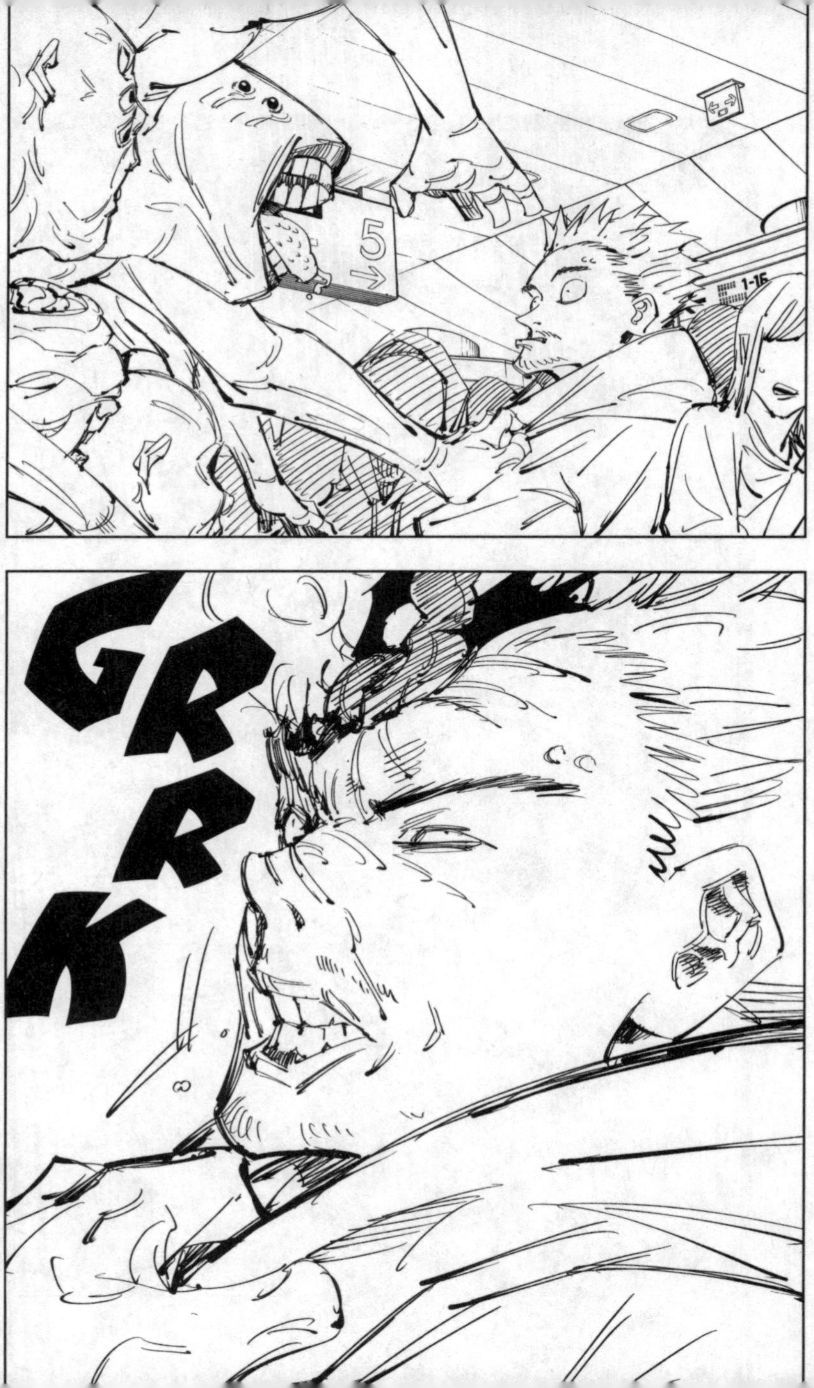
1-16
5
GRRK

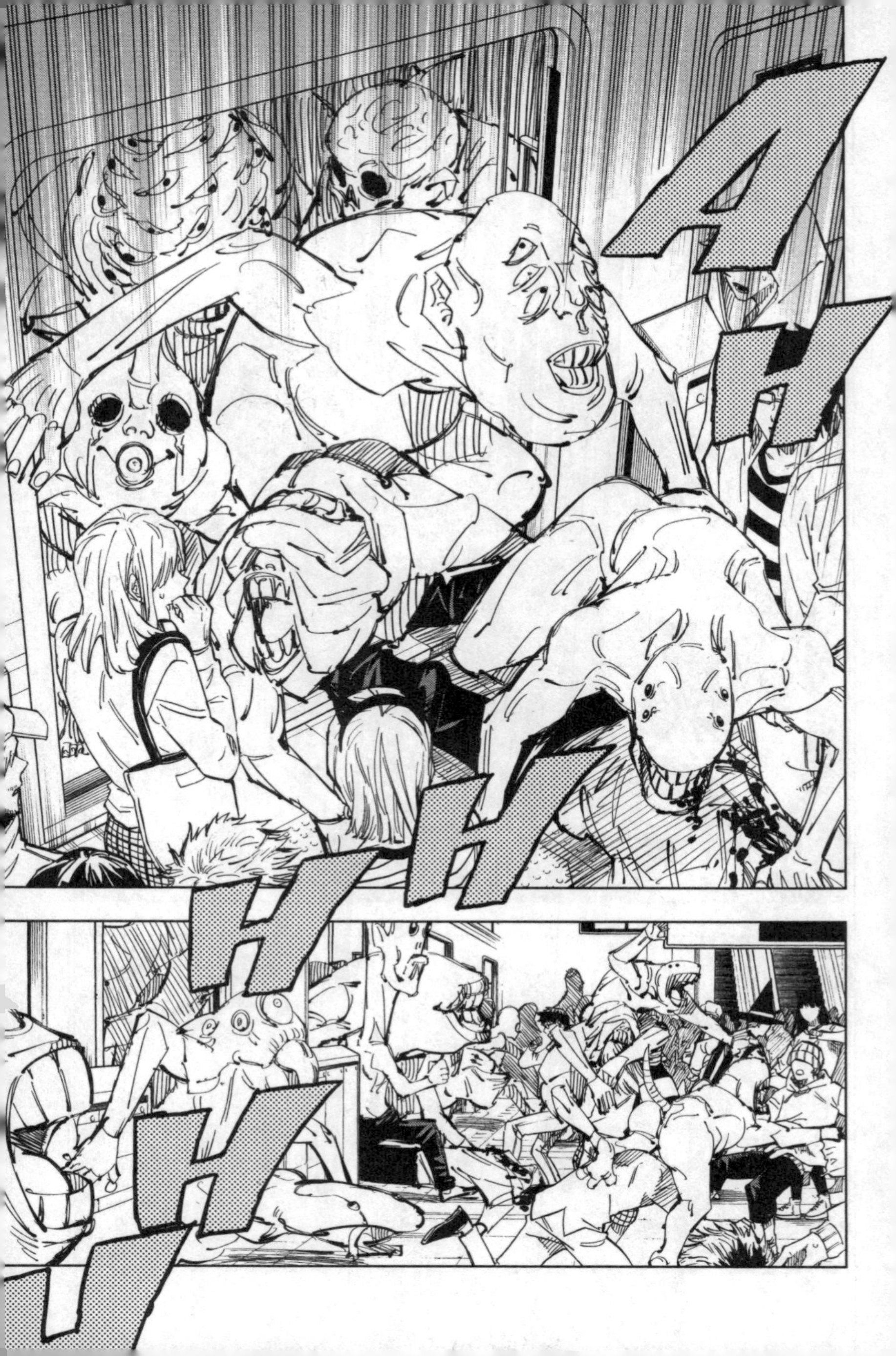
AHHHHH

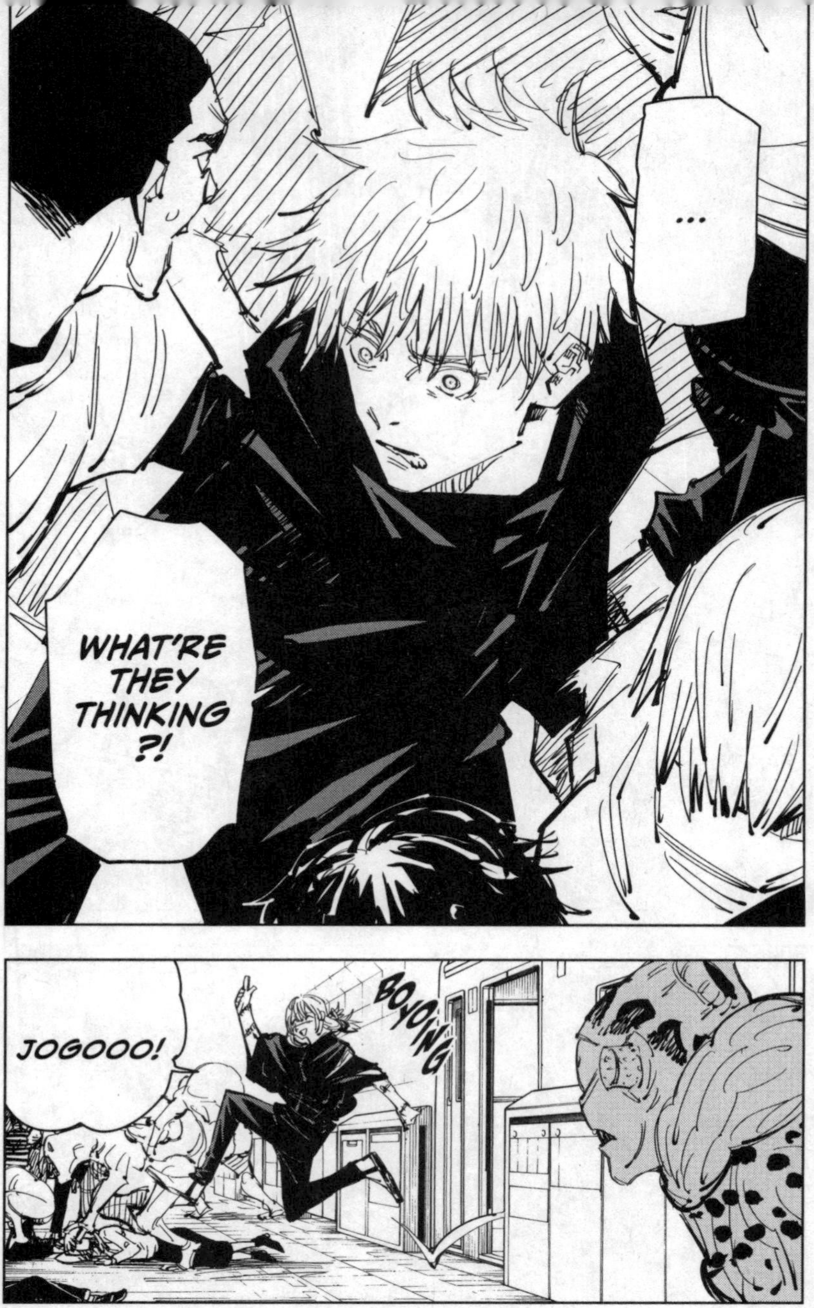
...
WHAT'RE THEY THINKING ?!
BOYOING
JOGOOO!

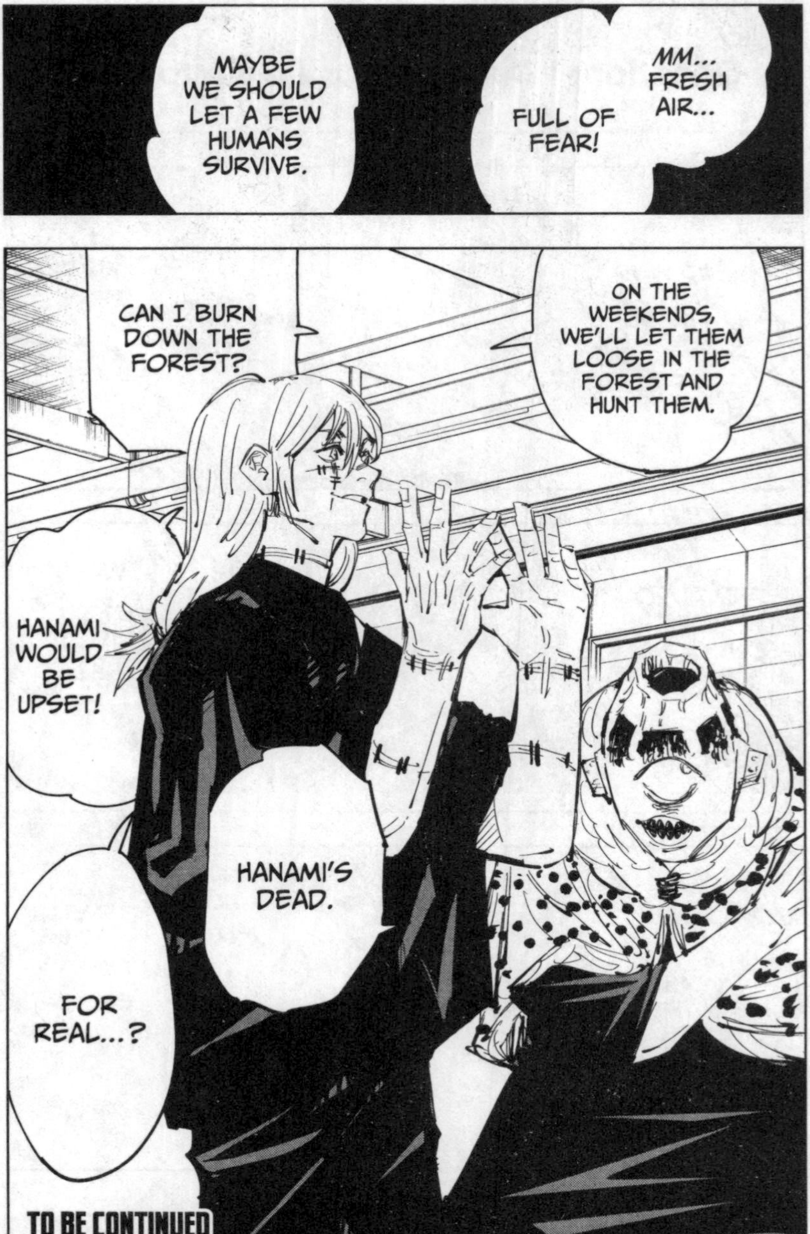
MM... FRESH AIR...
FULL OF FEAR!
MAYBE WE SHOULD LET A FEW HUMANS SURVIVE.
ON THE WEEKENDS, WE'LL LET THEM LOOSE IN THE FOREST AND HUNT THEM.
CAN I BURN DOWN THE FOREST?
HANAMI WOULD BE UPSET!
HANAMI'S DEAD.
FOR REAL...?
TO BE CONTINUED

Question: What is Satoru Gojo to you?

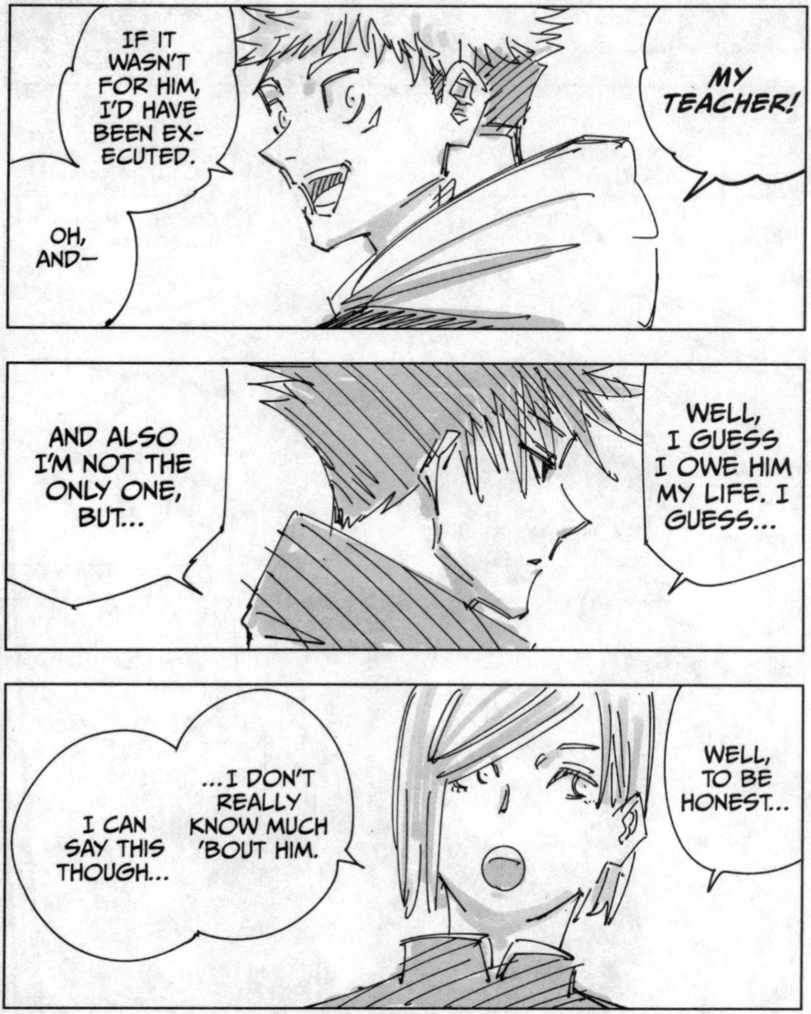

MY TEACHER!
IF IT WASN'T FOR HIM, I'D HAVE BEEN EX-ECUTED.
OH, AND—
WELL, I GUESS I OWE HIM MY LIFE. I GUESS...
AND ALSO I'M NOT THE ONLY ONE, BUT...
WELL, TO BE HONEST...
...I DON'T REALLY KNOW MUCH 'BOUT HIM.
I CAN SAY THIS THOUGH...

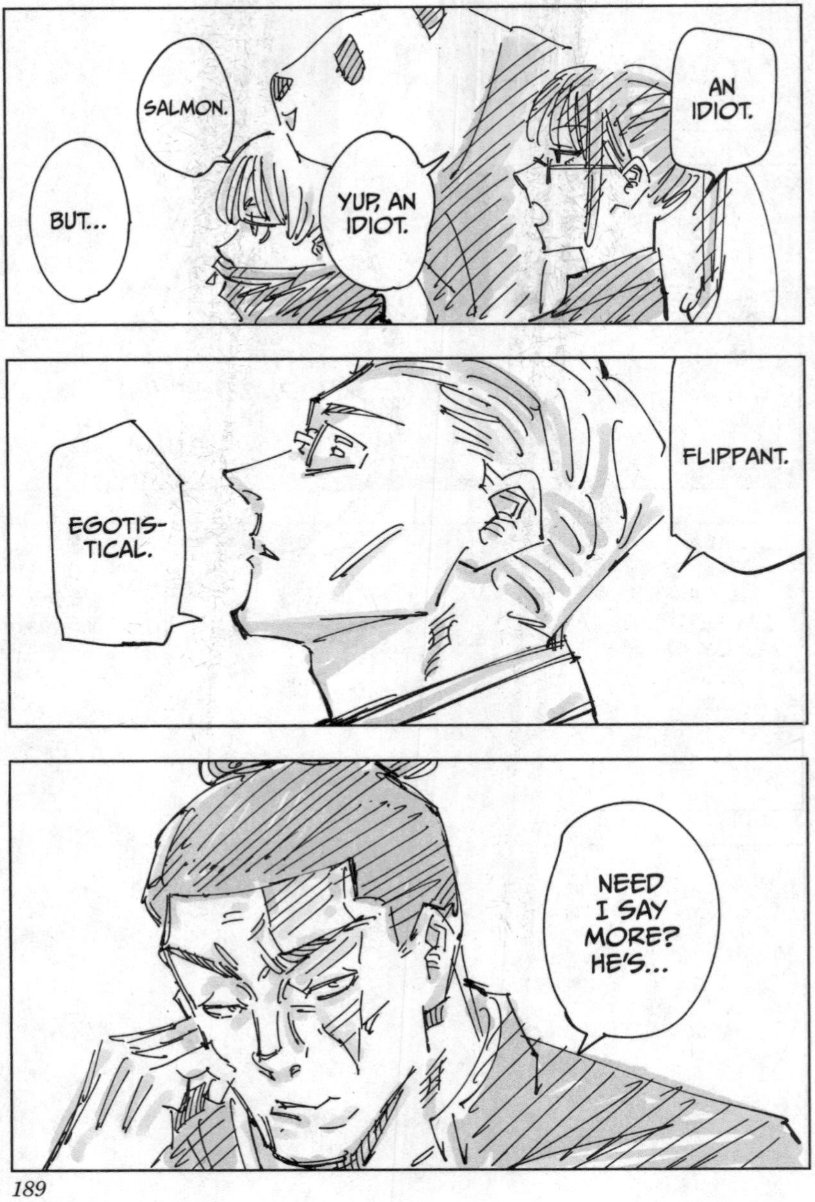
AN IDIOT.
YUP, AN IDIOT.
SALMON.
BUT...
FLIPPANT.
EGOTIS-TICAL.
NEED I SAY MORE? HE'S...

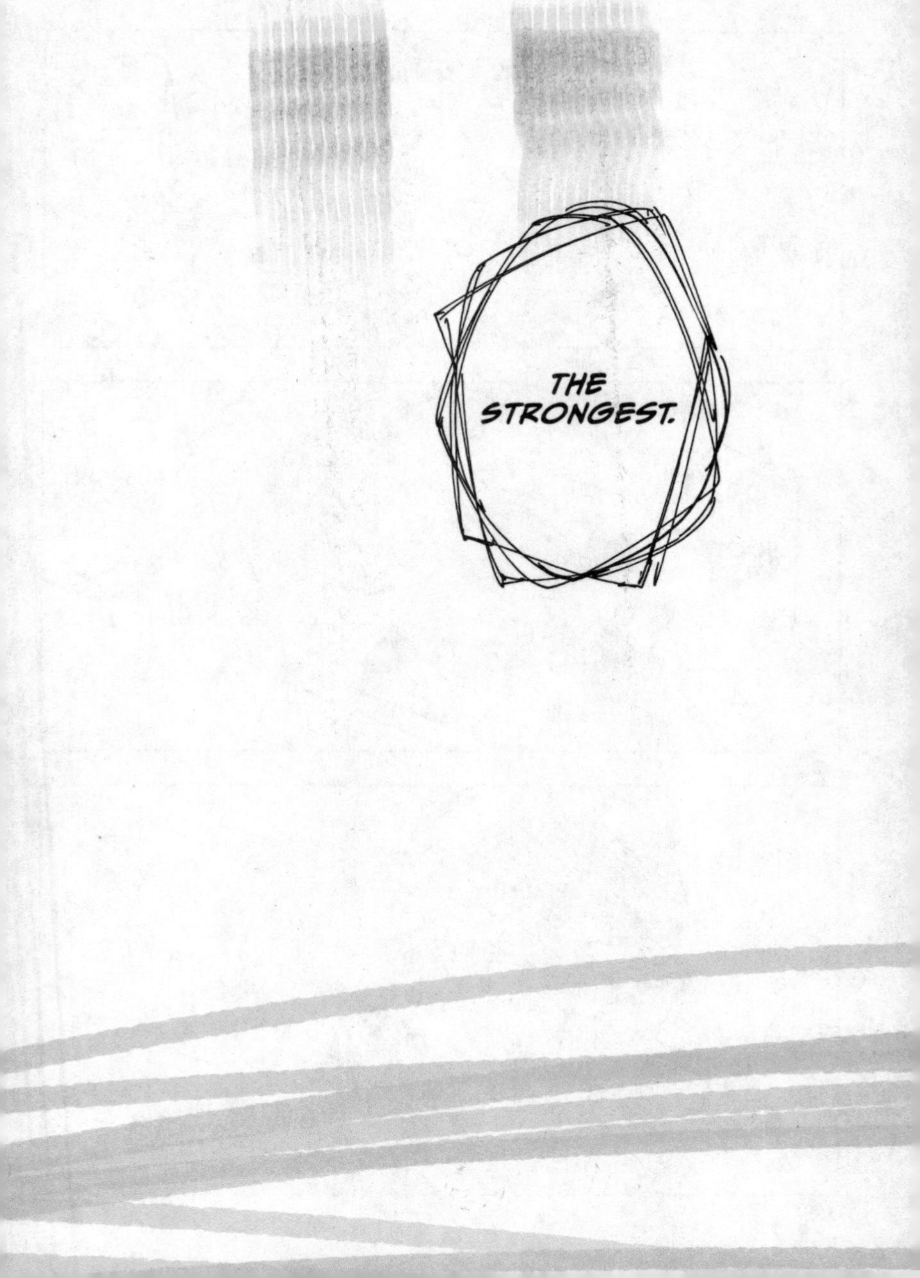
THE STRONGEST.

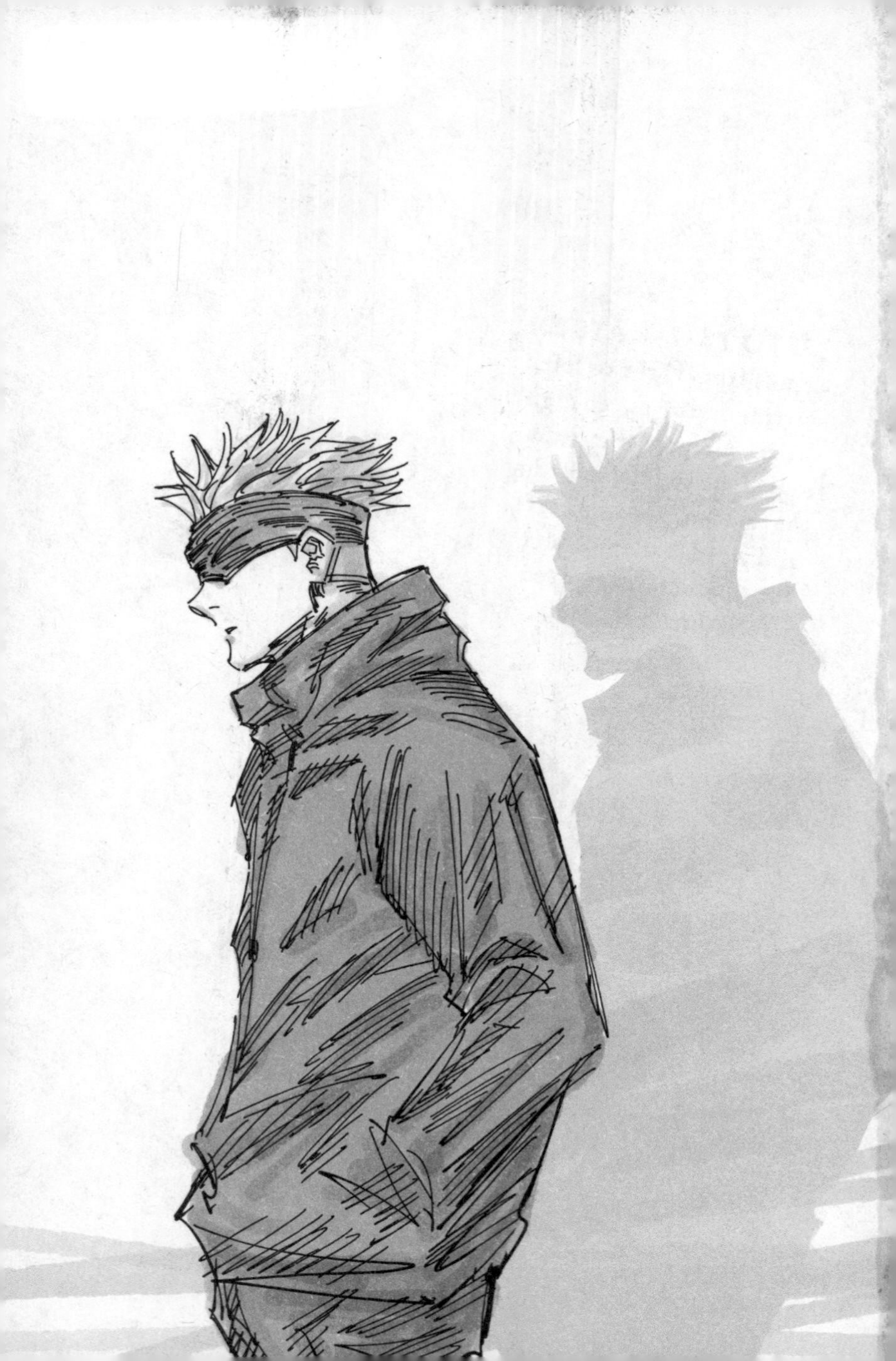

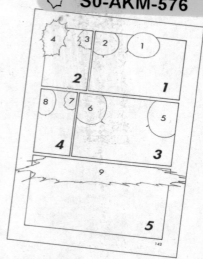

JUJUTSU KAISEN

reads from right to left, starting in the upper-right corner. Japanese is read from right to left, meaning that action, sound effects and word-balloon order are completely reversed from English order.

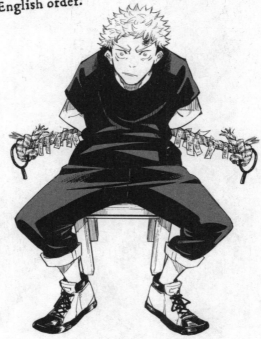